DATE DUE

2 Jun 73 QU			
30 Aug '73 DA	SEP 04 2001		
8 Feb '74 BB			
20 May 74 FD			
4 Dec '74 LC			
10 Jun 75 LM			
[illegible] EK			
4 Mar 76 DS			
[illegible] 76 DS			
[illegible] GE			
MAR 16 '77			
DEC [illegible] 1982			
APR 25 1986			

GAYLORD PRINTED IN U.S.A.

Population: Perspective, 1971

CALTECH POPULATION PROGRAM (Officers and Advisory Committee)

Harrison Brown, Professor of Science & Government, *Chairman* of Committee and *Director* of Program
James Bonner, Professor of Biology
David C. Elliot, Professor of History
Kenneth Frederick, Assistant Professor of Economics
Edwin S. Munger, Professor of Geography
Thayer Scudder, Professor of Anthropology
Alan Sweezy, Professor of Economics, *Associate Director* of Program

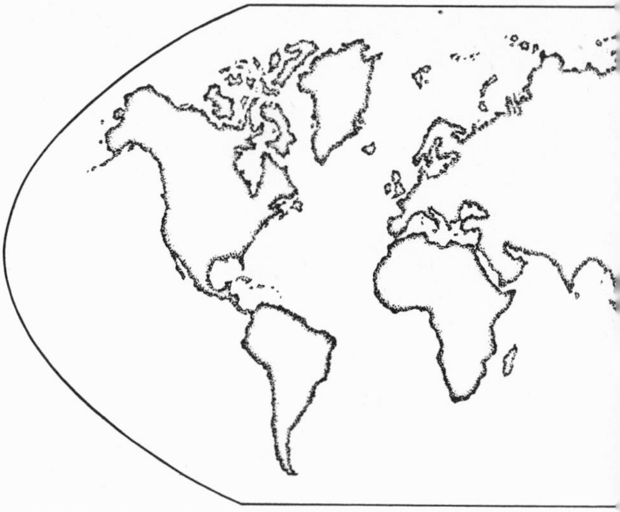

AMERICAN UNIVERSITIES FIELD STAFF

E. A. Bayne (Italy, Iran, Israel, Somalia) *Director,* Center for Mediterranean Studies
Victor D. Du Bois (West Africa)
Louis Dupree (Afghanistan, Pakistan)
Loren Fessler (China, Taiwan)
Charles F. Gallacher (Islamic Affairs, The Arab World) *Director of Studies*
Willard A. Hanna (Southeast Asia)
James Hooker (Malawi, Zambia, Rhodesia)
Alan W. Horton (United Arab Republic, Syria, Sudan) *Executive Director*
F. Roy Lockheimer (Japan)
Jon McLin (Common Market, NATA)
Norman N. Miller (Kenya, Tanzania, Uganda)
Richard W. Patch (Bolivia, Peru)
Albert Ravenholt (China, Southeast Asia)
Dennison I. Rusinow (Austria, Yugoslavia, Czechoslovakia)
Thomas G. Sanders (Brazil, Chile, Columbia)

Population: Perspective, 1971

The American Universities Field Staff

Edited with commentaries by

HARRISON BROWN
Professor of Geochemistry and of
Science & Government

and

ALAN SWEEZY
Professor of Economics

California Institute of Technology

FREEMAN, COOPER & COMPANY, PUBLISHERS
1736 Stockton Street, San Francisco, California 94133

First Printing—January, 1972

Printed in the United States of America

Library of Congress Catalogue Card Number 70-175103

ISBN 0-87735-011-6

Contents

Population: Perspective, 1971

Introduction

Harrison Brown

Humanity is now going through a period of rapid population growth and movement which is unprecedented in history, at least on any truly substantial scale. At the end of the Neolithic period there were probably no more than 10 million human beings in the world and the rate of population growth was extremely small. As the result of a sequence of revolutionary cultural changes, the rate of population growth increased as did population itself, with the result that by the turn of this century, there were some 1,600 million persons and the rate of growth had risen to about 0.7 per cent annually. By mid-1971, the world population had risen to some 3,700 million persons and the rate of growth had reached approximately 2 per cent annually.

This accelerating growth of world population has been the result of a sequence of technological innovations coupled with social changes which have greatly lowered mortality rates. With birth rates unaltered, at least for some time, populations grew rapidly.

But the diverse components of the agricultural, industrial, and scientific revolutions did not diffuse uniformly over the populated regions of the earth. In a particular group of countries, typified by the United States, Japan, and the countries of Europe, death rates fell and populations grew rapidly. But agricultural and industrial production increased even more rapidly than did population, with the result that the lot of the average person improved significantly with time. Eventually birth rates started to decline in these areas and this led to an even more rapid increase in per capita wealth. In relative terms these nations can now be called "rich."

Technologies which gave rise to a lowering of death rates spread to the rest of the world, where as a consequence populations also increased rapidly.

But, for a variety of reasons, agricultural and industrial production in those areas, typified by the nations of Africa, Asia, and Latin America, increased but very slowly. As a result, per capita wealth increased little, if at all. In relative terms these nations can be called "poor."

The per capita wealth in the rich countries is now some 13 times greater than that in the poor countries. Even more important, the differential in per capita wealth is increasing, in part because rates of population growth in the poor countries are rising while those in the rich countries are falling. The populations of the rich countries and their rates of growth are shown in Table 1.

Table 1. The Growth of Rich Nations Compared with Poor Nations
Mid-year Population (millions)

Year	*1930*		*1940*		*1950*		*1960*		*1970*
Population of world . .	2070		2295		2517		3005		3620
Increase in decade . .		10.9%		9.7%		19.4%		20.5%	
Population of rich nations	742		801		834		947		1050
Increase in decade . .		8.0%		4.1%		13.5%		11.4%	
Population in poor countries.	1328		1494		1683		2058		2570
Increase in decade . .		12.5%		12.7%		22.3%		24.7%	

Source: United Nations Demogarphic Yearbook

Changing technology also brought with it accelerated urbanization. In the rich countries the combination of increased farm productivity and the attractions of the city resulted in a flow of people from rural to urban areas, which led eventually to the urbanization of the majority of the population. Until recently, however, this process has taken place but very slowly in the poor countries.

During the past two decades the process of urbanization in the poor countries has been accelerating, as can be seen from Table 2, but only in small measure

Table 2. Division of Population between Urban and Rural (per cent)
(Calculated from data presented by Kingsley Davis in *World Urbanization 1950–1970, Volume I: Basic Data for Cities, Countries, and Regions*. Institute for International Studies, University of California, Berkeley.)

	1950		*1960*		*1970*	
	Rural	*Urban*	*Rural*	*Urban*	*Rural*	*Urban*
Rich countries. .	48.4	51.6	40.6	59.4	32.5	67.5
Poor countries. .	83.4	16.6	79.1	20.9	74.2	25.8
World	71.8	28.2	67.0	33.0	62.0	38.0

because of increasing farm productivity. Decreasing mortality rates have resulted in increased rural populations. With little new land available which can be placed under cultivation, rural unemployment and underemployment have been rising and the combination of this pressure plus the attraction of the city have accelerated the migration process. Indeed, people have been flowing into the cities of the poor countries faster than jobs have been created, with the result that urban unemployment and underemployment have also grown rapidly. In most of the cities of the poor countries vast slum areas have emerged such as the *bustees* of Calcutta, the *barriadas* of Lima, and the *favelas* of Rio de Janeiro.

Clearly, the processes which we see taking place around us today cannot continue for a very long time in the future, at least at present rates. The separation between the cultures of the rich and the poor is widening with each passing year and the strains which result may well prove to be intolerable. Present trends indicate that the next two or three decades will be critical. Within that period the world appears to be slated to experience dramatic and perhaps even explosive changes.

It is quite possible that present processes will lead to a more or less permanent division of the world into the cultures of the rich and the poor. But it is also possible that man will mobilize his genius to the end of creating a world in which all people can live their lives free from the fears of hunger, disease, and poverty. We know that from a purely technological point of view, if not from a social and political one, he can do this.

Rapid economic development of the poor countries seems essential if starvation, disease, and deprivation are to be eliminated. But what is of critical importance during the present phase of human development is the rate of economic development *per capita.* The average person in the poor countries must be relieved of the feeling of hopelessness. He must be able to see his personal position improve significantly during the course of his lifetime and be able to realize that the condition of his children will be even better than his own. But clearly if the real rate of economic growth of his country is 4.0 per cent per year and the rate of growth of population is 2.8 per cent per year, the rate of economic growth *per capita* is only 1.2 per cent per year, which corresponds to a doubling of income in something over 80 years. The prospect of waiting 80 years to increase per capita income from $100 to $200 is not likely to fill many citizens' hearts with joy.

Beyond slowing down the growth of per capita income, however, rapid population growth has a number of additional serious consequences. Large-scale internal migration has already been mentioned. A recent study prepared by the National Academy of Sciences* points out that rapid population growth worsens political and social conflicts among different ethnic, religious, linguistic, and social groups. High proportions of children hinder the improvement of education and profoundly affect health, welfare, and child development. Environmental effects can be substantial.

Clearly, everything possible should be done to stimulate the economic growth of the poor countries, but it is important that we appreciate that economic and social development and population growth cannot be divorced from each other. When economic and social development take place, population growth and migration are affected. Conversely, population growth and migration in turn affect eco-

---

* *Rapid Population Growth; Consequences and Policy Implications.* Published for the National Academy of Sciences by The Johns Hopkins University Press, Baltimore (1971).

nomic and social development. It is of the greatest importance that the complex interrelationships between such factors as population growth, migration, economic development, and cultural and political change be better understood than they are at present, for some measure of understanding must precede intelligent action.

For several years these problems have concerned a number of the faculty of the California Institute of Technology. In 1969 the decision was made to start a continuing program of population studies, with the financial support of the Agency for International Development. The Institute subsequently entered into a close working relationship with the American Universities Field Staff in this field. The latter organization, which is sponsored by a consortium of 11 universities, has a long and unexcelled tradition of reporting from the field on major global issues. Their writers, who are full-time Associates, are astute observers who spend long periods abroad and who are selected for their ability to cut across the boundaries of the academic disciplines in order to study societies in their totality. The Fieldstaff Associates produce some 20 papers each year dealing with population problems in the light of the advice, support, and criticism of a Caltech Advisory Committee on Population Programs, which is interdisciplinary in composition.

The project is primarily concerned with increasing our understanding of the population problem as it is related to different social and cultural patterns throughout the world. The causes of population growth and the means of its control, including both acceptable technology and adequate motivation, are related to social attitudes, religious beliefs, and economic conditions. What is true and what will work in one part of the world may be neither true nor efficacious in another. The field studies are conducted in such a way that our knowledge of demography may be combined effectively with an understanding in depth of local social and political conditions.

It is planned that once each year the Associates of the AUFS will come together with the interdisciplinary Committee from Caltech and a few additional selected experts, to review the significant happenings of the year and to plan the program of observations and study for the following year. The first of these meetings, which gave rise to this volume, was held in Pasadena in December 1970, the next in Rome in December 1971. It is planned to issue a similar volume annually, so that concerned persons can follow the developments regularly and systematically.

The Author

HARRISON BROWN is professor of geochemistry and of science and government at the California Institute of Technology, where he has been a member of the faculty since 1951. He is also foreign secretary of the National Academy of Sciences and vice-president of the International Council of Scientific Unions. Brown was graduated from the University of California at Berkeley in 1938 and obtained his Ph.D. from Johns Hopkins University in 1941. Before going to Caltech he was associated with the U.S. atomic energy program. He is the author of *The Challenge of Man's Future* and co-author of *The Next Hundred Years.*

Attitudes toward Limitation

Alan Sweezy

THE ELITE

This section deals with the attitudes toward population growth of the governing, or influential, elite in the countries covered by the Conference reports and discussion.

Reasons for Favoring a High or Increased Rate of Growth

We will first consider attitudes favoring maintenance or increase of the rate of population growth. From the Conference proceedings, four main reasons emerged for such attitudes: 1) a desire for power, either national or ethnic, 2) the belief in the existence of large untapped resources, 3) moral or religious objections to interfering with the natural course of events in the realm of sex and reproduction, 4) worry about a labor shortage, or an unfavorable age distribution, in some of the developed countries which have already reached a low rate of population growth. Numbers 1) and 2) are often closely linked together, the desire for greater power being supported by a firm belief in the existence of vast unexploited resources. In some cases it appears that number 3) might be an important element contributing to the development of the attitudes characterized under 1) and 2).

Reasons 1 and 2. Brazil and Malawi are outstanding examples of countries in which the governing elite, or at least important sections of it, favored continued high rates of population growth—now in the neighborhood of 3 per cent a year in both countries. In the former, the proponents of rapid growth have "a romantic vision of a Brazil with a large population and an inhabited interior." By the end of this century, with a population in excess of 200 million, "Brazil will emerge as one of the world's major nations." Brazilians of this persuasion believe that the growing population can be absorbed without difficulty because of "the nation's vast natural resources and, more recently, from the high indices of economic growth."

In Malawi "the President views the projected doubling [by 1990] of the population with favor. To those who declare that Malawi already is overpopulated, he retorts that this is untrue, especially when one considers new ways of using land and other resources." Disagreement with the President's views is expressed only in private: "no agency, private or public, is concerned openly with the topic [of birth control]. There are no projects which touch upon family planning, no national bodies associated with this sort of research, no cooperation with foreign organizations."

It has been suggested that President Banda has Greater Malawi aspirations. He often refers to the "indubitable historical fact that there once was a Malawi state spilling across northern Mozambique, eastern Zambia, and southern Tanzania." But he does not openly contest the national boundaries arbitrarily established in Africa by Europeans.

A similar attitude toward population growth was predominant in Indonesia in the Sukarno era. Sukarno himself held that Indonesia could easily support a population of 150 million. By way of contrast, informed opinion is beginning to move toward the view that with its present 120 million Indonesia is "already confronted with a population problem of crisis proportions." The Sukarno view was popular because it fitted in with the common ambition to achieve the international prestige and power to which the nation "would seem to be entitled as the world's fifth or sixth most populous and one of its most richly endowed."

In Brazil, Malawi, and Sukarno's Indonesia nationalistic aspirations form the basis for attitudes favoring rapid population growth. Ethnic rivalry is an even more pervasive reason. Many examples could be given. To cite only a few: In Kenya it was rumored that "during the Kikuyu oathings following the Mboya assassination one of the oaths was to avoid any family planning and to increase the Kikuyu numbers as rapidly as possible." Whether true or not, such rumors were bound to produce fears of being outnumbered in other tribes, notably the Luo, and to make them also reluctant to adopt family limitation. In this case the Kikuyu reaction was triggered not only by Mboya's assassination but also by other rumors that the Luo have grown larger in numbers than the Kikuyu—rumors, incidentally, that were stimulated by the 1969 census but are "totally unsubstantiated."

In the Ivory Coast the main problem is the presence of large numbers of workers from neighboring countries. While many of the leaders would favor the implementation of a program of birth control among the foreign Africans who reside in the Ivory Coast and compete with their own people for jobs, they are loath to see such a program established among themselves.

Ethnic rivalry is not confined to the less developed countries. In Belgium the question of birth control touches not only on the religious, but also on the linguistic, issue. "There has been some concern among French-speaking Belgians, especially since the early 1960s, about evidence showing that their relative numbers are decreasing; and there is a corresponding tendency among Flemish-speaking Belgians, especially those called *flamingants,* to be suspicious of vigorous promotion of birth control on the grounds that it is inspired by anti-Flemish feeling."

As is indicated by these examples, reluctance to limit population growth on ethnic grounds may be more defensive than aggressive. It is the fear of being swamped by the growth of other groups that makes people unwilling to limit their own numbers. The same thing also applies in international relations, especially in the relation of several nations to those that are contiguous. Thus the opposition leaders in Kenya criticize the government's support of family planning, on the ground that Uganda may outstrip them in numbers and in power. Among the reasons birth control has not been advocated in the Ivory Coast is "a genuine fear in the minds of many Ivoirien leaders that it will lead to a weakening of the country vis-à-vis its neighbors, especially Guinea and Ghana." The suggestion was made in the course of the discussion that to get around this difficulty family planning programs may have to be carried out on a regional basis.

As would be expected, xenophobic elements are strong in thinking about population policy in countries where rapid growth is favored on nationalistic or ethnic grounds. In Brazil in 1966–67, "family planners became the object of a hostile campaign charging them with 'genocide,' collusion with foreign powers against Brazilian interests, and undermining national morality." Even among educated people the assumption is common that it is unpatriotic to try to reduce the natural rate of population growth. In Malawi the leadership goes even further. Overpopulation, they hold, is a purely American phenomenon. "Discussion of the 'quality of life,' which so pervades American journals, seems singularly grotesque here. Americans have persuaded themselves that man has overrun the universe. In this part of Africa that assumption is rather silly." Malawians are inclined to think that what animates Westerners is "just the old-style racism tricked out in new garb."

Even in Kenya, where the official policy is favorable to family planning, opposition elements have seized on both the fear of neighboring countries and the suspicions of foreign influence to stir up trouble for the government. As a result, it has been "difficult to gain from high officials strong commitments in favor of family planning that could later be used against them."

Finally, it should be noted that even in countries where the dominant view favors rapid population growth there are likely to be significant dissenting opinions. Even in Malawi "there are people in and out of the Government who view unrestricted population growth with alarm," though they are careful to express this view in private only. In Brazil disagreement is open. "Articulate opinion in Brazil is deeply divided over family planning . . . Although it is still politically advantageous to oppose family planning in some circles, the climate for individuals and groups to express themselves and to act favorably is much more encouraging than in the past."

3) *Moral and religious objections to birth control.* Whether Dr. Banda is motivated by dreams of a Greater Malawi or not, he clearly has strong moral objections to birth control. "The Government, the ruling Party, and the Life President all are opposed to birth control, to population planning, and to the dissemination of any information about sex, which is considered to be a topic unsuited to the sensibilities of decent people." Dr. Banda's position on birth control is substantially the same as that of the American Medical Association 35 years ago when he was a student in the United States.

Similar attitudes are, of course, to be found elsewhere, although in none of the countries covered by the Conference are they held by the leadership with quite the same intensity as in Malawi. The Ivory Coast, for instance, is another country in which traditional attitudes are still strong. The dissemination of birth control literature is still prohibited by law. Many of the nation's leaders, however, "including President Houphouet-Boigny himself, a former medical doctor, clearly recognize the merits of a family control program." The problem is not yet felt to be serious enough, though, to justify an official change in policy.

The last three years have seen dramatic changes in Philippine attitudes toward population and family planning. Formerly, "birth control and contraceptives were subjects that all except a very small minority of professionals and scholars discussed only furtively. Government officials and politicians with rare exceptions studiously tried to avoid expressing any opinion publically. Now all of this is changing . . ."

A similar change occurred in Indonesia where, from being taboo in the Sukarno era, birth control and family planning have become topics of open and officially sanctioned discussion. In Brazil, as already noted, although official policy is pronatalist, opinion is divided. The Church is ambivalent. Although its official position "is adherence to *Humanae Vitae,* in practice the Brazilian Church is probably the most open to family planning of any in Latin America. Theologians have criticized the reasoning behind the Pope's position and offered justification for limiting and spacing children as a personal decision."

In general, as these examples suggest, there seems to have been a significant diminution of moral and religious objections to family planning in the last few years.

4) *Labor shortage.* While the less developed countries have been worrying about how to provide employment for their rapidly growing populations, the developed countries of Western Europe and Japan have been experiencing rapid economic growth with correspondingly high rates of employment and a negligible amount of unemployment. To the business man, trying to fill the rapidly increasing orders for his product, it appears that there is a severe labor shortage. Since these countries have low and still declining rates of population increase, it was probably inevitable that sooner or later someone would begin to blame the labor shortage on the slow growth of population.

This is just what has happened recently in Japan. Shortly after World War II the Japanese government legalized abortion. This was followed by a spectacular decline in fertility, which in less than a decade reached the long-run replacement level (a net reproduction rate of 1), where it has remained ever since. This means that while the population of Japan is still increasing it will, if fertility stays low, continue to slow down and before long stop growing entirely.

While Japanese fertility was falling and the rate of population growth slowing down, Japan has for more than a decade been enjoying an extraordinary economic boom. As in all periods of boom there have, of course, been shortages —of materials, of capital equipment, and of labor. The only thing that is different about this boom from others that have occurred in other countries and at other times is that business men and their spokesmen in political life have begun to associate the shortage of labor with the decline in fertility and to call for a reversal of Japan's policies with respect to birth control and population growth. "Conservative Prime Minister Eisaku Satō, reflecting concern over labor shortage among his business supporters, has called for an increase in the birth rate."

Actually, the kind of labor shortage Japan has been experiencing has nothing to do with either the rate of population growth or the level of efficiency in the use of labor. (An improvement in efficiency has been suggested as an alternative solution to the problem.) A labor shortage is always a concomitant of an economic boom, and booms can occur under widely differing circumstances: with zero or rapid population growth, on high or low levels of efficiency. The cause of a boom is simply an excess of aggregate demand over aggregate supply. It is even possible that under some conditions more rapid growth of population might, while increasing supply, increase demand, through its effect on investment, even more, thus accentuating rather than moderating the boom and with it the labor shortage.

Recent U. S. history provides a good example of the lack of correlation between labor shortage and the growth of labor supply. From 1957 to 1963 the growth of the labor force was relatively slow (800,000 per year) while labor was relatively abundant (unemployment averaged 6 per cent). From 1965 to 1969 the labor force grew much more rapidly (1,600,000 per year) but the labor market was unusually tight (3.7 per cent average unemployment).

The Japanese government can get rid of the labor shortage any time it wants by applying more restrictive fiscal and monetary measures. That it might be reluctant to do so is understandable since such measures would increase unemployment. Both shortage and surplus of labor have their good and their bad features: a shortage is usually accompanied by an undesirable degree of inflation, an evil that has to be set off against the opposite evil of unemployment.

A different source of confusion is the failure to distinguish between total and *per capita* national product. Total product will almost surely grow faster if the labor force is increasing than if it is not (at least in the developed countries where there is an adequate supply of capital and organizing ability). In the case of Belgium, for instance, invidious comparison with other OEEC countries has sometimes been made on the basis of the growth of total GNP alone. But except perhaps for military power—and even that is doubtful under conditions of modern warfare—total national product is irrelevant. The proper measure of welfare is *per capita* product and that is likely to grow *faster* the slower the rate of increase in population and labor force (*1*).*

A different problem posed by slow population growth is the altered age distribution of the population and the labor force. This has caused some concern in Japan and in Belgium and other countries of Western Europe. It is widely assumed that the increased average age of the work force, which results from the slowing of population growth, would have an unfavorable effect on productivity. It is far from clear, however, that this assumption is valid. An older work force is also a more experienced work force. Whether the gain in experience outweighs the loss in youthful vigor is not known. This is a question on which more research needs to be done.

Reasons for Reducing the Rate of Population Growth

1) *Land.* Following Malthus and the other classical economists the population problem has traditionally been conceived of primarily in terms of food (*2*). Food, in turn, is thought of as depending on the amount of land available. If a country has large unoccupied areas, or if its population density is low, the usual judgment is that it has no population problem. Correspondingly, a country with little or no land to spare is considered to have a pressing need to limit its numbers.

While this is only one element in the complex of problems associated with population growth, it is, nonetheless, an important one. Food is, of course, a basic necessity and a country with large reserves of good agricultural land can contemplate the growth of its population with more complacency than a country without such reserves.

There is considerable evidence already of pressure on natural resources, especially agricultural land, in the countries covered at the Conference. Bolivia "already is hard pressed to provide subsistence for its existing population." The problem in "the rural highland areas is steady reduction of size of land holdings as they are redistributed to heirs of a deceased."

In Indonesia President Suharto said in his 1967 Budget Message to Parliament: "Looking into the future we should courageously face the fact that the increase of population is not in balance with the increase of available food supplies, whether produced at home or imported." Afghanistan "is attempting to achieve self-sufficiency in foodstuffs by 1973" but this is "a probably impossible goal."

In the Ivory Coast "land pressures in the populous forest regions of the south are already very great and a number of conflicts between newcomers and the old settlers have occurred."

If Kenya's present rate of population growth continues, the potentially productive acres per person will sink from 4.2 (1965) to 2.6 in 1980 and 1.3 in 2000. What this means is well summarized in the following passage: "Because of limited supplies of land and other resources, long-term diminishing economic returns for the people will result, unless more capital, more trained labor, and

---

* Such a numeral refers to "Notes" at the end of an article.

technological innovations come into the equation. Cultivated land is currently limited to 4.2 acres per person, capital is still in short supply, and the improvement in labor skills is slow."

Even Brazil and Malawi, whose leaders look with such favor on continuing rapid population growth, have at least regional land/labor problems: Brazil in the Northeast and Malawi in the settled areas of the South.

So far as food supply is concerned there are two possible escape routes from pressure on land. One is to adopt new techniques which give higher yields from the land already under cultivation. This is the essence of the Green Revolution. New seed varieties have been combined with much greater amounts of fertilizer and water to produce spectacular increases in the yield of such crops as rice and wheat. The chief results so far have been in southeast Asia. It will be necessary in subsequent reports to keep close tabs on the spread of such techniques to Africa and South America.

The other escape route is to open up new land. Not all countries have this option—Hong Kong, for example!—but most of those covered in the Conference do have large areas that are either unoccupied or very thinly settled. The big questions, of course, are how good is the land and how much capital investment will it take to open it up and make it productive?

In some areas the investment would be so large and the yield so small as to make development utterly unfeasible. In the Stalin era grandiose plans were formulated for agricultural development in the Arctic. Experience soon led to the conclusion that such development on a large scale would be grossly uneconomic. Similarly, many areas are so mountainous or rocky or have such poor soil that development is out of the question. An interesting special case is that of the Amazonian jungles in Brazil. While supporting luxuriant vegetation in its native state, this area is considered by some experts unsuited for cultivation. The problem is that once the jungle is cleared the heavy rains soon leach the nutrients out of the soil.

Two of the most common problems in bringing more land into cultivation are water and transportation. The southern region of Malawi has 7.8 million acres of which "half is theoretically arable; only 20% is currently being farmed. Communications and water are needed, of course, to bring the rest under the hoe and this is what the government is attempting to do." The Ivoirien leaders' lack of concern about population growth is based, partly, at least, on the conviction that "the continued prosperity of the country can accomplish any miracle" including conversion of the "parched, arid lands of the northern savannah into pleasant, salubrious places easily able to accommodate the nation's peoples."

The Brazilian government is constructing highways that will cut the Amazon region from east to west and from north to south that are aimed specifically at the settlement of the unemployed, poverty-stricken surplus population of the Northeast. Opinions differ sharply as to the wisdom of these projects: proponents see a rich inland empire developing, while critics fear that the vast expenditures required will result in no more than a trickle of resettlement into what they consider a basically unpromising area for agricultural development (3).

In Bolivia transportation presents fantastic difficulties: "Topography, road conditions, and expenses of transportation are beyond the belief of anyone who has not traveled for months in eastern and northern Bolivia. Roads and bridges are being built, but a truck inching up the grade from Villa Tunari in the Chapare with the load of bananas for Cochabamba may still expect a quarter of his load to freeze and be ruined on the high pass. From a sugar and rice importing country Bolivia now has a surplus of both. Rice rots for lack of transportation, and quotas have been strictly imposed on sugar growers. Bolivia's problems with tropical products can only be solved with enormous expenditures in transportation facilities."

2) *Capital.* The problem of capital formation is pervasive. Not only is capital required to open up new lands—in some cases vast amounts of capital—but it is also necessary to introduce such new techniques as those of the Green Revolution, to expand employment in non-agricultural pursuits, to provide educational and health facilities, and finally to raise the standard of living in line with the rapidly rising expectations of peoples all over the world.

Capital formation involves the diversion of a part of current output to building for the future. Manpower and materials, which might be used to satisfy current consumer wants, are used instead to build roads, irrigation systems, factories, and schools which will help satisfy consumer wants only at some time in the future. In a relatively poor society the margin over essential current consumption is small; hence this amount of building that can be done each year for the future is likewise small.

Population growth means one of two things: either (1) a part of current capital formation—in the case of rapid growth, a large part—must be used merely to provide the additional people with equipment, buildings, etc., on the existing level, thus reducing the amount that can be used for improvement; or (2) the additional people are left out and all the capital is concentrated on improving the lot of the in-group. This perpetuates, or gives rise to, what has been aptly called a dualistic society; one sector with jobs and a rising standard of living, the other unemployed or underemployed, scraping along on a bare subsistence level.

The concern engendered by the problem of capital formation is not with the absolute size of population but rather with its rate of growth. Critics of the present government's policy would undoubtedly be willing to grant that Brazil could eventually support 200 million people at a satisfactory standard of living but they would insist that it makes a great deal of difference how soon that figure is reached.

Awareness of this problem is spreading. One of the clearest statements is contained in the paper on population issued by the Government of Ghana in March 1969:

> The size of our present population does not pose immediate problems for us. However, the rate at which the population is increasing will very certainly create serious social, economic and political difficulties before the turn of the century (*4*).

In a seminar on population and development at University College in Nairobi the drag on Kenya's economic progress was described in the following terms:

> Population growth impinges on development by increased pressure on the land, by speeding up the consumption of non-replaceable natural resources, by slowing the rate at which capital is accumulated, and by reducing the rate of growth of resources and equipment that can be used by the labor force.

Nearly all major economists in Brazil "have publicly insisted that a more moderate rate of population growth will ease the burden of future social and economic development." The outstanding exception is the Minister of Finance, Antonio Delfim Neto, who "holds that the present economic growth rate can absorb the current population increase."

3) *Education.* Many illustrations could be given of the inadequacy of current rates of capital formation in the less developed countries to do all the things the people are demanding and the governments are trying to do. One of the clearest is in the field of education.

In Hong Kong the competition for entrance into the better schools is so intense that "many families have to ante up for private tutors in order to keep their children in the better schools."

Although the government of the Ivory Coast has greatly increased its allotment to education in the national budget, "it is doubtful that even with this sizeable increase it will be able to resolve the urgent problem of educating the nation's youth in view of the inordinately high cost which such education involves."

> Currently some 60 per cent of primary age children are enrolled in Kenya. The government plans an annual increase of 4 per cent. Under present population growth rates the total number receiving no education in 1990 will be twice the present number. If fertility were reduced by 50 per cent in the next 15 years, the government's goal of universal primary education would be possible by 1990.
>
> Brazil's educational problems are legion . . . While awareness of these problems is growing . . . governmental good will is undermined by the high proportion of youth in the population. Any effective solution will demand additional public funds, reducing the amount of capital available to keep the economy growing at politically acceptable rates. It is interesting to note that the leading supporter of family planning in the Brazilian government is the Minister of Education.
>
> The Indonesian population responds so enthusiastically to modern educational and medical services that the government's truly heroic efforts in those areas of activity have not at all kept up with the demands.

In rural areas in the Philippines, "the average youngster receives only four years of schooling. A chronic shortage of textbooks plus over-crowded classrooms means that many acquire but a smattering of learning."

Even in Malawi, whose leadership is so scornful of the idea that population growth might constitute a problem, the educational situation is described in the following terms:

> Malawians have a reputation for hard work and thrift, and a high regard for education . . . Despite this emphasis on getting ahead, only a minority of Malawians is literate in any language. About 17 per cent of the school-age population was in school in 1966. The 51 secondary schools cannot cope with the qualified demand for places . . .

4) *Employment.* As population grows, so—with a lag—does the labor force. Where are the additional workers to find employment? Basically, there are three possibilities: (*a*) through more intensive labor methods of cultivation in the existing agricultural sector; (*b*) through the opening up of new lands; and (*c*) through the expansion of industry and other non-agricultural sectors of the economy.

(*a*) seems to offer little hope. Agriculture is already labor intensive in most of the less developed countries. As improved methods are introduced it seems much more likely that they will employ less rather than more labor. This is what has happened in the developed countries and early indications are that it is beginning to happen in the countries touched by the Green Revolution (5).

(*b*) should provide employment in rough proportion to the amount of land opened up (6). But in view of the difficulties mentioned above and the large amounts of capital required, it seems unrealistic to expect that large numbers of workers will find employment in this way.

We are thus left with (*c*) as the main possibility for absorbing the growth in the labor supply—plus, it seems likely, a substantial number of workers displaced in agriculture as productivity rises. But because it requires capital and organizing ability, both of which are in short supply, the expansion of industry lags behind the demand for jobs in practically all countries with high rates of population growth. The result is a piling up of unemployed or underemployed labor in the *favelas* or *barrios* which are such a characteristic—and depressing—feature of the rapidly growing cities of the less developed countries.

Brazil provides an outstanding example of this whole process.

> The percentage of persons employed in the primary sector is declining, although it is still much too high for a 'modern' economy. The agricultural sector is expelling excess population . . . Work opportunities in industry have not kept pace with the influx of population . . . The increase of population in the cities without compensatory employment has created large contingents of people living what is often called a "marginal" existence. Although the most obvious sign has been the mushrooming squatter settlements (favelas), the underlying problem is a low income level and what seem to be substantial levels of underemployment.

Similar reports come from Indonesia, the Philippines, Kenya, the Ivory Coast, and Bolivia. In all of them the labor force is growing faster than satisfactory employment opportunities, people are moving from the country to the cities, urban slums with deplorable housing and health conditions are proliferating. Concern over this kind of development is perhaps the most important reason growing sections of the elite in these countries are beginning to realize the need to slow down population growth.

In some respects Malawi may constitute an exception. President Banda is reported to be determined to prevent the growth of favelas in his country. His remedy is to keep people employed on the land. With that end in view no tractors are being imported into the country. Whether this laudable policy will succeed in the face of a three per cent or more annual growth in population is open to serious question. It is reported that even now in Malawi "there is a huge population of teen-age males, a majority not in school and not at work." Moreover, there are some 200,000 Malawians working outside the country. Considering that the total population is between four and five million this is a very large number—the comparable figure for the United States would be ten million. What will happen if the countries in which these 200,000 work decide in response to labor supply pressures of their own to close their doors to foreign workers?

5) *Environment.* The scope of concern about the effects of population growth has broadened greatly in recent years. Traditionally, people worried only about food and other means of subsistence. Many discussions of population are still couched in these terms. But increasingly attention has shifted from food to the total output of goods and services. The question: Will the population be able to feed itself? has given way to the larger question: What effect will population growth have on gross national product?

Still more recently, the scope of concern has again been broadening to include the effects of growth on the environment. This has been particularly true in the developed countries. To judge by reports at the Conference there is still little interest in the less developed countries in environmental problems. Is this because they do not have such problems? Evidence that will be introduced shortly suggests that the reason is rather that the standard of living is still so low that people are absorbed by other, to them more pressing, concerns.

In some respects, of course, their environmental problems are less serious than those of the developed countries. But if they succeed in raising their standard of living, as almost all of them are trying to do (7), pollution and other undesirable concomitants of economic growth will grow correspondingly worse. Japan provides a good example of what happens when a poor, densely populated country takes off on the path of rapid economic development. Growth has been so fast that Japan's GNP is now the third largest in the world. *Per capita* output is still less than that of most Western countries but it is approaching the Western European level. By the first two tests mentioned above, i.e., the ability to feed its people and to increase the total amount of goods and services available to them, Japan has had a spectacularly successful record.

The effect of growth on the environment, however, has been badly neglected:

> Japan today finds that its large industrial facilities, although generally bright and shiny, are increasingly being surrounded by the blight of indus-

trial pollution, of the atmosphere, the countryside, the rivers, and the coastal sea. Housing is woefully inadequate; environmental engineering has only begun to be developed; and the rapidity of the spread of the urban sprawl remains relatively unmanaged.

From this and other reports it appears that pollution and congestion may be worse in Japan than anywhere else in the world. Further population growth, now that Japan has reached a relatively advanced stage of economic development, would clearly add that much more to the already excessive burden on the environment.

Although it has not yet reached the Japanese level of industrial development, Brazil is already experiencing serious environmental problems. "Brazil's cities also suffer from urban problems common to developed countries—like smog, deficient transportation, health services, education, and sanitary facilities."

In one respect these problems—especially health, sanitation, and housing—are actually worse in the less developed countries since they lack the resources to cope with them.

In the Philippines, for example,

> Newcomers to the cities create new slums . . . Renting a few hundred square meters or simply squatting on public land, they collect galvanized metal roofing, scraps of lumber, and hammer flat five-gallon kerosene cans to erect close-packed shacks. Water for these proliferating communities usually is available from public faucets. However, sewage pipes rarely are laid in and garbage collection is at a minimum. Resulting health problems can prove even more stubborn to correct than they were in the rural *barrios* where these migrants came from.

Rapid population growth adds to environmental problems in many ways: it increases the congestion in the cities, it dilutes the capital available to build the necessary social infrastructure, it increases the pressure to use harmful pesticides in order to increase the food supply, it hastens the destruction of wildlife preserves and areas of natural beauty. In some countries—Kenya and Malawi are notable examples—the last named factor is of immediate, as well as long-run, significance because of its detrimental effect on the tourist trade.

THE PEOPLE

Interest in family planning is by no means synonymous with interest in population control. In both the developed and the less developed countries many people have supported family planning purely for its effects on maternal and child welfare without any thought as to how it might influence population growth. Some demographers have warned, on the other hand, that family planning by itself may not be enough to bring population growth within manageable limits.

Up to now, voluntary family planning, however, seems to be the only policy instrument those who are concerned to reduce population growth are willing to support. Everywhere there is strong emphasis on voluntarism, even in countries whose governments are not adverse to authoritarian methods in other areas.

In Yugoslavia interviews with family planning workers revealed "opposition to any 'population policies' as state intervention in a private sphere."

Tom Mboya when Minister for Economic Planning in Kenya, after warning that population growth could exceed economic growth, went on to say:

> I must also warn against those who in their enthusiasm for family planning go around preaching the scare of population explosion. This may be the problem in some countries but it is certainly not the prompting factor in Kenya. . . . It has never been the Government's intention to introduce birth control or family planning by compulsory or legislative measures.

To have any impact on population growth, family planning programs must not only be widely accepted but must also lead the acceptors to reduce significantly the size of their families. What do we know about the attitudes both toward family planning and toward family size?

In the developed countries the transition from high to low fertility took place without any prompting or encouragement by governments. On the contrary, the official stance of both church and state was opposed to birth control and family limitation. Many countries have had laws prohibiting the dissemination of birth control information or the sale of contraceptive devices. Some of those laws are still on the books, though no attempt is made to enforce them. In Belgium, for instance, a bill before Parliament which would bring the legal situation more into conformity with practice has "lain dormant partly because of the general political sensitivity to the subject and partly because those who might be thought the logical supporters of reform—private groups engaged in birth control programs, etc.— prefer the evil they know—a very restrictive law that is almost completely unenforced—to the one they fear—a liberalized but somewhat restrictive law that might be rigorously enforced."

The conclusion has often been drawn from the fertility history of the developed countries that a) family limitation will spontaneously catch on at a certain stage in socio-economic development, and b) there is no possibility of getting people to practice family limitation until this stage has been reached.

The latter assumption is crucial for population policy. If it is strictly true, governments would do well to concentrate on indirect measures designed to hasten socio-economic development rather than on direct efforts to get people to adopt family planning.

As to the former, there are two different explanations of the way in which development affects fertility.

1) The first is economic. In the less developed countries children are regarded as a source of old age security and as a welcome addition to the agricultural labor supply. The strength of these motives decreases as society becomes industrialized and urbanized. This change in attitude toward fertility is reinforced by a decline in infant and child mortality since it is not necessary to have as many children to insure a high probability that the desired number will survive.

Along with the decline in the advantages goes an increase in the economic disadvantages of having children (*a*) there is an increase in the cost of rearing, and especially of educating, children; (*b*) the competition of consumer goods and of extra-familial activities becomes more intense.

An important question is, will the historical experience of the developed countries have to be repeated in the underdeveloped countries? Some of the motives for limiting family size that have just been mentioned seem to be appearing at an earlier stage in the developmental process.

The desire to educate children, for instance, is already prominent in most of the countries covered at the Conference. Mention has already been made of the fact that "the Indonesian population responds so enthusiastically to modern educational and medical services that the government has not been at all able to keep up with the demand." In the Philippines, "as literacy grew with the public schools . . . new values entered the society . . . When ordinary Filipinos saw that graduates of these schools actually could enter government on merit and sometimes quickly become prominent, they developed an extraordinary confidence in education as an avenue to advancement." Malawi, Kenya, Brazil, and the Ivory Coast provide other examples of the strong desire on the part of the people to have their children educated.

The competition of consumer goods may also begin to have an influence at an earlier stage than it did in Western society. In the Philippines, for instance, "both Christian and democratic values foster aspirations galloping far ahead of employment and income opportunities." As "consumption appetites are aroused by the numerous transistor radios, ever fewer Filipinos are content with circumstances of the past . . ."

It is too early to tell whether the desire for education and for consumer goods will have a significant effect on fertility. The fact that such desires exist already, however, should at least help to dispel the deterministic pessimism of those who argue that interest in limiting family size cannot appear until a later state in economic development (8).

2) The alternative emphasis in the theory of demographic transition is on ideas. According to this view, while economic factors are not ruled out they are less important in explaining the decline in fertility in the West than the change in ideas which occurred in the 19th and 20th centuries. The hope, of course, is that, through contact with the West and through educational and propaganda efforts, ideas in the less developed countries can be changed more quickly than in the past. Two sets of ideas that seem to be particularly important for fertility behavior are:

a) It is wrong to interfere with "nature" in the realm of sex and reproduction. This has already been mentioned in connection with the attitude of leaders in certain countries. It is an equally or more important obstacle to the acceptance of family planning by the mass of the people. This idea appears in many forms, varying from the Belgian bishops' earlier injunction to confessors to be alert in asking, "Do you commit yourself totally to divine Providence in the generation of children?" to the barren woman's fear in Kenya "of being accused of witchcraft or of supernatural punishments."

Many Ivoiriens, like other Africans, are convinced "that one ought not to try to interfere with events or try to influence them—especially where the birth of children is concerned—because such is God's will. This feeling is reinforced by both the pagan religions and the Islamic and Christian sects to which many Ivoiriens belong." The vast majority of Indonesians "regard fecundity as a sign of the special blessings and bounty of God."

Similar beliefs and inhibitions are common in other less developed countries. More research is needed on how serious an obstacle they are likely to be to the acceptance of family planning. To what extent are they losing their force already? How are they affected by the rapid increase in education of the young? By increased knowledge of the possibility and the techniques of birth control?

b) Studies of fertility in the West—both of the change over time and of the differences between socio-economic groups at a given point in time—put much emphasis on the importance of the idea of improving one's lot in life (or one's children's lot). In pre-modern society a fatalistic attitude was common. This is still true on the lower socio-economic levels in the developed countries (9) and among the mass of the people in the less developed countries. "Social-psychological characteristics affecting family planning that would apply to much of rural Kenya include a high degree of fatalism, or the individual's feeling that he lacks the ability to control the future." In Indonesia, "whatever the cultural and religious obstacles to family planning, it seems probable that the greatest will be merely the difficulty of persuading the human individual—and keeping him or her persuaded—that systematic family planning is worth all the trouble."

At what stage in economic and cultural development does the idea of taking purposeful action to improve one's lot catch on? Is it a result of change in the mode of production or of the emergence of a rational outlook on life? Can the latter develop ahead of the former?

A special factor affecting the disposition to plan for the future that received considerable attention at the Conference is land tenure. Several participants suggested that a shift from tenancy to outright ownership of land may have a significant effect on fertility. An excellent statement of this thesis is contained in the report on the Philippines:

> Prevalence of share-tenancy, especially in most rice growing regions, fortifies this pressure for more children and especially sons. For self-defeating as it is in the national economy, the fact is that all the tenant has to sell is his labor and that of his family. It is only when he becomes at least a lease holder or, better yet, an owner that the farmer's attitude on this score changes—and then but gradually. As he begins to think of himself as a property holder, a new set of criteria conditions his actions. Does he want to have two or three sons among whom the farm must be divided?

An observer who has traveled extensively in rural Yugoslavia notes that "families with more than two children are exceptions of increasing rarity. The reasons offered: not enough land and a desire to avoid further splintering of already small holdings . . ."

A special factor in Yugoslavia is a law requiring equal treatment of male and female heirs. "The postwar law has been implemented only gradually . . . While it may be only a minor factor, a Belgrade sociologist who has done extensive demographic field work tells me that she finds a significant correlation between the rate of fertility decline and the extent to which the law is observed . . ."

It was also suggested that changes in land tenure may have had a significant effect on fertility in Taiwan.

While suggestive, these examples are far from conclusive. Somewhat contradictory evidence was reported from Egypt and Zambia. Clearly more detailed studies of the relation between changes in tenure and in fertility are needed. The less developed countries should provide a good laboratory over the course of the next decade or so. Hopefully, it will be possible to find cases, either in past or future experience, where tenure differs while other conditions are substantially the same.

Another factor that may affect fertility is information. People may have no clear understanding of the fact that it is possible to limit family size; or, if possible, how to do it. Ignorance may, of course, be a product of the belief system; if people think it is impious or immoral to control family size or if they think planning for the future is futile, they will be unlikely to acquire knowledge about the means. Information, however, may still play an independent role. For while beliefs inimical to family limitation may keep people from acquiring information on their own, they may not be strong enough to keep people from being influenced by information presented to them from the outside.

Several examples of the possibility of such influence were reported to the Conference. In remote rural areas of Afghanistan, for instance, people who had heard about birth control on radio broadcasts from Kabul wanted to know how they could obtain contraceptive supplies. In the Philippines press and radio are "now beginning to make family planning a topic of conversation even among otherwise traditional or rural *barrio* folk."

A survey of attitudes toward family planning of 2,000 respondents in the Djakarta area by the Social Science Department of the University of Indonesia in 1967 showed that "a majority was favorably inclined but that few had any real knowledge of the subject." Likewise a KAP survey sponsored by the Indonesian Family Planning Association showed that "levels of public information with regard to family planning are extremely low but there exists a strong positive attitude toward the acquisition of information."

Similarly, favorable attitudes toward learning more about family planning methods together with little knowledge and less practice were reported for samples of the urban population in both Kenya and Brazil. Reports from Malawi are conflicting. Some welfare workers maintain the attitude of women is "overwhelmingly pronatal . . . others have argued that women are avid for contraceptive education, that, given the chance, they express a very lively fear of being trapped into successive pregnancies . . ."

While it by no means assures success of family planning programs, widespread ignorance combined with a professed desire to learn more at least suggests that it may be possible to speed up the decline in fertility by spreading knowledge and access to the means of family limitation.

Evidence that adoption of family planning does not have to wait on social and economic development comes from Korea, where in rural, non-modernized areas people are already practicing family planning on a large scale. An example of rapid adaptation to new social and economic conditions came from Italy where, it was reported, workers who have moved to the north from the high fertility south have about the same fertility as the native northerners.

It was suggested that family planning may itself act as an agent of social change.

> Any innovation that creates a profound change in the way things have happened for centuries is going to influence people's social attitudes and particularly the ones most closely related to the change. The abstract argument between the advocates of social change on the one hand and family planning on the other is rather sterile, since what you have is complicated interactions of various factors leading to the desired results, not one factor versus another.

What, finally, is the role of birth control technology? One view is that technology is of little importance. In Belgium, for instance, where fertility is low, the majority of couples still use *coitus interruptus* and the rhythm method. A 1970 estimate of the St. Pierre physicians is "that some 17 per cent of the relevant groups of Belgium women use the pill, under 1 per cent the loop, and only some 20 per cent of the couples use any of the modern means." In this respect Belgium is fairly typical of Western Europe, where the great decline in fertility of the 19th and early 20th centuries came about without extensive use of even appliance methods of contraception. The "modern" methods, pill and IUD, were, of course, unknown until long after the decline had reached its low point.

> Belgian students of the subject conclude from these and other data on the low rate of modern contraceptive use, from the low birth rate, and from clinical experience at St. Pierre and elsewhere that the rate of illicit abortions is quite high. The range of guesstimates is from 80,000–200,000 per year. Assuming the midpoint of that spread, 140,000, to be the correct figure, it roughly equals the number of births in the country in 1968 (141,242).

Many demographers have concluded from this experience that the techniques of birth control are unimportant, that motivation is the overriding factor.

The opposite view, that techniques are, or, at least, may be, important, finds support in what has happened in countries where abortion has been legalized. Japan is, of course, the outstanding example. Following the passage in 1948 of the Eugenic Protection Law, which, in spite of nominal restrictions, in practice made abortions obtainable on demand, fertility dropped with unprecedented speed. The gross reproduction rate, which was 2.5 in 1925 and 2.0 in 1940, went up to 2.2 in 1947. Then following the legalization of abortion it fell to 1.15 in 1955 and has remained at, or slightly above, 1.0 since then.

Marked declines in fertility also occurred in the socialist countries of Eastern Europe in the period following liberalization of their abortion laws. In Yugoslavia abortion was first legalized in 1952, the motivation being a "desire to reduce the incidence of illegal abortions performed under unsatisfactory conditions, with attendant dangers to life and health." The gross reproduction rate dropped from 1.89 in 1950 to 1.26 in 1967. Other factors were no doubt involved in the drop in fertility in both Japan and Eastern Europe but the timing and the speed of the decline suggest that increased availability of abortion made a significant contribution.

Further evidence that the availability of an acceptable technique does make a difference, at least in the short run, is provided by recent experience in Rumania. A very restrictive law on abortion was reintroduced there in 1966. The birth rate shot up from an average of 14.3 in 1966 to 27.3 in 1967. It has since dropped, but only part way back to its previous level (23.3 in 1969). This indicates quite clearly that while people are shifting to other methods of control the adaptation takes time and still is far from complete.

In both Japan and Yugoslavia efforts have been made by governments and family planning groups to persuade people to shift from abortion to contraceptives as a means of birth control. Some of the reasons these efforts have met with only partial success are indicated in the following report on population attitudes in Yugoslavia.

> The reasons offered at this level are the ones one would expect: "it takes the fun out of it" and "my husband wouldn't approve, but doesn't know when I have an abortion" are perhaps the commonest. One knows, for example, of a Vojvodina peasant who had five abortions that her husband was unaware of, all in the three years between the births of their first (female) and second (male) children; or of girls who insist that their partners use neither condom nor coitus interruptus because they "would rather take a chance." They know exactly where to go for a quick pregnancy test or an abortion, but are vague about other possibilities because they are simply not interested.

The widespread existence of such attitudes combined with the difficulties that have attended the use of the pill and the IUD suggests the need for a redefinition of the ideal means of fertility control. "What we need is a non-toxic, completely effective substance which, when self-administered on a single occasion, would insure the non-pregnant state at the completion of a monthly cycle. So far our methods of fertility control, because they rely heavily on foresight, have been limited in their efficiency in all societies, including our own. If we can invoke hindsight, and if the method can be self-administered, there could be a quantum jump in the speed and effectiveness of family planning programs around the world."

It now appears that as a result of recent research on the prostaglandins such a method may actually become available within the next few years. The prostaglandins are fatty acid substances which occur naturally in the body. They were identified initially in semen in the 1930s. It is now known that there is a group of 14 or 16 such substances which have somewhat different characteristics. The most important from the point of view of fertility control are the prostaglandins E-2 and F-2-alpha, which are particularly effective in stimulating the contraction of the uterine muscles. They have been used for a couple of years now to induce labor at term and they are very effective at this. Dr. Karim in Uganda has administered them to more than 700 women for the induction of labor.

A little more than a year ago some of the researchers hit on the idea of using the prostaglandins for emptying the uterus much earlier in term. The initial studies were done with intravenous injection, which is somewhat difficult and extends over a period of 6 to 20 hours. In September 1970, however, Dr. Karim and others reported at a meeting held under the auspices of the New York Academy of Science that, when administered by the vaginal route, prostaglandin was effective in inducing the menses.

In the view of one of the participants in the Conference who has followed the prostaglandin developments closely, "this could be a fundamental breakthrough in fertility control. It will take some additional time to bring to fruition. But there are so many buttressing findings by multiple parties in multiple countries that there seems good reason for optimism. Because we are dealing with a natural substance there are unlikely to be any of the ordinary problems of toxicity. A few years hence it seems likely that women will have available through drugstores—thus circumventing the clinical bottleneck—medicated tampons or tablets which they can insert to bring on the menses any time they want to. This means that a woman will have complete control of her fertility with at most three or four acts per year, which would subject her to the influence of the drug for less than a total of 24 hours annually, which means that the problems of prolonged administration which exist with some of the current means would not apply."

While not denying the importance of motivation, the optimists at the Conference endorsed the idea of a trade-off between the strength of motivation and ease of controlling fertility. The prostaglandins offer the hope of a shift in the terms of this trade-off which could have a significant impact on population growth in the latter part of the 20th century.

Notes

1. Even this measure needs to be adjusted, as pointed out below, for the costs of overcrowding which has occurred in many urban areas.
2. In classical economics "food" stands for the basic necessities of life.
3. An intermediate position on the possibilities of resettlement is suggested in the following comment: "It is a mistake to think that the interior of Brazil is nothing but the Amazonian jungle. A half a day down the highway from Belem to Brasilia you start emerging onto the planalto, where people are raising cattle. Now as to the highways: their justification is partly for security, but it is already known that there are extensive mineral resources which could not be exploited up to now because of their isolation. Brazilians may be naive when they think of areas like the Amazon being 'settled' in the sense of having

people all over the place. On the other hand, it is realistic to assume that there can be poles of population and economic growth where there are minerals, where agricultural land might be better than ordinary, at cross-roads, etc."

4. *Studies in Family Planning*, Number 44, August, 1969.
5. Rice may be something of an exception. While California farmers can plant rice by airplane and harvest with combines, throughout nearly all of Asia rice seedlings are transplanted by hand. No satisfactory machines for doing this job have yet been developed. Irrigation, preferably all year around, is fundamental to the Green Revolution in the tropics, which frequently increases the agricultural year from five to twelve months. This means just that much more employment on the land and fewer men who flock to the cities in the dry season seeking cash employment.
6. With qualification, of course, for differences in quality which affect the kinds of products and the appropriate methods of cultivation. The report on Bolivia, for example, says that much of the lowlands "is suitable only for cattle and would not support even the national average population."
7. Malawi may be an exception.
8. The importance of both education and competing consumer goods is emphasized in the following report from Brazil: "Middle class Brazilians all say the same thing about family planning: it is so expensive nowadays to bring up children that we only have two. What this means is undoubtedly linked to giving children what people in the middle class expect to give them. This is education, but it is also clothes, travel, recreation, etc. . . . Many poor people somehow survive without any of the amenities we consider important. If they get some rice and beans most days they make it. In the middle or upper lower class, however, many people have heard of birth control and even use it themselves. They may live in a favela, but they try to send their children to school, aspire to a television set and to have some furniture in their house. There seems to be a line in the lower class of Latin America which separates those for whom life is survival from those for whom life involves options, however limited, of education and consumption."
9. See, for example, L. Rainwater: *Family Design*, Chicago, 1965.

The Author

ALAN SWEEZY obtained his B.A. in history in 1929 and his Ph.D. in economics in 1934 from Harvard. He taught economics at Harvard from 1934 to 1938 and at Williams from 1940 to 1947. In between he was in the Division of Research and Statistics of the Federal Reserve Board in Washington. Since the fall of 1949 he has been at Caltech, where he is professor of economics and associate director of the population studies program. Dr. Sweezy became interested, during the depression of the 1930s, in the role of population growth in the Keynesian theory of employment and income. He wrote several articles dealing with this subject, including "Population Growth and Investment Opportunity," which appeared in the *Quarterly Journal of Economics*, November, 1940. In

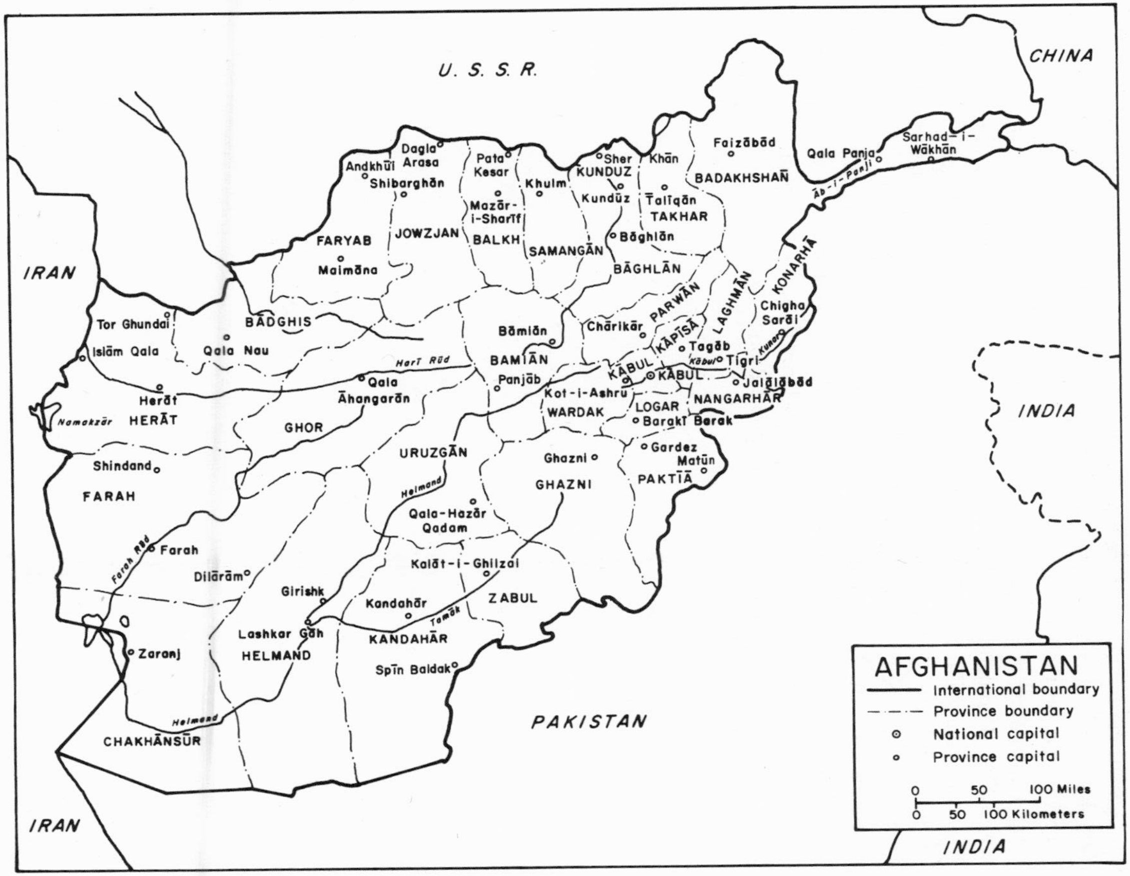
AFGHANISTAN
International boundary
Province boundary
National capital
Province capital
0 50 100 Miles
0 50 100 Kilometers
U. S. S. R.
CHINA
IRAN
IRAN
INDIA
INDIA
PAKISTAN
Sarhad-i-Wākhān
Qala Panja
Āb-i-Panja
Faizābād
BADAKHSHĀN
Sher Khān
KUNDUZ
Kundūz
Tāliqān
TAKHAR
Bāghlān
BĀGHLĀN
Khulm
SAMANGĀN
Pata Kesar
Mazār-i-Sharīf
BALKH
Dagla Arasa
Andkhūī
Shibarghān
JOWZJAN
FARYAB
Maimāna
BĀDGHIS
Qala Nau
Tor Ghundai
Islām Qala
Herāt
HERĀT
Namakzār
Harī Rūd
Qala Āhangarān
GHOR
Bāmiān
BAMIĀN
Panjāb
Chārikār
PARWĀN
KĀPĪSĀ
Tagāb
LAGHMĀN
KONARHĀ
Chigha Sarāi
Kunar
Tīgri
Kābul
KĀBUL
KĀBUL
Jalālābād
NANGARHĀR
Kot-i-Ashru
WARDAK
LOGAR
Barakī Barak
Gardez
Matūn
PAKTĪĀ
Ghazni
GHAZNI
URUZGĀN
Helmand
Qala-Hazār Qadam
Kalāt-i-Ghilzai
ZABUL
Kandahār
Tarnak
KANDAHĀR
Spīn Baldak
Shindand
FARAH
Farah
Farah Rūd
Dilārām
Girishk
Lashkar Gāh
HELMAND
Zaranj
Helmand
CHAKHĀNSŪR

recent years he has returned to the study of population and since the spring of 1968 has given a course on population problems at Caltech. He has written several papers on the causes and consequences of population growth: "The Economic Explanation of Fertility Changes in the United States," *Population Studies,* July, 1971; "Population, GNP, and the Environment" in *Are Our Descendants Doomed?,* Viking Press Inc., 1971; "The Economic Meaning of a Labor Shortage," *Science,* 3 July 1970. In addition to his academic work on population problems Dr. Sweezy has been active in organizations dealing with family planning and population growth. He is currently president of Pasadena Planned Parenthood and a member of the board of directors of Planned Parenthood—World Population. He is also a member of Zero Population Growth and has spoken and written on the economic implications of a stable population.

Afghanistan

Louis Dupree

Afghanistan, a landlocked country about the size of Texas (250,000 square miles), is not densely populated but, in the absence of a census, the estimate of 15 million inhabitants may be far from the fact. Agriculture and grazing are the mainstays of the economy. The people are Muslims and about 95 per cent of them are nonliterate (*1*).

The statistics used in this review, drawn from data available through agencies of the United Nations, U.S.A.I.D., and ministries of the government of Afghanistan, are at best intelligent estimates. The lack of reliable statistics may obscure existing population problems in Afghanistan while at the same time obstructing any sophisticated planning for population control.

Population Profile

Estimates of the rate of population growth vary from 1.9 to 2.5 per cent annually. The population will probably double in about 30 years. The death rate is an estimated 100/1000 during the first year of life; by five years of age, 40 per cent mortality, usually caused by complications accompanying gastrointestinal disturbances. Life expectancy cannot be defined but if one survives the first five years, and is not cut down in a feud, one may achieve a ripe old age.

The population of Afghanistan presents a mosaic of ethnic and linguistic groups (*2*). The boundaries between these elements, however, have tended to grow fuzzy as development programs have opened new employment opportunities and as educational opportunities have expanded. Three major physical types live in Afghanistan (*3*). The basic type apparently relates to the Mediterranean substock of the Caucasoid peoples, who stretch from the Pillars of Hercules on both sides of the Mediterranean Sea through the Arab Near East, Anatolia, Iran, and Afghanistan, into the North-West Frontier Province of West Pakistan. Modified Mongoloids dominate north of the Hindu Kush, but intensive miscegenation has produced such end products as freckle-faced, pug-nosed, blue-eyed, blond Tajik or Uzbak, complete with the classic Mongoloid epicanthic eyefold and high cheek bones.

About 30 per cent of the cattlemen and sheep and goat herders of the high mountain area of Nuristan (eastern Afghanistan) have a recessive blondism (blue or mixed eyes with red or blond hair). The phenomenon is accounted for in part by the people's practice of endogamy and the relative isolation of the region, reinforced by the presence of an extensive cloud cover most of the year.

The third major physical type, Veddoid, is limited to the Brahui, but modified through intermarriage with the Baluch and Farsiwan (Persian speakers of western Afghanistan). The Brahui appear to be related ultimately to the dark-skinned Dravidian speakers of India south of the Narbada River.

Language presents a complex picture. Four major language families (Indo-European, Uralic-Altaic, Mongolian, Dravidian) and probably a fifth (Semitic) are represented, as well as numerous dialects. Indo-Iranian subfamilies of the Indo-European family dominate, with Persian (Dari or Farsi) and Pashto being the most important. Dari is the *lingua franca* of the country, although about 50 per cent of Afghans have Pashto as their mother tongue. Tajiks speak Tajiki dialects of Dari. The mongoloid-looking Hazara speak Hazaragi; the Aimak, also Mongoloid, speak Dari dialects with many Turkic loan words. Other Indo-European speakers include: Baluch, the Wakhi-Pamiri peoples, and the Dardic speakers of Nuristan and surrounding areas.

The several Turkic dialects of Uralic-Altaic include those spoken by the Uzbak, Turkoman, and Kirghiz of northern and northeastern Afghanistan. The Brahui speak Dravidian, but usually also know either Baluch, Dari, or Pashto, depending on which other groups live nearby. Scattered throughout central and northern Afghanistan are small groups of Moghol, once Mongolian speakers, but now primarily Dari speakers, although Mongolian loan words have been identified. Several tribes of Arabic speakers—some nomadic, some seminomadic, some sedentary—live in north Afghanistan, but most simply claim to be "Arab," and speak mainly Dari.

The complex situation sketchily discussed above has led to the evolution of a peasant-tribal society, the most common type in the world today. However defined, the peasant-tribal society has, at the minimum, the following attributes, all of which affect population dynamics:

(1) *Nonliteracy.* A factor limiting communication and a population's awareness of itself.

(2) *Ecological Time-Energy Relationship.* Most of the people spend the greatest part of their time engaged in basic food production. About 90 per cent of Afghans are farmers, herders, or combinations of the two.

(3) *Mobility.* Peasant-tribal societies are characterized by limited social, economic, political, and geographic mobility. In the social sphere, limited mobility helps to insure group survival at the expense of individual choice. In

Afghanistan, preferred mates, for example, are father's brother's daughters, and the individual's role as leader or follower relates to family status. Economically, a man's occupation will generally be that of his father. Geographically, even nomads lack real mobility, for they follow the same paths from summer to winter pasturages and back again.

(*4*) *Kinship Replaces Government.* Various kin units substitute for many of the normal institutional interactions which occur between government and governed in the Western sense. The peasant-tribal society is, generally speaking, uni-institutional; i.e., the range of choices in almost every decision relates in one way or another to kinship. Reciprocal rights and obligations between individuals and groups are tightly defined and include everything from the right to name a child to social welfare and warfare.

The above attributes have helped to perpetuate the peasant-tribal society of Afghanistan. Since attitudes are possibly more important than simple technological changes, we should consider for a moment just what attitudes a peasant or tribesman is born into. He is born into an inward-looking society, or, to put it another way, he is born into a *set of answers.* Conversely, in the literate, pluralistic, industrialized societies of the West, a man is born into a set of questions, or an outward-looking society.

In Afghanistan, the answers come mainly from Islam, but we must differentiate between literate and nonliterate Islam, the two often being at opposite attitudinal poles. Nonliterate Muslims—as well as literate Traditionalist Muslim thinkers, and almost all Westerners, consider Islam to be rigidly deterministic; i.e., all things happen because Allah has willed them. Traditionalist religious leaders, who have a vested interest in the status quo, encourage their flocks in this belief. In the essence of Islam (not available to most Muslims because of their nonliteracy), however, free will plays an important role. Islam means "submission," but, in the interpretations of most Modernists, not a blind submission to an impersonal divine force. Instead, submission must be to a way of life or essence, only after careful examination and acceptance of its precepts and concepts: a belief in Allah and order in the universe; the equality of all believers before Allah; social justice among men.

Population Distribution and Movement

Three recent studies on manpower (Chupir, Givens, Hendrikson) deserve mention. Chupir (1967) valiantly tries to arrive at sensible population figures, and then project them toward possible manpower needs from 1967–1972. Population estimates, however, vary from 7 to 17 million, depending on who uses which figures for whatever purpose. Chupir, a Russian manpower expert who worked with the Ministry of Planning in Kabul, derives his total population estimates from prior estimates of urban populations, which, in turn, had been derived from three other estimates:

(*1*) A series of sample employment surveys cursorily carried out by foreign technicians in Kabul, Qandahar, Herat, Ghazni, Mazar-i-Sharif, Kunduz, Giriskh, etc. estimate that 1.02 million Afghans live in urban areas. These piecemeal surveys were undertaken between 1960 and 1966. Only those in Kabul have been repeated, and only since 1967. Adequate control is lacking, moreover, for questionnaires are mailed exclusively to industrial plants registered with the government and then without instructions or supervisory checking. Most plants simply do not return the forms, or, if they do, with only the most perfunctory information. It must be pointed out that the inadequate samples, the natural tendency of the Afghan to protect his group's privacy, and the use of Western-oriented questionnaires and interview techniques leave the conclusions of these surveys, however tentative, open to question.

(2) *A Population and Agricultural Survey of 500 Villages* (1963), undertaken by the Ministry of Planning, which resulted in an estimate of .97 millions for the urban scene.

(3) Humlum (1959), a Danish geographer, gives the figure 1.18 millions for the urban population in his classic work.

Chupir, nevertheless, says of his report that the "accuracy of estimates herein is not open to great doubt." He does concede that "no estimated data can substitute for the results of a population census."

Although the average of the urban population estimates in the three studies is 1.06 million, Chupir arrived at the ultimate figure of 1.02 millions. After considering the various estimates of the proportion of urban to rural population, he appears to have flipped a mental coin and assigned 10 per cent of the total population to cities. His estimate is possibly as close to reality as the lack of hard data allows. Accordingly, he came up with 13.4 million as Afghanistan's total population in 1961, but it must be emphasized once again that he based his mathematical gymnastics on nothing but estimates. In the deepest recesses of my nonstatistical brain and from my experience of twenty years of travels in Afghanistan, I feel the figure to be grossly overstated.

Chupir criticized the long accepted (by Afghans at least) annual population growth figure of 1.75 per cent that was based primarily on data from surrounding countries, including the Central Asian Republic of the U.S.S.R. He finally accepted an estimate of between 2.2 and 2.5 per cent for use in the Second Five Year Plan (1962–69). Using 2.3 per cent, he concluded the population should be 16.9 million in 1972.

Table 1 shows Chupir's projections from 1966–67 to 1971–72. When—and if—Afghanistan ever takes a census, it will be interesting to compare the results with these estimates of estimates, which (along with subsequent reports by the Robert Nathan Associates team, an American economic advisory group working in the Ministry of Planning) form the basis for much of Afghanistan's official statistical manipulations.

The Afghan government (Survey of Progress: 1968–1969), on the basis of Chupir, subject to modifications by Hendrikson (former chief of the West German economic advisory commission in the Ministry of Planning) and the Nathan team, accepts the percentage breakdown of labor force distribution shown in Table 2.

In my opinion, the total percentage for agricultural and related activities (including herding) in the rural area should be closer to 90 per cent than 86.1 per cent; possibly *over* 90 per cent would be more accurate. The 3.8 million

Table 1. Population Estimates for Afghanistan, 1966–72

	1966/67					*1971/72*				
	Total	*By zones*				*Total*	*By zones*			
	Thous. persons	*East and North East*	*North and North West*	*South and South West*	*Cen-tral*	*Thous. person*	*East and North East*	*North and North West*	*South and South West*	*Cen-tral*
Total	15080	—	—	—	—	16890	—	—	—	—
Nomads	2730	—	—	—	—	3000	—	—	—	—
Others	12350	5430	2540	3310	1070	13890	6090	2860	3730	1210
Of Others										
(a) Urban	1480	810	314	300	56	1960	1080	410	394	76
(b) Rural	10870	4620	2226	3010	1014	11930	5010	2750	3336	1134
Male, all ages	6422	2823	1321	1721	557	7223	3167	1487	1940	629
Female, all ages	5928	2607	1219	1589	513	6667	2923	1373	1790	581
Ages 15–60	6150	2704	1265	1648	533	6900	3030	1420	1850	600
(a) Urban-all	715	394	152	143	26	925	515	195	182	33
Male	365	201	78	73	13	472	263	99	93	17
Female	350	193	74	70	13	458	252	96	89	16
(b) Rural-all	5435	2310	1113	1505	507	5975	2515	1225	1668	567
Male	2772	1178	568	768	258	3047	1283	625	850	289
Female	2663	1123	545	737	279	2928	1232	600	818	278

Source: Chupir

Table 2

	Number	Per Cent
Agriculture	2,942,000	77.0
Industry, handicrafts	231,000	6.0
Construction, mining	83,000	2.2
Transportation, communications	30,000	.8
Education	12,000	.3
Health	6,000	.2
Trade	106,000	2.8
Civil Service	60,000	1.6
Misc. activities, rural area	250,000	9.1
Totals	3,720,000	100.0

figure for the working force means that only 24.8 per cent of the total 15.4 million Afghans (official 1969 figure) constitute the labor force. (About two million nomads and seminomads, included in the over-all estimate of population, have been excluded from categorization in the labor force.) In India the comparable figure is 37 per cent; in Iran, 23 per cent; in Pakistan, 28 per cent; in Jordan, 15 per cent.

Hendrikson's report in 1968 mentions that approximately 4,100 women were employed in 1967, a remarkable figure since few women worked outside the family group before 1959, the year the Daud government unofficially—but effectively—sanctioned the voluntary abolition of purdah and the removal of the veil (*4*). Today, in urban areas, women work in all the ministries, in business offices, and in some factories.

The Givens report to U.S.A.I.D./Afghanistan (1967) goes into more detail about female employment but gives a figure of 2,500 in 1965/66, with only 180 in the private sector; of the remainder, 1,109 were employed in education, 398 in health, and 419 in other civil service jobs.

One noteworthy fact about the labor force in Afghanistan is that 51 per cent of all educated persons (defined as those with at least a ninth grade education) work for the Ministry of Education (*5*).

Givens' report, like those of Chupir and Hendrikson, is interested primarily in manpower resources and utilization, but along the way, he discusses items of demographic importance. For example, he says:

> Since education alone does not create jobs, and by itself it does not insure capable, imaginative participation in the labor force, overeducation can be a serious form of waste. It is important to avoid overinvestment in particular segments of education.
>
> A disturbing sign of overinvestment appears when unemployment or downgraded levels of employment appear among educated persons. It is reported that this begins to show among graduates of the Faculties of Science and Letters, for example, at the University of Kabul. This should be watched in

> every field, and procedures for this purpose will be suggested. Whether restriction of educational output or qualitative changes in content should be the remedy is a matter for analysis; if no better alternative remedy is practicable or accessible, then restriction of numbers in such situations may be wise. In a field where the problem is not one of qualitative relevance to job opportunities and requirements, the remedy may be found in an active program of promotion to extend the fields of employment for graduates. (pp. 17–18)

The present cabinet has rejected Givens' suggestion of restriction as an alternative. Instead, it has encouraged increased enrollment in Kabul University, reasoning that, under its proposed decentralization of schools to the provinces, all graduates of KU can be utilized for provincial development. The ideal cannot be faulted, but the question of how to induce the educated elite to leave the big city has yet to be seriously considered.

Migration patterns. It must again be emphasized that no really significant demographic studies have been undertaken, and that the discussion below is primarily qualitative and tentative. The migration patterns described here exclude the nomadic-seminomadic-semisedentary patterns, focusing rather on those seasonal rural-urban migrations related to part-time economic specialties, which may in time bring a larger permanent labor force to the cities.

First, however, three historical rural-rural migrations which have affected several regional population patterns should be briefly mentioned. The first occurred in the late nineteenth century, during the reign of Amir Abdur Rahman Khan (1880–1901), when he forcibly moved tens of thousands of his opponents from south to north of the Hindu Kush. Included in the groups were nomads as well as farmers, and the whole social, economic, and political scene in the north was altered. Antigovernment in the south, the transplanted Pushtun tribesmen became bulwarks of government policy in the non-Pushtun north. The nomads rapidly adjusted, becoming important traders and culture-communicators along their new routes of travel, as well as money lenders (6). Very quickly they became major landowners in the region, and many groups eventually became semisedentary; most became seminomadic (7). The pattern began to change with the introduction of a new motorable road over the Hindu Kush at Shibar Pass in 1933 and subsequent expansion of the road system, culminating in the intensive development of the area's infrastructure after World War II.

The last great forced migration occurred just after World War II when the government moved large numbers of rebellious Safi Pushtun to the north.

The second major pattern of movements resulted from Russia's attempts to pacify (in some instances to reconquer) the former Czarist Empire in Muslim Central Asia during the 1920s. To escape the Soviets, Turkoman, Uzbak, Tajik, and Kirghiz flowed across the border, the last groups trickling in just after World War II. These groups brought a great boost to the raising of *qarakul* (Persian Lamb) and to carpet weaving, which together now account for most of Afghani-

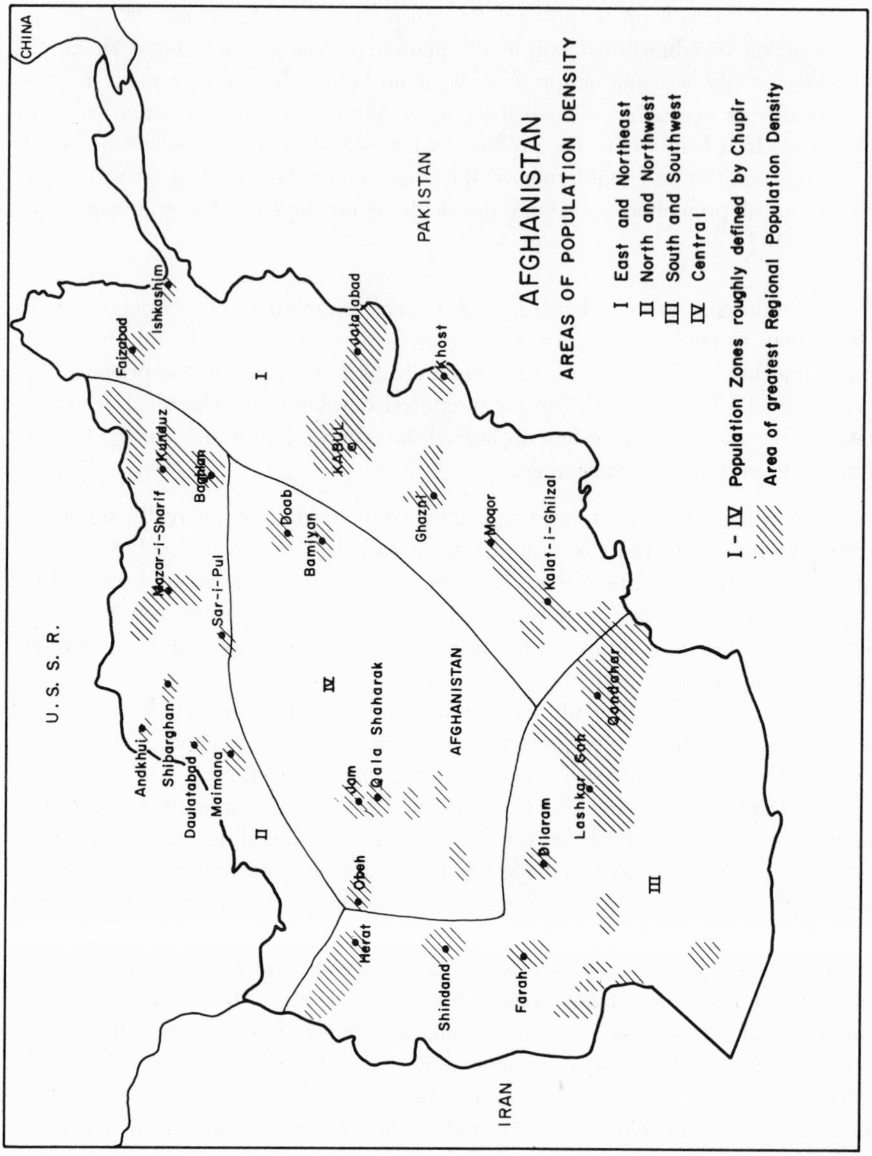
AFGHANISTAN
AREAS OF POPULATION DENSITY
I East and Northeast
II North and Northwest
III South and Southwest
IV Central
I - IV Population Zones roughly defined by Chupir
Area of greatest Regional Population Density
CHINA
PAKISTAN
U. S. S. R.
IRAN
AFGHANISTAN
Faizabad
Ishkashim
Jalalabad
Khost
KABUL
Kunduz
Baghlan
Mazar-i-Sharif
Doab
Bamiyan
Ghazni
Moqor
Kalat-i-Ghilzai
Sar-i-Pul
Qandahar
Qala Shaharak
Jam
Andkhui
Shibarghan
Daulatabad
Maimana
Obeh
Herat
Shindand
Farah
Dilaram
Lashkar Gah

stan's hard-currency exports. But the minority groups of the north feel negelected by the Pushtun-dominated central government.

The third category of rural-rural migrations of importance have been the mainly voluntary movements associated with the opening up of new agricultural lands made available by irrigation projects primarily in the north (Kunduz, Baghlan, Pul-i-Khumri), but also in the Helmand-Arghandab Valleys of the south. New projects are under way near Jalalabad in the east, near Charikar north of Kabul, and east of Herat in the northwest.

Some seasonal rural-rural migrations relate to the nonagricultural period, when certain groups travel to specific areas where they have traditional, well-defined work relations. Usually these groups move as family units, either nuclear families or simply the males, depending on the type of work and the distance to be traveled. For example, seasonal (late summer, early fall) collectors of asafedita in the foothills of north-central Afghanistan usually consist of small groups of related males who travel to predetermined areas under contract. Andar Ghilzai Pushtun males specialize in the construction and repair of the intricate networks of underground canals (*ganat*, Dari; *karez*, Pashto), which finger from the water table in the foothills to the arable plains. Every spring, thousands upon thousands of Afghans (including some urban types who look on the exercise as an outing) pay a fee to the government for permission to roam the mountains of the north, collecting wild pistachio nuts. Also in the north, seasonal migrants help plant rice in June, reap wheat in summer and early fall, reap rice and pick cotton from September to December. Seasonal specialists from the upper Andarab Valley (an estimated 40 per cent of the entire population) of central Afghanistan move in winter to lower altitudes to husk rice and extract oil from oilseeds (8). Almost invariably, the participants in the seasonal rural-rural movements return to their own villages as the annual need for their part-time specialties subsidies.

A growing number of such seasonal migrations involve a rural-urban movement. From the mountainous valleys surrounding or adjacent to the various small-scale industrial complexes (textiles, cement, fruit processing, etc.), particularly in the north near Kunduz, Baghlan, Pul-i-Khumri, and in the central mountains near Kabul, Gulbahar, and Jabal-us-Seraj, come men to work in the agricultural off-season (9). The valleys of the Panjsher and Farkhar contribute significant numbers, partly because cheap imports, as well as the growth of the new industries, have diminished the importance of local handicrafts. The same cheap imports, along with other, culturally oriented factors, keep many Afghan factories in a constant state of underproduction. In addition, many plant operators complain about the instability of the work force. Semitrained after working one season, and using their wages to purchase desirable items (cloth, lanterns, guns, transistor radios, iron implements, maybe a horse or other livestock), workmen often go home to their mountain villages and do not return until after the next harvest or perhaps a few years. This same pattern was mentioned to me in both 1959 and 1964 by certain Soviet factory administrators in Soviet Central Asia. They simply could not understand why Tajik and Uzbak workmen would come from remote valleys, work for several months in a factory and then return home.

Groetzbach's study (1969) suggests that 80 per cent of the inhabitants of the upper Andarab and Farkhar valleys go to towns and cities to work in the winter, returning to their farming occupations in early spring and remaining until late summer or early fall.

A unique type of rural-urban migration developed after World War II in response to the needs of the thousands of foreign technicians who have passed through and still pass through Afghanistan. From the Panjsher Valley north of Kabul, many Tajik (other groups from other areas have increased in the past five years, particularly Hazara) more or less permanently settled in various districts of Kabul city, working as cooks and servants. Surplus labor in the technically (not socially) oriented terms of the West has existed in Afghanistan for at least several decades. Most of the individuals working as servants have maintained close in-group ties with their villages and families, and, with the improved transportation-communications networks, have been able to maintain their contacts with a high level of intensity. Money saved (and the servant class receives high wages compared to many others in the Afghan labor force) at first went almost exclusively into purchase of land, the traditional way to increase income and sociopolitical prestige. Now, however, many invest in lorries, which have rapidly replaced camels as the major unit of transport along the main (usually paved) roads. Others lend financial support to close relatives in rented or purchased shops in nearby towns and cities.

The important thing to remember about all these new activities is that they are undertaken to strengthen one's hand in one's own family and home village. Although *urban-based,* therefore, these new operations are ultimately *rural-oriented.*

In practice, however, the pull of the city grabs an increasing number of migrants, who become permanent residents, slowly shifting their loyalties to urban institutions. Few admit this trend exists, for the articulated ideal still relates to the vertical kinship structure in the village. One concrete evidence of the shift is that a small but growing minority of parents will approve nonkin urban wives for their sons. (Sedentary villagers prefer to keep daughters locally anchored.)

The Hazara, Mongoloid-looking, Persian speakers also migrate to Kabul and other urban centers in the winter. There they are generally discriminated against by other groups so they frequently work as coolie labor, gathering each morning at specific points for traditional shapeups (*10*). Many Hazara work as servants for middle- and upper-class Afghan families. Others have gained control of much of the firewood supply, so necessary to keep Kabul homes warm in winter. However, coal and, to a lesser degree, oil (plus increased government efforts at forest conservation) have diminished this activity.

From the above listing of population movements, the most significant conclusion is that rural-urban migrants still maintain strong ties (i.e., reciprocal rights and obligations) to their home villages, and, after taking advantage of the new economic opportunities, return home and use their earnings to intensify the traditional patterns.

Few Afghans emigrate to other countries. Even most of the Jews who left for Israel returned because of discrimination at the hands of the Ashkenazim. Some Afghans, however, do go overseas for advanced training; almost all eventually return, bringing with them as many goodies as possible for their families. Some have been known to mail their textbooks home with hard currency stuffed between the pages.

The National Economy

Afghanistan is an agricultural country, with about 90 per cent of the population engaged in agricultural and related activities (including herding). Agricultural products account for more than 85 per cent of the GNP and practically all of the exports. The nation is attempting to achieve self-sufficiency in foodstuffs by 1973, a probably impossible goal. The vagaries of nature influence the annual crop output to a great degree, and there has been no substantial increase in production over the past few years when relatively reliable statistics have been kept.

Occasionally food shortages can be critical in a year when precipitation drops off. The 1969–70 growing season suffered a drought and Afghanistan currently faces a potential shortfall of about 200,000 tons of foodstuffs. Only the urban centers will suffer, however, for the rural population always manages to keep enough for its own needs. Probably wheat loans from the United States and the Soviet Union will fill the gap, as has happened in previous periods of need.

The growing industrial sphere is designed around two objectives: to save hard currency by producing items locally instead of importing them; to increase exports by volume and to command higher prices, thereby gaining more income through quality control on such items as Persian lambskins, sausage casings, carpets, fruits, and nuts.

Major exports are: dried fruits and nuts, *qarakul* skins, raw cotton, carpets and rugs, fresh fruit. Major imports: sugar, tea, petroleum products, textiles. Major trade partners are: the Soviet Union, India, Pakistan, United Kingdom, the United States, and Japan.

The relationship of nomadism to the national economy deserves some attention because nomads and seminomads have long been considered parasites by both Afghan and foreign planners. Nomads seldom pay taxes, nor do they serve in the army. They smuggle, or at least sell smuggled goods along their routes of migration. However, I maintain—as have others, e.g., Kolars (*11*)—that nomads and villagers live in a set of basic symbiotic relationships, the destruction of which would rend the fabric of Afghan society, as happened in Soviet Central Asia and Iran. For example: nomads supply meat and dairy products in exchange for grains and vegetables; nomads' flocks graze over reaped fields and deposit manure which replaces nitrogen in the soil; nomads act as communicators between regions; they sell luxury and commodity items; they lend money and often become landowners when farmers default (a major source of tension).

Population and Development

A good many studies of Afghan development have been conducted over the years. Most of them gather dust in the Afghan ministries for which they were done and rest quietly also in the archives of the United Nations and of the various countries that have extended aid. Some have been widely read but few have been accepted as a basis for policy and fewer still have been even partially implemented.

Three studies deserve special mention in this Report: the Joint Afghan-Russian 50 Year Plan for the city of Kabul; the Kabul Household Expenditure Survey; the Lashkar Gah (now called Bost, the name changes periodically and may once again be Lashkar Gah by the time this Report is presented) Household Expenditure Survey, the last two named being reported in the *Survey of Progress: 1968–69.*

The Russian plan (the Russians call it a joint effort by courtesy only) for Kabul envisions a population growth to 800,000 in 50 years beginning with a 1962 estimate of 380,000. This figure includes much of the area surrounding Kabul, which, within a half century, should be tightly integrated as suburbia. The proposals add up to a planner's dream—or perhaps fantasy. The plan recommends a central administrative and business area of about 450 hectares with interconnected thoroughfares and pedestrian walkways. Included in it would be the Royal Palace complex, an interesting suggestion from a nation once dedicated to the overthrow of all monarchies. A park and zoo complex would sit south of Bala Hissar, an historic fortress overlooking Kabul. In essence, the plan calls for the gradual demolition of practically all of old Kabul as it stands today, and its re-creation as an urban paradise. Speaking of paradise, the atheistic planners included numerous mosques (listed as "other institutions" in the English and Russian versions of the plan, but as *masjid* in the Dari version) to be located in residential districts and the central area. If the implementation of this plan, already under way, forces the various ministries concerned to cooperate more effectively than on previous projects, the plan might just succeed. At least it has made an encouraging start.

The Kabul Household Expenditure Survey (KHES) was conducted jointly by the Directorate-General of Census and Sampling, Department of Statistics of the Ministry of Planning, and the Ministry of Agriculture and Irrigation. They had the reluctant cooperation of Kabul Municipality. A first effort, carried out in the summer of 1968 by semitrained (and less interested) Afghan students, KHES officially covered 1,685 families. The sample was said to comprise 2.4 per cent of all households in Greater Kabul, which includes five districts in the inner city and ten in the suburbs. The 15-page questionnaire attempted to extract detailed information about demographic characteristics of Kabul and household expenditure, income, and occupational patterns.

It is doubtful, however, whether many in the nonliterate population of Kabul (or even in the literate segment, for that matter) responded accurately to questions about their income, or the number of sons in the family. They would not risk having their taxes increased or their unregistered sons drafted into the armed forces. But the survey has produced the only new figures available to the general public as of this writing, so the statistics will be of historic interest if nothing else. A few general comparisons with the 1965–66 survey may be in order.

(*1*) The average number of persons per household was calculated to be seven, an increase of .7 per household over the 1965–66 estimate.

(*2*) Of the 11,870 persons listed in the KHES, 53 per cent were males, 47 per cent females (compared with 56 per cent male, 44 per cent female in the 1965–66 survey).

(*3*) KHES: 23 per cent of the population earned cash incomes; 27 per cent in 1965–66.

(*4*) KHES: 48.1 per cent of population, ages 0–14; 1965–66, 44.8 per cent.
KHES: 2.9 per cent, age 65-plus; 1965–66, 3.2 per cent.
KHES: 49 per cent, 15–64 years old; 1965–66, 52 per cent.
(Therefore, theoretically over 50 per cent of the people are economically inactive, being too young or too old to work. In fact, however, many under 15 and over 65 *do* work).

(*5*) KHES: 6 per cent of the households averaged quarterly incomes of 30,000-plus afghanis: 8 per cent of the total sample lived in these households, which earned 49.1 per cent of the income reported for the total surveyed sample; 35 per cent of the total sample had fixed incomes. No 1965–66 data.

(*6*) Average monthly income about 681 afghanis (or $9.08) per person, or average estimated annual per capita income of 8,180 afghanis ($109). Fixed income about 18 per cent of total, rest from seasonal labor. No 1965–66 data.

(*7*) Of total sample, 41.1 per cent males were income earners; only 2.4 per cent of women. No 1965–66 data.

(*8*) Of all the households 60 per cent were privately owned; probably an overestimate. No 1965–66 data.

(*9*) About 50 per cent of the sample resided in houses with one or two rooms. No 1965–66 data.

(*10*) About 34 per cent do not have potable drinking water; 27 per cent do not have electricity. No 1965–66 data.

Capitalizing on the identified successes and failures of the KHES, the same institutions (but in cooperation this time with the Helmand-Arghandab Valley Authority) conducted a similar survey in January–February 1969 at Lashkar Gah, capital of Helmand Province. The Lashkar Gah Household Expenditure Survey included urban and rural elements (Table 3), neither being defined. Furthermore,

Table 3

	No. households surveyed	*Pop.*	*% of Total*
Urban	829	4,844	17.7
Rural (19 rural villages in LG Municipality)	3,622	22,563	82.3
Totals	4,451	27,407	100.0

the area had for a decade or more been the center of a major American effort in

Afghanistan, and many in the urban area had been trained in the United States or by Americans in Afghanistan. Thus, the findings cannot be taken as representative of the country as a whole.

The total urban population and seven of the 19 villages (1,114 households with a population of 6,929) were surveyed; total households in the survey, 4,451.

The LGHES came up with the following important demographic estimates. The more important tabular results are found in Appendix A.

(*1*) Each rural household contained an average of 6.2 members; urban, 5.8.

(*2*) Children from 0–14 constituted 50.1 per cent of the population surveyed; 65-plus, 3 per cent; 15–64 (the theoretical economically productive years in developed societies), 46.9 per cent.

(*3*) Urban sex ratio: over-all, 795 females to 1,000 males; ratio between ages 35–44, 339 females to 1,000 males, probably because many males come from Kabul to work for the provincial government and leave their families in the big city.

(*4*) Rural sex ratio: over-all, 883 females to 1,000 males, and it must be remembered that Muslim peasants often decline to mention the number of small girls in the household. The female over male imbalance from ages 20–34 (Appendix A, Table 5) possibly results from two factors: men leaving for military service and seasonal labor.

(*5*) Literacy of males above five years is 32.7 per cent, high for the country as a whole because Lashkar Gah is a provincial center with many outsiders shipped in as administrators; female literacy also high, 5.7 per cent. Of the total literates, 13 per cent had finished the ninth grade or higher. For Kabul, the figure is 14 per cent. Both percentages are obviously high for the rest of Afghanistan.

(*6*) 42.5 per cent of urban age group 10–59 had jobs; rural, 41.5 per cent. Of the total working group, 78.1 per cent were males between 10–59; 1.2 per cent, females (obviously means only active nonagricultural wage earners, for 100 per cent of rural females work, except those too young and too old).

(*7*) Annual per capita income of the urban area, $74; rural, $62.

(*8*) LGHES roughly estimates a 1.7 per cent natural rate of population increase, but to quote the survey's tentative results: "This figure cannot be made the reliable basis for projection and policy purposes, and, surely, there is urgent need for accurate information in this regard." (p. 55) The low figure once again may relate to the artificiality of the population in the provincial center of Lashkar Gah.

Another important offshoot of developmental projects, particularly those dealing with infrastructure, has been the creation of skilled workmen (electricians, mechanics, crane operators, drivers, etc.), either working for private companies or serving as conscripts in the Labour Corps (*12*). When a regional project (dam, irrigation, road, airport) is finished, however, a sizable percentage of the specialists return home, often with documents certifying their skills, which prove to be virtually useless in the villages. Along with other conscripts from the military, these skilled workmen sometimes become part of a semi-idle force, dissatisfied with the traditional power elite but not strong enough to rock the boat. Those who become true dissidents leave and seek jobs in other development projects, but jobs become scarcer as the major infrastructure nears completion. Those who remain in the villages have slowly, without plan or formal structure, coalesced into social and incipient informal power units that grow in importance as the new experiment in democracy penetrates more deeply into the rural scene. Intensive central planning is needed to pursue internal regional and provincial infrastructure projects in order to take advantage of this trained labor force.

The studies mentioned in this Report have all used Western models or Western-designed questionnaires or assumptions concerning economic patterns and population growth, but the inward-looking society of Afghanistan and other developing areas should probably be examined more critically, at least initially, in the realm of the qualitative rather than the quantitative. The attitudes and values of a society and their gradual shift toward outward-looking concepts are more significant than the number of toilet seats per capita or even an increase in literacy per se. However, an over-all census is just as obviously an important first step.

Population and Society

"Education is the nation's fastest growing industry" (Givens, p. 15), as can be seen from Table 4, and from the fact that expenditures on education in the

Table 4. Education, 1963–1969

National Summary	*1963/4*	*1964/5*	*1965/6*	*1966/7*	*1967/8*	*1968/9*
Schools	1,719	1,876	2,085	2,298	2,561	2,628
Village	989	1,052	1,213	1,320	1,426	1,359
Elemen. & Second.	653	743	789	885	1,030	1,150
Vocational & High	77	81	83	93	107	119
Students	295,169	345,728	403,852	443,459	497,879	540,743
Village	65,557	69,795	84,059	88,137	96,321	92,997
Elemen. & Second.	216,148	260,942	302,230	334,796	377,688	419,159
Vocational & High	13,464	14,991	17,563	20,526	23,870	28,587
Teachers	6,550	7,675	8,525	9,824	11,640	13,349
Village	989	1,166	1,241	1,339	1,536	1,894
Elemen. & Second.	4,766	5,698	6,452	7,598	8,706	10,059
Vocational & High	795	811	832	887	1,398	1,396

Source: Survey of Progress, 1968–1969

ordinary budget are second only to those for defense, and fourth in the development budget.

The harsh fact remains, however, that many schools still have no (or untrained) teachers and the entire system encourages rote learning. Education is still status-oriented and not development-oriented, although a new team in the Ministry of Education, under the leadership of the Minister, Dr. Abdul Kayeum, has started an experiment in decentralization. Several junior colleges will be founded in regional urban centers and oriented toward regional development.

The educational system would then become a true pyramid, with more and more people achieving basic literacy to use as a development tool, and more and more students reaching the top, but the bulk remaining in their home regions, involved in the creation of an outward-looking society. But that is for the future, because in 1968, 62 per cent of all students in Afghanistan lived in Kabul Province, which has only 8 per cent of the total population.

In contrast to the progress in the field of education, public health programs have advanced but little (even on paper) since World War II (Table 5). In

Table 5. Health, 1963–1969

	1963/4	*1964/5*	*1965/6*	*1966/7*	*1967/8*	*1968/9*
Hospitals	59	59	63	63	65	65
Beds	1,997	2,717	2,187	2,197	2,232	2,355
Pharmacies	166	188	189	239	251	259
Laboratories	15	15	15	15	15	15
X-Rays	15	15	16	16	16	16
Medical personnel						
Physicians	375	396	496	527	582	632
Asst. physicians	43	43	19	19	19	19
Foreign physicians	6	18	11	11	11	11
Male nurses	367	399	269	269	269	269
Female nurses	80	89	90	90	90	90
Asst. nurses	29	32	36	36	36	36
Pharmacists	119	143	143	169	189	210
Lab. technicians	35	50	50	50	50	50
Lab. assistants	15	15	18	18	18	18
Technicians	9	10	11	11	11	11
Inoculators	63	69	73	73	73	73
Surgery assists.	56	68	132	161	176	196
Sanitorium techns.	38	46	38	38	38	38
Midwives	38	43	38	38	38	38
Asst. dentists	38	43	38	38	38	45
Radiographers	4	7	4	4	4	4

Source: Survey of Progress, 1968–1969

1970, 77 of the 164 clinics were without doctors and, according to Ministry of Health statistics, only 15 per cent of patients outside Kabul are women and children. Of the clinics, 67 per cent are outside Kabul, and the Ministry hopes to open between five to ten new ones annually, a very ambitious goal. In view of the relative lack of health facilities, it is unlikely that Afghanistan's population growth will accelerate in the near future.

As mentioned previously, most social welfare in Afghanistan takes place in the bosom of the family. However, the government reportedly has increased the number of orphanages and homes for the aged and plans others. In addition, the Afghan Women's Institute, the Volunteer Women's Association, and the Women's Welfare Society plus the Red Crescent Society (similar to the Red Cross) engage in limited charitable work. But for some time to come, social welfare in the rural areas will be a part of the reciprocal rights and obligations of the kin-oriented group.

Population and Polity

The Royal Government of Afghanistan has, as yet, done little to help (or hinder) family planning. The Afghan Family Guidance Association (AFGA) founded in July 1968 has made a modest, successful beginning in Kabul (five clinics in and around the city), but has found varying receptions in its attempts to open centers in other towns and cities (Lashkar Gah, Herat, Mazar-i-Sharif; others are planned for Qandahar and Jalalabad). AFGA also has established a training center for doctors, nurses, and midwives, and has instituted a series of week-long courses to acquaint them with family planning policies, practices, and programs.

Positive and negative attitudes towards family planning split along ideological lines. Among Islamic leaders, the Traditionalists disapprove, the Modernists approve. Both sides use the Quran and the Hadiths (Sayings of the Prophet Mohammad) to support their arguments. AFGA has published a 16-page, illustrated booklet in Persian (compiled by Dr. Amir Mohammad Mohebzada) which uses quotations from the Quran to plump for personal hygiene, public sanitation, and family planning. AFGA also uses publications from other Muslim countries to justify the program. Emphasis is always on individual choice, not group acceptance, a key Modernist principle.

Since the war for family planning is just beginning, the shape of the battle is not yet clear, but, obviously, most Afghan literates favor some sort of birth control, as do many of the rural women tired of having annual babies. Dangerous, unsanitary abortions take the lives of many rural women each year, but the number remains unknown. The desire for sons (as a means to increased economic potential and political power for the family), plus the ultra-masculine superiority complex among Afghan males, militates against a wide-scale acceptance of the idea of family planning in the rural areas.

A modest start has been made, however, and the government-controlled press and Radio Afghanistan (which has a 40-minute daily program on family problems and plans more) have perceptibly increased their focus on the modern family during the past year. In addition, although AFGA receives little direct financial help from the government, the cabinet recently decided to incorporate the concept of voluntary family guidance into the basic health service programs. The emphasis is on the voluntary aspect in the hope of mollifying conservative religious factions.

The pill is available in the various AFGA clinics, but Afghan doctors are pushing the IUD (Lippes Loop) as the most effective device for Afghanistan. A proposed Knowledge-Attitudes-Practices (KAP) survey should throw light on the problems of how to disseminate pills, IUDs, and family planning know-how.

Population Work and Research

U.S.A.I.D./Afghanistan has agreed to underwrite a KAP survey beginning in 1970 and terminating in 1974. The research plan, according to Dr. Abdul Ghafar Aziz, Secretary-General of AFGA, divides Afghanistan into six ecological zones, with the following provinces being at the center of the respective zones: Kabul,

Mazar-i-Sharif, Kunduz, Qandahar, Herat, Ningrahar. The ideal would be to take one urban and one rural sample for each zone, but the cost may prove prohibitive, so Dr. Aziz suggests combining the following: Kabul-Ningrahar, Qandahar-Herat, Kunduz-Mazar-i-Sharif.

Few would underestimate the difficulties involved in doing surveys among nonliterates, urban or rural. Those proposing the KAP emphasize that the individual (male and female) and the married couple, not the household, should be the primary sample unit. Obviously, kinship structure, kinship interaction, the generational power structure, and in-group decision-making dynamics must be examined in some detail. While the heart of the KAP study will be to gather information on knowledge about, attitudes concerning, and practices involving birth control and family planning, enough data should be collected to make possible more accurate estimates of rural vs. urban population, with relatively specific data on age, sex, marital status, and occupation.

At the time these paragraphs were written, Washington had not announced selection of the KAP contractor.

Technically, AFGA is a private, voluntary organization, but it collects no more than $400 a year from its membership, which numbers less than 200. On matters of policy, AFGA consults with the Ministry of Public Health, and practically all the medical personnel working in AFGA clinics (except the central clinic) are employees of the government on part-time loan to AFGA.

International Planned Parenthood Foundation, acting as a contractor for U.S.A.I.D., contributed about $20,800 during the first year's operations, and A.I.D. gave a direct commodity grant of about $3,500. Also with A.I.D. support, three Ministry of Public Health officials visited six Asian countries in order to study family planning. Other A.I.D. grants made possible the following: two AFGA officials participated in a workshop on communications and family planning in Bangkok; other Afghan doctors attended seminars in England, Yugoslavia, and the United States (Tulane University Medical Center). A.I.D. money also brought an American gynecologist to Afghanistan for several months to advise Afghan doctors. Currently, several medical technicians, both men and women, are in the United States undergoing training in family planning. Finally, A.I.D. assisted directly in the purchase of office supplies. Since 1968, A.I.D. has contributed almost $100,000 to the programs, and its contributions will probably increase considerably as the KAP survey gets under way and more Afghans receive scholarships for study abroad.

The American Women's Association in Kabul made posters for public distribution in order to publicize AFGA, which hopes to solicit specific support from Care-Medico (powdered milk, doctors, nurses, technicians), the Peace Corps (social workers, nurses), and UNESCO (lab equipment) as the program develops.

Conclusions

After two and a half years of operation, AFGA has become as well-entrenched as possible given the circumstances, and if it continues to grow at the present rate, possibly it may have an impact on the Afghan demographic scene, particularly in the urban areas. But this is for the future and the present is fraught with political pitfalls and cultural barriers, some of which may prove insurmountable.

The Royal Government of Afghanistan either controls or has a critical role in all national enterprises, public or private. However, coordination is hardly known among the ministries, each of which jealously guards its prerogatives, with the result that there is much duplication of effort. In spite of the pervasive influence of government, little consistency exists in decision-making. Also, many in the bureaucracy prefer to carry on the steady, dull, ordinary, daily business of government instead of going into the countryside to become involved in the exciting but occupationally unstable and relatively uncoordinated business of development. The characteristic passivity is shared by the whole class of *tawildar*, the storekeepers who keep everything from huge electric generators and trucks to pencils and paper clips under lock and key. Often it requires the signature of a minister or deputy minister to shake anything loose from these tightfisted, single-minded functionaries (*13*).

On the whole, the bureaucracy has not yet been offered pay and status inducements that would generate pro-development attitudes.

The educational system, although it now may be undergoing a basic revolution, primarily prepares Afghans to fill time-serving bureaucratic jobs. Possibly, more functionally-oriented institutions along the polytechnic lines of Europe and the United States should be developed in the provinces. As literacy increases, such a revised approach to education may become established policy.

A census would be of major help in all areas of developmental policy and planning, including those relating to population problems. The United Nations' Technical Assistance Administration had tentatively agreed to assist during 1968–69, but everything bogged down in a bureaucratic quagmire. Possibly the proposed KAP survey will evolve into a proper census over the next few years. Meanwhile, Afghanistan has opportunities afforded few developing countries. Most Afro-Asian nations that formerly were colonies inherited administrative institutions geared to the bookkeeping of empire rather than to the fostering of development. Never having been a colony, Afghanistan could, with some vigorous pushing on the part of the King and the cabinet, create an administrative atmosphere keyed to development.

Afghanistan's infrastructure is totally a creation of the post-World War II Cold War competition between East and West. It is almost completely development-oriented (although certain strategic aspects are certainly present; e.g., military aid, airfields, roads from Central Asia to Pakistan and Iran).

The infrastructure now permits intensified sustained contacts in zones of previous relative inaccessibility. The usual trends will possibly develop: increased yields per acre and increased acreage under production; increased literacy; improved health conditions; attendant movements to urban areas with all the horrors this conjures; hopefully, expanded industrial and commercial opportunities, and so forth. But the key to successful development is not in the improvements noted in individual areas but in a coordinated plan of action and, more important, in its active implementation.

Afghanistan has created the atmosphere for an evolutionary movement of social, political, and economic forces in its new parliamentary system within the framework of a constitutional monarchy. But, unless coordination and cooperation among the monarchy, the cabinet, the parliament, and the various ministries are achieved at the center, and then linked to the various provinces, the chaos of political musical chairs and repeated coups d'état, the experience of most developing nations, can occur.

Given the ingredients discussed in this Report, possibly we should agree with Myrdal (*14*). For man apparently has the socio-psychological bent for creating technological advances which immediately benefit man, but ultimately become destructive (DDT, the gasoline engine, detergents, the no-return bottles). Other mammals, more controlled by environment, adapt—or die. Man attempts to control his environment, and the environment begins to die.

Possibly the Field Staff, report-oriented rather than action-oriented, has an important function in man's attempts at population control: to record the initial technical progress which seems almost always to attend pilot projects, and then to report on such failures as may occur when programs are introduced on a wide scale, as well as on the successes which can be hoped for as the ultimate outcome.

Notes

1. In this Report, I have attempted to avoid unnecessarily repeating items discussed in Louis Dupree, *Population Dynamics in Afghanistan* (LD-7-'70), Fieldstaff Reports, South Asia Series, Vol. XIV, No. 7, 1970.
2. Term "mosaic" borrowed from C.S. Coon's *Caravan* (New York, 1951).
3. G.F. Debets, *Physical Anthropology of Afghanistan: I–II*. Illustrations and Notes by Louis Dupree. Translated by Eugene V. Prostov. Edited by Henry Field. Russian Translation Series of the Peabody Museum of Archaeology and Ethnology, Vol. V, No. 1. Peabody Museum, Harvard University, Cambridge, Mass. 1970.
4. Louis Dupree, *An Informal Talk with Prime Minister Daud* (LD-3-'59), Fieldstaff Reports, South Asia Series, Vol. III, No. 2, 1959.
5. *Survey of Progress:* 1968–1969, Department of Statistics, Ministry of Planning, Royal Government of Afghanistan, Kabul, September 1969, p. 37.
6. K. Ferdinand, "Nomadism and studies in Pushtun nomadism," *Wazhma,* Kabul, 1960; K. Ferdinand, "Nomad expansion and commerce in central Afghanistan," *Folk,* Copenhagen, 1962; Louis Dupree, *The Green and the Black* (LD-5-'63), Fieldstaff Reports, South Asia Series, Vol. VII, No. 5, 1963; and Louis Dupree, *Aq Kupruk: A Town in North Afghanistan,* Parts I and II, (LD-9, 10-'66), Fieldstaff Reports, South Asia Series, Vol. X, Nos. 9 and 10, 1966.
7. For purposes of this Report, the following terms need to be defined: *sedentary farmers,* agriculturalists who live permanently in the same village and move only when forced to, or in order to accept a better farming opportunity; *semisedentary farmers,* agriculturalists who own livestock which are moved

in summer to highland pastures or taken on migration by less than 50 per cent of the group, which returns in winter to the base village; *seminomadic herdsmen,* herdsmen who practice some agriculture, and more than 50 per cent of the group moves seasonally with the flocks, returning to the base village in the winter; *nomadic herdsmen,* groups which move from winter to summer pasturages and back again.

8. J. Uberoi, Social Organization of the Tajiks of Andarab Valley (Thesis, Australian National University, Canberra), 1964.
9. C. Jentsch, "Structural changes of nomadism in Afghanistan," *The Geographical Review of Afghanistan,* Kabul, 1969.
10. H. Amoss, "Dani-zul: Village in transition," *American Historical Anthropology: Essays in Honor of Leslie Spier,* eds., W. Taylor and C. Riley, Carbondale, 1967.
11. J. Kolars, "Locational aspects of cultural ecology: The case for the goat in non-western agriculture," *Geographical Review,* Vol. 5, No. 4, 577–584, 1966.
12. All healthy adult Afghan males are eligible for two years' conscription, and in many cases, especially in rural areas, are literally selected by relatives, friends, and neighbors. Service is in one of the following: army, air force, police (urban), gendarmerie (rural), or the Labour Corps of the Ministry of Public Works.
13. For details, see Louis Dupree, *Afghanistan: 1968* (LD-4-'68), Fieldstaff Reports, South Asia Series, Vol. XII, No. 5, 1968.
14. Gunnar Myrdal, *Asian Drama* (New York, 1968).

References

Chupir, V., "Population and Manpower in Afghanistan: 1345–1350 (1966/67–1971/72)," Royal Afghan Government, Ministry of Planning (mimeo.), Kabul, March 1967.

Givens, M., "Human Resources Development and Manpower Utilization in Afghanistan," USAID/Kabul (mimeo.), May 1967.

Groetzbach, E., "Some economic processes and their regional differentiation in the Hindu Kush, Afghanistan," *Geographical Review of Afghanistan,* Kabul, 1969.

Hendrikson, K., "The Need for Skilled Workers During the Third Five Year Plan and the Capacities of the Required Training Centers in Afghanistan," German Economic Advisory Group (mimeo.), Kabul, 1968.

Humlum, J., *La géographie de l'Afghanistan,* Copenhagen, 1959.

"Population and Agricultural Survey of 500 Villages," Royal Government of Afghanistan, Ministry of Planning (mimeo.), Kabul, 1963.

The Author

LOUIS DUPREE has specialized in the Indo-European language areas of the Middle East and Central Asia, emphasizing Afghanistan and Iran. His anthropology studies at Harvard University earned him the B.A. (1949), M.A. (1953), and

Ph.D. (1954) degrees. Dr. Dupree has made two field trips to Afghanistan for the American Museum of Natural History, of which he is a Research Associate, and one to Iran for the University of Pennsylvania. A former Associate Professor of Middle Eastern Studies at the Air University, he joined the Field Staff in 1959. Concurrent with his Fieldstaff appointment, he is an Adjunct Professor of Anthropology at Pennsylvania State University. His published works include nine monographs and numerous articles and reviews in such varied publications as *The Nation*, the *Economist*, *Evergreen Review*, and the *Middle East Journal*. He is based in Kabul to observe developments in Afghanistan, Pakistan, and Soviet Central Asia, particularly in regard to their relationships with the United States.

Table 1. Composition of Families, Urban Areas

Number of persons	*Number of households*	*% of total*
Single	78	9.41
2–3 persons	135	16.29
4–6 persons	288	34.74
7–9 persons	213	25.69
10 and over	115	13.87
Totals	829	100.00

Source: Survey of Progress, 1968–1969

Table 2. Composition of Households, Rural Areas

Number of persons	*Number of households*	*% of total*
Single	37	1.02
2–3 persons	557	15.38
4–6 persons	1,787	49.34
7–9 persons	747	20.62
10 and over	494	13.64
Totals	3,622	100.00

Table 3. Composition of Population by Age

Age group	*No. of persons*	*% of total*
0–4	5,569	20.3
5–9	5,034	18.4
10–14	3,118	11.4
15–19	1,985	7.2
20–24	1,973	7.2
25–29	1,816	6.6
30–34	2,081	7.6
35–39	1,312	4.8
40–44	1,286	4.7
45–49	783	2.8
50–54	827	3.0
55–59	375	1.4
60–64	431	1.6
65 and over	817	3.0
Totals	27,407	100.00

Table 4. Composition of Population by Age and Sex, Urban Areas

Age groups	Number of persons Male	Female	Proportion Male	Female
0–4	498	459	52.0	48.0
5–9	413	409	50.2	49.8
10–14	393	238	62.3	37.7
15–19	208	152	57.8	42.2
20–24	201	172	53.9	46.1
25–29	185	181	50.5	49.5
30–34	168	188	47.2	52.8
35–39	201	69	74.4	25.6
40–44	158	53	74.9	25.1
45–49	99	59	62.7	37.3
50–54	56	59	48.7	51.3
55–59	33	30	52.4	47.6
60–64	36	33	52.2	47.8
65 and over	50	43	53.8	46.2
Totals	2,699	2,145	55.7	44.3

Table 5. Composition of Population by Age and Sex, Rural Areas

Age groups	Number of persons Male	Female	Proportion Male	Female
0–4	2,512	2,100	54.5	45.5
5–9	2,337	1,875	55.5	44.5
10–14	1,375	1,112	55.3	44.7
15–19	875	750	53.8	46.2
20–24	700	900	43.8	56.2
25–29	575	875	39.7	60.3
30–34	800	925	46.4	53.6
35–39	680	362	65.3	34.7
40–44	575	500	53.5	46.5
45–49	375	250	60.0	40.0
50–54	337	375	47.3	52.7
55–59	187	125	59.9	40.1
60–64	225	137	62.2	37.8
65 and over	424	300	58.6	41.4
Totals	11,977	10,586	53.1	46.9

Table 6. Literacy by Age and Sex

Age groups	*Total population*	*Males*	*Females*
0–9	678	500	178
10–14	1,184	983	202
15–19	684	617	67
20–24	440	376	64
25–34	516	462	54
35–44	443	429	13
45–54	239	229	10
55–64	118	118	—
65 and over	105	105	—
Totals	4,407	3,819	588

Table 7. Classification of Workers by Sector

	Industry	*Agri-culture*	*Construc-tion & building*	*Trans. & comm.*	*Other social services*	*Total*
Urban	183	71	223	54	733	1,264
Rural	189	2,898	290	75	1,840	5,292
Totals	372	2,969	513	129	2,573	6,556

Table 8. Expenditure: % of Various Items

	Food	*Clothing*	*Rent*	*Fuel*	*Miscellaneous*
Urban	60.7	8.6	5.3	9.6	15.8
Rural	65.6	7.6	1.2	7.3	18.3

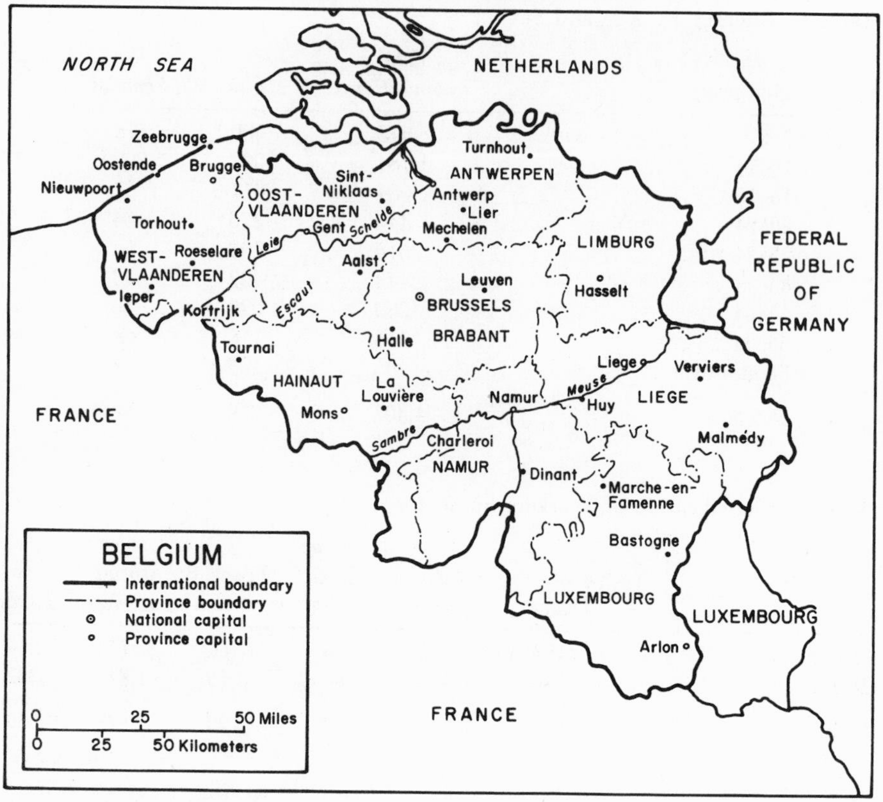
NORTH SEA
NETHERLANDS
Zeebrugge
Oostende
Brugge
Nieuwpoort
Sint-
Niklaas
Turnhout
ANTWERPEN
Antwerp
Lier
Mechelen
OOST-
VLAANDEREN
Gent
Leie
Schelde
Torhout
Roeselare
WEST-
VLAANDEREN
Ieper
Kortrijk
Aalst
Escaut
LIMBURG
Leuven
Hasselt
BRUSSELS
Halle
BRABANT
Tournai
HAINAUT
La
Louvière
Mons
Namur
Liege
Verviers
Meuse
Huy
LIEGE
Malmedy
FEDERAL
REPUBLIC
OF
GERMANY
FRANCE
Sambre
Charleroi
NAMUR
Dinant
Marche-en-
Famenne
Bastogne
LUXEMBOURG
LUXEMBOURG
Arlon
BELGIUM
International boundary
Province boundary
National capital
Province capital
0 25 50 Miles
0 25 50 Kilometers
FRANCE

Belgium

Jon McLin

Population Profile

Belgium is one of the most densely populated polities in the world (315 per square km). However, the dominant concern reflected in its demographic literature in recent years has been that the birth rate and rate of natural increase are too low. Many Belgians believe that an overacceptance by the populace of Malthusian doctrine—that efforts should be made deliberately to reduce fertility in order to offset an inherent tendency toward overpopulation—is having adverse economic, social, and political consequences. Prominent among these effects are the implications that population trends are thought to have for the sensitive balance between Flemings and Walloons, the country's two principal linguistic groups.

Zero population growth has not yet arrived in Belgium, but if present trends continue it is not far away. The birth rate began to decline around 1880 (it had already begun around 1860 in the Walloon part of the country), when it was 31/1000, and continued to fall until the 1930s, when it stabilized at around 16–17. After World War II, following a brief "baby boom" that was less pronounced than in some European countries, it first levelled off, then (after 1964) dropped again; in 1968 it was down to 14.66. The drop is mainly due to a decline in married fertility, not to a change in nuptiality.

The death rate, by contrast, has been rising, at least in relative terms. In 1870–80 it was among the lowest for industrializing countries, but by 1961 was higher (at 11.6) than that of all comparable countries except Austria and Britain. By 1968 it was 12.59. This change in relative position reflects the comparative aging of the Belgian population. As the following tables show, there has been both an increase in numbers of those over 65 and a shift towards the older cohorts within the economically-active age groups.

The very slow rate of natural increase—2.07 in 1968—has been somewhat supplemented by a net immigration that in 1968 amounted to 6,342 or .66/1000. During that year the resulting net increase in population was 2.73/1000. The average annual increase during the period 1961–68 was 6.05/1000.

4,717,790 or 48.87 per cent of the total population of 9,631,910, as of December 31, 1968, was male. Distribution by age, when compared with that of Belgium's Common Market neighbors, brings out strikingly the aged character of the Belgian population (*1*).

Most Belgian demographic data, including the foregoing, are reliable. Only the figures on linguistic identification are subject to some dispute. That problem is complicated by mixed marriages, bilingualism, pretensions based on the socially more prestigious role of French, and political sensitivities. The most recent census, that of 1961, omitted the sections on linguistic identification. Most figures given below are based on accepted conventions concerning which communes are Flemish and which are French-speaking, with Brussels—the main mixed area—

Table 1. Age-Specific Distribution of Population

Age	*1880*	*1930*	*1947*	*1961*	*1970 (est.)*	*1985 (est.)*
Under 20	427	309	282	304	305	313
20–65	510	615	611	574	553	551
Over 65	63	76	107	122	142	136
Total	1,000	1,000	1,000	1,000	1,000	1,000
20–40	553	540	473	469		
40–65	447	460	527	531		
Total	1,000	1,000	1,000	1,000		

Source: Joseph Stassart, "Structure par Age et Croissance Economique," *Population et Famille*, Nos. 6–7 (1965)

Table 2. Age Distribution of Population in Common Market Countries, End of 1967

Age	*Germany*	*France*	*Italy*	*Netherlands*	*Belgium*	*Luxembourg*
0–14	23%	25%	22%	28%	24%	23%
15–19	7	9	9	9	7	6
20–29	14	13	14	15	13	13
30–39	14	13	14	12	13	14
40–49	12	12	13	12	13	13
50–64	18	15	16	14	11	18
65+	13	11	10	10	19	12

treated separately. As an example of the order of magnitude of dispute, a recent survey in Brussels, carefully done by a team of researchers from U.L.B. (the Free University of Brussels), concluded that the population of that city is about 82 per cent French-speaking to 18 per cent Flemish. The usual estimate previously had been 75/25 per cent.

Population Distribution and Movement

The country is highly urban. Over 70 per cent of the population lived in communes of over 2,500 inhabitants at the time of the last census, in 1961. All but the largest of these (which experienced a move to the suburbs) had shown substantial growth since the previous census, while most of the smaller communes had lost population. In the center of the country, the conurbation that includes Ghent, Antwerp, and Brussels groups 41 per cent of the population on only 16 per cent of the territory. It remains true, however, that some 70 per cent of the communes have populations of under 2,500.

Most of the population is concentrated north of the Sambre and Meuse rivers. This cleavage between thinly and densely populated areas coincides only in part with the linguistic dividing line, which runs east and west between Courtrai (Kortrÿk) and Tongres (Tongeren). Not all of the French-speaking area is sparsely populated, for the cities of Brussels, Charleroi, Mons, Namur, and Liège are predominantly French-speaking. Nevertheless, most of the sparsely populated area is in Wallony.

There is substantial regional variation in the age pyramids. Indeed, an analysis of the 1961 census revealed that regional pyramids show more similarity with contiguous regions in neighboring countries—between Limburg and the Netherlands, East Belgium and Germany, the Flemish littoral and the English coastal region—than with each other. But a recent trend toward uniformity in birth rates will produce a more homogeneous future pattern. Between 1938 and 1960 there was a general trend towards uniformity in the birth rate, both between and within linguistic regions. The high rate areas of 1938 (mainly in Flanders) were generally falling and the low rate areas (mainly in Wallony) generally rising. Before World War II the birth rate in Wallony and Brussels had fallen to around 12/1000, while in Flanders it was nearly 20. By 1961, the rate in Flanders had descended to 18.85, while in Wallony it had risen to 15.80 (aided by a higher rate among immigrants in the Walloon region), and in Brussels to 14.42. The recent drop has been general: in 1968 the crude birth rates were 15.55 for the Flemish region, 13.78 for Wallony, and 13.02 for Brussels.

Only in the province of Limburg, which is relatively rural and adjoins the Netherlands, is there a significant departure from this pattern. Birth rates there have been significantly higher, death rates substantially lower, than in other parts of the country in recent years. In 1968, the crude rates were 18.6 and 7.8, respectively, for the province.

The present composition of the population is changing rapidly, notwithstanding a certain uniformization in regional birth rates, for differences in past birth rates are now making themselves felt in higher death rates in Wallony and higher rates of natural increase in Flanders. The distribution of the population according to linguistic group as of the end of 1967, and its natural increase during 1968, is shown in Table 3.

Table 3. Linguistic-Group Distribution of Population

	1967	*Increase or decrease during 1968*
Flemish-speaking region	5,348,039	+23,000
French-speaking region	3,117,388	− 2,356
German-speaking region	60,993	+ 374
Brussels (75–85% French-speaking) region	1,079,181	− 1,051

The aged character of the population may be measured by the fact that there are 81 persons of economically inactive ages (under 20, over 64) for every 100 of active age. The labor force in 1968 numbered 3,717,000, which broke down as follows:

Industry	1,622,000
Agriculture	201,000
Services	1,783,000
Military	111,000
Unemployed	110,000
Unfilled Vacancies	6,700
	(3.0%)

Of the civilian labor force, 2,457,000 were men, and 1,149,000 were women.

It may be supposed that there is some underemployment in the declining industries, especially coal mining, that are still protected by government subsidy from even more serious contraction than they have undergone.

Internal migration in Belgium has followed a familiar pattern in that it has been primarily toward urban centers and, more specifically, toward those urban centers endowed with diversified industrial structures. It has been fairly constant throughout this century in direction and rhythm. Net gainers since 1948 have been the provinces of Brabant (surrounding Brussels), Antwerp, and Liège, which have always gained. Most immigration has been to the region around Brussels between Charleroi and Malines. In most parts of the country (with the exception of Campine) the natural movement of the population has been so slight that migration could have a substantial effect on total population trends. In 1968, there were 530,764 internal migrations, results of which are shown in Table 4.

The presence of substantial numbers of foreign workers on Belgian soil is nothing new, but the pattern has changed somewhat in recent years. Already in the late nineteenth century substantial numbers of foreign migrants were employed in Belgium. Whereas in those days most came from neighboring countries (and, during the interwar period, from Poland), the recent immigration has been primarily Mediterranean (54 per cent of the total, as of 1961), especially

Table 4

Region	*Natural rate of increase*	*Net immigration*	*Net rate of growth*
Flemish area	4.28/1000	.47/1000	4.75/1000
French-speaking area . . .	−.75/1000	1.53/1000	.78/1000
Brussels	−.97/1000	−1.02/1000	−1.99/1000

Italian (44 per cent of the total), in origin. The 1961 census listed 453,486 foreigners as resident in Belgium, an increase of 85,767 over 1947. Well over half the increase consisted of women. While the earlier immigration resulted mainly from individual decisions and initiatives, the recent inflow has been organized and sponsored by governments.

Not that the Belgian government has done much to encourage permanent settlement by the migrants. It has sought immigrants mainly as a function of the level of economic activity. Only in 1964 was naturalization legislation eased somewhat to make it possible for some immigrants to remain, even though there has been occasional discussion of actively encouraging immigration in order to rejuvenate the population and—on the premise that most immigrants would be from Latin countries and thus natural allies of the Walloons—redress the Flemish/Walloon balance. The lack of special schools for immigrants is aimed less at assimilation than at limiting the influence of the government of the country of origin over the migrants. Immigrants face the usual complex of social problems—language, housing, separation from families (many Italians, though fewer Sicilians, leave their families behind), adjustment to the climate. These social requirements have become more important as more families have come to join the men in Belgium. There has also been a decrease in the proportion of foreigners who are economically active. Whereas in 1947 the figure was 52.7 per cent (compared to 37.4 per cent of the Belgian population), by 1961 it was down to 40.7 per cent (36.4 per cent of the Belgian population).

In spite of this trend, and of the remittances which migrant workers continue to send out of the country, the Belgian government still sees itself a gainer. Not only does the foreign immigration help offset a general shortage of labor, it also goes willingly into the mining, metallurgical, and household occupations which Belgians are increasingly reluctant to perform. About 60 per cent of the Italian immigrants, and 80 per cent of the total of male immigrants, are in extractive industries. In 1968, there were 57,122 new arrivals, as against 44,348 departures. The latter reflect mainly the temporary nature of most foreigners' work visits, as relatively few Belgians emigrate.

Population and the Economy

Belgium's 1968 GNP (in 1963 prices) was $17 billion, or $2,160 per capita, which puts it about in the middle of the range of OECD countries. The economy is heavily trade-dependent—exports amounted to 38.0 per cent and imports to 38.8 per cent of the Belgian-Luxembourgeoise Economic Union's GNP in 1968.

This is the highest proportion of any OECD country. Roughly two-thirds of the exports go to other EEC countries. The structure of economic activity is heavily weighted in favor of industry (including mining) and tertiary activity.

Table 5

	% of Civilian labor force	*% of Gross domestic product at current prices*
Agriculture, forestry, and fishing	5.6	5.4
Mining, manufacturing, construction, water, gas, and electricity	44.9	41.1
Other activities	49.6	53.5

Source: OECD

As these data reveal, such underemployment as persists is mostly in the second category, reflecting mainly the still incomplete rundown of mining activity since the turnaround in the coal market in the 1950s.

The main economic trend since World War II has been this decline in economic activity in the southern part of the country—where the coal reserves are mainly located—and the relative buoyancy of the Flemish littoral and its immediate hinterland. The changing economics of fuel prices and transport have been mainly responsible for this growth, led as it is by such activities as coastal refining, assembly and steelmaking plants, as well as by the ports of Antwerp (the EEC's second largest, after Rotterdam) and Ghent themselves. General manufacturing is centered in mid-Belgium.

Internal migration, though substantial, has not alone sufficed to get labor to the places where jobs now are. There is also a substantial commuter traffic, subsidized by means of economically advantageous railway passes. And many unemployed or underemployed workers, particularly in older age groups, cannot or will not seek work elsewhere. It is to cater to them, their families and their regions, that the government follows a "regional" policy of providing financial inducements to direct new, job-creating investments towards those areas. The policy is complicated by the fact that most such regions are in Wallony. Flemish areas demand comparable assistance on grounds of linguistic balance, but these claims run into problems with the EEC's competition policy, since the regions do not qualify as economically depressed.

It is the convergence, and mutally reinforcing character, of the economic and demographic trends in the Flemish and Walloon parts of the country that goes far to explain the intensification of their mutual hostilities in recent years.

Population and Development

The average annual rate of growth of GNP in Belgium from 1958–1968 was 4.3 per cent (3.7 per cent per capita). This represented a significant increase from the rate of the early and mid-fifties, before the formation of the

EEC; from 1950–55 the national income grew at an average rate of only 3.25 per cent. The country nonetheless is the slowest grower (Luxembourg excepted) in the EEC. Some analysis has been done of the causes of this performance, and it is worth explaining in view of the light it sheds on modernization and on the question—a controversial one in the Belgian literature—of what economic consequences demographic trends have had.

The Belgian controversy concerns the degree to which the country's low fertility and the unfavorable age structure associated with it are responsible for this lack of economic dynamism. The argument sometimes made is that the comparatively high proportion of the population in the economically inactive age groups, and a distribution that is not necessarily ideal within the economically active groups, may deny the economy the kind of labor inputs necessary for satisfactory growth.

The data from Denison's analysis are summarized in Table 6, which expresses the contribution of various factors to the growth, during the period 1950–1962, of the United States, Belgium, and Northwest Europe.

Details of these comparisons may be found in Denison, but a couple of comments are appropriate here. First, it is interesting to note that in certain structural respects the Belgian data resemble those for the United States more closely than those for Northwest Europe. Not only are over-all growth rates similar (2), but some important single factors—such as the economic contribution of a better-educated labor force or of conversion of productive factors from agricultural to industrial use—are also very close. Second, while the data do not refute the argument that Belgium's relatively poor performance is partly attributable to demographic factors—the contribution from employment levels was indeed smaller than the average for Northwest Europe—they do put that argument in diminished perspective. Belgium's retard is general, not specific. And to the extent that it is attributable to labor, the impact is slight: (*1*) in age-sex composition, Belgium actually underwent changes from 1950–62 more favorable than the Northwest European average; (*2*) the smaller contribution from employment levels in Belgium was largely offset by the quality of the Belgian work force, as reflected in their educational level. The shortage of labor from within the Belgian population would perhaps have been even more serious had there not been a relatively plentiful supply of migrant labor—which may not always be available. Another mitigating factor was that unemployment was at a relatively high level during the early part of the period, thus providing a source that, again, wouldn't always recur for expanding employment levels.

Nevertheless, the population-employment factor remains a minor one. Doctors seeking to prescribe remedies for slow-growing economies would do better to look elsewhere, such as at the factors affecting output per unit of input. In 1961 France had a higher proportion of its population in the economically inactive age groups than Belgium; but its growth rate from 1958–68 was the second highest in the EEC. Table 7, also from Denison, gives a better perspective on the role played by employment.

Interpreting these figures, it should of course be kept in mind that higher employment levels—to the extent they represent population increases rather than

Table 6. Sources of Growth of Total National Income (Col. I) and National Income per Person Employed (Col. II), 1950–1962

	U.S.A. Col. I	*U.S.A.* Col. II	*Belgium* Col. I	*Belgium* Col. II	*N.W. Europe* Col. I	*N.W. Europe* Col. II
Rate of growth of national income (%)	3.32	2.15	3.20	2.64	4.76	3.80
Percentage points attributable to:						
Total factor input	1.95	.79	1.17	.62	1.69	.73
Labor	1.12	.22	.76	.36	.83	.12
Employment	.90	—	.40	—	.71	—
Hours of work	−.17	−.17	−.15	−.15	−.14	−.14
Age-sex composition	−.10	−.10	.08	.08	.03	.03
Education	.49	.49	.43	.43	.23	.23
Capital	.83	.60	.41	.28	.86	.65
Dwellings	.25	.21	.02	−.01	.07	.04
International assets	.05	.04	−.06	−.06	−.03	−.04
Nonresidential structures and equipment	.43	.29	.39	.31	.64	.51
Inventories	.10	.06	.06	.04	.18	.14
Land	.00	−.03	.00	−.02	.00	−.04
Output per unit of input	1.37	1.36	2.03	2.02	3.07	3.07
Advances of knowledge	.76	.75	.76	.76	.76	.76
Changes in the lag in the application of knowledge, general efficiency, and errors and omissions						
Reduction in age of capital	—	—	—	—	.02	.02
Other	—	—	.08	.07	.54	.54
Improved allocation of resources						
Contraction of agricultural inputs	.25	.25	.20	.20	.46	.46
Contraction of nonagricultural self-employment	.04	.04	.15	.15	.14	.14
Reduction of international trade barriers	.00	.00	.16	.16	.08	.08
Balancing of the capital stock	—	—	.17	.17	.08	.08
Deflation procedures	—	—	—	—	.07	.07
Economies of scale						
Growth of national market measured in U.S. prices	.30	.30	.33	.33	.41	.41
Income elasticities	—	—	.11	.11	.46	.46
Independent growth local markets	.06	.06	.07	.07	.06	.06
Irregularities in pressure of demand	−.04	−.04	—	—	−.01	−.01

Table 7. Employment Growth Rate and Its Contribution to Growth Rate of Total National Income for Selected Countries, 1950–1962

Area	*Employment growth rates (percentages)*	*Contribution to growth rate of national income (percentages)*
United States	1.1	.9
Northwest Europe	.9	.7
Belgium	.5	.4
Denmark	.9	.7
France	.1	.1
Germany	2.0	1.5
Netherlands	1.0	.8
Norway	.2	.1
United Kingdom	.7	.5
Italy	.6	.4

an increase in the portion of the population employed or in the hours worked—contribute much less to the *per capita* growth rate, not indicated in Denison's figures, than to the *total* growth rate.

This interpretation of Belgium's economic performance is strengthened by the faster growth rates the country has enjoyed in recent years. Since there have been no substantial changes in employment levels over the last decade, the quickening in the rate of growth must be attributable to other factors. In the absence of analysis as systematic as Denison's, one can only speculate that the main causes are changes in the level of international assets (as a result of a deliberate policy of encouraging foreign investment); in the stimulus from lowered trade barriers, as the EEC has become a full customs union; and in economies of scale. The result should be encouraging to those who fear the potentially adverse economic effects of near-stable populations. Not only are alternative sources of growth and development (besides labor inputs) theoretically available, but on the evidence the Belgian population has demonstrated a willingness and ability to apply them and to accept the change that they entail.

Population and Society

Literacy is near-universal among the autochthonous population, which is what matters demographically, given the transitory status of most immigrants. Communications are advanced and widespread: there were (as of January 1, 1968) 186 television receivers, 181 telephones, and (January 1, 1969) 187 passenger cars per 1,000 inhabitants. The country is small enough to be traversed in a few hours by car. Military service and large-scale internal tourist movements to the Ardennes and the seashore insure high levels of at least superficial exposure to the country's various ethnic groups and geographic regions.

A contributory health service run by a Socialist Party-affiliated cooperative (*Mutuelle*) brings relatively low-cost health care to the working-class population. At the end of 1967, there were 151 doctors, 65 pharmacists and 827 hospital beds per 100,000 inhabitants.

The most significant thing about regional differences in educational levels

Table 8. Indicators of Educational Levels

Per cent of population in full-time school or university attendance (1966–1967): 15.8%

Per cent of age-groups in full-time education (1965–1966)

3 . . .	86.8	13	98.6	19	23.1
4 . . .	95.5	14	86.3	20	15.8
5 . . .	99.9	15	72.5	21	12.6
6 . . .	100.0	16	58.1	22	6.9
7 . . .	100.0	17	44.0	23	5.0
12 . . .	98.6	18	32.1	24	2.9

is that, contrary to a widely-held view, they do *not* in any direct way coincide with ethnic divisions. A study of educational levels of the three principal regions found that, on the basis of an index of 100 for the national average, regional indices were 91.07 for the Flemish region; 90.42 for Wallony; and 154.22 for Brussels. Since Brussels is predominantly French-speaking, there is a slight disparity among language groups that does not appear in the first two figures. But the study makes clear that this is incidental; that the determinants of local educational levels are socio-professional backgrounds and, relatedly, degree of urbanization.

Population and Polity

Belgium's present legal regime governing birth control is embodied in a 1923 statute which is severely restrictive. It outlaws the distribution of contraceptive devices and of birth control information that has a commercial intent. Abortion is outlawed. For the past several years there has been before Parliament a bill• which would considerably liberalize the legal situation and presumably bring law somewhat more into conformity with practice. It has lain dormant partly because of the general political sensitivity to the subject and partly because those who might be thought the logical supporters of reform—private groups engaged in birth control programs, etc.—prefer the evil they know—a very restrictive law that is almost completely unenforced, insofar as contraceptive devices are concerned—to the one they fear—a liberalized but somewhat restrictive law that might be rigorously enforced. The present situation in practice is that contraceptive devices are generally available, subject only to occasional personal scruples of Catholic physicians; birth control information is not disseminated in either an unsolicited or commercial way, but is available to those who seek it from nonprofit organizations like the local affiliate of the International Planned

Parenthood Federation. And abortion, though illegal, is widely practiced, mainly outside medical channels. (See concluding section.)

Birth control questions touch on two sensitive points in Belgium: the religious issue and the linguistic issue. The latter has been mentioned elsewhere in this paper and need only be restated here in summary form: there has been some concern among French-speaking Belgians, especially since the early 1960s, about evidence showing that their relative numbers are decreasing; and there is a corresponding tendency among Flemish-speaking Belgians, especially the militants or *flamingants,* to be suspicious of vigorous promotion of birth control on the grounds that it is inspired by anti-Flemish feeling.

The religious issue is related to this but is also important in its own right. The religious cleavage to some extent coincides with the linguistic one, for although both ethnic groups are predominantly Catholic, the more devout Catholics tend to be Flemish and the non-Catholic minority is mainly concentrated in the French-speaking population. The general problem of church-state relations, moreover, has been a burning political issue on occasion. The most recent instance, involving public aid to parochial schools, was in 1963.

The Belgian Church is somewhat divided internally on birth control questions. The current Belgian primate, Cardinal Suenens, has of course been a kind of leader of His Holiness's Loyal Opposition to *Humanae Vitae,* and the upper echelons of the Church have followed his lead. But the rural parish priests have not entirely caught up with this sea-change in the position of the Belgian Church since 1909. In that year, the then primate, Cardinal Mercier, issued a pastoral letter aimed at discouraging the idea of birth control, and this was followed by the "Instructions Against Onanism," issued by the Belgian bishops to curés and confessors. It called upon them to be vigorous in opposing the view that marital intercourse could have as its primary object ends other than procreation, and towards that end confessors were to be especially alert in asking such questions as "Do you commit yourself totally to divine Providence in the generation of children?" Husbands using "such instruments" were to be considered rapists, "to whom a woman must then oppose the resistance which a virgin must offer an attacker." Persons guilty of practicing contraception would be punished, it was held, by the premature death of their children.

Faced with these multiple sensitivities successive Belgian governments have avoided consistent demographic policies, although they have taken a number of half-measures that are germane. Relatively generous family allowances and childbirth allowances are provided, but these are justified on the grounds of "family policy" rather than encouragement to have children. Modest subsidies are also provided to the privately-operated family planning clinics on the same grounds. These measures seem to have had no noticeable effect on fertility; yet the Sauvy Report recommended a much enlarged package of such allowances as part of the natalist policy it advocated for Wallony.

Public attitudes toward birth control are changing in Belgium as elsewhere, but it would be as surprising for the government to adopt a policy of consistent and outspoken support for birth control as for it to take the opposite course and adopt a comprehensive natalist policy. What is more likely is growing real (if quiet) public support for contraceptive programs with the aim of reducing not the birth rate but the rate of abortions.

Population Work and Research

The principal family planning programs are those of La famille heureuse, the Belgian organization affiliated with the IPPF, and of l'Hopital universitaire St. Pierre of Brussels. The former organization was founded in 1962. It operates some family planning clinics, which dispense information, not devices, and conducts experimental programs in a few Belgian schools on population problems and sex education. Its main activity has been to hold clinics for young doctors in order to have a multiplier effect. It has found a substantial clientele for its programs, in Flanders and Wallony alike, and the limiting factor in their expansion has been money. The work of the gynecological division of St. Pierre has been a natural extension of its normal services. In addition to research, the main work has been, again, training clinics for Belgian physicians, and some speakers have been sent to talk to groups in provincial towns on population problems.

The most important body of demographic research in Belgium is that done by the Centre d'Etude de la Population et de la Famille within the Ministry of Public Health and the Family. The center was founded in 1963 as a response to the notorious Sauvy Report, which more than anything else provoked the heightened interest in demographic questions in Belgium. That report, commissioned and published by the Conseil économique wallon, and written by the then director of the Institut national d'études démographiques in Paris, sounded the alarm on the demographic trends in Wallony and proposed a set of vigorously natalist measures to reverse the trend. The center's publication, *Population et Famille,* has appeared some three times each year since 1963 and contains the richest body of analysis available on the country's demographic trends.

The Institute of Sociology of the Free University of Brussels has done and is doing good work on sociological aspects of demographic trends. Economists at the University of Louvain have studied the economic aspects. European regional problems associated with the population movements are studied by economists and geographers in Bruges at the College of Europe and the Conference of Regions of Northwest Europe. And physicians in St. Pierre's gynecological division try to make some statistical sense out of their clinical experience relating to birth control. They also give from three to four seminars per year on population problems for doctors from French-speaking African and from Southern European countries.

Belgian participation in international agencies concerned with population has been as ambivalent as its own domestic policy. A few years ago the Belgian government threatened to withdraw from the World Health Organization rather than consent to have population control regarded as a health question and thus treated by the WHO. It did not participate in the OECD project on demographic trends in Western Europe and North America. Its own foreign aid program, and that of the EEC in which it participates, have no birth control projects.

More recently, there has been a change towards quiet support for international agencies' work in birth control. Specifically, Belgium is one of the countries which make financial contributions to support the population program of the OECD's Development Centre, and its delegate to that program obtained a mandate to play a serious and constructive, though "low profile," role in its work. Consideration was recently being given by the government to contributing to the IPPF's program in Africa.

As in other relatively developed countries the role of organized programs in birth control is far less consequential than the spontaneous changes, unorganized and without official encouragement, in individual behavior. Nonetheless, the strongly positive response to the modest programs of such institutions as St. Pierre and the Famille heureuse suggests that they filled a real need and that in the absence of budgetary limitations they would find themselves doing a still more active job, partly in respect to the problem of abortion. The Centre d'Etude de la Population et de la Famille provides reliable data and analysis useful not only for those concerned with family and birth control policies but also for economists, geographers, urban planners, and the like.

Conclusions

Belgium's main population-related problem is one not so much of demography as of physical and mental health. It concerns the kind of birth control that is practiced and in particular the problem of abortion. Table 9 gives the results

Table 9. Number of Women (of Childbearing Age and Able to Conceive) Using Various Means of Contraception

	Flanders	%	*Wallony*	%	*Brussels*	%	*Belgium* %
Coitus interruptus	778	65.8	327	52.2	180	54.0	60.7
Rhythm method	498	42.1	268	42.7	169	50.8	43.2
Oral contraceptive	138	11.7	56	8.9	50	15.0	11.3
Condom	97	8.2	71	11.3	39	11.7	9.4
Douche	87	7.4	134	21.4	74	22.2	12.9
Diaphragm	19	1.6		1.3	33	9.9	2.4
Others	35	3.0		1.1	14	4.2	3.8
Undetermined	19	1.6		2.1	2	.6	1.6
Totals	1,182	141.4	627	141.0	333	168.5	145.3

Source: R. L. Cliquet, "L'étude de la fertilité et de la contraception dans le cadre de l'enquête nationale sur la fertilité et fecondité conjugales. Quelques résultats provisoires," *Population et Famille*, No. 15 (1968)

of a survey conducted in 1966 on contraceptive use.

For comparison, the 1970 estimate of the St. Pierre physicians (based largely on sales figures of pharmaceutical companies) is that some 17 per cent (200,000) of the relevant groups of Belgian women use the pill, under 1 per cent the loop; and only some 20 per cent of the couples use any of the modern means.

Belgian students of the subject conclude from these and other data on the low rate of modern contraceptive use, from the low birth rate, and from clinical experience at St. Pierre and elsewhere that the rate of illicit abortions is quite high (3). The range of guesstimates is from 80,000–200,000 per year. Assuming the midpoint of that spread, 140,000, to be the correct figure, it roughly equals the number of births in the country in 1968 (141,242). Belgian physicians appear to take seriously the legal ban on abortions, so the overwhelming majority of these must be performed without medical help, with results that can only be surmised. Some two thirds of the cases are thought to involve married women who already have two or more children.

There is some evidence that the situation is improving. Rising sales of oral contraceptives, evidence that among young people the use of modern practices is more common, and random testimony from rural physicians that the number of abortions is declining are all encouraging. But there is a long way to go. It is for this reason as much as any other that some Socialist and Liberal parliamentarians have proposed abolishing the 1923 statute, in order to liberate the flow of information on birth control techniques.

Compared to this question the other main, would-be issue—the differential rates of growth in Flanders and Wallony and their economic and political consequences—is a nonproblem. While there are serious difficulties, both political and economic, in the relations between the main linguistic groups, the demographic element makes only a minor and, in my view, nondetermining contribution.

The main demographic significance of the Belgian case may well prove to be its suggestiveness of the social problems associated with near-stable populations. Its rate of natural increase is among the lowest in the world. The duration of the trend towards declining fertility, and general conditions at present (population density, urbanization, increased availability of modern contraceptives), provide no reason to expect the trend to change. The social problems associated with the age distribution that goes with a stable population would perhaps repay study. The possible mitigating effect on those problems of participation in far-reaching European and Atlantic arrangements for trade, investment, and migration should also be examined. The problems might well have been more acute if the society had been less open.

The main problems with which Belgium will have to deal in the foreseeable future are the linguistic issue; ideological and generational differences about the nature of the society; and the environmental problems shared with other developed countries and exaggerated by a high population density. Present demographic trends mildly aggravate the first; have no apparent impact on the second; and render the third somewhat more manageable than it would otherwise be. But in none of the three cases can a prediction be made mainly on the basis of demographic considerations.

Notes

1. More detail may be found in Jean Morsa, "Fécondité, nupialité et composition par âge," *Population et Famille* No. 5 (1965), and Henriette Damas, "Les régions démographiques de la Belgique," *ibid.*, No. 11 (1967). The figures in this table are calculated from data in the 1969 supplement to the 1967–68 employment statistics published by the Statistical Office of the European Communities.
2. The United States growth rate accelerated after 1962, however.
3. It is also possible that these means used with determination are more effective than is usually thought.

References

Centre d'Etudes Politiques, Economiques et Sociales, "La population belge," *Documents-CEPESS* 1963, No. 2.

Conseil Economique Wallon, *Le rapport Sauvy sur le problème de l'économie et de la population en Wallonie.* Liège: Editions du Conseil économique wallon, 1962.

Henriette Damas, "Les régions démographiques de la Belgique," *Population et Famille,* No. 11 (1967).

Jean Morsa, "Tendances récentes de la fécondité belge," *Population et Famille,* No. 1 (1963).

The Author

JON McLIN has been concerned with the study of international organizations and the affairs of Western Europe since 1960. After receiving the B.S. degree in physics from Washington and Lee University, he was awarded a Rhodes Scholarship to Oxford University, which granted him the B.A. degree in 1962. For the following three years he studied at The Johns Hopkins School of Advanced International Studies and did field research in Canada and Europe, receiving the Ph.D. degree in 1966. In 1965, he joined the political science department of the University of Alabama, where in addition to his teaching duties he served as Assistant Dean for International Programs. Mr. McLin is the author of *Canada's Changing Defense Policy, 1957–63: The Problems of a Middle Power in Alliance.* He joined AUFS in 1968 to report from Brussels on the re-emergence of Europe as a political and social entity.

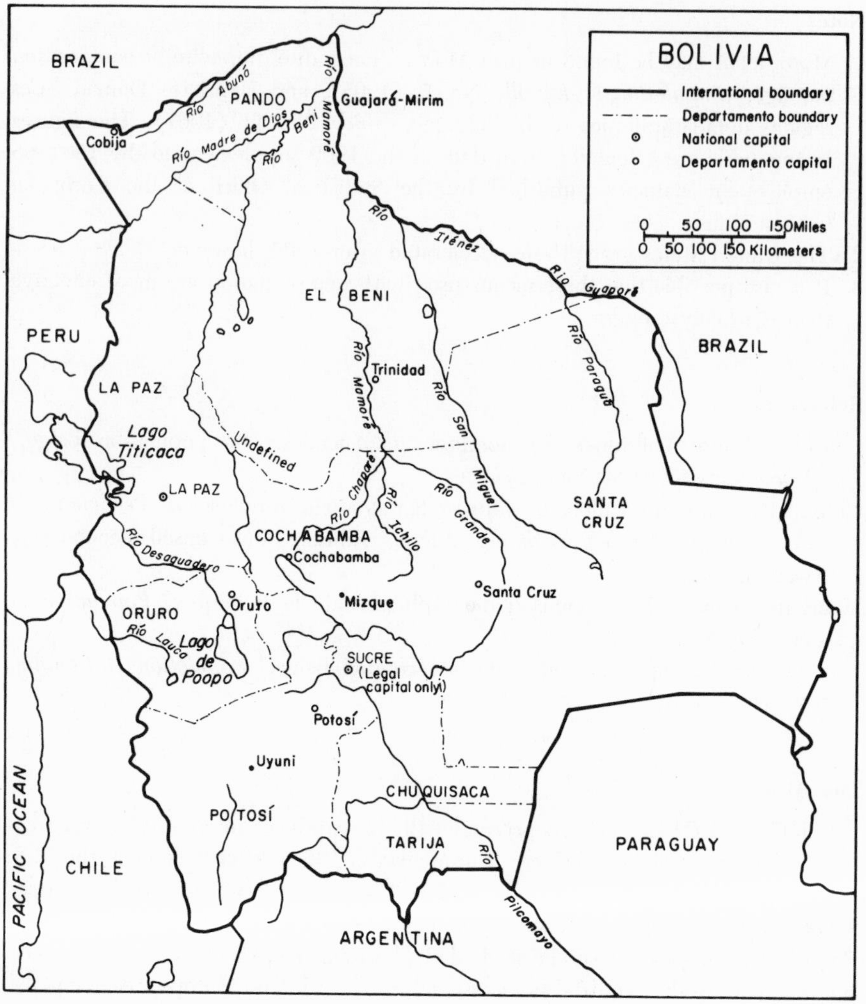

BOLIVIA
International boundary
Departamento boundary
National capital
Departamento capital
0 50 100 150 Miles
0 50 100 150 Kilometers
BRAZIL
PANDO
Río Abunã
Guajará-Mirim
Río Mamoré
Río Beni
Cobija
Río Madre de Dios
Río Iténez
Río Guaporé
EL BENI
Río Paraguá
BRAZIL
PERU
Trinidad
LA PAZ
Río San Miguel
Lago Titicaca
Undefined
Río Chaparé
LA PAZ
Río Ichilo
Río Grande
SANTA CRUZ
COCHABAMBA
Cochabamba
Río Desaguadero
Santa Cruz
Oruro
Mizque
ORURO
Río Lauca
Lago de Poopo
SUCRE (Legal capital only)
Potosí
Uyuni
CHUQUISACA
POTOSÍ
PACIFIC OCEAN
TARIJA
PARAGUAY
CHILE
Río Pilcomayo
ARGENTINA

Bolivia

Richard W. Patch

Population Profile

The Department of Social Affairs of the Organization of American States made a valiant effort to pull together statistics from eighteen sources relating to the population of Bolivia. The resulting tables are published in *Datos Básicos de Población en América Latina, 1970*. These data have been examined by the writer, together with Bolivia's Minister of Finance and Statistics, and by the Director of Statistics and Census of the Republic. Our conclusion was that the statistics are guesses but the guesses are as good as any available.

The crude birth rate is stable at 44/1000. The death rate declined from 21/1000 in 1960 to 19/1000 in 1970. However, the infant mortality rate *increased* from 103 per 1,000 of live births in 1960 to 108 per 1,000 live births in 1970. Births and deaths are both underestimated.

CELADE, in its *Boletín Demográfico,* estimates an annual growth rate of 22 per 1,000 inhabitants in 1960 and a rate of 24 per 1,000 inhabitants in 1970. This includes international migration. But migration into and out of Bolivia has small significance in comparison with natural increase. Given these figures the population of Bolivia should double in 29 years, from 4,658,000 in 1970 to 9,316,000 in 1999, whereas the population of Latin America as a whole will double in only 24 years.

In 1960 there were 688 minors under five years of age per 1,000 women between the ages of 15 and 49. In 1970 there were 728 minors under five years of age per 1,000 women between the ages of 15 and 49.

CELADE in its *Proyección de la Población de Bolivia* estimates (without distinction by sex) that life expectancy at birth was 41 years in 1960. In 1970 life expectancy is 46 years. The most common causes of death are tuberculosis, pneumonia, associated broncho-pulmonary diseases, and gastrointestinal diseases.

Bolivia's birth rate (44/1000) is higher than the average of Latin American countries (38/1000). CELADE believes, and I agree, that this birth rate was approximately the same in 1960 and may be projected to 1980.

The infant mortality rate is high, at 108 per 1,000 live births, compared with an average of 81 for all Latin America and only 58 for Argentina. Bolivia's rate of infant mortality is increasing while the average for Latin American countries has decreased slightly, from 82 to 81 per 1,000 live births.

The death rate in Bolivia declined only from 21 to 19 per 1,000 inhabitants in the ten years from 1960 to 1970. In the same decade the death rate in all of Latin America declined from 11 to 9 per 1,000 inhabitants.

The sudden arrival of modern medicine has had mixed results in Bolivia. Physicians are concentrated in the cities of La Paz, Cochabamba, Santa Cruz, Sucre, and Tarija. Interns, often against their will, are required to spend two years of service in populous rural areas that are otherwise without doctors.

There is a potentially dangerous belief by both patients and doctors that for any illness there must be a specific drug or herb remedy. Much of the population still depends on the *curandero* and on herbs and the like sold by *mestiza* women in markets from *ita'payllo* (an artichoke-like plant with spines containing an irritant) for abortion, to 20 grams of *melisa* leaf, 20 grams of mint, 15 grams of *manzanilla,* and 25 grams of *reqaliz* to regulate menstruation. Llama fetuses are sold for protection against witchcraft.

Perhaps more dangerous is the faith placed in sophisticated, though little tested, drugs flowing from Europe. The drugs are sold without prescription, usually on the recommendation of a druggist who has no medical training. Instructions are in Spanish, French, or German and are used by persons literate in no language. There is little information about dosages or potential incompatibility of drugs from Belgium, France, Germany, Italy, Peru, Switzerland, and Brazil. Drugs from the United States are disappearing from the Bolivian market.

Often medical care is a haphazard mixture of modern drugs and techniques with local remedies used for centuries. As recently as 1955 I was "cupped" and would have been bled had I permitted it, in the provincial capital of Cliza. Since then new drugs have arrived in vast numbers. To cite a more typical case, a child with labored breathing on the altiplano may be trucked in near freezing air to the nearest village which has a pharmacy. The pharmacist, who may only recently have realized the profit potential shifting from native *curandero* to a man in a white uniform, sells an antibiotic injection, which is then administered by an assistant. The needle may or may not be sterile; the assistant may or may not wash his hands or pause to determine if the injection is intramuscular or intravenous. There is no question of the child's allergy or rejection history. If fortunate he is soon trucked home again and given aspirin with caffein to cut the fever. If still more fortunate he may live.

In rural areas, where two thirds of Bolivia's population live, the present state of modern medical attention and the fascination with drugs may have contributed to an increasing infant mortality rate and nearly maintained the high death rate of Bolivian adults. But, Bolivian rural people are becoming more literate, more independent, and less awed by a white medical coat. Nevertheless, it may be another ten years before the death rate is substantially reduced by rational medical practices.

Reliability of data. The specifically Bolivian data are unreliable. There has been no national census since 1950 and the 1970 census of the city of La Paz is in gross error (*1*). After six months official figures had not been released on La Paz because "correction factors" were still being applied. But there is a certain chronological and internal consistency in the figures compiled by the Organization of American States which make it necessary to take them seriously: the statistics probably indicate major trends and major differences with the rest of Latin America and the world.

Population Distribution and Movement

According to *Datos Básicos de Población en América Latina, 1970,* the population of Bolivia was 3,696,000 in 1960, divided between 1,104,000 urban inhabitants and 2,592,000 rural inhabitants. By 1970, in a total population of 4,658,000 inhabitants, 1,652,000 were classified as urban, 3,006,000, rural.

The increase of population of the cities may be attributed both to substantial rural-urban migration and to natural urban growth. The relatively rapid growth of the cities is evident in the great expansion of *barrios marginales* around such cities as La Paz. The *barrios* have reached so high in the mountains above La Paz that they are built on precipitous inclines and many are washed away by the heavy summer rains. The urban sprawl has reached El Alto on the altiplano, although water there must be distributed by cistern truck.

The rural population, widely scattered over sometimes impenetrable terrain, has never been counted. Estimates of 2,592,000 rural inhabitants in 1960, 3,006,000 in 1970, and a projection of 3,486,000 in 1980 are in reality "guesstimates," and probably underestimate the rural population. Given existing communications technology, and lack of adequate transportation, population sampling in rural Bolivia is not feasible; nor is counting the *campesino* clusters around Lake Titicaca, in the Cochabamba valleys, and in the north of Potosí. One encounters similar problems in estimating the number of colonists who have moved to live near sea level in northern and eastern Bolivia among meandering tributaries of the Amazon. Considering the paucity of reliable rural data, it seems unwise at this time to accept the figures which show the urban population growing at a faster rate than the rural population.

The urban population is more promiscuous than the rural population, where family and community ties are stronger. But urban dwellers are almost entirely wage workers at very low levels and both men and women increasingly have knowledge of and access to contraceptives. Their use seems to be increasing among women who do not want to have a child a year, and among men who realize that they cannot buy adequate food and clothing for a large family. In the countryside, on the other hand, contraceptives are little known. Children are not the burden they are in the city although usually there is insufficient land to give them a future as *campesinos*. Nevertheless, a large family seems the only insurance for old age—which comes rapidly.

Internal migration. Bolivia has the most successful program of colonization in Latin America. A study I directed in 1960 showed there was an already substantial spontaneous flow of colonists to the under-inhabited lowlands north and east of the Andes. The Bolivian government and the Inter-American Development Bank combined to provide an administrative structure, based on aspirations and problems of colonists who had resettled with their own resources, that would facilitate a greater flow of migrants from the highlands to the lowlands. Bolivia's Ten Year Plan, fashioned in the halcyon days of the Alliance for Progress, called for movement of 700,000 persons to the lowlands in ten years. The goal will not be reached but it will be approached despite drastic funding cuts.

Urban-urban migrations are also of significant proportions. The city of Santa Cruz is fulfilling expectations of becoming one of the most important cities in Bolivia. It is attracting persons from other cities because it has become the center of growing, oil-producing, eastern Bolivia. It has the country's only paved highway, to Cochabamba. (La Paz is still trying to link itself with pavement to Oruro.) Sucre (Bolivia's legal capital) and Cochabamba are stagnant. Tarija has suffered floods. Movement is toward Santa Cruz and La Paz. La Paz has reached the physical limit of its expansion unless there is a huge capital investment to shore up the mountainsides, replacing the water and sewerage systems, greatly extending both of them, and giving electricity and telephone service to the *barrios marginales*. Santa Cruz, however, is awarded special state grants for its petroleum and gas contribution. Its services and potential for expansion are superior to those of La Paz.

Emigration. Seasonal migration reaches as far into the center of the country as the Cochabamba valleys. From there and other densely populated *campesino* areas farther south, there is a regular flow of Bolivian workers to harvest the cane crop of the sugar fields of northern Argentina. Usually they return to their home communities in six months. There is little family separation and it has no important effect on demographic growth.

Permanent emigration among the wealthy and professional classes became a phenomenon after the Nationalistic Revolutionary Movement (MNR) revolution of 1952. Some engineers and others returned to Bolivia after the fall of the MNR in 1964, but with increasing "national socialism" after September 1969, professionals are again leaving Bolivia.

Foreign remittances to Bolivia are minimum and by no means compensate for dollars sent abroad for Bolivian students, and for the habit among the well-to-do of maintaining accounts and holding savings in foreign banks. Only the prospect of a 300 per cent or more return attracts this capital back to Bolivia. Bolivia is extremely capital-poor and unemployment is rising. The present Torres government shelved the ousted Ovando's project to raise the $17-a-month minimum wage. Even cheap contraceptives are a problem. Plastic spirals, inserted in La Paz for a fee of $100, are out of the question.

Population and the Economy

Much of Bolivia appears to be underpopulated, but most of this area cannot be settled without mammoth technological development. The country has four inhabitants per square kilometer and 32 inhabitants per cultivable square kilometer. This compares with 14 and 49 for all of Latin America. The estimate for Bolivia must be evaluated carefully because highly trained soil experts do not agree upon the cultivability of most of Bolivia's lowlands. Apparently much is suitable only for cattle grazing and would not support even the national average population.

The river valleys of the eastern Andean foothills, the alluvial fans, and the piedmont plains, seem well adapted to intensive agriculture. As with present colonists in these areas, a projected 700,000 colonists could live in conditions of agricultural surplus. The problem is what to do with the surplus. Topography, road conditions, and expenses of transportation are beyond the belief of anyone who has not traveled for months in eastern and northern Bolivia. Roads and bridges are being built, but a trucker inching up the grade from Villa Tunari in the Chapare with the load of bananas for Cochabamba may still expect a quarter of his load to freeze and be ruined on the high pass. From a sugar and rice importing country Bolivia now has a surplus of both. Rice rots for lack of transportation, and quotas have been strictly imposed on sugar growers. Bolivia's problems with tropical products can be solved only with enormous expenditures in transportation facilities.

Trucks can arrive at La Paz from Caranavi at the foot of the Nor Yungas with intact loads of bananas, oranges, tangerines, grapefruit, and coca. Coca is a mild stimulant that probably neither helps nor hinders anyone. Bananas have become a staple in La Paz, either fresh or fried; oranges and tangerines are eaten, without enthusiasm; foreigners will eat grapefruit. Milk is abundantly produced in Cochabamba, where the milk plant does not work at full capacity, but it arrives in La Paz diluted and polluted. Families who can afford to do so buy evaporated milk imported from Denmark. Bolivia produces a surplus of meat—"surplus" in the sense that there is more beef than Bolivians can afford to buy. Much beef goes by plane from the eastern Beni to Lima, Peru. Staples on the altiplano are potatoes, *quinua,* and a little mutton. Foot-trodden *tunta* and *chuño* (forms of dehydrated potatoes) are no longer altiplano staples because the former is worth a dollar a pound in La Paz, the latter half a dollar. Chickens, eggs, cheese, *tunta, chuño,* and truck vegetables are marketed in La Paz and are seldom savored by people of the altiplano.

Bolivia is the only country in the Western Hemisphere without an outlet to the sea. Overseas shipments must be sent through the Chilean ports of Antofagasta or Arica after a long rail haul down the western Andes. Diplomatic relations between Chile and Bolivia have been interrupted since 1962. Access to the sea through national territory remains a critical political question.

Bolivia's natural wealth is most obviously in minerals, but her so-called resources have often resembled plagues. The native population declined severely in the sixteenth, seventeenth, and part of the eighteenth centuries when Spaniards brutally exploited literal mountains of silver (Potosí). Nitrates became important for fertilizers in the nineteenth century. Chile took Bolivia's nitrate-rich coast in the War of the Pacific. Rubber became valuable. Brazil took Bolivia's northern, tropical province of Acre. Tin became especially valuable in the twentieth century and Bolivia seemed to have some of the largest reserves in the world. Three individuals gained control over the larger mines and made fortunes which they invested abroad. The large mines were nationalized October 31, 1952, after the MNR revolution of April 1952. As state enterprises the large mines have been dismal failures. Working conditions, health care, and mortality are appalling.

Petroleum and gas in eastern Bolivia have become the newest resource. Standard Oil holdings were nationalized in 1937. Then, with the government oil company (YPFB) a successful operation, the MNR government allowed new concessions to independent oil companies. The only operation which found reserves was the Bolivian Gulf Oil Company. It exported oil through a trans-Andean pipeline. Gas was discovered and a pipeline was under construction to Argentina. Bolivian Gulf was nationalized in October 1969 soon after General Ovando took the presidency. After that no one would buy Bolivian oil, and the gas pipeline was abandoned.

Bolivia's natural resources have undermined rather than aided the country's people and "their" governments. Tin miners' wages, for instance, were arbitrarily halved although the world price of tin was reaching all-time highs. Now Bolivia has built its own smelter although half a dozen commissions have said it would be uneconomic. Bolivian refineries produce all ordinary gasoline, kerosene, and lubricants now needed in the country.

Most unskilled laborers work at, or near, the minimum wage of $17 a month: for a man with family this is not a subsistence wage. The labor supply greatly exceeds demand. Only the controlled low price of some basic food products allows much of the urban population to live. The rural population lives from the land and low prices give it little incentive to increase productivity.

Population and Development

There is a direct relation between Bolivia's lack of technological progress, lack of industrial development, lack of housing, only slight increase in agricultural productivity, and the very high death rate.

There are few parts of Latin America as insular as Bolivia, although it borders on five countries. Bolivia's boundary with Chile is the nearly uninhabitable Atacama Desert. The border with Peru runs from the Andes in the south to tropical rain forest in the north. Northern and eastern Bolivia are bounded by the almost unvisited frontiers of Brazil's and Paraguay's tropical rain forest, and by the Gran Chaco, which can be a desert in the dry season and a bottomless pit in the rains. The southern frontier with Argentina is remote from any cities. Bolivia is closed in upon itself and the result has been economic calamity.

Bolivia is the fifth largest country in South America but it is a topographical curiosity and a chronological monster. The culture of most of the population remains rooted in the sixteenth century. Embellishments of 450 years have taken their respective places, and the resulting mixture is strange: witches, witchcraft against witchcraft, and a persistent belief in Mother Earth—the Pachamama. Desiccated llama fetuses are placed in the cornerstone of modern buildings. At best births are attended by midwives, more often the woman's mother, grandmother, or aunt.

Many *campesinos* still use the *taclla,* a short hoe-spade inherited from the Incas. Until 1955 a wanderer from Andalusia in the Spain of 1555 would have found a familiar home in Bolivia's eastern Santa Cruz. The pallets were of straw, most light was by candle, and the rains turned sandy streets into quagmires. Even the accent of southern Spain remained, until modified by completion of the Cochabamba-Santa Cruz highway in 1955, which linked far-away Santa Cruz with the rest of Bolivia and presumably the world.

Today La Paz and Santa Cruz have some electricity, telephones, taxis, and drinking water. For the last three years La Paz has had television, a single state channel which repeats movies and cartoons so often that workers have threatened to strike. High buildings have risen in La Paz, but many are only half completed and their future is now in doubt. Anyone who drinks the water from the taps of La Paz takes a great risk. The mains have been corroding and bursting for thirty years. Sewer lines were laid in the same trenches. For no apparent reason the municipality shuts off the water in La Paz from 11 P.M. to 2 A.M. Sewerage and all leaks into the empty water mains and finally emerges from water taps as an orange-colored liquid. From this can be imagined other services.

Modern technology in Bolivia, superficially imposed on beliefs and practices of centuries past, is often incongruent, misunderstood, liable to fail at any time. Many appliances will function with La Paz's peculiar combination of 220 volts and 50 cycles. The voltage varies, however, from zero to sudden bursts which burn out the motors of cheap refrigerators (at $500). Even auxiliary generators in private clinics do not function. There is a modern computer center in the office of the National Agrarian Reform Council but it required a trip to the United States to obtain special print-out paper for land titles. Examples may be multiplied. A final example will suffice: the problem of heat, living at eleven to twelve thousand feet above sea level in La Paz. Daytime temperatures are tolerable if a person has a pair of sweaters and keeps active. On cloudy days and at night the temperature can go below freezing in two or three hours. Firewood is prohibitively expensive on the near-treeless altiplano. There is no coal. There are no gas lines. The usual solution is to put on another sweater and go to bed at dark.

Population and Society

Bolivia is divided into two main groups. The "indigenous" group speaks Aymará or Quechua as its first language and composes 55 to 60 per cent of the total population. The second group speaks Spanish as its first language and is 40 to 45 per cent of the total population. Indigenous speakers are by no means as culturally isolated as the indigenous speakers of Peru and Ecuador. They move easily in the cities and dominate many markets.

The percentage of illiterates over 15 years of age is put at 60 per cent. This figure seems low and many functionally illiterate persons probably were included.

Socio-intellectual mobility is great in Bolivia, compared with the similar populations of Peru and Ecuador. The revolution of 1952 was a culminating mark in a long process of integration of "Indians" and "mestizos."

Public health situation. Public health programs are among the most rudimentary of the world. They consist mainly of massive but sporadic vaccination campaigns—against typhoid and smallpox in La Paz, and against cholera and similar diseases when the Ministry of Public Health determines that they have reached epidemic proportions in outlying areas. The most successful program, sponsored by the United Nations, went far toward total eradication of malaria in the northern and eastern lowlands.

There appear to be no family health programs, nor special assistance in maternal welfare. A large part of public health medicines is donated by other countries, notably Argentina. The main functioning hospital is the Workers Hospital in La Paz, where social security benefits are provided by the National Office of Social Security. The hospital is overcrowded and conditions are extremely poor. Other patients go to private clinics which are not well equipped and are managed without public regulation. A seriously ill person with the money to do so goes to the United States, Chile, or Argentina for treatment.

Educational profile. There is an estimated total of 1,195,000 children of primary school age (five to fifteen years old) in the country. Of this number 720,000 are enrolled in primary schools, with 18,000 teachers. There are some 145,000 youths enrolled in public and private secondary schools, and 21,000 enrolled in colleges and universities. Indigenous-speaking *campesinos* have been eager to enroll their children in schools, and have themselves built many primary school buildings in rural areas. Three special normal schools for preparation of teachers from rural areas and for rural areas have greatly aided the government in its promise to provide teachers for rural schools. Thus, many rural previously monolingual indigenous children have the same access to primary schools as Spanish-speaking children in the towns and cities. However, relatively few rural children continue to secondary schools. There is no barrier to continuance except the economic one of living away from home. It is nearly the same in the universities, where no one is very sure of his "ethnic background" and progress depends on performance and politics. But practical problems are great for *campesino* youths wishing to continue to secondary schools and universities.

The quality of education is abominable. The primary school graduate is lucky if he learns to read, write, and do simple sums. A few private secondary schools ("colleges") polish this a bit. Public secondary schools and many private secondary schools are already so involved in national politics that general education is bypassed. Students of a secondary school in La Paz took and wrecked the interior of the building housing the Ministry of Education in September 1970. The school year had to be suspended and became a factor in the downfall of

President Ovando early in October. Politics in the national universities are even more intensive. They involve strikes, hunger strikes, manning barricades, ventures with jungle *guerrilleros,* mock funerals, and very real funerals. Apparently a few students get some guidance and, working mostly on their own, achieve a certain education.

Population and Polity

Current legal situation. It would be a meaningless exercise to try to separate the legal status of family planning programs and laws governing availability of contraceptives and abortion from the current political situation.

Bolivia has no law, no constitutional government, no respected legal authorities, and two capital cities. This does not mean that Bolivia is a "banana republic" or a "tin tiger." It does mean that Bolivia is now ruled by decrees which vary from week to week. In practice this nearly amounts to common law—what is usually done by most people cannot be sanctioned unless the government is willing to risk another coup.

In practice there are no family planning programs which have had any impact. Contraceptives are freely available to anyone. Abortion is practiced as a matter of course, by physicians in clinics, for anyone willing to pay the modest cost (2).

Contraceptives have little place within marriage. Some urban women use the pill, men do not favor the condom. Most urban and many rural men understand use of the condom but it is widely rejected in the countryside. It is accepted in the larger cities for uses before and outside marriage.

Contraceptive information is obtained by word of mouth. The only publicity campaign which has come to Bolivia was aimed at druggists, in November 1968, and promoted the sale of plastic spirals. The promotion is a failure because physicians charge $100 for IUD insertion. In contrast, supposed aphrodisiacs are commonly sold by native *curanderos,* and male hormone products have a steady sale in pharmacies.

Only a few individuals and organizations in Bolivia have shown any interest in family planning. The Roman Catholic Church in Bolivia has taken no firm stand against contraception and there is little discussion of the issue. News of the pill has spread fairly widely in large cities and it has been adopted predominantly by women of the wealthy and professional classes.

Conclusions

The basic problem in Bolivia is population maldistribution, not overpopulation as such. On a smaller scale the problem in the rural highland areas is steady reduction of size of land holdings as they are redistributed to heirs of a deceased. In the larger cities, such as La Paz, the population is becoming impacted, undernourished, and unproductive.

Colonization movement to the lowlands is important and significant. It has had some effect on stabilizing the rate of increase in densely populated rural areas. But the rate of internal migration is not matching the rate of natural increase. Present population maldistribution will continue until the north and east are fully opened, and that requires technological development beyond that which Bolivia is now capable of providing.

Family planning will be resisted by a majority but an urban minority practicing various methods of contraception will slowly increase. More rational use of modern medical techniques and drugs will sharply cut the death rate and raise the rate of natural increase to levels as high as any in Latin America. Bolivia, with its geographical problems and its small, disturbed, economic base on which to build, already is hard pressed to provide subsistence for its existing population. With its illiteracy, its ignorance, and essential family conservatism, Bolivia will be a major test of family planning programs.

Notes

1. See Richard W. Patch, *The La Paz Census of 1970* (RWP-4-'70), Fieldstaff Reports, West Coast South America Series, Vol. XVII, No. 12, 1970.
2. See Richard W. Patch, *Attitudes Toward Sex, Reproduction, and Contraception in Bolivia and Peru* (RWP-3-'70), Fieldstaff Reports, West Coast South America Series, Vol. XVII, No. 11, 1970.

References

Centro Latinoamericano de Demografía (CELADE). *Proyección de la Población de Bolivia,* Serie C No. 9. Santiago, 1963, Cuadro 5.

CELADE. *Boletín Demográfico,* año 2, Vol. III, Santiago enero 1969. Cuadros 2, 3 y 4.

CELADE. *Boletín Demográfico,* año 1, Vol. II, Santiago, octubre 1968. Cuadros 1, 2 y 4.

Organización de los Estados Americanos (OEA). *Datos Básicos de Población en América Latina, 1970.* Washington, D. C., 1970.

The Author

RICHARD W. PATCH, a Professor of Anthropology at the State University of New York at Buffalo, studied at Deep Springs College, California, and Cornell University, which awarded him a Ph.D. in 1956. A former Fellow of the Institute of Current World Affairs, Dr. Patch taught at Tulane University and then joined the Field Staff for a decade beginning in 1957. From 1963 to 1968 he held a concurrent appointment as Visiting Professor of Anthropology at the University of Wisconsin. Beginning his field studies in 1951 in the Peruvian Andes in association with the Vicos Project, in 1954 he originated social research on Bolivian agrarian reform and in 1963 directed a study of internal migration there. Dr. Patch has been a member of several missions of the Inter-American Development Bank to Bolivia as well as a member of the Latin American Science Board of the

National Academy of Sciences. Best known of his writings are *Social Implications of the Bolivian Agrarian Reform* (thesis) and a section of *Social Change in Latin America Today.*

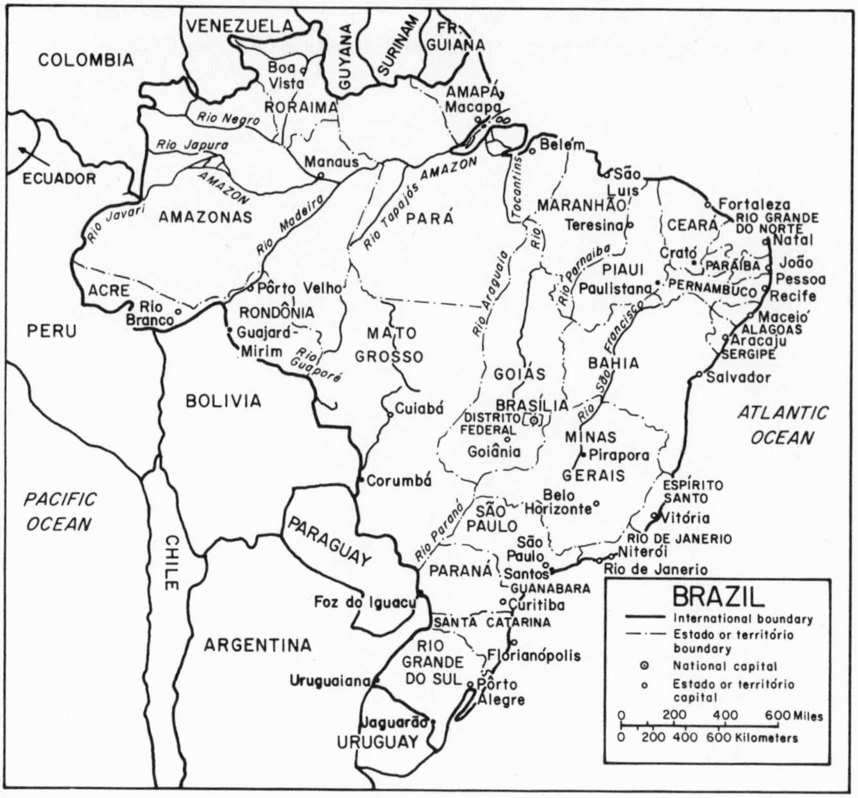
VENEZUELA
COLOMBIA
GUYANA
SURINAM
FR. GUIANA
Boa Vista
RORAIMA
AMAPÁ
Macapá
Rio Negro
Rio Japura
Manaus
Belém
ECUADOR
AMAZON
São Luis
Rio Javari
AMAZONAS
Rio Madeira
Rio Tapajós
PARÁ
Tocantins
MARANHÃO
Fortaleza
Teresina
CEARÁ
RIO GRANDE DO NORTE
Natal
Rio Araguaia
Rio Parnaiba
Crató
PARAÍBA
João Pessoa
PIAUI
Paulistana
PERNAMBUCO
Recife
ACRE
Pôrto Velho
Rio Branco
RONDÔNIA
PERU
Guajará-Mirim
MATO GROSSO
Maceió
ALAGOAS
Aracaju
SERGIPE
Rio Guaporé
GOIÁS
BAHIA
Salvador
Rio São Francisco
BOLIVIA
Cuiabá
BRASÍLIA
DISTRITO FEDERAL
MINAS GERAIS
ATLANTIC OCEAN
Goiânia
Pirapora
Corumbá
ESPÍRITO SANTO
PACIFIC OCEAN
Belo Horizonte
SÃO PAULO
Vitória
Rio Paraná
PARAGUAY
RIO DE JANERIO
São Paulo
Niterói
CHILE
PARANÁ
Santos
Rio de Janerio
GUANABARA
Foz do Iguacu
Curitiba
SANTA CATARINA
ARGENTINA
RIO GRANDE DO SUL
Florianópolis
Uruguaiana
Pôrto Alegre
Jaguarão
URUGUAY
BRAZIL
International boundary
Estado or território boundary
National capital
Estado or território capital
0 200 400 600 Miles
0 200 400 600 Kilometers

Brazil

Thomas G. Sanders

Early in the 1970s the population of Brazil will reach 100 million and before the end of this century exceed 200 million (*1*). Brazil will emerge as one of the world's major nations, in population as well as size. Its annual rate of population increase, which was approximately 3 per cent between 1950 and 1960, and 2.7 per cent between 1960 and 1970, will strain severely the resources available for the investments in production, education, health, and jobs which are also prerequisites for Brazil to become a significant nation.

Brazil is typical of most other Latin American countries in having entered a stage of reduced mortality resulting from medical and sanitary advances without a corresponding decline in levels of natality. Only 30 years ago, Brazil's population was increasing at less than 2 per cent annually, as the mortality rate hovered around 25/1000 while the natality index was about 44. During the forties and fifties public campaigns against transmittable diseases achieved dramatic results. The former figures dropped to a little over ten and life expectancy increased to a 1964 estimate of 54.2 years. The level of natality, however, declined only slightly, to 41 (*2*). The gap between those two sets of data provided nearly all of the 3 per cent increase, since migration, which was important as a population increment before 1934, is now negligible (*3*).

Continued high fertility and reduction of infant and child mortality have made Brazil a country of dependent youth: approximately 42 per cent of the population is 14 years old or under (*4*). This index of dependence introduces additional burdens on heads of households and on society, which are called upon to invest in the future of their young people. Brazil's population pyramid, unlike that of developed countries, is perfectly proportional, with the largest number of individuals in the lowest age group and declining gradually ascending upward in age (*5*).

The women of Brazil continue to have high rates of fertility despite "modernizing" processes that might be expected to lead to reductions. Previous census figures show that women in cities produce about two thirds as many children as those in rural areas, and Brazil is rapidly urbanizing (*6*). Likewise, educational levels are improving, and there seems to be a clear inverse correlation between years of education and fertility (*7*). States with a substantial urban population and relatively high standards of education, like Guanabara, São Paulo, and Rio Grande do Sul, have markedly lower natality rates than predominantly rural northeastern states like Rio Grande do Norte, Paraíba, Ceará, and Pernambuco (*8*). Nevertheless, the "modern" segment of the population continues to be a minority. Most Brazilians are poor and whether they live in the country, in provincial towns, or in the lower class areas of the cities, they have very low levels of education and lack means of information for determining the number of children they will have.

Mortality rates and causes of death vary in different parts of the country. Official data, which depend on civil registers, are not reliable indicators of mortality (or natality), but supplementary studies of the capital cities of various states reveal sharp discrepancies. Rio de Janeiro has an infant mortality rate of 65.3/1000 and São Paulo 75.1, whereas Maceió and Teresina, capitals of the northeastern states of Alagoas and Piauí, have 213.6 and 246.3. The general mortality rate of São Paulo is 9.1/1000 and that of Maceió, 16.6. The states of Guanabara and São Paulo have a mortality rate of nine and an infant mortality figure of 75, while the northeastern region offers a contrasting 18 and 176 (*9*).

In cities like São Paulo, the chief causes of death are those common to developed countries, diseases of the circulatory system and cancer, but in most of the northeastern capitals, they are digestive disorders, infections, and malnutrition, which take a heavy toll of children (*10*). The southeastern region, with the major industrial cities of Rio de Janeiro, São Paulo, and Belo Horizonte, has 69.1 per cent of the doctors and 44 per cent of the nation's population, while the Northeast, with 30 per cent of the population, has only 13.5 per cent of the doctors. In both regions medical personnel are heavily concentrated in the cities. The Southeast also has 56.2 per cent of the nation's hospital beds, the Northeast, 15.6 per cent (*11*).

Comparative figures on rural and urban morbidity and mortality do not exist. Nevertheless, the contrasts between cities, states, and regions indicate that the lower the level of income and availability of medical personnel and facilities, the higher will be the rates of mortality and the shorter the life span. We may consequently assume that many rural areas of Brazil have higher indices of mortality and infant mortality than the capitals of the northeastern states.

Estimates of future trends in Brazilian population characteristics involve guesswork because of deficiencies in statistics. Brazil long had a tradition of sophistication in demographic analysis because of the influence of Dr. Giorgio Mortara, director of the Instituto Brasileiro de Geografia e Estatística, and the censuses of 1940 and 1950 were considered the most accurate in Latin America. The census of 1960, however, dropped sharply in quality and was never fully tabulated, so that many projections continue to rely on the 1940 and 1950 data.

The census of 1970, which is now being tabulated, represents a return to the former standard and will be helpful in remedying our present lack of information.

Information on births, marriages, and deaths in Brazil is drawn, theoretically, from the civil register. While this functions well in the more urban and developed regions, it is estimated that in some states of the North, less than 10 per cent of births are recorded, the figures on death being somewhat better. Given these deficiencies, demographers are inclined to use the census data for their estimates.

No records are kept of internal migration and emigration. Analysts of internal migration usually resort to the census and lists of lodgers in centers that receive and arrange work for migrants.

Determination of urban-rural population composition is hampered by the use of an administrative rather than numerical determination of urban centers. Within each *municipio* (geographical township), the *sede* (administrative center) and *vilas* (small towns) are classified as urban and the rest of the area rural. Since many of these urban centers have populations smaller than common international urban criteria (generally 2500 inhabitants), it is believed that the urban population of Brazil is overestimated.

Color is another commonly cited characteristic of the Brazilian population whose validity is questionable. Brazil is probably the world's leading racial melting pot, absorbing Africans, American Indians, northern and southern Europeans, and, in the twentieth century, Orientals, into a fusion based on a tradition of miscegenation. Many Brazilians have physical characteristics of three of these. Accurate determination of race is impeded by two cultural factors: (1) In Brazil race is based not simply on color, but on other features like hair and physical characteristics. (2) There is a bias in terms of attractiveness and prestige in favor of White characteristics so that individuals tend to identify themselves as lighter than they are. Thus a light mulatto is inclined to call himself White, and a Black may call himself a *moreno*. Brazilian racial data are based in recent censuses on self-identification within four categories: White, Black, Oriental, and *pardo* (mixed). In 1950, 61.8 per cent of those in the census called themselves White, a figure which is unquestionably an exaggeration (*12*).

A similar problem of self-definition exists in literacy, which is politically important because only literates can vote. In Brazil the criterion is ability to write one's name. Although by this standard illiteracy has steadily declined with each decade to less than 40 per cent of the population, this does not accurately define the capacity of the population to read and interpret the world around them. Educated people are clearly a minority concentrated in urban centers.

Despite the dubiousness of figures on urban-rural distribution of the population, the use of a consistent criterion shows Brazil to be in a process of rapid urbanization. In 1960 the population was estimated to be 54.1 per cent rural, but during the past decade Brazil made the transition to a predominantly urban country. From 1960 to 1970 annual urban population growth was 4.6 per cent, while rural was 1.1 per cent (*13*). The expansion of major cities has been phenomenal. Greater São Paulo increased from 2,449,000 in 1950 to an estimate of over 8,000,000 in 1970, and Greater Rio more than doubled in the past 20 years. The fastest growing large city is Belo Horizonte, which was founded in the late nineteenth century, had 353,000 people in 1950, and today with its environs is calculated to have 1,728,000. The large urban centers have not been the only beneficiaries of this process. Historically an agrarian country, Brazil in 1960 had 72 cities with more than 100,000 people. Capitals of states like Fortaleza (Ceará) and Salvador (Bahia) are approaching a million inhabitants, while provincial cities like Campinas (São Paulo) and Campos (Rio de Janeiro) now have over 300,000 (*14*).

Preliminary indications from the census of 1970 suggest that the large cities themselves have not reached the estimated projections and that part of the anticipated increase is going instead to "suburbs" where housing is cheaper and life more tranquil. Lower class suburbs of Rio de Janeiro, for example, are now major cities. Nova Iguaçú grew 129.8 per cent between 1950 and 1960, reaching an estimated population in 1968 of 478,319. Duque de Caxias grew 132.1 per cent and in 1968 had 324,261. São João de Meriti grew 134.4 per cent to reach 255,201. São Gonçalo and Niterói, which are also considered suburbs of Rio, had, in 1968, 329,764 and 303,375 inhabitants respectively (*15*).

The expansion of population in the cities is the result not merely of natural increase but of internal migration. The origins of this movement of people lie in Brazil's backward rural sector, which is dominated by largeholdings (latifúndios) and smallholdings (minifúndios). Neither structure is capable of absorbing the large population increases in rural areas, which are also the centers of poverty, illiteracy, and disease. From the rural areas migrants tend to go first to provincial cities and state capitals, and often from there to urban agglomerations. The chief areas of expulsion have been the rural regions and small towns of Minas Gerais, Bahia, and the Northeast, especially the coastal zone (*mata*), where sugar culture traditionally dominated. Other important sources of migrants are the depressed agricultural states of Espírito Santo and Rio de Janeiro in the Southeast, and certain rural regions of Rio Grande do Sul in the South, where land is no longer available for the numerous progeny of families of Italian and German descent.

The dominant migratory stream runs from the Northeast and Minas Gerais to São Paulo and Rio de Janeiro. According to the now out-of-date figures of 1950, the state of São Paulo had 513,000 inhabitants born in Minas Gerais, 190,000 in Bahia, and lesser numbers from other northeastern states (*16*). Since the chief expansion of these urbanized states has come since 1950, we may assume that today these figures are several times as large. Guanabara has absorbed heavily from Minas Gerais, the neighboring state of Rio de Janeiro, and Bahia.

Other migratory currents have moved toward the empty spaces of the interior. One goes from the Northeast toward the Amazon, passing by the fertile areas in the state of Maranhão opened during the last decade by the Northeast Development Agency (Sudene). The government is currently constructing highways that will cut the Amazon region from East to West and from North to South, which are aimed specifically at encouraging this resettlement. Another stream has as its objective the huge pastoral states of Goiás and Mato Grosso, with the greatest intensity of settlement around the new metropolis of Brasília and nearby Goiânia (both of which have over 300,000 inhabitants). The final current has drawn people from Rio Grande do Sul and São Paulo into northern and western Paraná (which was the most rapidly growing state in the 1950s) and southern Mato Grosso (*17*).

Seasonal migration and emigration in Brazil have been little studied. The best known cases of the former involve *sertanejos* from the interior of the Northeast and Bahia who harvest cash crops like sugar on the littoral. During 1970, hundreds of thousands of *sertanejos* were also participating in "work fronts," public works projects to provide income for victims of one of the Northeast's periodic droughts. The *sertanejo* is also known for his tendency to migrate to a southern city, work or try to get a job for several years, and then return. As to external migration, Brazil has no statistics. There is considerable evidence, however, that Brazilians are encroaching on the thinly settled frontier areas of neighbors like Paraguay, where a major attraction has been the lack of coffee export taxes, and Bolivia.

Although Brazil has a large and growing population, many Brazilians are unaware of the high costs for jobs, education, and health that this entails and believe that it can be absorbed without difficulty. This view is encouraged by the nation's extensive natural resources, the long-time policy of importing labor, and, more recently, the high indices of economic growth. Brazil had a population density of only 8.3 inhabitants per square kilometer in 1960, with a range of over 3,000 in Guanabara to less than one in Amazonas (*18*).

Despite low productivity in relation to area cultivated and low levels of consumption, the country is self-sufficient in major food products except wheat. Its two major agricultural exports are coffee (the world's largest producer) and cotton. Many Brazilians, however, are poorly nourished because of low levels of agricultural technology and purchasing power, the high cost of marketing products, and ignorance about nutrition. The bulk of potential agricultural land is scarcely utilized.

Brazil also has extensive mineral resources, especially iron, and including quartz, manganese, zinc, and aluminum. Coal and petroleum reserves are believed to be substantial, though their scope is undetermined. Great progress has occurred in recent decades in exploiting these natural resources, though difficulties of transportation and lack of energy and capital continue to limit potential.

Since World War II, industry has spearheaded the nation's development. The triangle defined by São Paulo, Rio de Janeiro, and Belo Horizonte is the chief beneficiary of industrial growth, though attempts have been made to spread it to other regions, especially the Northeast, through fiscal incentives. The economic crisis of the early 1960s occurred largely because the country had reached a saturation point in substituting imports, and present government policy aims at diversifying exports, especially of manufactured goods (which now compose 12.3 per cent of all exports). Brazil is the largest industrial nation in Latin America. It produces all types of consumer and capital commodities, including automobiles, airplanes, and ocean-going vessels, and is currently establishing petrochemical complexes in São Paulo and Bahia. Government and foreign enterprises dominate heavy industry, but current economic policy seeks to strengthen the Brazilian private sector. Chief trading partners are, in order, the United States, West Germany, Italy, the Netherlands, England, and France.

In the decade of 1959–1969, the Brazilian economy grew at an annual rate of 5.9 per cent (agriculture, 4.3 per cent; industry, 6.6 per cent; and services, 6.1 per cent), but in 1968 the GNP increase was 8.5 per cent, in 1969, 9.0 per cent, and in 1970, about the same. The surface dynamism of the economy hides, however, certain human problems. One is the poor distribution of income, the most inequitable in Latin America. The upper one per cent of income earners receives 28.05 per cent of personal income, while the lower 90 per cent receives 46.51 per cent (*19*). Given a per capita income of $350–$400 a year, this relegates the majority of the population to bare subsistence.

Another problem is the discrepancy between participation and productivity among the various economic sectors. The primary sector has 53.7 per cent of the population and only 27.6 per cent of national production. The secondary sector employs 13.08 per cent of the work force and provides 21.56 per cent of the national product (*20*). Between 1950 and 1960, employment opportunities increased 2.8 per cent over-all (1.7 per cent in the primary sector, 2.3 per cent in secondary, and 5.2 per cent in tertiary) (*21*). The percentage of persons employed in the primary sector is declining, although it is still much too high, in relationship to productivity, for a "modern" economy. The agricultural sector is expelling excess population. Work opportunities in industry, which supply the chief pull factor in internal migration and urbanization, have not kept pace with the influx of population. Current Brazilian industrial growth, being capital and technology intensive, has not significantly increased its percentage of employment so that services have had to expand to absorb the urban migrants.

The increase of population in the cities without compensatory employment has created large contingents of individuals living what is often called in Latin America a "marginal" existence. Although the most obvious sign has been the mushrooming squatter settlements (*favelas*), the underlying problem is a low income level and what seem to be substantial levels of underemployment. While official government figures on unemployment are modest (and dubious), not exceeding 3 per cent (*22*), underemployment statistics are not available. Brazil's cities also suffer from urban problems common to developed countries—like smog, inadequate transportation, health services, education, and sanitary facilities—but have limited resources to confront them.

The development of communications (especially the radio), highway construction, migration, and increased literacy suggest that even rural and backward Brazilians are undergoing changes in attitude. The act of leaving the countryside and moving to a city indicates a sharp break with the past, which will especially affect one's children. The industrialization of Brazil, by creating jobs in factories and expanding middle class positions in business and public administration, diversified the traditional class structure. Yet the persistent dualism of Brazilian society is reflected in two class structures, the traditional static one based on agrarian paternalism, and a modern urban one offering chances of upward mobility (*23*).

Analysis of social class and mobility in Brazil is hampered by disagreement over the definition of class and by lack of data. In 1950, one compilation indicated that 70 per cent of the population was in the lower class, 26 per cent in three categories of middle class, and 4 per cent in the upper class (*24*). A number of studies of social mobility undertaken a decade ago by Bertram Hutchinson showed that in six cities (operating with six class categories), two fifths of the migrants stayed in the same class as their fathers, two fifths assumed a higher status, and one fifth a lower one. Individuals who immigrated from abroad were more likely to rise (48.6 per cent), as were those who originated from another large city (41.8 per cent) (*25*).

It has long been noted that immigrants played a disproportionate role in the economic development of São Paulo. Examining a sample in that city Hutchinson remarked that "the increase of industry in São Paulo is not only largely a result of intense foreign immigration; the economic development itself is a powerful force which continues to attract migrating movements from outside the Brazilian population" (*26*).

An associate of Hutchinson discounted increased educational opportunities and argued that certain personality characteristics were the chief stimuli to social mobility: "capacity to act with a certain independence of the environment, a greater ability to initiate and organize, the power to struggle for control of the social and other forces of the environment . . . , signs of manifest and potential anxiety combined with the difficulties of regulating them. Therefore, the basic necessity of eliminating the anxiety makes the individual confront situations which produce anxiety and try to solve them" (*27*). Hutchinson refers to Italians and their children, whose "desire for individual realization is stronger than ordinary," but the same can be said for other ethnic groups which have made the South Brazil's most prosperous region: Germans, Japanese, Middle Easterners. The Hutchinson studies indicate, then, that urbanization and education do not automatically lead to social mobility, but that a factor of initiative is required as well.

The failure of Brazil's educational system to respond to the demand for qualified personnel has long been cited as a major obstacle to the nation's development. Although progress has occurred, the statistics still do not reflect the modernity evident in such other areas as industry. There is now a growing awareness of the value of investing in education, indicated by the appointment of one of Brazil's most capable public figures, Jarbas Passarinho, as Minister of Education (following some undistinguished predecessors), and the economist Mário Henrique Simonsen, to head up literacy programs.

Education is deficient on all levels. Illiteracy declined from 65 per cent in 1920 to a government estimate in 1970 of 32.1 per cent (22.3 per cent in urban areas and 43.6 per cent in the countryside) (*28*). Yet the growth in population has resulted in an increase in absolute numbers, so that today there are 16,500,000 illiterates over 14 years old. Moreover, as we have noted, many "literates" can write their names, but cannot read and write.

Brazil's educational pyramid (*29*) reveals the loss of talent due to deficiencies in the schools resulting in failure of pupils, and the inability of families to maintain their children in the system. Of each 1,000 pupils who enter, only 395 pass to the second year, and a mere 181 complete primary education. Of these, 101 enter secondary school, and 35 finish. Although matriculations on the secondary level increased 238 per cent in the past decade, only 22 per cent of the population between 11 and 18 attend school. Brazil has a mere 400,000 university students (an increase of 301.4 per cent in ten years) out of a population of 95 million, and few of those who enter university come from the lower class (*30*).

Brazil's educational problems are legion (*31*). In 1967, only 3.5 per cent of national income was going to public education. Some 70 per cent of the schools have only one room, and a majority of the teachers do not meet the government qualifications to teach on the level that they do. Qualifying examinations (*vestibulares*), based on memorization, weed out candidates for secondary and university education. Private schools enroll 48 per cent of the pupils on the secondary level. Curricula and career selections of university students reflect traditional patterns of prestige rather than the development needs of the country.

While awareness of educational problems is growing, so that literacy training, strengthening of all levels of schooling, and development of technology are considered national priorities, governmental good will is undermined by the high proportion of youth in the population. Any effective solution will demand extensive public funds, reducing the amount of capital available to keep the economy growing at politically acceptable rates.

Further public resources are also required to produce healthy adults. Although advances were made in the forties and fifties in checking such diseases as malaria, tuberculosis, and typhoid fever, much remains to be done. Life expectancy continues low, especially in the poorer states, chiefly because half of deaths occur among children under five. Transmittable diseases are responsible for 40 per cent of deaths, and 90 per cent of these come from infectious diarrhea, grippe, pneumonia, tuberculosis, measles, and tetanus (32). While health standards are reasonably good in the more prosperous cities, where medical personnel and hospitals are concentrated, over 2,000 *municipios* do not even have a doctor. A substantial part of the population does not consult trained persons when they are sick.

Improvement of health is hampered by the dispersion of responsibility. Many hospitals and clinics are private; the federal government focuses on campaigns against major national diseases; the states have major responsibility for general health care; and the *municipios* handle sanitary systems and water supply. The National Social Security Institute is heavily involved in health, through agreements with other institutions to cover its participants. This scattering of authority hinders the development of comprehensive programs of maternal and child care, which is available for those who seek it and can pay, but is not effectively promoted by public entities. The Ministry of Health recognizes maternal-child care as one of its three priorities and is presently formulating a plan to do something about it.

Brazil's response to population growth has always been conditioned by awareness of the lightly settled areas of the country and the desire for a large population to fill them, incorporate them into the rest of the country, guarantee national security, and promote the use of natural resources. Legal policy is pronatalist: the Ministry of Labor gives a supplement to families with more than six children; and federal and state governments, as well as the National Social Security Institute, give employees bonuses for each new birth. Abortion and propaganda for contraception are illegal, but the prevalence of abortion makes the law unenforceable.

Contraceptives are freely sold in pharmacies, though publicity about the negative effects of progesterone pills recently led to restriction of their sale to holders of prescriptions. In 1967 a law, which did not pass, was introduced in Congress providing for limitation of natality as a health measure under the aegis of the medical profession. Similarly unsuccessful measures were submitted to the state legislatures of São Paulo and Paraná.

Articulate opinion in Brazil is deeply divided over family planning. Newspapers and magazines are publishing an ever-increasing number of articles and editorials on the population crisis, abortion, contraceptive methods, and public opinion on these matters (*33*). Almost any distinguished visitor to Brazil, be he statesman or rock music singer, is likely to be asked in press interviews his opinion on birth control.

In 1966 and 1967, family planners became the object of a hostile campaign charging them with "genocide," collusion with foreign powers against Brazilian interests, and undermining national morality. The chief pressure group involved was a small group of doctors, calling themselves the Association of Doctors of the State of Guanabara. At the request of the Minister of Health, the Federal Council of Medicine rendered a judgment entirely favorable to family planning, which contended that "no one . . . can deny the ethical legitimacy of voluntary regulation of fecundity, and the action of the doctor is not only a right but a moral obligation toward the individual and the collectivity" (*34*). A parliamentary committee of inquiry also investigated the charges, but when confronted with the testimony of numerous specialists, did not undertake action. More prevalent than these organized attacks is a common ignorance, even among educated people, of the economic and social consequences of population growth and the assumption that it is unpatriotic to try to reduce the natural rate.

The present government policy toward family planning is ambivalent, but not closed. Two cabinet members, the Minister of Finance and the Minister of Justice, are publicly opposed, but several others are explicitly or implicitly in favor. In June 1970, President Emílio Garrastazu Médici acknowledged the existence of a population problem and spoke somewhat ambiguously of public responsibility. "The Brazilian public figure cannot copy lines of politico-administrative action of peoples with gradual and controlled population increase if our reality is demographic explosion. . . . He who speaks of a demographically young nation soon discerns the economically active minority in contrast with the immense contingent in which consumption surpasses production. . . . It violates our sensibility for the State to undertake as its problem of control of natality, when we are convinced that it can only enter the intimacy of the family through education, respecting the inalienable power of decision of each one" (*35*). Despite its tentativeness, this position represents a distinct advance over that of former President Artur da Costa e Silva, whose major statement on the matter was an enthusiastic congratulation of Pope Paul VI for the encyclical, *Humanae Vitae*.

Although it is still politically advantageous to oppose family planning in some circles, the climate for individuals and groups to express themselves favorably and act is much more encouraging than in the past. The potentially most important elite group favoring an official policy of population control is economists, who have exceptional prestige and influence in Brazil's military-technocratic developmental model. Nearly all major economists, both within and outside the government, have publicly insisted that a more moderate rate of population growth will ease the burden of future social and economic development. The exception is the most important one, Minister of Finance Antônio Delfim Neto, who holds that the present economic growth rate can absorb the current population increase. A ten-year development plan drawn up in 1968 urged the "adoption of an adequate rate of population expansion that will allow the progressive utilization of the country's natural resources and the effective occupation of her territory" (*36*).

Another important elite group predominantly favoring family planning on health grounds is gynecologists and obstetricians. Although there is sufficient divergency among them to prevent them from acting in unison, in key crises many of them have lent their prestige to family planning.

The officials of the Armed Forces are divided. It is important to recognize that they come from and live on the salaries of the middle class, an economic fact which represents a counterbalancing force to aspirations for a large population. Two major military men who have emphasized population as a problem are General Aurélio Lyra Tavares, head of the junta which assumed power on Costa e Silva's fatal illness, and Marshal Cordeiro de Farias, one of the chief leaders of the Revolution of 1964. The Escola Superior da Guerra (Higher War College) invites both advocates and opponents to present their position, and according to observers at these sessions, the debate afterwards indicated a majority sentiment in favor of family planning. The best known advocate of family planning in Brazil, the geographer and economist Glycon de Paiva, is a former president of the graduates of the Escola Superior da Guerra.

The Catholic Church, to which about 90 per cent of Brazilians belong, is ambivalent. The official position of the hierarchy is adherence to the norms outlined in *Humanae Vitae,* but in practice the Brazilian Church is probably the most open to family planning of any in Latin America. Theologians, especially, have criticized the reasoning behind the Pope's position and offered justifications for limiting and spacing children as a personal decision. The moral teachings of the Church influence only a tiny minority of Brazilians, those who regularly attend mass and are acquainted with the official positions (*37*).

Public opinion also seems to favor family planning. In 1966 an inquiry in ten cities involving 3,000 interviews revealed that 92 per cent favored access of couples to information for deciding the number of children. A poll by the magazine, *Realidade,* in July 1970, which asked, "Do you think that Brazil should adopt an official policy of control of natality?" received affirmative answers from 54 per cent of those in the upper class, 62 per cent in the middle class, and 64 per cent in the lower class (*38*).

In urban areas limitation of births seems to be common. A study by the Latin American Center of Demography several years ago showed that 58.1 per cent of the women surveyed in Rio de Janeiro were using contraceptives, ranging from 42.5 per cent among those with no education to 74 per cent among those who had attended universities (*39*). As early as 1965, it was estimated that Brazil had over a million, and perhaps a million and a half, abortions a year (*40*). Family planning leaders estimate that in 1970, 3,250,000 women were using the pill.

The chief organization promoting family planning is a private institution, Bemfam (Brazilian Society of Family Welfare) which was founded in 1965 and is headed by Dr. Walter Rodrigues. Bemfam now has 60 clinics in various parts of the country, though it lays great emphasis on promotion of awareness about family planning through seminars on population problems and the training of medical and paramedical personnel. Bemfam has grown steadily, and currently has more requests for its services than its financial resources and personnel can meet. Perhaps the most encouraging aspect of Bemfam's operations is the willingness of municipal and state governments to provide facilities for family planning; the state of Espírito Santo, for example, has agreed to let Bemfam give contraceptive information in any of its health centers. Bemfam also has a number of its clinics in university hospitals. The organization is affiliated with and largely supported by the International Planned Parenthood Association, with the Ford Foundation assisting in research and evaluation (*41*). The lack of a public policy on population has not inhibited the expansion of private efforts like that of Bemfam. A small organization in São Paulo, the Family Orientation Service, also offers birth control information as part of its family counseling activities.

Population as a field of study is still underdeveloped in Brazil. A number of government entities have demographic interests, the principal one being the Brazilian Institute of Geography and Statistics, which conducts the census and has published numerous analyses of population (*42*). The Institute of Research in Applied Economics of the Ministry of Planning recently established a department of demography, reflecting a heightened awareness of the relevance of population factors to economic and social planning. Other government agencies—the state of São Paulo, the Bank of the Northeast, the Northeast Development Agency, and the Amazon Development Agency—also have teams studying demographic matters. In Brazil the major centers of population studies are public and policy-planning oriented.

Some universities also have professors, and, in a few instances, institutes engaged in population studies, but well-trained persons and resources are minimal. The Faculty of Hygiene and Public Health of the University of São Paulo offers the only real demographic training in the country, an intensive three-month course. The most important academic research project in population is a study of fertility and reproductive behavior in a sample of 3,000 women being conducted by the Brazilian Center for Planning and Analysis of São Paulo and financed by the Ford Foundation. Ford also subsidizes medical research related to demography in two institutions: (1) In the Federal University of Bahia, a team, under the direction of Dr. Elsimar Coutinho, is studying aspects of reproductive biology and has already published 28 articles in international journals on the results. (2) The Federal University of Rio de Janeiro is examining medical, psychological, and social factors associated with oral contraceptives and intrauterine devices.

Brazil is sometimes regarded as the world's leading demographic problem, a society careening toward 200 million people without a care or countervailing force. Such an image underestimates the modernity of the educated segment of Brazilian society, the influence of important individuals who with considerable courage advocate limiting population, and the realistic technicism which determines governmental decisions. The quality, seriousness, and quantity of public discussion is constantly improving; and Bemfam, although it is small in relation to the total population, has the support of many influential people.

Despite the silence of the federal government, a number of state and municipal governments have committed themselves to including family planning under public health services. Medical personnel have been trained in contraceptive practices by Bemfam and presumably are applying this information in their clinical work. A number of Brazilians who are well acquainted with the status of family planning in their country believe that the gradual expansion of these services on the lower level will lead within a few years, perhaps five, to a quiet commitment by the federal government as well.

The early 1970s will witness a confrontation between the two points of view on family planning. The opponents will be fortified by euphoria over the country's economic growth and policies like road building, regional development, and colonization, which will intensify the romantic vision with a large population and an inhabited interior. The census of 1970 has already bolstered them by showing a decline in natality, especially in the cities.

The supporters of family planning, on the other hand, will also find ammunition in the census data, and armed with the oracles of leading economists, will turn the discussion to the quality of life in a future Brazil and the injustice of abandoning most of the population to ignorance and multiplication. The family planners will be realistic and moderate. They know that a high rate of population growth is inevitable for many years because of low levels of education, insufficient medical personnel, and the backwardness and isolation of rural life. They also know that Brazil is a more than ordinarily difficult country to carry out any kind of program involving a change in attitude of the masses.

The deciding factor will be the rationality of decision-makers. Gradually, in its paternalistic way, the federal government will move toward a population policy. Whatever is done will have a peculiar Brazilian flavor, marked by slowness, inefficiency, and a mixture of stubbornness and toleration toward outside experts who criticize but know little about the special difficulties Brazil offers for the implantation of such a program.

Both family planners and sophisticated opponents like Minister Delfim Neto know that more clinics alone will not solve Brazil's population problem. A nation divided into a traditional and a modern sector, with high levels of illiteracy and semiliteracy, and a substantial percentage of its people who never or hardly ever see a doctor, cannot control its population in a way that meets the needs of family well-being, economic betterment, and national aspirations. Only Brazil as a developed country—the common ground on which both supporters and opponents of family planning can meet—can do that. Economic growth and education (as a key element in incorporating the masses) are more fundamental national priorities. At the same time, however, they are indispensable to effective family planning. An early official commitment to a program of population control, on the other hand, will gradually contribute to these national priorities. As higher standards of living and education contribute to a reduction of family size, availability of information on reduction of family size will lead to higher standards of living and education.

Notes

1. Cf. Appendix—1 for past and future population estimates. The curve of population growth is in Appendix—10.
2. Cf. Appendix—2.
3. *Ibid.* Data on the number and national origins of immigrants are in Appendix—3.
4. Appendix—4.
5. Appendix—5.
6. Appendix—6(a).
7. Appendix—6(b).
8. Appendix—6(c).
9. Appendix—7.
10. *Anuário Estatístico do Brasil, 1969* (Rio de Janeiro: Instituto Brasileiro de Geografia e Estatística, 1969), pp. 81–105.
11. *Saúde e Saneamento: Diagnóstico Prelíminar,* Plano Decenal de Desenvolvimento Econômico e Social (Rio de Janeiro: Ministério de Planejamento e Coordenação Econômica, Escritório de Pesquisa Econômica Aplicada, 1966), p. 82.
12. Appendix—8 has figures on racial composition according to the census of 1950, comparative figures for selected states, and estimates of literacy rates by race.
13. Appendices—9, 10.
14. For data on Brazilian cities, cf. Kingsley Davis, *World Urbanization, 1950–1970* (Berkeley: University of California, Institute of International Studies, 1969), vol. I.
15. *Anuário Estatístico do Brasil, 1969,* p. 45.
16. Appendix—11(c).
17. For data on regional gains and losses, see Appendix—11(e). The map in Appendix—12 indicates the chief flows of internal migration.
18. Appendices—11, 12, 13.
19. "Nas mãos de poucos, a renda do Brasil," *Jornal do Brasil* (May 31, 1970).
20. *Ibid.*
21. Mário Henrique Simonsen, *Brasil 2001* (Rio de Janeiro: Apec, 1969), p. 53. Cf. Appendix—14 for a breakdown of the economically active population by sectors.
22. *Populacão-Mão de Obra,* Pesquisa Nacional por Amostra de Domicílios (Rio de Janeiro: Instituto Brasileiro de Geografia e Estatística, 1969).
23. For an analysis of the two systems of social structure, cf. L.A. Costa Pinto, "As classes sociais no Brasil," *Sociologia e Desenvolvimento* (Rio de Janeiro: Civilização Brasileira, 1970), pp. 213–57.
24. *Ibid.,* p. 43. This analysis is based on the census data of 1950.
25. Bertram Hutchinson, "Urban Social Mobility Rates in Brazil Related to Mi-

gration and Changing Occupational Structure," *América Latina,* VI (julho-setembro de 1963), 47–61.

26. Bertram Hutchinson, *Mobilidade e Trabalho* (Rio de Janeiro: Centro Brasileiro de Pesquisas Educacionais, 1960), p. 12.
27. Carolina Martuscelli Bori, "O Indivíduo e a mobilidade: características psicológicas relacionadas com a mobilidade social," *ibid.,* p. 278.
28. Appendix—15.
29. Appendix—16.
30. A recent compilation of educational data and trends was published in *O Globo* (September 14, 1970).
31. Of continuing value is the analysis of Brazilian education by Frank Bonilla, "Brazil," *Education and Political Development,* ed. James S. Coleman (Princeton: Princeton University Press, 1965), pp. 195–221.
32. *Saúde e Saneamento: Diagnóstico Preliminar,* p. 82.
33. The divergence may be illustrated by editorials from Rio de Janeiro's two most respected newspapers. According to *Jornal do Brasil* (May 9, 1967), "Our country constitutes one of the special cases in which the demographic explosion does not represent a problem. Recent experience shows that we are able to grow between 6 per cent and 7 per cent per year. With the population increasing at 3 per cent, this means an increment of product per inhabitant of 3 per cent to 4 per cent a year, a perfectly satisfactory rhythm." *Correio da Manhã* (Jan. 11, 1967), on the other hand, argues, "The government cannot remain indifferent to the problem. The State cannot, obviously, force the use of contraceptives or other methods of family planning . . . , but it can and must make these methods as accessible as various vaccines. It has the moral obligation to instruct the poor classes in the use of these remedies and facilitate their acquisition."
34. *O Contrôle da Natalidade: Documentos Brasileiros* (Rio de Janeiro: Bemfam, n.d.), p. 12.
35. "Govêrno não faz contrôle," *Veja* (June 10, 1970).
36. The plan adds: "Our analysis of recent trends shows that the foreseeable rate of demographic growth is very high, reaching 3 per cent per year. Considering the need for new jobs, for investments in the economic infrastructure, and for social overhead capital, this fact suggests that the community should take into consideration the effects of a slower rate of over-all demographic growth, accompanied by some regional resettlement of the population." Cited by Rubens Vaz da Costa, "Brazil: A Prodigy of Growth," *Population Bulletin,* XXV (September 1969), pp. 96–97.
37. Cf. Thomas G. Sanders, *The Relationship between Population Planning and Belief Systems: The Catholic Church in Latin America* [TGS-5-'70], Fieldstaff Reports, West Coast South America Series, Vol. XVII, No. 7, 1970.
38. "O que o brasileiro pensa do Brasil," *Realidade* (julho de 1970), p. 29.
39. Carmen A. Miró and Ferdinand Rath, "Preliminary Findings of Comparative Fertility Surveys in Three Latin American Cities," *Millbank Memorial Fund Quarterly,* XLIII, no. 4, part 2 (October 1965), 58. Cf. also, Sugiyama Iutaka, "A estratificação social e o uso diferencial de métodos anticoncepcionais no

Brasil urbano," *América Latina,* VIII (jan-marco de 1965), 101–19. This study shows that more than one half of those interviewed (58.3 per cent) used some contraceptive method, with higher incidence in the upper class.

40. Octávio Rodrigues Lima, "Abôrto Provocado: Considerações sôbre un inquérito realizado no Brasil," *Vozes,* LXI (nov. de 1967), 971–79. Cf. also Bertram Hutchinson, "Induced Abortion in Brazilian Married Women," *América Latina,* VI (out-dez. de 1964), 21–34, in which 9.2 per cent of a sample of married women in the state of Guanabara admitted to at least one induced abortion.

41. On Bemfam, cf. Walter Rodrigues, "Progress and Problems of Family Planning in Brazil," *Demography,* V, no. 2 (1968), 800–10.

42. Cf. *Publicações do Laboratório de Estatística* (Rio de Janeiro: Instituto Brasileiro de Geografia e Estatística, 1967).

References

Costa, Rubens Vaz da *et al.,* "Brazil: A Prodigy of Growth," *Population Bulletin,* XXV (September 1969).

Contribuições para o Estudo da Demografia no Brasil (Rio de Janeiro: Instituto Brasileiro de Geografia e Estatística, 1961).

Diégues Júnior, Manuel, *Imigração, Urbanização, Industrialização* (Rio de Janeiro: Instituto Nacional de Estudos Pedagógicos, 1964).

Hutchinson, Bertram, *Mobilidade e Trabalho* (Rio de Janeiro: Centro Brasileiro de Pesquisas Educacionais, 1960).

Salzado, F. M. e N. Freire-Maia, *Populações Brasileiras: Aspectos Demográficos, Genéticos e Antropológicos* (São Paulo: Nacional, 1967).

The Author

THOMAS G. SANDERS, who reports on several countries of Latin America, was formerly an Associate Professor of Religious Studies at Brown University. He received his A.B. in history from Duke University in 1952, and after studies at Union Theological Seminary in New York and the University of Copenhagen (as a Fulbright Scholar), he received his Ph.D. in religion from Columbia University in 1958. Dr. Sanders is the author of *Protestant Concepts of Church and State* and numerous articles on church-state theory and problems, and he contributed a chapter on Brazil to *Churches and States: The Religious Institution and Modernization.* In 1966 he became a Fellow of the Institute for Current World Affairs to work on various aspects of the relationship between Catholicism and development in Latin America. For the Field Staff he writes principally on Chile, Brazil and Colombia.

Brazil

Sanders

Table 1. The Population of Brazil

1900	17,984,000	1970	93,549,000
1910	22,216,000	1975	108,354,300
1920	27,404,000	1980	125,503,200
1930	33,568,000	1985	145,866,100
1940	41,114,000	1990	168,372,700
1950	51,976,000	2000	225,885,700
1960	70,141,200		

Source: Future projections are from "Estimativas da População, 1970–2000," Documento No. 7 (19-2-69) Rio de Janeiro: Instituto Brasileiro de Geografia e Estatística, 1969.

Table 2. Annual Rates of Population Increase

Year	*Global (%)*	*Natural (%)*	*Migratory (%)*	*Natality*	*Mortality*
1872–1890	2.01	1.63	.38	46.5/1000	30.2/1000
1890–1900	2.42	1.82	.60	46.0	27.8
1900–1920	2.12	1.86	.22	45.0	26.4
1920–1940	2.05	1.87	.18	44.0	25.3
1940–1950	2.38	2.34	.04	43.5	20.1
1950–1960	3.00	3.00	.00	41.5	11.5

Source: Demografia: Diagnóstico Preliminar (Plano Decenal de Desenvolvimento Econômico e Social) Rio de Janeiro: Ministério de Planejamento e Coordenação Econômica, Escritório de Pesquisa Econômica Aplicada, 1966, p. 39.

Table 3. Immigration

(*a.*) Entrance of immigrants into Brazil

1851–1860	120,000
1861–1870	95,000
1871–1880	215,000
1881–1890	530,000
1891–1900	1,125,000
1901–1910	670,000
1911–1920	795,000
1921–1930	835,000
1931–1940	285,000
1941–1950	130,000
1968	12,521

Source: Contribuições para o Estudo da Demografia no Brasil. Rio de Janeiro: Instituto Brasileiro de Geografia e Estatística, 1961, p. 124. *Anuário Estatística do Brasil, 1969.* Rio de Janeiro: IBGE, 1969, p. 111

(*b.*) National origins of immigrants (1819–1959)

Portugal	31.04%
Italy	29.17%
Spain	12.54%
Germany	4.64%
Japan	4.03%
Russia	2.27%

Source: Manuel Diegues Junior, *Imigração, Urbanização, Industrialização.* Rio de Janeiro: Instituto Nacional de Estudos Pedagógicos, 1964, pp. 26–28

Table 4. Population Structure, Age-Sex Specific Structure (1960) in thousands

Age	*Total*	(%)	*Male*	*Female*
0–4	11,970.0	15.97	6,019.6	5,950.4
5–9	9,851.7	14.48	4,927.4	4,924.3
10–14	8,092.5	12.22	4,011.2	4,081.3
15–19	7,293.4	10.19	3,647.4	3,646.0
20–24	6,060.4	8.79	3,044.5	3,015.9
25–29	5,116.2	7.43	2,567.4	2,548.8
30–34	4,502.8	6.42	2,241.2	2,261.6
35–39	3,870.1	5.52	1,924.8	1,945.3
40–44	3,264.4	4.65	1,636.4	1,628.0
45–49	2,726.6	3.89	1,368.6	1,358.0
50–54	2,270.4	3.24	1,135.1	1,135.3
55–59	1,800.8	2.57	894.3	906.5
60–64	1,332.7	1.90	654.8	677.9
65–69	925.2	1.32	448.8	476.4
70 plus	1,064.0	1.52	482.8	581.2
Total population				
(1960)			35,004.3	35,136.9
(1970)			46,372.9	46,890.3

Source: Censo Fiscal da União, 1968 Rio de Janeiro: Ministério da Fazenda, Secretaria da Receita Federal, 1969, p. 15

Life expectancy	*Male*	*Female*
1940–1950 . . .	40–42	44–46
1950–1960 . . .	48–51	53–55
Average over-all (1960): 52.5 . . .		

Source: Demografia: Diagnóstico Preliminar (Plano Decenal de Desenvolvimento Econômico e Social) Rio de Janeiro: Ministério de Planejamento e Coordinação Econômica, Escritório de Pesquisa Econômica Aplicada, 1966, p. 45

 Table 5. Composition of Population by Age, 1960

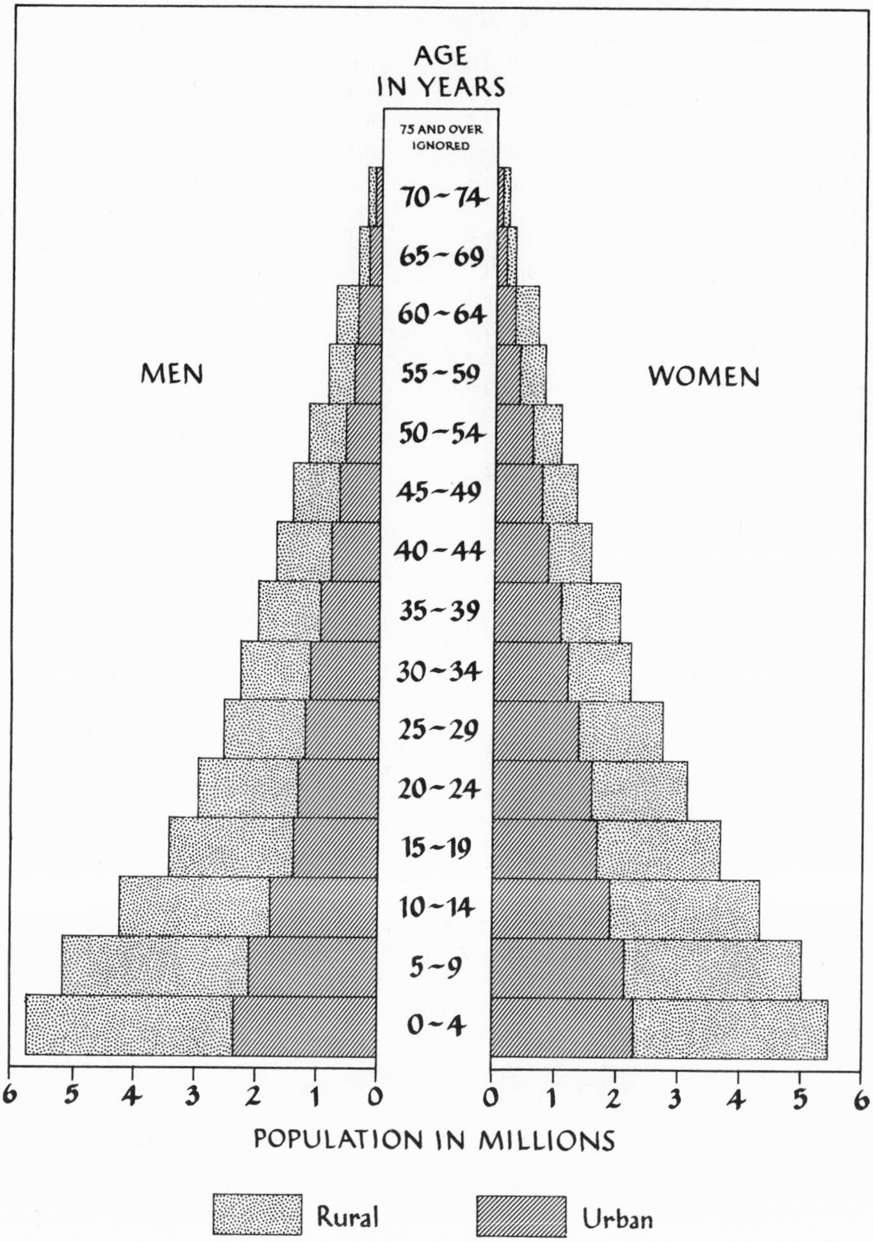

Source: Anuário Estatistico do Brasil, 1969, Rio de Janeiro: Instituto Brasileiro de Geografia e Estatística, 1969, p. 43

Table 6. Fertility Factors and Patterns

(*a.*) Urban-rural fertility. Based on the "fertility ratio," the number of children 0–4/1000 women aged 15–49

	Urban	*Rural*	*Ratio*
1920 . . .	411	646	.64
1940 . . .	440	709	.62
1950 . . .	482	735	.66

Source: J. V. D. Saunders, *Differential Fertility in Brazil* Gainesville: Univ. of Florida Press, 1958. Summarized in Murray Gendell, "Fertility and Development in Brazil," *Demography*, IV, no. 1 (1967), 147

(*b.*) Education. Live births by educational level in a sample of women in Rio de Janeiro

All women	2.25
No education	3.33
1–3 years	2.93
4 or more years primary . . .	2.46
Complete primary	2.17
1–3 secondary	1.63
4 or more secondary	1.43
Complete secondary	1.38
Less than 5 yrs. university . .	1.05
Five or more yrs. university	1.21

Source: Carmen A. Miró and Ferdinand Rath, "Preliminary Findings of Comparative Fertility Surveys in Three Latin American Cities," *Millbank Memorial Fund Quarterly*, XLIII, no. 4, part 2 (October 1965), p. 51

(*c.*) Comparative natality rates (by states)

Guanabara	28/1000
São Paulo	38
Rio Grande do Sul . . .	38
Rio Grande do Norte . .	52
Paraíba	51
Ceará	49
Pernambuco	49

Source: Alguns Aspectos da População do Brasil, Segundo o Censo de 1960. Rio de Janeiro: Instituto Brasileiro de Geografia e Estatística, 1969, p. 16

Table 7. Mortality (est.) 1964

Brazil	*Mortality rate*	*Infant mortality rate*	*Average life span*	*Productive life (at age 15)*
Brazil	13/1000	112/1000	54.2 yrs.	40.2 yrs.
Eighteen state capitals	10.7	S78.3		
North	11	S67	57.9	39
Northeast	18	176	48.9	
Center-West	12	74	56.5	40.2
Southeast I	13	89	54.8	39.4
(ES,MG,RJ)				
Southeast II	9	75	60.7	41.3
(GB,SP)				
South	10	73	58.6	39.6

Source: Saúde e Saneamento: Diagnóstico Preliminar (Plano Decenal de Desenvolvimento Econômico e Social). Rio de Janeiro: Ministério de Planejamento a Coordenação Econômica, Escritório de Pesquisa Econômica Aplicada, 1966, pp. 34–35.

Cities (1968)	*Mortality rate*	*Infant mortality rate*
São Paulo (SP)	9.1/1000	75.1/1000
Rio de Janeiro (GB)	9.8	65.3
Recife (PE)	13.0	153.9
Natal (RGN)	14.6	158.0
Salvador (BA)	13.0	154.3
Maceió (AL)	16.6	213.6
Teresina (PI)	9.9	246.3

Source: Anuário Estatístico do Brasil, 1969, Rio de Janeiro: Instituto Brasileiro de Estatística, 1969, p. 80

Table 8. Racial Composition (1950), by Self-Identification in Census

61.8%	*branco* (white)
26.6%	*pardo* (mixed)
11.0%	*prêto* (black)
0.6%	*oriental*
0.2%	*indígenas*

Comparison by states (%)	*branco*	*pardo*	*prêto*	*oriental*
Piauí	28.0	59.1	12.9	
Bahia	29.6	51.2	19.2	
Acre	30.1	64.7	5.2	
Pará	29.0	65.6	8.2	0.1
Maranhão	33.8	50.4	15.8	
Santa Catarina	94.8	1.5	3.7	
Rio Grande do Sul	89.3	5.5	5.2	
Paraná	86.5	7.3	4.3	1.9
São Paulo	85.8	3.2	8.0	3.0
Literacy rates by race (%)				
Literates over 5 years old	52.73	26.75	23.52	73.59
Literates over 20 years old	59.31	31.69	25.82	77.88
Men over 20 years old	65.77	38.15	31.84	86.04
Women over 20 years old	52.85	25.47	20.10	68.21

Source: F. M. Salzano e N. Freire-Maia, *Populações Brasileiras: Aspectos Demográficos, Genéticos e Antropológicos* (São Paulo: Nacional, 1967), p. 37; and *Contribuições para o Estudo da Demografia no Brasil* (Rio de Janeiro: Instituto Brasileiro de Geografia e Estatística, 1961), p. 396

Table 9. Urban-Rural Population Distribution and Projections

Year	*Urban*	%	*Rural*	%
1960	33,197,400	45.9	39,085,500	54.1
1970	52,857,600	55.9	41,547,000	44.1
1975	64,819,700	58.3	44,809,300	41.7
1980	79,566,700	63.1	46,472,300	36.9
By selected states				
Amazonas				
1960	234,200		470,600	
1970	369,800		552,000	
1980	581,600		651,500	
Piauí				
1960	301,000		974,300	
1970	530,600		1,096,600	
1980	893,600		1,201,700	
Sergipe				
1960	298,700		468,700	
1970	443,400		512,900	
1980	648,800		658,700	
Guanabara				
1960	3,164,800		82,200	
1970	4,238,900		98,500	
1980	5,569,600		113,700	
Rio de Janeiro				
1960	2,039,600		1,301,200	
1970	3,306,700		1,342,800	
1980	4,853,900		1,410,800	
São Paulo				
1960	8,001,100		4,737,500	
1970	12,201,500		5,056,700	
1980	17,394,600		5,442,000	

Source: Censo Fiscal da União, 1968, Rio de Janeiro: Ministério da Fazenda, Secretaria da Receita Federal, 1969, p. 13

Urban-Rural Population by Sex, with Projections

Year		*Urban*	*Rural*
1960	Male	15,618,200	19,386,100
	Female	16,868,700	18,268,200
1970	Male	24,897,800	21,504,000
	Female	26,972,600	19,917,700
1980	Male	37,369,900	23,816,700
	Female	40,484,000	21,321,400

Source: Censo Fiscal da União, Rio de Janeiro: Ministério da Fazenda, Secretaria da Receita Federal, 1969, p. 16

TERRITORIAL DISTRIBUTION OF POPULATION—1960

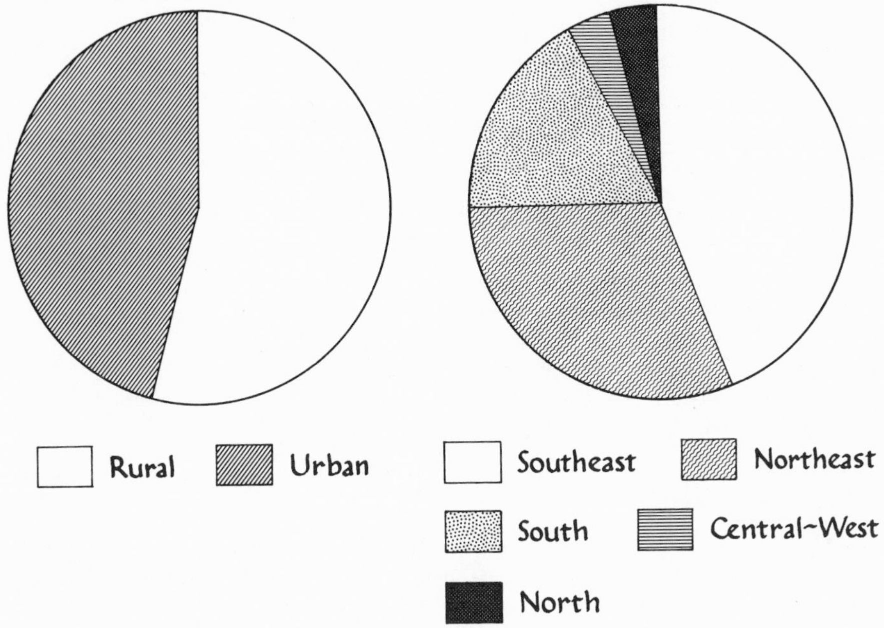

Table 10. Population, 1870–1970

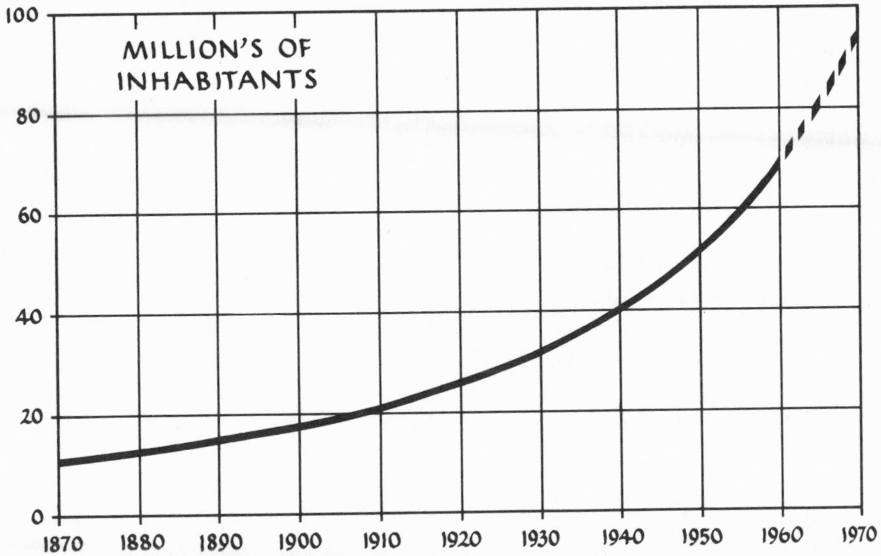

Source: Anuário Estatistico do Brasil, 1969, Rio de Janeiro: Instituto Brasileiro de Geografia e Estatística, 1969, p. 39

Table 11.

(*a.*) Internal Migration

(1.) Brazilians residing in a different state from that of birth. (2.) Brazilians residing in a different region from that of birth.

Year	*(1)*	*(2)*
1940	8.5%	3.3%
1950	10.3%	4.3%
1960	18.2%	5.8%

Source: Demografia: Diagnóstico Preliminar (Plano Decenal de Desenvolvimento Econômico e Social) Rio de Janerio: Ministério de Planejamento e Coordenação Econômica, Escritório de Pesquisa Econômica Aplicada, 1966, pp. 85–86

(*b.*) States with largest number of immigrants, 1950

(Number of individuals in census born in a different state)

São Paulo	1,064,000
Distrito Federal (GB)	930,000
Paraná	661,000
Rio de Janeiro	366,000
Goiás	281,000

Proportion of immigrants (per cent)

Distrito Federal (GB)	42.92
Paraná	32.44
Goiás	23.23
Rio de Janeiro	16.19
Minas Gerais	15.54
São Paulo	12.61

Source: Contribuições para o Estudo da Demografia do Brasil, Rio de Janeiro: Instituto Brasileiro de Geografia e Estatística, 1961, p. 371

(*c.*) In the state of São Paulo, in 1950, there were:

513,000 born in	Minas Gerais
190,000	Bahia
63,000	Pernambuco
57,000	Alagoas
56,000	Rio de Janeiro

In the state of Paraná, in 1950, there were:

352,000 born in	São Paulo
157,000	Minas Gerais
63,000	Santa Catarina

In the Distrito Federal (Guanabara), in 1950, there were:

360,000 born in	Rio de Janeiro
192,000	Minas Gerais
56,000	Espírito Santo

Source: Ibid., p. 382

(*d.*) States with largest numbers of emigrants (1950)

Minas Gerais	1,367,000
São Paulo	507,000
Rio de Janeiro	504,000
Bahia	430,000
Pernambuco	311,000
Ceará	268,000
Paraíba	247,000
Alagoas	207,000
Rio Grande do Sul	206,000

By Proportion

Rio de Janeiro	21.06%
Alagoas	16.81%
Espírito Santo	16.25%
Minas Gerais	15.47%
Sergipe	15.03%
Paraíba	13.28%
Piauí	13.13%

Source: Ibid., pp. 370–71

(*e.*) **Gain or loss (—) of regions, in exchanges of individuals with other regions**

	North	*Northeast*	*East*	*South*	*Center-West*
North		−97,210	25,436	4,111	7,334
Northeast . . .	97,210		219,511	185,805	73,022
East	−25,436	−219,511		844,301	204,901
South	−4,111	−185,805	−844,301		15,548
Center-West . . .	7,334	−73,022	−204,901	−15,548	
Total gain or loss .	74,997	−575,548	−804,255	1,018,669	286,137

Source: Ibid., p. 367

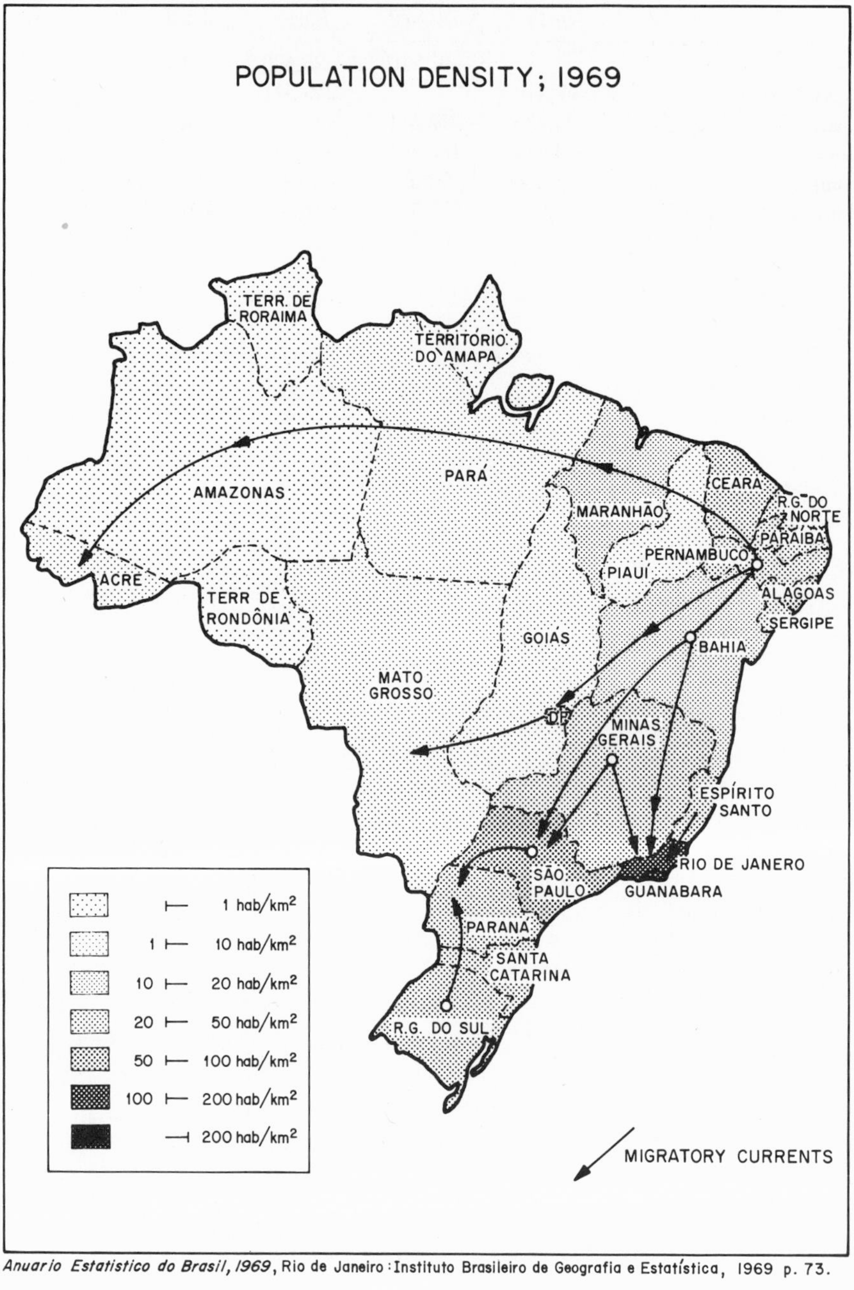

Anuario Estatistico do Brasil, 1969, Rio de Janeiro : Instituto Brasileiro de Geografia e Estatística, 1969 p. 73.

Source: Anuário Estatístico do Brasil, 1969, Rio de Janeiro: Instituto Brasileiro de Geografia e Estatística, 1969, p. 73

Table 13

(a.) Population Density

Year	*National density*
1900	2.1/sq. km
1920	3.2
1940	4.9
1950	6.1
1960	8.3

Source: Demografia: Diagnóstico Preliminar (Plano Decenal de Desenvolvimento Econômico e Social). Rio de Janeiro: Ministério de Planejamento e Coordenação Econômica, EPEA, 1966, p. 37.

(*b.*) Comparative Densities

Latin America . . .	10/sq. km
France	83
India	136
England	303

(*c.*) Selected States, 1968

Guanabara . . .	3,176.46/sq. km
Rio de Janeiro . .	105.03
São Paulo . . .	67.05
Distrito Federal .	63.40
Alagoas	50.54
Amazonas . . .	0.57
Acre	1.32
Pará	1.55
Mato Grosso . .	1.10
Goiás	4.26

(*d.*) Regions

North	0.7/sq. km
Center-west	1.6
Northeast	14.6
South	21.1
Southeast	33.6

Source: Censo Fiscal da União, 1968, Rio de Janeiro: Ministério da Fazenda, Secretaria da Receita Federal, 1969, p. 10.

Comments:

The North and Northeast have 64.2 per cent of national territory and 7.9 per cent of the population.

The Northeast has 18.2 per cent of national territory and 31.6 per cent of population.

The South and Southeast have 17.6 per cent of national territory and 31.6 per cent of the population.

In 1872 the Northeast had 46.7 per cent of the population and in 1960, 31.6 per cent.

In the same period the Southeast increased from 40.4 per cent to 43.8 per cent; the South from 7.26 per cent to 16.73 per cent; the Center-west from 2.22 per cent to 4.24 per cent.

Table 14.

(*a.*) Economically Active Population (1960)

Sectors	*Total*	(%)
Agriculture, livestock, forestry	11,697,798	51.54
Extractive industries	573,443	2.53
Manufacturing industries	2,005,775	8.86
Construction	785,014	3.47
Commerce	1,520,046	6.71
Services	2,732,148	12.06
Transportation, communications, storage	1,088,798	4.81
Others	2,248,241	9.92
Totals (male . . . 18,597,163) (female . . . 4,054,100)	22,651,263	

Source: Censo Fiscal da União, 1968, Rio de Janeiro: Ministério da Fazenda, Secretaria da Receita Federal, 1969, pp. 19–20

(*b.*) Tendencies in Economically Active Population

	1940	*1950*	*1960*
Agriculture, livestock, forestry	64.1%	57.8%	51.54%
Extractive industries	2.6	2.8	2.53
Manufacturing industries	7.7	9.4	8.86
Construction	1.8	3.4	3.47
Commerce	5.1	5.6	6.71
Services	9.7	9.8	12.06
Transportation, communications, storage	3.4	4.1	4.91
Others	5.6	7.2	9.92

Source: Murray Gendell, "Fertility and Development in Brazil," *Demography* IV, no. 1 (1967), p. 145

Table 15

(*a.*) Rate of Literacy of Those over 15 Years Old

Year	(%)
1900	34.66
1920	35.06
1940	43.78
1950	49.31
1960	60.52

Source: Censo Demografico: Resultados Preliminares, Rio de Janeiro: Instituto Brasileiro de Geografia e Estatística, 1965, preface

(*b.*) Rate of Literacy by Age, 1960

Age	(%)
5–9	19.71
10–14	61.13
15–19	66.59
20–29	66.10
30–39	62.41
40–49	55.69
50 plus	47.47

Source: Ibid., p. 2

Table 16. Brazilian Educational Pyramid 1954/1964

Level	*Series*	*Indices of matriculation*
Primary . .	1st	1000
	2nd	395
	3rd	282
	4th	181
Ginasio . . .	1st	101
	2nd	80
	3rd	65
	4th	53
Colegio . . .	1st	51
	2nd	41
	3rd	35

Source: Mário Henrique Simonsen, *Brasil 2001,* Rio de Janeiro: Apec, 1969, p. 225 (from Instituto de Pesquisa Econômica Aplicada, Ministério de Planejamento)

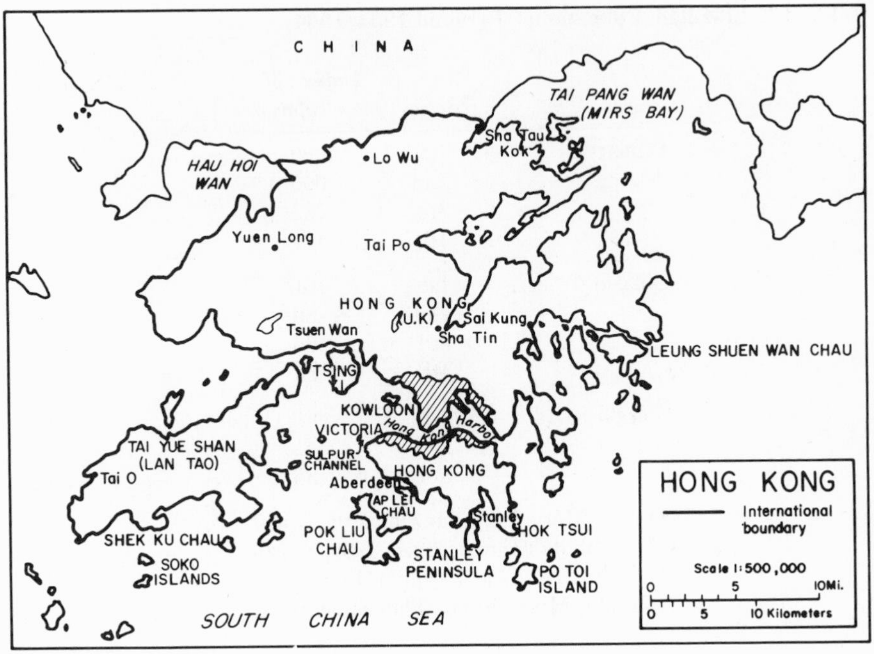
CHINA
TAI PANG WAN (MIRS BAY)
Sha Tau Kok
Lo Wu
HAU HOI WAN
Yuen Long
Tai Po
HONG KONG (U.K)
Sai Kung
Sha Tin
Tsuen Wan
LEUNG SHUEN WAN CHAU
TSING I
KOWLOON
VICTORIA
Hong Kong Harbor
TAI YUE SHAN (LAN TAO)
SULPUR CHANNEL
HONG KONG
Tai O
Aberdeen
AP LEI CHAU
Stanley
HOK TSUI
SHEK KU CHAU
POK LIU CHAU
STANLEY PENINSULA
SOKO ISLANDS
PO TOI ISLAND
SOUTH CHINA SEA
HONG KONG
International boundary
Scale 1:500,000
0 5 10Mi.
0 5 10 Kilometers

Hong Kong

Loren Fessler

Population Profile

Hong Kong is a British Crown Colony in which more than four million people, nearly 99 per cent of them Chinese, live on less than 500 square miles of rock, earth, and floating deck space. The crude birth rate, on the basis of 1969 calculations, is 20.7/1000 and the crude death rate about 4.8, resulting in a natural increase rate of around 1.6 (*1*). According to 1961 figures the life expectancy for females at birth is 70.51 years and 63.64 for males.

Historically immigration and emigration have been important factors affecting the size of the Colony's population. The movement of people into or away from Hong Kong has been, and to some extent still is, influenced by the degree of economic and political security in mainland China, the political and economic situation in Hong Kong itself, and the willingness of countries elsewhere to accept immigrants from Hong Kong.

In 1962, accordingly, Hong Kong experienced a net population increase of well more than 100,000 above its yearly average when people in neighboring Kwangtung and Fukien provinces, reacting to fears of renewed food shortages, fled to Hong Kong. During Hong Kong's 1967–68 "disorders" large numbers of people, especially well-to-do aliens and Chinese, left for safer areas. And, in recent years, with some relaxation or broadening of the American quota system, increased numbers of Chinese have migrated to the United States.

Hong Kong population watchers do not see either immigration or emigration factors seriously affecting the present or near-future scene in terms of numbers, or in terms of social or economic impact. By 1969, for example, it was officially estimated that of a total increase of some 65,000 in the population, less than 1,800 was due to an "inward increase in migration" (*2*).

An approximation of the structure of Hong Kong's population can be drawn from the following two tables, both constructed according to 1961 census data. The first table gives rounded numbers for the 1961 population according to age and sex plus the low projections for 1966 and 1971. Table 2 gives a medium projection, in percentage terms, for population distribution by age and sex for the same periods (3).

Following the 1966 by-census and reinterpretation of data made possible in the light of more recent developments, the projections have been revised downwards. For example, at the end of June 1970 the population was estimated at 4,089,000. At a rate of 1.6 natural increase, the population at the end of June 1971 was expected to be around 4,150,000—considerably below the 4,388,700 projection for July 1, 1971 total shown in the low projection, Table 1. According to the Census and Statistics Department, the crude birth rate between 1962 and 1969 declined from 36.8 to 20.7, a 41.2 per cent drop. About 9 per cent of this drop is attributed to changes in the age structure, while 8 per cent is attributed to a decrease in the proportion of women married. The remaining 24 per cent decrease in fertility is believed due to a genuine drop in age specific fertility rates. Table 3 shows these declines, including the decline in proportion of women married, in age specific fertility rates between 1961 and 1969.

The reason why population projections have had to be reworked downward is Hong Kong's continuing fertility decline. The crude birth rate dropped from 37.9 in 1958 to 20.7 at the end of 1969. An early and important part of this de-

Table 1. Population of Hong Kong by Age and Sex 1961–1971, Low Projection (as of 1st July, rounded to nearest hundred)

Age groups	*1961*		*1966*		*1971*	
	Male	*Female*	*Male*	*Female*	*Male*	*Female*
0–4	267,100	252,000	269,900	252,100	294,400	275,000
5–9	226,400	210,300	269,600	253,300	270,000	251,600
10–14	183,200	163,100	237,100	218,500	274,600	257,200
15–19	96,700	80,500	197,500	173,600	243,900	223,400
20–24	111,400	90,900	112,900	91,700	204,900	178,700
25–29	141,100	119,200	127,000	101,900	119,900	96,900
30–34	141,100	122,800	150,300	129,100	130,400	106,400
35–39	125,900	113,400	145,700	130,800	151,400	132,300
40–44	107,000	96,400	128,200	119,300	145,100	132,600
45–49	87,400	81,500	107,300	100,800	126,000	120,200
50–54	60,800	64,800	85,400	84,700	103,000	100,700
55–59	38,300	51,000	57,700	67,100	79,400	83,700
60–64	23,500	39,600	34,400	52,100	50,600	65,100
65–69	13,400	28,300	19,700	39,000	28,200	48,900
70–74	7,500	18,400	10,300	25,900	14,700	34,400
75–79	3,600	10,100	5,000	14,900	6,700	20,500
80 & over	1,900	5,700	2,600	9,500	3,500	14,400
Totals	1,636,300	1,548,000	1,960,600	1,864,300	2,246,700	2,142,000

Table 2. Percentage of Age and Sex Distribution of Population, Hong Kong 1961–1971, Medium Projection

Age groups	1961 Base population Male	Female	1966 Medium projection Male	Female	1971 Medium projection Male	Female
0–4	8.39	7.91	7.22	6.74	7.24	6.76
5–9	7.11	6.60	6.90	6.45	6.09	5.65
10–14	5.75	5.12	6.15	5.63	6.01	5.57
15–19	3.04	2.53	5.20	4.53	5.47	4.94
20–24	3.50	2.85	3.09	2.48	4.71	4.04
25–29	4.43	3.74	3.42	2.73	2.95	2.33
30–34	4.43	3.86	3.91	3.40	3.05	2.52
35–39	3.95	3.56	3.75	3.42	3.35	3.02
40–44	3.36	3.03	3.29	3.10	3.17	2.98
45–49	2.75	2.56	2.75	2.62	2.74	2.69
50–54	1.91	2.04	2.19	2.21	2.24	2.26
55–59	1.20	1.60	1.48	1.76	1.74	1.89
60–64	0.74	1.24	0.89	1.37	1.13	1.49
65–69	0.42	0.89	0.51	1.02	0.64	1.12
70–74	0.24	0.58	0.27	0.68	0.35	0.79
75–79	0.11	0.32	0.13	0.39	0.16	0.47
80 & over	0.06	0.18	0.07	0.25	0.10	0.34
Totals	51.39	48.61	51.22	48.78	51.14	48.86

Table 3

Age	*1961*	*1969*
15–19	47	18.8
20–24	238	141.8
25–29	313	234.7
30–34	231	166.1
35–39	139	89.1

Source: The Hong Kong Family Planning Association 19th Annual Report 1969–1970

cline was the distortions in the age-distribution factor in the population; as a result of the Pacific War, Hong Kong's population had a smaller than normal percentage of women in the child-bearing age brackets. Since 1965, however, the continuing decline in the birth rate has been due in very large part to a real decline in the fertility of married women. These declines, according to demographers in Hong Kong and the United States, are "of very great importance" and "are likely to have long-term effects and to be cumulative in their impact" (*4*).

Despite the increasing numbers and percentages of women of high child-bearing age in the population, there is evidence indicating that family planning efforts have been paying off. The Hong Kong Family Planning Association feels that its work has contributed to the fertility decline, but is careful in its claims and cautious about the future. The Association notes "an increasing tendency of younger, lower parity and better educated women" to practice birth control. The accent, they observe, is on spacing rather than limiting birth by users of all forms of contraception. HKFPA, citing a study done in cooperation with the University of Michigan Population Studies Center on the distribution of birth control device acceptors during 1961–1968 and on the relationship between the characteristics of these acceptors with the pattern of fertility decline, feels there is "evidence that the organized intervention of the Family Planning Association probably accounts for a significant part of the fertility decline."

The HKFPA cautions that "the age distribution in Hong Kong is undergoing changes which tend to favor high birth rates, inasmuch as any modest decline in the fertility level after 1967 would be negated by the increasing proportion of women of child bearing age." To hold the birth rate at 20.0 the HKFPA estimates it will have to increase its 1969 rate of 30,000 acceptors by 10 per cent for each year from 1970 to 1976 (*5*).

Hong Kong has some serious health problems, connected in part to crowded living and working conditions. Programs to improve preventive measures and expand health facilities have had considerable success in the last decade. In 1959 the infant mortality rate was 48.3 and the maternal mortality rate 0.73; at the end of 1968 those rates were 22.8 and 0.14 respectively. Tuberculosis has long been a serious problem, particularly in areas densely populated with low income people. In 1957 out of every 100,000 people who died, some 103 perished of TB; by 1968 the rate had gone down almost one third, but still stood at nearly 38 per 100,000. No other infectious disease even approaches TB as a cause of death (*6*).

Extrapolating from recent trends, it seems likely that fertility rates, and with them birth and natural increase rates, will continue to decline in Hong Kong. Assuming the Colony remains economically viable, expenditures—both capital and recurrent—in health facilities are likely to increase, resulting in some decrease in the rates of morbidity and mortality where public health is a factor.

Statistics on Hong Kong's population are generally reliable and recently a Census and Statistics Department was created. In view of an increasing awareness of the economic usefulness of such statistics, it seems reasonable to expect that information on most aspects of Hong Kong's population will become more detailed and probably even more accurate.

Distribution and Movement

In the last two decades the physical location of Hong Kong's population has undergone considerable change. In 1950 the Colony's economy was based primarily on its traditional role as an entrepot for goods to and from China. Population densities were heaviest near the dock and commercial areas of Hong Kong

Island and the Kowloon peninsula. Aside from some shipbuilding and a bit of light industry there was not much of what could be called factory areas. Few buildings exceeded four stories. Excepting some blocks of quarters for government employees and staff of some of the larger companies, there was little in the way of high density housing. Beginning in 1950 Hong Kong was forced, by events over which it had little control, to alter its ways of making a living—from simple trade to manufacturing-cum-trade.

Hong Kong has long had a predominately urban population. Recent estimates put the percentage of people who live in the built up areas of Hong Kong and Kowloon at from 73 to 85 per cent. While this distribution is probably not drastically different from earlier patterns, there are two important quantitative differences. First, dwellings now have from three to five times as many stories as before. Second, built up areas are spreading in an oil-drop pattern into what used to be rural areas. If one accepts the estimate that 85 per cent of the population lives in the urban areas of Hong Kong and Kowloon, this means that about 3.4 million people are stacked up on some 15 square miles of land. By comparison, the roughly eight million residents of the five boroughs of New York City have 320 square miles in which to spread out and somewhat up (7).

At the end of 1969, some 1,523,000 of Hong Kong's approximately four million citizens—just under 40 per cent of the population—was estimated as being employed (8). A breakdown of the employment by type is shown in Table 4.

Table 4

Manufacturing	600,000
Services	367,000
Commerce	254,000
Construction	94,000
Agriculture, forestry, and fishing	80,000
Communications	104,000
Public utilities	15,000
Mining, quarrying	5,000
Other	5,000
Total	1,524,000

Unemployment does not seem to be a serious problem and there is a fairly high labor turnover in the manufacturing industries as workers seek better jobs. Underemployment or very low pay is probably the most potentially troublesome problem for workers, especially in Hong Kong's many tiny workshops (called factories) and in the service industries. Among the less than 6 per cent of the labor force estimated to be in farming, forestry, and fishing, subsistence level employment is probably more the rule than the exception.

While rural birth rates and infant mortality rates are higher than those in urban areas, this has little influence on Hong Kong's over-all population patterns. The percentage of rural population appears to be decreasing and will likely continue to do so. Hong Kong's marine population, primarily dependent on fishing and cargo handling, is also on the decline. Between 1961 and 1966 the number decreased 25 per cent (*9*). This is due in part to a trend away from sailing to motorized vessels—which require fewer people to operate.

The question of internal migration thus does not seem of great importance in Hong Kong. As urban areas expand into the countryside there is less area for rice farming, and there have been changes in the pattern of agriculture—primarily a shift away from rice to vegetables. The Colony government is giving of late some attention to the problems of diversifying and modernizing agriculture.

The crowded cities, towns, and rural villages of South China have traditionally supplied migrants to Southeast Asia and, to a lesser extent, to other areas of the world. Hong Kong residents have also participated in the "export" of muscle and brains and still do. The yearbook, *Hong Kong 1970*, records an emigration of workers numbering 2,368 in 1967, 2,643 in 1968, and 2,650 in 1969. A good many people in Hong Kong—and especially in the New Territories—do get remittances from relatives abroad, but not apparently in quantities to be of economic or social significance.

The Economy

As mentioned previously, Hong Kong's economy, and thus the livelihood of the population, has changed radically in the last two decades. Until the Korean War and the United Nations' embargo on trade with the People's Republic of China, Hong Kong's main commercial activity consisted primarily of importing manufactured goods and raw materials for re-exporting them elsewhere. Mainland China was a major trading partner. The Korean War and the flight of Chinese capitalists and factory technicians changed that. Gradually Hong Kong's fledgling textile, plastics, and other light industrial plants multiplied and the volume of locally produced exports grew. Between 1959 and 1969, for example, the value of Hong Kong manufactured items exported more than quadrupled, from about US$353 million to more than $1.66 billion. The labor force in the manufacturing industry during that same period more than doubled, from just over 200,000 to around 500,000 men and women (*10*).

This growth in Hong Kong's manufacturing industry came about despite the fact that Hong Kong has almost no natural resources and that much of its raw materials as well as finished products must travel great distances from suppliers and to buyers (*11*). Compensating factors, however, have contributed to Hong Kong's success: commercial and industrial know-how, both Chinese and British; a stable, yet nearly laissez-faire money market; a minimum of red tape; a generally stable political situation and comparatively uncorrupt legal system; a good supply of unskilled and trainable labor; an excellent harbor and cargo handling system; competent administrators; tolerance on the part of the big neighbor, plus the local will to survive.

In the same way that Hong Kong's manufacturing industries depend almost entirely on imported raw materials, the Colony's population depends almost entirely on imported food—a significant portion of it from the People's Republic of China (*12*). Fresh water, which used to be a serious problem in Hong Kong, also comes in part from China. Thanks to recent reservoir development the Colony could get along if China turned off the tap during the dry season, but strict rationing, with all the administrative and social problems that entails, would be required. The authorities in Hong Kong have worked out a system of stockpiling reserves and of contracting for the purchase of staple foods from a variety of suppliers in order to minimize problems for the Colony should either crop failures or politics make it difficult for supplies from any one source to reach Hong Kong. The thought of what an embargo could do to Hong Kong and the people who live there is very much a factor in Hong Kong planning.

Development

Hong Kong is a city undergoing rapid change. The physical change is both extensive and obvious. The social change is probably as great but less apparent.

The switch from a primarily entrepot to a primarily manufacturing economy has resulted in the growth—at first spontaneous and then planned—of vast new industrial areas. The industrial success, plus the inadequacy of existing housing facilities for the people coming into Hong Kong to participate in that industrial life, has required the building of large government-operated and government-subsidized housing developments. The linking of industry with living and business areas has put great strain on Hong Kong's communications system. New roads have had to be built and old streets widened. New bus lines have been added, new cross-harbor ferry services instituted, and new docks constructed. A cross-harbor tunnel is under construction and the Colony's airport is being expanded to accommodate jumbo jets and millions of passengers. An area is being developed for handling containerized ocean freight.

As Hong Kong's first big industrial enterprise—textiles—developed, prospered, and came into extensive competition with both highly automated enterprises and cheap labor-intensive enterprises around the world, a trend to bigger plants, using more automated processes and fewer though more skillful and better trained workers, began. Then came the electronics industry, specializing in hard-to-automate processes—but processes requiring fairly skilled and increasingly ambitious workers. The most recent export-dollar earner has been the wig industry, where hand labor is still very important. And all the while tiny "factories," in some cases employing only two or three workers, have continued to provide work for tens of thousands of laborers and to turn out a great variety of goods.

Hong Kong industry is in a process of flux—giant gleaming factories with rather high levels of pay and fringe benefits constitute part of the scene. So too do grimy little sweatshops where the pay and welfare of employees depend very much on the personality and individual success—or failure—of their employer and his enterprise. Technical innovation and shrewdness in marketing seem to be the key to the goals of economic progress or simple survival.

The housing picture is less complicated. In the early 1950s the situation was degrading for the individual and dangerous for the society. Human beings lived in conditions so crowded and so lacking in basic sanitation facilities that it was a blessing in disguise when one tragic fire after another eventually culminated in a huge holocaust which forced the Hong Kong government into the housing business. By 1970 more than 40 per cent of the population lived in government-owned or government-aided housing. By 1971 the percentage was about 45 per cent, and by 1976 more than half of Hong Kong's residents will rely in whole or part on the government for a place to live. The accommodations vary: none are terribly stimulating and some are depressing. But they are secure against most of Nature's blows and equipped with at least minimum levels of sanitation. The social scene with its potential development and problems is another matter (*13*).

Hong Kong's major ecological problem is space; there isn't much elbow room for either work or play. Smog from oil-burning electric power plants has been an issue in recent years. Decibel levels from aircraft—which sometimes must make their landing approaches over heavily-populated areas in Kowloon—have been another. As the middle class grows, so does car ownership. Parking and severe traffic congestion are increasing problems. Air pollution from motor vehicles has not yet become a much publicized issue. The greatest offenders are the large public buses of the two privately-owned major bus companies and the smaller (nine to 14 seats) minibuses. There is an "excessive smoke" charge in Hong Kong traffic regulations, but it seems to be seldom enforced. Hong Kong police are sometimes accused of being overly indulgent when dealing with large government-favored enterprises like the bus companies and of being overly cautious about the minibuses, whose owners and drivers have strong left-wing support which can and does cause problems for the police.

In Hong Kong, private citizens and government officials alike have only recently begun to think much about the problem of pollution and environment. The Labor Department now has what is called a "smoke abatement adviser" and the Agricultural Department works with a committee formed several years ago on the use of the limited countryside. At the end of 1970 and early 1971, Hong Kong newspapers ran numerous stories about the lethal refuse from New Territories factories being dumped into a river there, killing ducks, pigs, fish, and endangering oyster beds. Government action at that time, according to press stories, seemed limited mainly to advice and requests, indicating that legislation to deal with this particular kind of problem is probably not yet on Hong Kong's books.

What does all this material change mean for the minds and mores of the people involved? What are their attitudes toward this change of which they are a part, and how have they been reacting to it?

On a rather basic level, the process of Hong Kong's becoming an increasingly modernized society with an economy based heavily on manufacturing has brought about predictable social changes. Prominent among these are some loosening of family ties—particularly the bond of strong parental authority—and an increasing degree of freedom and demand for equal rights among women (*14*). A continually rising level of expectations has accompanied an increase in the size and importance of a middle class in Hong Kong, and a rising level of literacy and education in general as government housing projects include provisions for schools.

Among some intellectuals there is concern, possibly increasing, about civic responsibility and the role of the individual and family in Hong Kong's day-to-day management and future existence; two decades ago this was a matter for a very small group—mostly foreigners and wealthy Chinese favored by those foreigners.

As Hong Kong grows more crowded, there seems to be greater competition for places in good schools. Reasonably good civil service jobs and education abroad depend on passing exams. Those who fail must take poorer jobs, and their chances of getting out of hemmed-in Hong Kong go down.

Difficult to define or document is a feeling of physical and psychic claustrophobia in Hong Kong. The Colony is small but it is difficult to go anywhere else. If a regime in China should decide to cause trouble in Hong Kong, life there could become very difficult. And, in 1997—less than three decades away—all but a small portion of Britain's holdings on the Kowloon peninsula and all of the New Territories are due to revert to China when the 99-year lease expires. This knowledge gives many food for thought, and some find it difficult to digest.

The Society

Residents and critical visitors often say Hong Kong is a society without culture, a society with little interest beyond the good investment, the bowl of rice, the Jockey Club tote board, and local football. This is not completely fair. Hong Kong does not have a great local cultural tradition to fall back on, and its citizens do concentrate much of their attention on the flying dollar. Still—whether it be for "cultural" or for escape reasons—people are interested in theatre. Cantonese opera on stage, film, and television draws large audiences. Even Peking opera and Mandarin dialect films are becoming popular. Religious festivals are well attended. There are some art galleries. In recent years two public libraries have been established by the Urban Council and in 1968 had approximately 250,000 volumes, about two thirds in Chinese, between them. The two universities both offer extramural courses—some in Cantonese, some in English, and some in Mandarin. People who are bright can move up the economic scale through the education ladder. The majority of those who move on to university, however, probably come from families with cash to spare for their sons and daughters to afford extra tutoring in an educational system where promotion depends heavily on exam results.

The physical well-being of the population of Hong Kong is the responsibility of the Medical and Health Department of the Hong Kong government and a number of other offices. The level of public health, as indicated by the decline in deaths from TB referred to earlier, has improved in recent years. As the population becomes better educated and as levels of expectation rise, that trend is likely to continue—barring severe economic or political troubles.

On the family level, the main concern is TB, and more than 90 per cent of all children born in Hong Kong now receive BCG vaccination against TB within three days of birth. The vast majority of children are now born in hospitals or maternity homes, and the government Maternal and Child Health Service offers free maternal and child care at approximately 30 full or part-time centers. These centers have educational as well as immunization and treatment functions. Government subsidizes a service whereby school children receive treatment from private practitioners for little more than US$1.00 per year. Out of a total of more than a million students enrolled in 1968, however, less than 44,000 were taking part in this scheme (*15*).

In addition to government-run or subsidized programs, which include several very large and apparently well-equipped general hospitals, Hong Kong has a large number of hospitals and clinics run by charitable and/or private organizations. The situation, in sum, is fairly good.

Statistics on education in Hong Kong present some interesting contradictions. According to the *Statistical Yearbook*, 1965, the literacy rate for males and females in the 20–24 age bracket in 1961 was 94.0 and 81.1 per cent, respectively. But according to the 1966 by-census, more than 24 per cent of Hong Kong's total population had not been to kindergarten or other kind of school. Slightly more than 48 per cent were then in, or had reached, the first six grades, about 20 per cent had made junior and senior high, about 5 per cent were being or had been educated by private tutor, roughly 2 per cent were in or had graduated from college or graduate school, and just over one per cent were enrolled in or had graduated from technical, vocational, or teacher training schools.

The high percentage of the population listed as illiterate or never in school reflects three variables in the population composition. Older people—those born before World War II, for example—constitute a sizable portion in this category. A second variable is place of origin. Persons born in China had and, to some extent, still have less chance for education than those born in Hong Kong. Finally, women tended, and to some extent still tend, to get to school in lesser numbers, and for shorter periods than do men. The highest rate of illiteracy reported in 1965 was among women, and in that category older women predominate. Among about 210,000 men and women 60 years and older, 128,000 had never been to school.

The old pattern of limited education is changing. In 1966 while almost 200,000 out of 521,000 boys and girls between the ages of five and nine had not been to school (just under 40 per cent), the "no school" share in the 10–14 category drops to only about 16,000 in 429,000 or less than 4 per cent (*16*).

The quality of education in Hong Kong, as in most places, comes under criticism from time to time. There is still great store put on the passing of exams controlling entrance to higher levels of education. The most desirable schools, i.e., those schools with the highest standards, are government-run and/or government-subsidized and are the schools which produce the highest percentages of examination passers. While tuition costs are lower in the government-run schools than in the subsidized and strictly private schools, many families have to retain private tutors in order to keep their children in the better schools. Competition is fierce and there is frequently a spate of suicides following exams.

For a rapidly industrializing society the number of students in technical school seems small. The number of students and variety of training have increased, however, in recent years.

Polity

The government of Hong Kong, while under some pressure to do so, has not adopted an official population policy. The Hong Kong Family Planning Association, a private organization, has been the primary force behind programs aimed at limiting the size and improving the quality of the population. The Family Planning Association is, in fact, a semi-official body and about 40 per cent of its recurrent budget comes from the Department of Medicine and Health.

Contraceptives of all kinds are readily available, through both social service and commercial suppliers. There are three full-time birth control clinics and forty-odd part-time clinics where both information about and devices for birth control can be obtained. Hundreds, perhaps thousands, of pharmacies sell condoms, the pill, and other devices with no questions asked (*17*).

Abortion in Hong Kong is illegal and, from newspaper accounts of prosecutions following deaths, rather widespread. At one time, according to rumor, women were going from Hong Kong to Canton for legal and free or low cost abortions. It is unlikely, however, that such visitors accounted for a significant percentage of Hong Kong women having abortions.

There have been no recent changes in government policy or regulations regarding population and birth control. Indications are that, as in other sectors of social activity, the Colony government prefers to preserve the status quo and work within the traditional private or semi-official groups already existing.

Party politics in the sense of the term as used in the West or even in Japan is not an important factor in the operation of government in Hong Kong. There are, in fact, no political parties functioning as such. There are two small "associations" which run candidates for the Urban Council, a body giving a few elected civic-minded people some face and some experience but very little power in the business of running city government. The Chinese Communist Party is not a legally constituted association in Hong Kong. While the CCP does function openly in the Colony, it does not seem to have concerned itself with population policy. Such politics as may be involved in consideration of population policy most likely involves traditional pressure groups like the Catholic Church, conservative Chinese elders, young and professedly liberal Westerners, and Asians affected by Western ideas. Despite the fact that Hong Kong is a British Crown Colony and is, in many ways, run like a colony, the British administrators are fairly sensitive to local opinions and pressures. As one member of the Establishment puts it, "The Governor cannot always pressure through everything he would like to and population policy just doesn't have as high a priority as many other issues. In this case, there is a reluctance on the part of government to tilt with Chinese tradition over what might be termed 'inappropriate Western notions' which would confuse people and make them less amenable to other more important matters."

In recent years there has been some pressure to legalize abortion, following

London's policy. Here action has been stalled by what is probably a combination of Catholicism with conservatism and status-quoism on the part of both the government and the population in general.

Population Work and Research

Hong Kong's Family Planning Association has a history going back to 1936. Aside from preparing public opinion and training people for work in this field, little significant action was taken prior to the advent of the IUD and pill. The work done in the last decade or so by the FPA and a few other groups has been the subject of a number of surveys. The Population Council's Country Profiles article "Hong Kong" in November 1969 describes some of the programs and research completed or under way at that time (*18*).

These programs and studies include:

(*1*) "The Urban Family Life Survey on Family Planning," completed in 1968. This study was designed to furnish guidelines for future family planning policy. Findings indicated: (*a*) The desire to limit family size increased with a woman's age. At ages 25–29 more than half of the women surveyed indicated they would not like to have more children; for women 30 and over, 80 per cent wanted no more children. (*b*) Limitation of family size increased with parity. While 68 per cent of the mothers with two children wanted no more, women of low parity and older women of high parity least favored family planning. (*c*) Oral pills and the IUD constituted 50 per cent of contraceptive methods offered to women who asked about family planning. (*d*) Women in their thirties had the highest rate of contraceptive users, and 42 per cent of Hong Kong's married women were practicing some form of contraception. (*e*) Among women under 25 using contraceptives, 34 per cent had begun the practice before their second pregnancy. (*f*) The women who wanted no more children but refused to practice contraception tend to be those who had married relatively young and had relatively little education.

(*2*) "Age-Specific Birth Rate Study, 1967," completed in 1968 by the HKFPA and the Population Studies Center of the University of Michigan. This study concluded that the 1967 decline in birth rate was a genuine decline in the fertility rate of married women and not the result of changes in age or marital status distributions.

(*3*) "Oral Pill Follow-up Study," designed to evaluate use-effectiveness and extended use-effectiveness of pills, which have become increasingly popular in Hong Kong. Initial findings were that discontinuation rates for pills seemed to be slightly higher than for IUDs.

(*4*) "Analysis of the Acceptance Rates, 1961–1968," a study to determine among which groups the Family Planning Association had had the most success in getting people to practice family planning. Preliminary conclusions are that younger women, women of lower parity, and better educated women have been more willing than others to accept family planning.

(*5*) "Plastic Condom Study," a planned study to compare the relative acceptability and effectiveness of plastic and rubber condoms.

(*6*) "The Postpartum Program." The Family Planning Association has been participating in the postpartum program sponsored and financed by the Population Council since 1966, operating, as of 1969, in three Maternal and Child Health Centers and six hospitals.

The office which seems to be most concerned with demographic research and training in Hong Kong is the Census and Statistics Department. This office in 1961 conducted Hong Kong's first census in 30 years and the first census ever using modern census-taking and analyzing techniques. A by-census was taken in 1966 and by 1970 demographers in the department had been busy for more than a year planning the 1971 census. The data obtained and projections following the censuses in 1961 and 1966 have been subjected to close scrutiny by members of the Census and Statistics Department and by outside demographers as well.

Hong Kong has had considerable experience in cooperating with foreign and international organizations on matters of population. The major organizations recently have been: the International Planned Parenthood Federation; the American Friends Service Committee; the Oxford Committee for Family Relief; the Unitarian Service Committee of Canada; and the Population Council.

Hong Kong's work on population control has been effective. The birth rate is down significantly and women coming into childbearing age are being made aware of birth control techniques. Some progress has been made in spreading the idea that fewer children per family can mean a better life for all members of that family. On the administrative level, by broadening the scope of information included in its censuses and by refining the techniques for analyzing census data, the government has been able, and increasingly will be better able, to plan for the needs of the people of Hong Kong. In sum, Hong Kong's population work is good and likely to get better, assuming political stability and adequate funding.

Conclusions

With such an optimistic assessment of population work in Hong Kong, it would be all too easy to be complacent about the problems of population in that well-ordered Crown Colony. Some of Hong Kong's planners, however, are not at all complacent. Among the problems worrying administrators in Hong Kong is the fact that the Colony has one of the highest population densities in the world. It is even more crowded than Singapore, which in 1967 had 3,367 persons per square kilometer. Hong Kong has 3,770 persons for each square kilometer, while Taiwan and Japan have only 360 and 275 respectively (*19*). The Hong Kong Public Works Department, drawing on population projections made in 1968 after the 1966 by-census, has based its estimates for future housing projects on what it calls a Medium II projection for the next fifteen years. Those projections have been:

1971	4.16 million
1976	4.62 million
1981	5.15 million
1986	5.76 million

When the 1971 census figures have been completed it will be possible to judge better how accurate these projections are.

Housing in this crowded city state is a crucial problem which has been handled with enough success to avoid serious trouble so far. Sufficient government and government-aided housing has been provided to give reasonably sanitary and weather-secure shelter to just less than 50 per cent of the population. Private housing supplies the needs of a good portion of the rest of the population, but roughly 10 per cent still lives in squatter shacks. And, on the basis of estimates in 1969, the government will be required to continue its role in the provision of housing. In 1966 it was estimated that 84 per cent of the population could not afford unsubsidized self-contained private accommodations. This percentage, it is estimated, may go down as incomes go up, but the projection for 1986 is that about 65 per cent of the population will still be in need of subsidized, project-style housing (*20*).

The encouraging thing about this potentially troublesome situation is that the government is aware there are problems and is moving to meet at least some of them. There is awareness of the desirability of smaller families. There is also awareness that mere shelter from the elements and places to shower and defecate are not enough for hundreds of thousands of people in a place as confined as Hong Kong. More thought is going into planning *better* individual living units and better communal facilities in Hong Kong's vast housing projects.

If the present tendencies continue—a lowering of the rate of population growth plus continued high level of government expenditure on the quantity and quality of housing and communal facilities, the people of Hong Kong should remain a relatively quiescent, productive force in a rapidly changing society.

Notes

1. This figure is from January talk with K. W. J. Topley, Commissioner, Census and Statistics Department, Hong Kong Government. The discrepancy, says Topley, arises out of different methods of tabulation used by the Registrar General and the Census and Statistics Department. Attempts are being made to coordinate.
2. *Hong Kong 1969* (official yearbook), The Government Printer, 1970, p. 214, and *Country Profiles,* "Hong Kong," issued by The Population Council and the International Institute for the Study of Human Reproduction, Columbia University, November 1969, p. 2.
3. Tables from *Census 1961*, The Government Printer, Hong Kong.
4. See *Studies in Family Planning,* No. 44, August 1969, "Hong Kong: The Continuing Fertility Decline, 1967," by Freedman, Namboothiri, Adlakha and Chan. Population Council. . . .
5. Hong Kong Family Planning Association, *19th Annual Report, 1969–70*, p. 29.
6. *Hong Kong 1969, op. cit.*, tables in Appendix.
7. The 85 per cent figure is from "Hong Kong," *Country Profiles, op. cit.*, p. 1; the 73 per cent from *Reports on Population Family Planning,* "Population and Family Planning Programs: A Factbook," Number two (1970 Edition), July 1970, Population Council. . . . , p. 26.
8. *Hong Kong 1969, op. cit.*, p. 26.

9. *Ibid.*, p. 216.
10. *Ibid.*, tables in Appendix.
11. *Ibid.*, p. 1.
12. According to notes from a personal briefing either from an official of Hong Kong's Department of Commerce and Industry or from a member of the American Consulate General in Hong Kong, the percentage (in terms of value) of food used in Hong Kong and coming from mainland China in 1966 was 59 per cent; in 1969, 48 per cent of Hong Kong's food came from mainland China.
13. *Town Planning in Hong Kong*, by Crown Lands and Survey Office, Public Works Department, Hong Kong, June 1969, mimeographed, pp. 22–26.
14. Women are the prime movers in the Hong Kong Family Association; female nurses recently shook the Hong Kong Establishment by threatening a strike for equal pay; for years women have been pressuring against nineteenth century regulations allowing Chinese males to take secondary wives; and even some women faculty members have been making unhappy noises about getting less pay than men for equal work.
15. *Hong Kong 1969, op. cit.*, pp. 114 and 337.
16. *The Census And You 1966,* by K.M.A. Barnett, The Government Printer, Hong Kong, 1967, p. 13.
17. *Country Profiles,* "Hong Kong," *op. cit.*, p. 4.
18. *Ibid.*, pp. 6–7.
19. *Reports on Population/Family Planning, op. cit.*, pp. 26, 28, and 30.
20. *Town Planning in Hong Kong, op. cit.*, pp. 22–26.

References

Hong Kong 1969 (official yearbook), The Government Printer, 1970.

Census 1961, The Government Printer, Hong Kong. This is in three volumes with many tables.

Country Profiles, "Hong Kong," issued by The Population Council and the International Institute for the Study of Human Reproduction, Columbia University, November 1969.

Hong Kong Monthly Digest of Statistics, Census and Statistics Department, Hong Kong Government.

K.M.A. Barnett, *The Census And You 1966,* Government Printer, Hong Kong, 1967.

Town Planning in Hong Kong, Crown Lands and Survey Office, Public Works Department, Hong Kong, June 1969, mimeographed.

The Author

LOREN FESSLER has maintained an interest in China since 1945. As a Harvard undergraduate, he spent a year at Lingnan University in Canton on an exchange student scholarship. Following graduate work at the University of Washington, Mr. Fessler began a career in East Asian journalism that lasted twelve years. Though he traveled extensively throughout the area, his primary responsibility was China reporting and analysis; his principal employer was Time-Life News Service. He has also written for other publications including the *New York Times,* the *Mainland China Review,* and the *Washington Post.* His book *China* was published in 1963. Returning to Harvard in 1967 to enter the program of Regional Studies—East Asia, he received his M.A. degree in June 1968. An Associate of the American Universities Field Staff since January 1969, Mr. Fessler reports on China from the vantage point of Hong Kong.

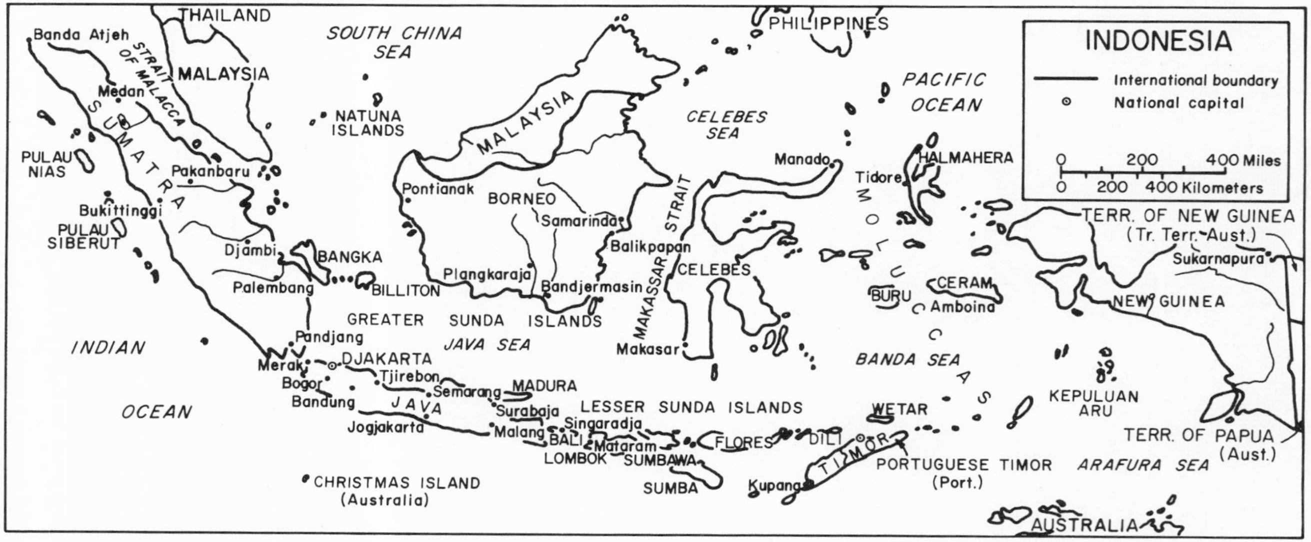
INDONESIA
International boundary
National capital
0 200 400 Miles
0 200 400 Kilometers
Banda Atjeh
THAILAND
MALAYSIA
STRAIT OF MALACCA
Medan
SUMATRA
PULAU NIAS
Pakanbaru
Bukittinggi
PULAU SIBERUT
Djambi
Palembang
BANGKA
BILLITON
SOUTH CHINA SEA
NATUNA ISLANDS
MALAYSIA
Pontianak
BORNEO
Samarinda
Balikpapan
Plangkaraja
Bandjermasin
GREATER SUNDA ISLANDS
JAVA SEA
INDIAN OCEAN
Pandjang
Merak
DJAKARTA
Bogor
Bandung
Tjirebon
Semarang
MADURA
JAVA
Jogjakarta
Surabaja
Malang
BALI
LOMBOK
Singaradja
Mataram
SUMBAWA
SUMBA
CHRISTMAS ISLAND (Australia)
LESSER SUNDA ISLANDS
FLORES
Kupang
DILI
TIMOR
PORTUGUESE TIMOR (Port.)
WETAR
MAKASSAR STRAIT
Makasar
CELEBES
CELEBES SEA
Manado
PHILIPPINES
PACIFIC OCEAN
HALMAHERA
Tidore
MOLUCCAS
BURU
CERAM
Amboina
BANDA SEA
KEPULUAN ARU
ARAFURA SEA
AUSTRALIA
TERR. OF NEW GUINEA (Tr. Terr.-Aust.)
Sukarnapura
NEW GUINEA
TERR. OF PAPUA (Aust.)

Indonesia

Willard A. Hanna

Population Profile

The Republic of Indonesia, with a population today of about 121 million people, has staged one of the world's most spectacular and long-sustained demographic escalations. Each generation, beginning at least a century and a half ago, appears to have experienced a doubling of population, which shows no signs of abating. The focus of greatest population pressure has been the island of Java, plus adjacent Madura and Bali. Here, packed into 7¼ per cent of the nation's land area of 575,450 square miles, live 67 per cent of its people—some 80 million persons, or an average of well over 500 per square kilometer.

Great areas of Java, Madura, and Bali—like the rest of the archipelago—are marvelous evidence of man's industrious and artistic adjustment to a luxuriant tropical environment. But as viable societies, Java, Madura, and Bali were already critically overburdened two generations ago. Today, as Indonesians themselves are just barely beginning to realize, these three key islands are rapidly becoming disaster areas. Realistic population control programs which should have been undertaken at least ten years ago are just now being initiated. According to the once hallowed "Teachings of Sukarno" the nation could (and therefore should and would) support a population of 250 million. Under President Suharto, the nation is setting itself to perform the multiple miracle of political, economic, and social regeneration after the Sukarno era disasters. If it is to have any chance of success, it must address itself resolutely to the control of that most basic of all human generative drives on the part of a prolific and in many respects an improvident people, the vast majority of whom regard fecundity as a sign of the special blessings and bounty of God. Even today the Bataks of Sumatra, who are by no means atypical in outlook, deem it propitious to repeat the traditional wedding wish: "May you have seventeen sons and sixteen daughters."

The over-all demographic situation in Indonesia is reflected in the following figures, all of them approximations which allow for at least a 10–20 per cent factor for error. The total population is in the neighborhood of 115–125 million, the official estimate as of 1970 being 121 million. Of this total, approximately 85 per cent live in rural and 15 per cent in urban areas. The annual rate of increase is on the order of 2.4–3.0 per cent per year—which means a doubling of the population within one generation. The fertility rate can be no less than 6.0. The crude birth rate is about 44–48/1000, the over-all death rate about 17–19/1000, the infant mortality rate is about 102–112/1000. At present only about 6.5 per cent of the population is over 55 years of age, but current attention to expanding and improving health services means a steadily increasing life expectancy. Well over half of the population is now under 20. The sex distribution is about 95 males per 100 females. The marriage age is low—the late teens and early twenties (according to a recent sample survey, 17.9 years for females and 23.6 for males). The incidence of celibacy is negligible. Simple mathematical projection of future population on the basis of present trends gives a figure of approximately 140 million in 1975, 160 million in 1980, and 185 million in 1985, beyond which few prudent persons care to peer. The not very remote alternatives would seem to be famine, pestilence, revolution—some natural or man-made disaster—or else an almost miraculously sudden and successful program of family planning.

All of the above figures are approximations. To be more precise would be to make arbitrary selection among the few authorities and to lend undue credence to figures which are at best ingenious extrapolations from inadequate and inaccurate evidence. Indonesian population reports of the colonial past were based at least as much upon conjecture as upon actual count. The first national census (1961) was more a triumph over bureaucratic inertia than a scrupulously scientific survey. Subsequent samplings have been more experimental than illuminating. Indonesian demography, like Indonesian statistical studies in general, has as yet had few serious practitioners either inside Indonesia or abroad. The Indonesian public itself, in any event, is unwilling and often unable to be exact in its responses to inquiries about such details as age or income. Refinement of rough figures like those given above remains preliminary and tentative. It is possible, for instance, to cite evidence that the rate of population increase is significantly lower on Java, Madura, and Bali than in the more sparsely populated outer islands, and smaller in urban than in rural areas. Sheer physical congestion, therefore, may already be exercising an inhibiting effect upon reproduction. The evidence, however, may be mere statistical illusion resulting from the application of different standards for census-taking at different times and places. The readily observable fact is that Java, Madura, and Bali are the focal points of an immediate and desperate population crisis which perhaps need not and certainly cannot be measured with any scientific precision in advance of calculating a crash program.

Population Distribution and Movement

The Indonesian population is one of great ethnic, linguistic, and cultural diversity scattered through a 3,000-mile-long equatorial archipelago made up of five huge and ill-linked major islands (Sumatra, Java, Sulawesi, two thirds of Kalimantan [Borneo], half of Irian Barat) and 1,000 others. The nation is also divided by regional rivalries and conflicts of almost all conceivable descriptions, including serious local resentment of the central government's neglect as well as of control and exploitation by it. Indonesia has recently been exposed to the physical and psychological hazards of three decades of disorders—the Japanese occupation, the anticolonial revolution, the turmoil of independence. It has the makings of at least half a dozen smaller and perhaps more viable independent entities. But despite all its disparities and adversities, Indonesia continues precariously to cohere as the inefficiently centralized Republic of Indonesia dominated by the overcrowded island of Java and the congested, chaotic capital city of Djakarta.

Indonesia's component parts hold together in part at least by reason of the common ambition, assiduously and dramatically cultivated during the Sukarno era, together to achieve the international prestige and power to which the nation would seem to be entitled as the world's fifth or sixth most populous and one of its most richly endowed. In terms of Sukarno's own aspiration and achievement, Indonesia is united on the basis of a shared sense of "national identity." This identity is in no small part dependent upon acceptance of three common denominators: a national language—Bahasa Indonesia, a highly developed form of Malay now spoken or at least understood by a good 60 per cent of the people; a national religion—Islam, to which some 90 per cent of the population adhere; the national ideology, the Pantjasila, the Five Principles of nationalism, internationalism, democracy, social justice, and religious freedom. The Pantjasila, ideally, makes for mutual tolerance and accommodation on the part of the heterogeneous elements of the population. These include a major racial minority of some four million Chinese (mainly Buddhist). It also includes various important religious minorities such as some seven million Christians (two million of them Catholic), and some two and a half million Hindus of Bali and Lombok. What this signifies for those who plan Indonesia's national programs, including those of population control, is that they are in fact dealing with a population which is much more homogeneous in its attitudes and reactions than might be assumed from the study of polychrome maps highlighting the nation's immense variety.

Indonesia's diverse peoples are no doubt growing at somewhat different rates and redistributing themselves in complex manner, but this is not subject to statistical demonstration. Neither immigration nor emigration is now a significant factor. Immigration had almost stopped in the years prior to World War II, and in the postwar years it has been legally and logistically all but impossible. In previous decades and centuries the most significant aspect of immigration was the fairly steady influx of highly industrious Chinese laborers, craftsmen, and traders. Most remained as permanent residents, thus establishing the distinct Chinese business communities which persist and thrive despite recurrent political and economic pressures and recent efforts at expulsion. These Chinese communities are concentrated in the urban areas but have their ramifications throughout the countryside. Arabs, Indians, and Pakistanis also entered Indonesia in prewar years, and some 50–100,000 of each community are now scattered throughout the archipelago, the major concentrations of the Indians and Pakistanis being in Sumatra.

Many Dutch and a few other Westerners once settled into Indonesia on a more or less permanent basis. In prewar days the Dutch numbered about 500,000, the great majority of them on Java. In the 1950s they numbered up to a quarter of a million, most of whom were in fact Dutch Eurasians. The Dutch Eurasians have been either assimilated or expelled; the ethnic Dutch were expelled in 1959. The Western community in Indonesia today numbers several tens of thousands of persons (including a new group of Dutch), members of the highly mobile cosmopolitan world of diplomacy, commerce, and technology.

In prewar years the Indonesians themselves, mainly Sumatrans, Javanese, and Makassarese (Buginese), migrated in significant numbers to nearby Singapore and Malaya, where a large part of the Malay population is of recent Indonesian origin. Postwar migration across the Straits has been a continuing but diminishing trickle. Seafaring people from Sulawesi (Minahasa) have traditionally moved at will into and out of the Southern Philippines. In postwar years some thousands of them have settled illegally in Mindanao. But these and similar movements—into Sarawak and Sabah (Malaysian Borneo) for instance—are on a minute scale in relation to the total population.

Although voluntary movement of settlers into and out of Indonesia has now all but ceased, interisland and rural-urban movement is a continuing and perhaps increasingly significant phenomenon. The complex Indonesian population has in fact already gone through a long process of mixing and blending. The Minangkabau of equatorial Sumatra, culturally and commercially the most adventurous of Indonesians, have been far-roving traders and more recently settlers, and the matriarchal females have of late begun to accompany or follow the males. The Bugis of Sulawesi have traditionally combined piracy with trade and settlement with conquest in spreading through the Riau Islands and into the Malay Peninsula. The Ambonese served the Dutch as clerks and soldiers and established their own enclaves. The Balinese were favored as slaves and servants and often chose to stay where they were taken. The Javanese, noted for their rigid and exclusive hierarchical system, have long been less independently venturesome than others. But tens of thousands of Javanese were settled by the Dutch as laborers in Sumatra. More were moved to Sumatra after independence. Yet more tens of thousands have fanned out all through Indonesia since independence as not always welcome members of the civil and military bureaucracy, many of whose individual members tend to take local roots. In years past intermarriage was much less common than was intermingling, but in recent years intermarriage too is on the increase. In the urban areas, most specially Djakarta, the population is truly polyglot. Any really detailed census of Indonesia would now certainly show at least 10 per cent of the people living far from their place of origin, if only by reason of mainly prewar migrations and the more recent drive from the farm to the city.

The accelerated pace of Indonesian urbanization is exemplified by the capital city of Djakarta. The capital attracted migrants from all parts of Indonesia during the Dutch colonial period and since then it has been steadily deluged with newcomers. Its population has grown by about 1,000 per cent from some 500,000 in 1940—inclusive of approximately 100,000 Dutch and 150,000 Chinese—to at least five million in 1970.

Dutch colonial Batavia was a compact and orderly city with imposing administrative, business, and residential areas. These highly modernized quarters, intended mainly for the Europeans and the Chinese, were surrounded and infiltrated by the Indonesian *kampongs.* Here the architecture was flimsy, amenities were meager, and congestion was already prejudicial to health and safety. Today Djakarta Raja (Greater Djakarta) is a vast, sprawling shambles of a city in which no urban services can begin to keep up with the demand. The new Djakarta boasts a façade of recently constructed modern structures—the offices and homes of the more fortunate members of the civil and military bureaucracy and of the other privileged classes. But at least 80 per cent of the population lives as or like squatters in wretched shantytowns where common urban amenities such as water and electricity scarcely penetrate.

What is true of Djakarta is true to a somewhat lesser degree of five other major cities (Surabaya, Bandung, Semarang, Medan, and Palembang), which, together with Djakarta, account for one-third of the urban population and have experienced comparable growth. Into these cities come migrants from all over Indonesia, attracted by the often illusory prospect of security, education, employment, housing, and opportunity. It is not only the larger cities—there are some 40 or more with populations over 100,000—which have grown bigger and denser and always more squalid, but also the 225 other towns now classified as urban and even the villages and the amorphous shoestring settlements. In parts of Java, Madura, and Bali, these latter now stretch out almost continuously among the pathways and waterways in a reticulation so intricate that the residents seem almost to be spilling back into the fields from which many of them were recently squeezed out. In the countryside itself the average land holding—most of it peasant owned rather than tenant farmed—has been reduced to a mere one hectare (2.4 acres). The peasants are industrious, and the combination of good soil, tropical climate, and widespread irrigation makes for two or more crops per year; but per capita income—urban as well as rural—is less than US$100.

The visible land pressure, and the obvious impossibility of all the population finding a livelihood in traditional farming, prompted the Dutch in the early twentieth century to give increasing attention to modern agricultural and industrial development. Almost inevitably, however, the emphasis fell upon new manifestations of an old system—estate agriculture for export products. In newly opened regions, especially Sumatra's east coast, and with newly introduced crops, specifically tobacco and rubber, the colonial government sought to invigorate and modernize the Indonesian economy. In the immediate prewar years (1935–1940) the Dutch recruited and transported annually up to about 12,000 laborers and their families and were given therefore to hailing transmigration as the solution both to Java's problem of excess population and to Sumatra's problem of development.

The new Indonesian leaders also beguiled themselves for two decades after independence with that cheerful fantasy. Indonesia's demographic problem, they maintained, was not one of proliferation but of maldistribution. The problem constituted in fact a glorious opportunity to draw upon Java's apparently limitless vitality and fecundity for the exploitation of the untapped resources of the outer islands—huge, relatively empty, presumably fertile, mineral- and timber-rich Kalimantan, Sumatra, Sulawesi, and even primitive, unexplored Irian Barat (West New Guinea), then under dispute with the Dutch, who obviously lacked the manpower to develop it. The Sukarno era planners conceived grandiose schemes for the transmigration of very large numbers of Javanese. An ephemeral "7 X 5 Year Plan," for instance, provided for the transmigration annually for 35 years of 600,000 Javanese. It seemed to escape attention, however, that this would not offset the two million annual increase.

The net result was the resettlement during the 1950s and early 1960s in good years of a reported total of up to 10,000 families of approximately 50,000 persons—a grand total of approximately 375,000 persons over the decade and a half. This minor movement of population was itself far more than cancelled out by reverse migration from the outer islands to Java, which included the back-tracking of no small percentage of disgruntled transmigrants. The transmigration schemes ran afoul of every conceivable difficulty concerning recruitment and screening of candidates, provision of transportation, clearing, leveling, draining, irrigation, and planting of land, building of shelter, delivery of promised seeds, tools, fertilizers, and other subsidies in cash and kind, training in new agricultural techniques, and organization of marketing facilities. No one appears to have foreseen the resentment toward Javanese interlopers on the part of the local people, the outbreak of regional insurrections, and more or less constant minor crises over mosquitoes, ants, rats, snakes, tigers, and elephants.

The Sukarno era fiasco proved conclusively that transmigration was a delusory solution to Indonesia's problems unless undertaken in a manner and on a scale of which the nation was and still is incapable. Nevertheless, during the Sukarno years, the theory of transmigration was part of the state dogma to which all had to subscribe or risk being branded as disloyal and counter-revolutionary. The handful of students and scholars who dabbled at all in demography therefore felt constrained mainly to manipulate the various possible formulas of transmigration in search of fresh inspiration. Even today, there persists the hope that some magical new formula can be discovered—a symbolic project which will somehow turn out to have potency as an incantation. Indeed, although in 1970 there were signs of a new sense of urgency and realism, between 1967 and 1969 the state planners seemed to have a mystical fixation upon an annual 600,000 "prevented births" which, for lack of any realistic action plan, proved as hypothetical as the annual migration Sumatra-wards of 600,000 unwilling Javanese.

Population and the Economy

Indonesia's net national produce is officially estimated to have risen Rp. 387,700 million in 1958 to Rp. 456,300 million in 1966 in terms of a constant 1960 rupiah—allowing, that is, for correction of inflationary factors. The average annual rate of increase was therefore approximately 1.75 per cent. Set off against a 2.5–3 per cent annual rate of population increase, this means a negative annual economic growth rate of approximately 0.75–1.25 per cent. The commonly accepted figure for the 1970 GNP is US$11 billion. The per capita income, according to various statistics and estimates, is somewhere within the range of US$30–100. The figure is highly conjectural, but the fact is that it has been close to the world's lowest and that it is dropping.

Much of Indonesia's rural population (about 85 per cent of the national total producing perhaps 60 per cent of the national income) earn and live at a low poverty level. But in rural, tropical Indonesia bare subsistence often offers as fringe benefits the beauty and bounty of nature. Much of the farmer's real returns thus escapes the net of the statistician. So too, in the past at least, did no small amount of the nation's export produce—rubber, tin, copra, spices, and other readily portable commodities which got smuggled overseas, not infrequently with enthusiastic official connivance. These moonlight exports produced much of the hard currency revenue which was squandered in luxurious living by the more resourceful and privileged classes. Any interpretation of statistical tables, therefore, must make generous allowances for both omissions and inventions. And all attempts at year-to-year comparison are complicated by the difficulty of correlation between rupiahs and foreign currency equivalents, especially since it is not often clear in what currency the original count or conjecture was made or even when. The rupiah, which was repeatedly devalued, was subject to such fantastic inflation that the 1958 price index of 100 had risen to 567,000 by late 1967. Official exchange rates between rupiahs and dollars, meanwhile, were multiple, arbitrary, and highly imaginative. Nevertheless, allowing for at least a 50 per cent factor for error, statistics confirm what the unaided eye can readily observe. Indonesia's vast wealth, real or potential, divided into some 120 million more or less equal parts, will soon not be sufficient to provide adequate food, clothing, and shelter, plus the health, education, and employment facilities which even the remoter rural people of the new generation have now been led to expect and demand.

The basic element of the Indonesian economy is its agriculture, which accounts for 50–60 per cent of the national income and employs well over 65 per cent of the total labor force. Peasant farming for production primarily of rice and other foodstuffs is still at least ten times as important in terms of crop values as is the estate sector, in which many peasants also work part time, for production of rubber, coffee, tea, and other export products. Both sectors have been in serious trouble for years. During the turbulent Sukarno years estate production dropped off sharply when incompetent and corrupt new managers took over the once phenomenally prosperous and productive Western-owned estates that had been confiscated or nationalized. During this period, also, large areas of estate land were occupied by land-hungry peasant squatters, who cut down rubber and tea to plant cassava and bananas. With the ambivalent assistance of the government, which sought at once and with some degree of success to improve agriculture and to maintain an artificial price system that channeled the profits from the farmer to the official, the peasants did manage significantly to increase both the acreage under cultivation and the annual yield. But the buts are massive and tragic.

Acreage and yield increased, but the per capita yield dropped and agriculture as a whole foundered. The watershed and forest reserves on Java were so depleted by farmers seeking land and firewood that soil erosion has become a major problem. Much of the irrigation system was badly neglected. And the systematic introduction of scientific farming and marketing techniques has been impeded by reason of the grave political and economic disruptions. Merely in order to prevent famine, Indonesia has been forced in recent years to spend approximately $100 million annually on rice imports. To put this figure in context, it means approximately 12 per cent of the value of all Indonesian imports at current rates, about 10 per cent of the value of its exports, or about 15 per cent of the annual value of international aid, or about 30 per cent of the annual outlay for national development. Achievement of self-sufficiency in rice production would thus signify a major breakthrough in the achievement of national rehabilitation and would release a large block of foreign exchange for other purposes.

Second only to the problem of providing 121 million Indonesians with sufficiency in rice production is that of giving them satisfactory employment. Available statistics indicate that well over 10 per cent of the 40 million labor force is unemployed, that about one third to one half is chronically underemployed, and that the rate of unemployment or underemployment is about 25 per cent higher in urban than in rural areas. It must be added that the labor force is usually estimated on the novel basis of approximately 80 per cent of the male and 30 per cent of the female population presumed to be ten years of age or older. Distinction between full employment and underemployment, furthermore, is extremely difficult to make. The evidence of one's eyes in Indonesia is that the farmers work long, hard hours in the fields but also that many of them are always on the road, trudging to and from town, and that the village houses and market places rarely lack for a large and leisurely society. In the cities one man rarely does a job which two can perform less efficiently and expeditiously, albeit more congenially. The pressure for jobs, in short, is enormous, and the accommodation to pressure is to stretch out the work. The dilemma is everywhere dramatized, in the country, for instance, by the ceremonious community performance of the rice harvest with every head or sheaf artistically arranged. In the city one observes the much less aesthetic spectacle of the newly arrived unskilled laborer who rents a trishaw, which becomes his twenty-four hour a day source of meager income and even his home, until such time as he can sublet the vehicle for twelve hours and himself rent sleeping space in a squatter shanty and establish a family.

Too many people, too few jobs, and the residual effects of the wildly unrealistic official policy of the Sukarno era with regard to jobs, pay, and daily necessities spell for Indonesia today what may be the most anomalous economic situation in the contemporary world. The Sukarno regime rejected all the conventional concepts of supply and demand, performance and reward. It made neither qualifications nor industriousness the criterion for employment, but only political expediency. It attempted to keep salaries and wages low and scarce commodities cheap. The government itself absorbed into its vastly inflated civil and military bureaucracy a conservatively estimated three million persons, including large numbers of the newly educated class. Their monthly wages and salaries were minute—the market equivalent in rupiahs of about US$1–25 to mention the extremes of the scale—but their prerogatives might be princely. For the higher-ups it meant prestige, plus homes, automobiles, trips overseas, and the opportunity, which few ignored, to become corrupted. The government thus temporarily defused a great deal of potential protest, but it also wrecked the economy and eventually precipitated the 1965 debacle.

The official Sukarno era policy with regard to rice illustrates some of the complexities and consequences of that policy. Cheap, plentiful rice symbolizes the good life which the national revolution was expected to achieve. The government therefore attempted to keep the markets abundantly stocked at a price the people could afford—one or two dollar cents per kilogram. In order to do so it resorted to virtually confiscatory purchases from the farmers and to expensively subsidized imports. It thus encouraged hoarding, blackmarketing, and a spiraling inflation, while also motivating the peasant to produce less and to consume more. The precedent of artificial wage-price controls had been set by the Dutch, but the degree of incompetence and corruption manifested by the Sukarno regime swiftly made effective control impossible. The ordinary peasant and worker bore the great burden of a deteriorating economic system.

The Indonesian worker today, whether on the estate or in the factory, can expect to earn no more than Rp. 100–2,000 ($0.25–$5.00) per month in cash. He also, perhaps, gets payment in kind (rice, textiles, cooking oil, etc.) to a total of about $1.25–6.25 in value. Depending upon his rating and luck, he may also get various health and educational benefits for his family. Today, as in former times, the really happy worker is the one who succeeds in establishing the colonial-feudal relationship with his employer whereby in return for loyal services he is enabled to bridge the great gap between income and outgo.

The dilemma of the Indonesian salary or wage earner at all levels is one which defies any real resolution short of the total national economic overhaul which the very dilemma itself seems to inhibit. At the upper level, both by reason of shortage of qualified personnel and inadequacy of payment, the Indonesian administrator, professional man, or technician, is forced to divide his time and effort among several positions and to supplement one or more official stipends by moonlighting and by other more or less licit economic maneuvers. His wife may hold a similar number of jobs. To maintain a car, a house, and family—since polygamy is not rare and devotion to both property and progeny runs high—on a basic single salary of no more than $25 per month calls for enormous ingenuity. No few Indonesians, including high civil and military officials, achieve a remarkably ostentatious and luxurious standard of living. The activities of a not particularly enterprising Corruption Eradication Team has done little to discourage such spectacles. It seems probable that the amount of money which is diverted each year from official to private bank accounts could quite easily pay for the nation's rice imports and much more besides. Along with rice and jobs, reform is an indispensable ingredient of Indonesian rehabilitation.

Rice and jobs are top priorities in the Suharto regime's new Rp. 1,420 million ($3,700 million) Five-Year Plan (1969–1974), and a beginning of reform is at least implicit within the planning process. The new plan was initiated for the fiscal year 1969 (April 1, 1969–April 1, 1970) after an interim period of emergency relief and stabilization subsequent to the national disasters of 1965–1966. It aimed at providing essential food, clothing, and shelter for the long-deprived people, repairing and improving the badly damaged infrastructure, and developing a soundly based new agricultural and industrial economy which would efficiently exploit local resources and manpower. The over-all objective was to achieve an annual economic growth rate 2.7 per cent greater than the rate of population increase. On the basis of early returns, it seems that most of the specific economic objectives are achievable. Are they adequate?

The basic target in peasant agriculture is the achievement of self-sufficiency in rice production. This means an increase by 50 per cent above the recent crop level. It is to be accomplished by greatly improving and extending the irrigation system, by increasing the amount of land under cultivation, and by introducing new seeds, fertilizers, pesticides, tools, and techniques. However, a sufficiency, or even an eventual surplus, of rice will not signify a national bonanza either in jobs or in dollars. By 1975, it is to be assumed, farm productivity per man hour will have been increased, thus perhaps worsening rather than improving the opportunity for farm labor. Even though attention is to be given to increase of production of vegetables, fruits, meats, and other cereals than rice, Indonesia will still have to import additional foodstuffs at an estimated cost in 1975 of $67 million. Meanwhile, other nearby agricultural nations will have improved their own situations to Indonesia's potential disadvantage as exporter or as importer.

The Five-Year Plan also calls for increases in the production of rubber, palm oil, copra, tobacco, coffee, tea, spices, etc., all export crops in which estate agriculture is much more important than peasant farms or small holdings. The increases are now calculated, however, more on the basis of rehabilitation than of new development. This is particularly true with regard to rubber, after oil the nation's second most important earner of foreign exchange. Genuine long-range revival of the rubber industry implies replanting on a scale so vast as to be inhibiting, especially in view of competition from Malaysia's already replanted estates and from Western synthetics. In short, in agriculture (as in fisheries, now scheduled for 45 per cent increase), Indonesia has yet to contemplate the enormous new programs which will make for anything more than somewhat improved subsistence and somewhat diminished unemployment.

The Five-Year Plan provides for a 300 per cent increase in production of textiles and of cement, and it mentions but does not actually schedule large-scale housing projects and various other methods of raising the standard of living. For the establishment of a firm new industrial base, the planners place their greatest expectations in the exploitation of timber (300 per cent increase) and petroleum (50 per cent increase). The nation's timber resources are almost inex-

haustible, and its oil deposits, as recent explorations show, may be quite fantastic.
But exploitation of timber and oil does not necessarily mean either sound development or a just sharing of the benefits between the people and the exploiters. Nor does it necessarily imply a rationalizing of the general industrial situation which, in the past, has resulted in the quick closure or in drastic production cutbacks of expensively subsidized new factories for which spare parts and raw materials were not provided and where standards of maintenance and of operation were at best deplorable. It does not now seem probable that industry, which has given employment to date to perhaps 6 per cent of the working population, can soon absorb double the present number of full employment rate, or that trade and commerce, which have employed an estimated 10 per cent, can soon expand without also increasing labor efficiency and thus restricting new openings. The over-all five-year target for industrial growth is 90 per cent which might, at best, double the industrial labor force (now perhaps two million). Much more than doubling is necessary in order to absorb a large part of a new generation of applicants—the estimated eight million or more young men and women of the 20–24-year age group who are already crowding themselves off the land.

Given a conceivable 5 per cent annual economic growth rate—that is, 25 per cent or more by 1975—given even a miraculous 10 per cent increase, or about 50 per cent by 1975, Indonesia will still not have made up for the progress it forfeited during 1950–1965, or even what it might already have achieved in the post-Sukarno period. It is impossible, on the basis of any scientific projection, to predict that by 1975 in economic terms Indonesia will not have dropped still farther behind its more rapidly advancing neighbor, Malaysia, or that it will be more able to meet the minimum expectations and demands of today's 121 million Indonesians, who will by then number more than 140 million.

Population and Development

Modern national development in Indonesia has been conceived of as a process of mass politicization and social activization, practiced by an already sophisticated national elite which has sought to inspire and to lead the awakening public in achievement of instant prestige and power. The early leaders—for the most part the well-educated and much-Westernized offspring of the traditional ruling class and of the indigenous colonial officials—tended to be at once impassioned and anticolonial rebels and doctrinaire social reformers. Inevitably they equated the elimination of alien capitalistic exploitation and the bestowal of welfare state social benefits with the achievement of national greatness. They devoted their own energies and channeled those of the public toward the eradication of submissiveness and ignorance. They did so by involving the people in revolutionary political, social, and cultural movements that recurrently assumed an aspect of militancy and belligerency. They succeeded brilliantly in raising revolutionary armies to fight the Dutch. They also established schools and hospitals, created political parties, recruited youth, women, peasants, workers, and others to join nation-wide mass movements. They excelled, as became apparent in the mid-1950s, in holding local, regional, national, and international conferences, in staging spectacular sports events, cultural festivals, political demonstrations, and Afro-Asian seminars and summits, and in mounting melodramatic "confrontations" with the Dutch, the Indonesian Chinese, the Western world in general, and nearby Singapore and Malaysia.

This revolutionary approach to development often proved at best merely wasteful and at worst outright destructive with regard to the nation's economic system. The first generation of Indonesian national leaders conceived and implemented a program of national development which critically undermined the economy. It dangerously overstimulated the demands of the people for adequate food, clothing, shelter, education, medical care, and job opportunity, which the revolution promised but which the nation could not and still cannot provide. The Sukarno regime squandered so many billions of Indonesia's own rupiahs and of the outside worlds' dollars and rubles that the new Indonesia inherited a US$2.5 billion mortgage and has had to reapply since for as much again. This is no vast sum in terms of contemporary international finance; but normal repayment of interest and principal would have consumed 60 per cent of all of Indonesia's export earnings in 1969–1970 and could still amount to 117 per cent of all 1973–1974 earnings.

The events of 1965–1966 induced a sober re-examination of the old concept of national development and the formulation of a new one. According to the new analysis, Indonesia must forego the irrational, destructive policies of the past and tailor its policy objectives to its own carefully measured dimensions. This has meant, first, a concentration of effort upon mere emergency economic relief for a foundering nation (1967); then a stabilization program to bring inflation under control and overhaul the administrative machinery (1968); and now a $3,700 million Five-Year Plan (1969–1974). The current objectives, as briefly summarized officially in English, are as follows: "the provision of food and clothing, the improvement of infrastructures, the improvement of housing for the common people, the provision of more employment and a higher spiritual welfare."

The primary emphasis, in other words, is to provide those basic daily necessities which the Sukarnoists assumed would be almost automatically forthcoming if only the nation successfully asserted its will to be great. The reversal of national priorities from emphasis upon will to emphasis upon work is as dramatic as it is difficult; and in rebuilding an economic infrastructure, the Suharto regime must at the same time maintain the dynamic and expensive social superstructure which was the genuine achievement of the Sukarno years. The Suharto regime, in brief, is confronted with the problem that Indonesia's social development is at least half a century ahead of its economic development. There is no way of speeding up the one without slowing down the other; but the self-evident logic of this conclusion is neither politically nor psychologically acceptable.

The social structure of the Indonesian nation can best be represented in graphic form as a long, sharply tapering white spire tipped with a gilded bulb, mounted upon a huge solid black base. The bulb represents the tiny but highly educated, sophisticated, and privileged ruling elite. Rashly oversimplified, this means the 50,000 top officials of the civil and military establishment and the

50,000 top business and professional people, who, together with their families, number in all about 500,000 persons. These Indonesians, much intermarried and closely interrelated in official, business, and social contacts, make and implement public policy and condition public opinion. In the Sukarno era this key component was dominated by an even smaller inner clique of feuding political cronies; in the early Suharto period it focused to a notable degree upon the military set. Influence and power have been passing of late to a younger group of civilian professionals and technicians. There are intimations, now and again, that in fact it is the youth who may force the new decisons—youths who themselves derive mainly from within this same very restricted milieu. Whatever the inadequacies of this analysis, the fact is that in Indonesia the intellectual elite group is still minute but powerful. It is susceptible to suggestion and influence by the Western world to a degree which was not true between 1950–1965, and it is far more experienced and accomplished in national and international affairs than were the leaders of the early 1950s. In working now for national development, the new group has shown the confidence and the courage to accept outside assistance to which obvious but tacit conditions are being attached.

The long tapering spire of the graph represents the ten million or so other Indonesians who have already moved into the modern world of dependence upon schools, shops, and clinics; newspapers and radio; electrical and sanitary facilities; and such possessions as sewing machines and motor scooters. It is largely urban, at least elementary school educated, fond of Western customs and dress (including white shirts), and it is the beginning of a genuine middle class. The very long taper allows for the many economic and social gradations between the subsistence level of the masses and the comfort and luxury of the elite.

The base, of course, is the mass of workers and peasants clad in black cotton shorts. It is the several tens of millions of ordinary Indonesians, to at least half of whom have already been brought schools, clinics, and political party branches well in advance of new seeds, fertilizers, tools, and vocational skills.

Population and Society

The Indonesians—most especially the Javanese—are frequently stereotyped as conservative, suspicious of change, and given to the most devious obstruction of any program which runs counter to the "true Indonesian way" of thinking or acting. It is generally true, however, that the individual Indonesian is alert and eager, ingenious and resourceful, capable of gracefully leaping the cultural gap between Kalimantan and Java, or between Djakarta and New York, Cairo, Peking, or Moscow. It now seems clear that too much has been made of the uniqueness of the "Indonesian identity"—by Sukarno, for instance, whose personal and political purposes it served to create the mystique of the distinctive Indonesian soul and spirit with which he and few others could effectively communicate. It seems time to re-emphasize the syncretism of Indonesian society. After all, over the centuries Indonesia has worked out a more than reasonably harmonious accommodation of such not easily compatible elements as the people of the Moluccas and Minangkabau, and of the Sudanese, Javanese, Bantamese and others of Java. It has managed at the same time to absorb and transform major elements of the civilizations of Hindu India, the Muslim world, and Western Europe.

The rural Indonesian born before about 1925, and already too old between 1945 and 1955 to be swept into the revolutionary movement, and the majority of others born before 1920, are probably fixed in their inherited preconceptions—but they are now the small and impotent minority. The great majority of Indonesians have experienced and accepted astounding alterations in their way of living and thinking. The impact of the Sukarno era with its nation-wide explosion of violence was sufficient to qualify the current generation of educated Indonesians for membership in a society of bewildered, change-conscious moderns. Indonesia, nevertheless, is a nation in which efforts deliberately calculated to induce change have repeatedly failed quite miserably or else have produced results quite other than those which were anticipated. This is evidence perhaps not so much of Indonesian resistance to innovation as of the parlous state—in Indonesia—of the still very imprecise science of social conditioning.

The Indonesian population responds so enthusiastically to modern educational and medical services, for instance, that the government's truly heroic efforts have not at all kept up with the demand. It takes little or no persuasion to get the child into school—not just the boy but also the girl, who might hold back or be held back in other Muslim countries—or to gain acceptance of the spray gun or inoculation needle. It is an unhappy fact, however, that a once-promising national campaign for the elimination of malaria rather quickly got mired down in the political and economic quagmire of the Sukarno regime. And dedication to education in general has not spelled similar dedication to vocational education to meet Indonesia's most pressing needs. The mass media, to mention another perplexing circumstance, promised in the early 1950s to be a prime instrument for modernization and for that reason gained generous national and international subsidy. The press, radio, motion pictures, and ultimately the TV were soon and quite ingeniously converted into vehicles for mass agitation rather than mass enlightenment, and have not yet clearly defined for themselves their new role.

The Indonesian educational record illustrates clearly the nation's capacity for achievement. As usual statistics are highly dubious, but the literacy rate, which was less than 7 per cent in prewar days, may now be 45 per cent or more among all those over ten years of age. In 1950 Indonesia had only a few hundred university-trained personnel of ethnic Indonesian origin. Today it turns out several thousand university graduates per year at home and sends hundreds of students to colleges and universities overseas. According to official report, of the total Indonesian population today, 32.4 per cent has now had an elementary school education, 1.6 per cent has studied at the secondary level, and 0.1 per cent at the university level. In terms of 1969 enrollment, this meant 15,900,000 in the elementary schools (almost one half of the elementary school age group), 1,600,000 in secondary schools, and 110,677 in some 75 national, provincial, or private universities. The greatest concentration of educational facilities, naturally, is in Java, but schools are found in the remotest villages, and every province now has at least one university.

The imperfections of the mushrooming system are easy to detect, and the Indonesians themselves are acutely aware of them. Standards have fallen off sharply at all levels from those of the rigid and exclusive colonial system. Teachers, textbooks, supplies, equipment, and classrooms are all in short supply. A shaky system of financing commonly leaves it up to the local community to provide buildings and to supplement the teacher's meager salary. Vocational education other than teacher training attracts few students, and trained teachers can frequently find more attractive and remunerative employment outside the schools. And almost always, at any level and in any except specialized fields, there are many times more graduates than there are appropriate job opportunities. Up until now, those with secondary or higher education have looked primarily to the government for employment. At the present time, in an attempt to reduce the bureaucracy, the government itself is trying to enforce a freeze on new inductions into the civil service. Yet pressure for education—and upon the educational system—will continue at an accelerating rate at all levels and the outlay for education will certainly rise quite sharply. Whether education in Indonesia will result in a greater degree of social adjustment or of alienation is difficult to predict, especially in view of the experience of 1965–1966. It was then the Indonesian students who shook down the rickety Sukarno regime which they had long and wildly applauded.

Everywhere in Indonesia today the younger generation can be readily reached by the spoken, the printed, and the broadcast Indonesian word. It is not now being effectively addressed, but the potential is there. The publishing industry, which flourished briefly in the early 1950s, has not caught up with the demand for textbooks and has deplorably neglected the publication of almost everything except official handouts, religious tracts, and the flimsiest of trivia. The daily newspapers manage to pack a remarkable amount of national and international news into some four to eight pages, but there is little variety among them and little enterprise in seeking out what is not distributed by government offices or provided through the several news agencies. At present there are some 100 dailies, the three or four largest of them having circulations of about 40,000–60,000, but the national total for all 100 is only about 500,000. An equal number of magazines commands comparable circulation. The government's national radio network reaches a large audience. It concentrates heavily upon music and entertainment but does provide some news and many routine official pronouncements. Government TV, with 75,000 registered sets, supplies viewers in the major urban areas of Java with a few hours' evening entertainment plus news and official announcements. The once promising motion picture industry has yet to be revived. The mass media thus await fresh new private or official attempts to invigorate it. The reappearance in 1968 of the crusading and long-suppressed or suspended daily, *Indonesia Raya*, may perhaps be a signal of over-all change.

The increasingly well-educated Indonesian public is also increasingly healthy. According to official statistics there are now about 5,000 registered physicians. These are overwhelmingly concentrated in urban centers and attached to government medical services; but government physicians also engage in part-time private practice and some venture at least on clinical visits into rural areas. At present

Indonesia has a total of approximately 1,000 hospitals with some 80,000 beds. There are also at least 2,500 clinics and another 2,500 polyclinics, the majority of the latter in nonurban areas and operated on a part-time basis. The larger hospitals have separate maternity and child-care centers and provide, insofar as equipment and personnel permit, the full range of clinical and surgical services expected of modern institutions. The more important Indonesian universities, notably the national universities in Djakarta, Surabaya, and Bandung, operate medical schools from which, at present, about 500 new doctors graduate each year. Indonesian standards of medical education are high and medical attention at its best is excellent. But the difficulties of ordinary medical practice, whether in government institutions or in private practice, are truly formidable.

Despite the undoubted decline in standards of medical services during the late Sukarno years, the habit has now been formed by the general public to patronize government health services wherever they are available and to place great confidence in the pill, the powder, the liquid, or the other treatments which may be prescribed.

One element of Indonesian health practice which ordinarily escapes report is the very common reliance upon the *dukun*, the practitioner of many indigenous arts which extend from the brewing of herbal remedies to soothsaying. The term *dukun* covers a wide variety of avocations, and the individual *dukun* may specialize in one or combine several. The great majority of Indonesians, whether in remote rural areas or at the highest level of modern officialdom, frequently resort to the *dukun*, whether for physical or spiritual counsel. The *dukun*, moreover, is an individual of immense real and potential influence, as became apparent in the course of the political maneuvering and intrigue which accompanied the downfall of Sukarno. Along with the schoolteacher and the leader in the mosque—which he may also be—the *dukun* is a figure to whose influence the national leaders give considerable thought. One specialized *dukun* is the *dukun beranak*, or midwife, of whom there are many thousands throughout the archipelago.

Population and Polity

That Indonesia is already confronted with a population problem of crisis proportions, and that population growth is subject to calculated control—these two facts are just barely beginning to register widely in Indonesia and to call forth any real degree of response. There has not yet developed a real sense of urgency about facing one more apparently irresolvable problem with which people have already been living for a long time. Anyone can see that everywhere people are packed ever more closely on the land and in the cities, and that everywhere there are always swarms of children. Everyone can also see that most of these people somehow manage to make do and that the children seem remarkably healthy, handsome, and happy.

The thinking Indonesian today has rejected the Sukarno doctrine that Indonesia can easily support a population of 250 million. This does not mean, however, that he has accepted the thesis that since it cannot support 120 million in 1970, it cannot risk 185 million in 1985. It is not that he will not agree, when questioned, that the population problem exists and must be faced. It is that very few care to define exactly the immediate problem and even fewer care to take the lead in sounding the alarm or in pressing a program.

The reasons are numerous. In the first place, Indonesians are fatigued with crisis. They have known little except crisis for thirty years, and they are now indisposed to stir in one more major ingredient. Second, after the euphoria and the hysteria of the Sukarno years, Indonesians are reluctant to associate themselves with any scheme which may prove to be unpopular or unsuccessful. Any project to limit reproduction seems likely to be both, given the universal Indonesian craving for children, and given also the precedent of almost consistent administrative failure in the implementation of plans. Third, even the ruling Indonesian elite lacks accurate information about the techniques of family planning—both the techniques of contraception and the techniques of introducing the public to a knowledge of them. Fourth, the elite groups themselves do not feel the need for planning their own families. They are a privileged class who can afford numerous children. They have homes, cars, and servants, and the assurance of preferential treatment with regard to hospitals, schools, and jobs.

It would be very difficult to assemble any impressive collection of speeches, newspaper articles, radio scripts, TV clips, or other evidence that Indonesia's national leaders are themselves genuinely convinced and eager to convince the public that family planning is a must. It would be difficult, for that matter, to assemble posters, booklets, books, or other information disseminated by those family planning agencies which already exist. Top national figures, including President Suharto, several of his ministers, and certain leaders of various religious groups, have made occasional public statements endorsing family planning. But there has been no energetic, sustained attempt to make the nation actively conscious of the problem or of the measures which can be taken to alleviate it. On the other hand, if strong support has not yet been forthcoming, neither has any vigorous, systematic, widespread opposition.

In Indonesia the *sine qua non* of a successful family planning project is continuous, enthusiastic, widely publicized top level official support. Such support may soon be forthcoming. As of January 22, 1970, President Suharto assumed personal responsibility for the program and set up a council of 11 persons of cabinet rank to make sure that a genuine project gets started—and continued. This was not the first such attempt, but it is by far the most promising. A new agency, the National Family Planning Coordinating Body, now replaces the moribund National Institute of Family Planning, which itself semisupplanted the experimental Indonesian Family Planning Association that launched an embryonic program which the NFPCB may now adopt and bring to maturity.

The main deterrents to acceptance of family planning will be: (1) The deeply rooted traditional emphasis upon early marriage, sexual fulfillment, and a large family; (2) the religious attitude of *Insjah Allah* (meaning both "It is according to the will of God," and "Let God's will be done"); (3) ignorance and improvidence; and (4) the personal sense of privacy and modesty. None of these factors seems likely to deter the normally responsive Indonesian from listening courteously to the family planning counselor and thus perhaps letting himself be recruited.

None unless, for instance, the village religious leaders, who have sometimes made a mad mix of religion and politics, should attempt to discredit family planning as a means for opposing the group in power, alleging Koranic grounds for personal and party vendettas. But persuading the Indonesian that family planning is acceptable and even desirable does not by any means signify that he or she is going to put it into practice. Even after listening and agreeing, the ordinary Indonesian will still be heavily influenced by the factors mentioned above.

The institution of the Indonesian family places a great premium of prestige upon its own perpetuation and aggrandizement. Traditionally, boys and girls are encouraged to marry quite young; the male feels impelled to prove his virility, the female her fecundity; and the more numerous the children the greater the sense of security against the hazards to life and property. To this instinctive and institutionalized drive for offspring is added the extraordinary deep and pervasive Indonesian love for children—more and more children, anybody's children. The Indonesian family in most areas is patrilineal but in some is matrilineal. In almost all cases it calls for close ties of the children to uncles, aunts, and other more distant relatives, as well as to family friends. The system encourages an attitude toward children which manifests itself commonly in lending, borrowing, giving, soliciting, and otherwise more or less formally and permanently passing children back and forth between families. Many children in Indonesia have both parents and foster parents who are almost equally indulgent. What might seem like an excess of children in a family which is unable to support them becomes an opportunity for relatives and friends, who are able and glad to provide material support, education, and affection. To this traditional form of child insurance is now added a contemporary administrative arrangement. The Indonesian government supplements its meager stipends with special allowances and rations; it adds a 5 per cent salary allowance and an extra ration of commodities for each child without setting any limit on numbers, and other employers are obliged to follow the official example. Having more children thus seems like one way of exacting more commensurate compensation for one's service.

The general Indonesian outlook toward propagation is fortified by the teachings of the Prophet Muhammad, who counseled his followers to be fruitful and multiply. In any event, the Indonesian Muslim, devout or not, is disposed to believe that whether or not he has children—and how many children he has—is a matter of *Insjah Allah.* The Indonesian Hindu has no rigid preconceptions, but all Hindu tradition weighs in favor of more offspring. The outlook of Indonesian Christians is not particularly different. Prominent Muslim, Hindu, and Christian leaders have made statements generally favorable to family planning (the Catholics accepting only the rhythm method), and certain church groups actually propose to engage in a program. Among those who have not been heard from, however, are leaders of the Pentecostal and evangelical sects which are very active in missionary work and sometimes educational and medical work as well, especially in the outer islands.

Whatever the cultural and religious obstacles to family planning, it seems probable that the greatest will be the difficulty of persuading the human individual —and keeping him or her persuaded—that systematic family planning is worth all the trouble. This cannot be done merely by setting up clinics, as has been the primary emphasis up to now. It necessitates a massive and sustained campaign of education, information, and also—for motivation must be aroused and maintained—inducement. The ordinary Indonesian between the ages of 14 and 40, the age group which must logically constitute the major target group, is quite capable of quickly comprehending the technical, social, and economic aspects of family planning, provided the explanation is clear, simple, forceful, and repeatedly presented.

In accepting family planning, furthermore, the ordinary Indonesian has to overcome a feeling of invasion of privacy—an affront both to his personal pride and to physical modesty. Whether or not one has children is assumed to be a matter of personal and family concern and not of government interest; and medical consultation means submission to physical examination. According to the teachings of the Prophet Muhammad, as generally interpreted in Indonesia, the devout female must under no circumstances permit any male other than her husband to view her genital organs. The Indonesian woman, therefore, frequently requires reassurance that at the clinic there be female personnel on duty, and even then, she is reluctant.

Certain special aspects of Indonesian family law and custom have a direct bearing upon prospects for the family planning program. Polygamy is legal and not uncommon; it is sanctioned not only by Muslim and Hindu tradition but also by pre-Hindu, pre-Muslim custom. Even though it has become all but prohibitive economically for the ordinary man to maintain more than one wife, some still aspire to the Muslim quota of four. Polygamy is especially popular in the rural areas among those who are or wish to seem to be men of substance and prestige. In urban areas it is the practice of some of the high ranking civil and military personnel who like to emulate their aristocratic forebears or the more recent example of the Sukarno clique, among whom multiple marital and extramarital involvement was the rage. Both Muslim and Hindu tradition also permit easy marriage and divorce procedures which may amount to little more than a statement of intent or an act of registration. In urban areas and at upper levels of society, to be sure, the technicalities have become much more complex, partly by reason of the frequent necessity for legal settlements with regard to property and children, partly because both the civil and the military bureaucracies frown upon the previous more carefree practices. But the strongest pressure for tightening up legal and extralegal provisions with regard to family matters is that which is exercised by Indonesian women's organizations.

One of the most conspicuous phenomena of independent Indonesia is the emergence of women's associations and federations of women's associations, and the spread of their activities from urban areas into towns and villages and even the rural *kampongs*. These relate to every aspect of community life from health and literacy to political and (in the late Sukarno era) military recruitment. The National Women's Congress (Kongres Wanita Indonesia, or KOWANI) now claims to coordinate the activities of about 40 national groups. Virtually every modern Indonesian woman belongs to one or more organizations and is exceedingly serious about the status role and rights of women. The wives of most of the top

Indonesian leaders are themselves active leaders of women's organizations, at whose meetings they seem to be daily in attendance. From the beginning, Indonesian family planners have found their most sympathetic audiences among women's groups, and at its Djakarta Congress on February 18–20, 1970, KOWANI voted to give full support to family planning.

KOWANI and other Indonesian groups, including those previously involved in family planning, have taken note of an anomalous legal situation which could lead to serious embarrassment or even impediments to the program. The Dutch colonial legal code, which is still being rewritten piecemeal, makes it a legal offense to encourage birth control in any way. The Attorney General has announced that he will not enforce this section of the code while awaiting action on its probable revision. In Indonesia, nevertheless, a legal technicality can suddenly and unexpectedly assume immense importance, so it is conceivable that some day a legalistic crisis might arise. Another still valid provision of the Dutch colonial code prohibits abortion, and this provision has not been called into question. The subject of abortion is not publicly discussed and there is no reliable information as to its prevalence. It is public knowledge, however, that many Indonesian women have resorted to the *dukun* in cases of unwanted pregnancy.

Population Work and Research

Population work to date has been marked by courageous but sporadic efforts on the part of a committed few, but also by confusion and repeated failure to convert nebulous plans into a realistically organized program. The obstacles have been enormous. It requires both courage and audacity even to conceive of a project which would have swift and significant impact upon a population of 121 million people. It is hard to believe, furthermore, that any vast new project could be carried out without—or even with—massive governmental participation. The highly centralized bureaucracy, a legacy of the Sukarno era, remains pervasive and stifling. Yet in the brief period since 1967 a family planning project has actually emerged with increasingly helpful government sponsorship. Past and present performance, however, is not particularly auspicious of the triumphant fulfillment of a bold new $31 million Five-Year Plan (1971–1974) to recruit six million acceptors and thus to reduce the national rate of increase by 0.5 per cent.

The magnitude of the problem can best be indicated by an account of the troubled history of the semiprivate Indonesian Planned Parenthood Association (IPPA), the low-level official Indonesian Family Planning Institute (IFPI), and now the top-level official National Family Planning Coordinating Body (NFPCB). These bodies have been charged successively and until recently quite confusingly with conflicting responsibility for developing and supervising projects which were in fact rather loosely delegated to the Ministry of Health and to the voluntary and semivoluntary efforts of various private and official citizens backstopped financially and logistically by foreign sponsors and donors. It would hardly have been possible deliberately to devise a procedural arrangement more certain to bog down. Yet special circumstances made such systemlessness virtually inevitable.

The IPPA, the pioneer organization for family planning in Indonesia and theoretically responsible until April 1, 1969, for the national program, was formed in Djakarta in 1957 and soon set up several branches. An anomalous, only semi-acknowledged appendage of the Ministry of Health, the IPPA remained for the next decade rather ephemeral in organization and activity. Before and especially after the establishment of the IPPA, various Indonesians who were concerned with its activities—doctors, nurses, and leaders of civic groups—observed family planning programs in Holland, India, Singapore, and elsewhere overseas, their visits being sponsored by national and international agencies interested in encouraging similar projects in Indonesia. Some of these attended short-term training courses and returned to Indonesia to introduce activities in a scattering of Indonesian government medical institutions, particularly maternity and child health centers. But facilities and supplies were scarce, clients were few, and the basic objective was improvement of health. In any event, the increasingly frenetic politics of the Sukarno years meant that programs had to be semisurreptitious. Sukarno and the Sukarnoists railed at family planning, but the Minister of Health, Dr. Subandrio (the wife of the Foreign Minister), tolerated it and even ambiguously encouraged it at times. Under these curious circumstances, the IPPA, which in 1963 accepted aid from the International Planned Parenthood Federation and the Pathfinder Fund, survived the Sukarno era, claiming seven or eight relatively permanent branches.

After the collapse of the Sukarno regime, various international agencies, whose subsidies sustain the Suharto regime, began to apply pressure for recognition of the population problem as one of top priority—not a secondary and deferrable question, as Suharto's own advisers were then disposed to think. The still rather amorphous IPPA reanimated itself, increased its branches suddenly to about 25 and its footholds in government clinics to about 150, and began to engage in carefully targeted lobbying. In consequence, family planning became politically respectable in Indonesia in 1967; in 1968 there came the beginnings of a potentially significant IPPA program; in 1969 the government itself openly, albeit reluctantly, accepted primary responsibility; in 1970 the government belatedly assumed almost complete control; and in 1971 the Master Plan was to go into effect.

For the family planners the first coup of the year 1967 was the staging of a Symposium on Contraception—then still a daring, in fact an illegal topic—held in Bandung under the sponsorship of the Faculty of Medicine of Padjadjaran University. The second coup was a National Conference on Family Planning which was held in Djakarta in February under the direct sponsorship of the IPPA. For this conference, the IPPA elicited statements of support from three key ministries (Health, Manpower, Social Affairs), from the dynamic young Governor of Greater Djakarta, and from leaders of the various religious communities. These two conferences served for a few days at least to focus a good deal of public and official attention upon the problem which President Suharto himself was persuaded to mention in his August 16, 1967 Budget Message to Parliament:

> Looking into the future we should courageously face the fact that the increase of the population is not in balance with increase of available food

> supplies, whether produced at home or imported. We should therefore pay serious attention to efforts at family planning, carried out within the realm of planned parenthood, which are justified by the ethics of religion and the ethics of the Pantjasila. This is a major problem which will affect the fate of our future generations. Therefore its implementation should be studied and planned very carefully.

The President's statement was not altogether unambiguous. He and some of his most influential advisers were of the opinion that family planning introduced social, cultural, religious, and political problems of extreme delicacy. They felt that any program should be clearly the result of voluntary individual and public decision and demand, not of government pressure. The government therefore resisted strong representations that it should establish a cabinet-level official agency. It decided to authorize the use of Ministry of Health facilities and personnel—which had been the mainstay of the program all along—but otherwise to rely upon private or semiprivate agencies. Specifically this meant the IPPA, which was advised to continue its program and to look to overseas bodies, private and official, for the funds and supplies which the government itself would find extremely difficult to provide.

The government's attempt to straddle the private vs. official agency problem resulted in an imprecise assignment and division of responsibilities. Most family planners were government officials, but it was impossible to define the chain or rather the maze of command. The government thus appointed an *ad hoc* committee, of which the Minister for People's Welfare was a member, to try to sort things out. This was the first of half a dozen committees, teams, task forces, and missions which took a dismayed look at family planning over the next several years, each set of findings seeming to make yet another inquiry the more urgent.

The original *ad hoc* committee reported to President Suharto in February of 1968 that it was the consensus of the family planners that there should be a large-scale national program beginning with a year of training and preparation (1968), followed by the initiation of projects in the major cities (1969), and later by the extension of activities into rural areas. All projects were to concentrate primarily on the key islands of Java, Madura, and Bali, and to rely principally upon the facilities of the Ministry of Health. The committee recommendations were extremely vague regarding timetable, targets, organization, and methodology —but did indicate that there was need for quite a good deal of calculation and coordination with regard both to personnel and logistics. President Suharto assigned responsibility to the Minister for Welfare to "coordinate, guide, and supervise all aspirations that exist among the people with regard to family planning." The Minister appointed a "Formation Team" of five persons, who themselves recruited an impressive panel of distinguished citizens, who in turn recommended that what was really needed was a national project under the supervision of an official agency. In late 1968, therefore, by a series of decrees emanating from the Ministry of People's Welfare, there was created the Indonesian Family Planning Institute.

The IFPI, unfortunately, lacked leadership, authority, and clearly defined responsibility. For months it had no head and no function. It gradually accumulated a professional staff of perhaps half a dozen part-time officials, all of whom carried numerous and onerous other responsibilities. It had almost no funds of its own, and it could not spend all of what it had, so cumbersome were the administrative procedures. It was dependent for clerical and other workers upon a hundred or so persons assigned from other government offices, for there was a freeze order on recruitment of new government employees. As a minor and not very prestigious appendage of the Ministry of People's Welfare, the IFPI was instructed to take over from the IPPA as of April 1, 1969, the supervision of clinics in Java, Madura, and Bali which were actually the prerogative of the Ministry of Health. It was also to coordinate the family planning activities of the Ministry of Defense, which was setting up programs in its own medical facilities. It was somehow at the same time to supervise the remaining activities of the IPPA, which retained general control over programs in the outer islands and which was also left in charge of training and information programs. The National Planning Agency (BAPPENAS), meanwhile, was writing into its new Five-Year Plan a chapter on family planning which seemed to come as a surprise to other family planners. While the IPPA and the IFPI were thinking in general terms of reaching perhaps 600,000 new acceptors over a five-year period, BAPPENAS was thinking in terms of an annual 600,000 "prevented births." In late 1968 BAPPENAS suddenly instructed the IPPA and the IFPI to set a target of 100,000 acceptors for Year I (April 1, 1969–April 1, 1970) of the Five-Year Plan and to double the target each succeeding year.

The Indonesian family planning program had barely got under way in 1967 and 1968 as an experiment on the part of the IPPA to determine what could be done, given the available facilities and resources and the inevitable Indonesian administrative confusion. This very tentative experiment was then successively, retroactively, and arbitrarily converted into a national five-year program to reach first 600,000, then three million—now six million—acceptors. The President and his advisors, BAPPENAS, the Ministry of People's Welfare, the Ministry of Health, the IFPI, and the IPPA have entertained at various times widely different impressions as to what either was already being done or should or could be done. The IPPA had established a creaky sort of *ad hoc* operating procedure which continued to function while ideas changed and clarified. Backstopped by foreign grants which supported its headquarters operation, it propagandized a bit with the public and more especially with officialdom for a project of significant scale. Meanwhile, it accepted delivery on miscellaneous grants of supplies and equipment from overseas agencies and moved them as best it could from dock to warehouse to clinic until, in mid-1969, the Ministry of Health took over those chancy logistic functions. It persuaded more and more Ministry of Health personnel to provide family planning services in government clinics—which meant that the already overburdened medical staff had to add a few hours per week to its routine schedules. It solicited rather sporadic statistical reports from the clinics, compiled over-all records, and engaged in a bit of analysis and research. But little effort was expended to persuade people to make the effort to visit the existing clinics where, if they happened to arrive on the right day and at the right hour, and if the staff and supplies were at hand, as was far from predictable, they might be initiated into the mysteries.

It was out of this set of circumstances that the IPPA, the IFPI, and the Ministry of Health attempted in 1969 to come up with something which would qualify as a coherent national program. In an effort to bring its own plans into conformity with various others, the Ministry of Health devised a One-Year Action Plan (April 1, 1969–April 1, 1970) which revealed by inadvertence just why inaction was inevitable. The Action Plan was mainly a discourse on history and theory. It made mention of several national targets—600,000 acceptors in five years, or possibly three million—but the Ministry's own target, it appeared, was "to reach one million mothers (of child bearing age) through information." What this information might be did not become apparent, but the target group was further defined as "Mothers of more than 3 children; Mothers visiting MCH centers; Mothers at the time of postpartum." According to the Ministry's analysis, "one major handicap [to family planning] is the continuing high mortality among children," a circumstance which disposed women to have child after child. The Ministry policy, therefore, would be "to give priority . . . . to the health of Mother and Child . . . . and to convince them that once a baby is born, it will live and reach an adult age; they should be convinced that it is not necessary to worry that the child will die because of illness." The remainder of the Action Plan consisted mainly of diffuse speculation as to what projects the IFPI and the IPPA might be undertaking. The IPPA and the IFPI, meanwhile, were relying upon the Ministry of Health not just to "inform" such mothers as might come its way but to provide the reassuring statistics on acceptors.

Statistical results for the years 1968 and 1969 for a total of some 400 clinics in which family planning services were offered were rather discouraging. The target each year was a somewhat flexible 100,000. The reported scores were 37,000 and 50,000 respectively. Out of the 25 million Indonesian women of reproductive age, perhaps as many as 37–50,000 deliberately chose not to give birth that year.

The biggest and until now the most successful family planning program in Indonesia is the one in Djakarta, which has been designated a pilot project and has had the enthusiastic support of the Governor. Djakarta, a city of five million, registered 8,757 new acceptors in 1968 and 14,036 in 1969. So far, studies of the relatively successful Djakarta experiment are not very revealing. One technical fact is that in Djakarta, as elsewhere in Indonesia, the IUD is the favored method. The national breakdown by region and device for the first 11 months of 1969 (the year-end report being unavailable at the time of writing) was as follows:

	IUD	*Oral*	*Other*
Java, Bali and Madura	20,308	9,006	6,146
Outer Islands	1,744	803	275

The explanation for the popularity of the IUD seems to be that the medical staff still most commonly recommends it, first because other methods cost more, second because, in the past at least, the supply of pills was precarious, and third because they distrust the ability and inclination of the patient to follow instructions.

The family planning clinics generally charge about Rp. 100–150 ($.25–.30) for insertion of the IUD and about Rp. 100 per monthly cycle of pills—both rather high in terms of a per capita income of perhaps $5.00 per month. The clinics may make certain additional coverage charges for forms, registration, consultation, or other not very clearly specified reasons. Supplies are also available at a few private pharmacies at about three to four times the cost at the clinics. The supplies used in the government clinics are donated by foreign agencies, and the proceeds from sales help to meet miscellaneous expenses. These expenses sometimes include inducement to clinical personnel by a modest supplement of their official stipend (which comes within the $1.00–$10.00 range) and the payment of finder's fees. As yet, not much attention has been given to the subject of motivating the technician, the finder, or the acceptor, but it has been discovered that a rupiah reward helps. Also, perhaps significantly, it seems that the traditional midwives, who are in an excellent position to exert influence, may be especially responsive.

The 1968–1969 trickle of statistics on acceptors and the perennial failure to rationalize the program resulted by mid-1969 in widespread realization that it was time for really drastic action. Two important things then happened. First, local and foreign pressures for a long, hard, new look at an ailing program—and patient reiteration of the point that more births offset more rupiahs and dollars in developmental outlays—resulted almost simultaneously in mid-1969 in the creation of a special IFPI Task Force and an invitation to the World Bank to send a special demographic mission. Second, President Suharto himself was persuaded to assume personal responsibility for creating a new organization and sponsoring a new program.

The Task Force, which consisted of persons who had had personal experience with the problems and the frustrations of the program, met in Djakarta from June 19 to July 31. It produced a remarkably candid critique in which the catalogue of failures added up to an administrative fiasco of complete discoordination. But instead of precise, systematic recommendations on how the program might be implemented, the Task Force resorted to generalities. Nevertheless, its report greatly simplified the work of the World Bank Mission, which arrived to find that the inquest on the old project had already been conducted. The five-man party spent a month in Indonesia (late September to late October) and eventually prepared a voluminous report which was made available for very limited official distribution in mid-1970. The report tactfully reiterated the criticisms of the Task Force and went on to make detailed recommendations for what amounts to total new organization and strategy. The Mission emphasized three main points. First, an effective administrative system must be set up so that decisions can be taken and acted upon. Second, field workers must be effectively recruited, trained, and deployed. Third, potential acceptors must be motivated. The Mission went on to analyze in great detail the specific requirements, including the establishment of 1,500 clinical centers with adequate staff, supplies, and equipment; and the employment of 500 administrators, 500 information workers, 5,000 full-time field workers, and 20,000 part-time personnel. The Mission recommended that both the previous target of three million acceptors in five years and the estimated budget of $15,500,000 be doubled, indicating that foreign agencies could be counted upon to supply whatever funds might be necessary. It accepted the suggestion that clinical activities should be conducted through the Ministry of Health as before and that the project should focus on Java, Madura, and Bali. The objective is to reduce the birth rate on these three key islands by 0.8 per cent and that of the nation as a whole, consequently, by 0.5 per cent.

It is on the basis of the Mission Report and the Task Force Report, plus the dismal experience of the last few years, that the new Indonesian National Family Planning Coordinating Body, to which President Suharto in June 1970 appointed an army general as executive head, will now undertake to slow down the rate of population growth, which still amounts to 3 per cent per annum compounded nightly.

The family planning agencies now active in Indonesia are the still nascent INFPCB, created in 1970 to replace the earlier and now defunct IFPI as the government's planning, coordinating, and action agency; the IPPA, organized in 1957 and now in the process of redefining its program; the Ministry of Health, which has always conducted the major part of the clinical programs; and the Ministry of Defense, which has undertaken a program of unreported scale in its own hospitals and clinics.

The INFPCB at present operates out of a Djakarta headquarters with a small administrative and service staff of about 50, which it inherited mainly from the IFPI, and with a few new professional appointees. It is in process of planning a major program with a large field staff of its own to recruit acceptors, who will be served in the Ministry of Health's duly expanded facilities. It is still much too early to be more specific about the organization or the program.

The IPPA has headquarters in Djakarta with an administrative and service staff of about 20 persons; it maintains a hundred or so regional offices, each of them staffed by a couple of part-time volunteers. The IPPA supervises family planning clinics in the outer islands and provides training for family planning personnel. It has set up a National Training Center in Djakarta with a staff of ten, mainly part-time workers. It also operates six provincial training centers. According to one set of statistics, by late 1968 these centers had already trained 400 physicians, 150 midwives/supervisors, and 150 other workers. According to another set, the annual training target is 300 in Djakarta and 2,200 in the provinces. The courses are given at irregular intervals, last from two days to two weeks, and register small groups of persons sent from various government agencies.

The Ministry of Health maintains some 1,000 hospitals, 2,500 clinics and 2,500 paraclinics (village extension projects) throughout Indonesia. Family planning programs can be carried out at all of these, potentially, as well as in new and expanded facilities now being contemplated. Some 400 clinics of the Ministry of Health are the basis of the present program, and new projects are posited upon Ministry of Health cooperation. It is impossible to make any clear or accurate report on the Ministry of Health and its activities without undertaking a major research project.

The Central Bureau of Statistics, which is itself still in the process of rehabilitation and reorganization, is undertaking a series of sample surveys in order to supplement the meager and not very reliable data of the 1961 census. The Statistics Bureau takes 40,000 selected families as its sample target and compiles information regarding employment, income, and expenditure in addition to basic demographic data. As yet the activities of the Statistics Bureau have not been well coordinated with those of other government agencies. The answers to the questions which the family planners would like to ask must be extrapolated from Statistics Bureau findings which are neither clear nor very current. Only the results of the first survey (1963) have yet been released.

The University of Indonesia in Djakarta has established a small new Institute of Demography with two trained demographers on the staff who have undertaken a very limited range of teaching and research activities. The most significant project to date is an evaluation of a family planning program in Bekasi, a rural area of 800,000 population not far from Djakarta, which has been designated as a pilot project area. Findings are not yet available.

The medical schools of several Indonesian universities have undertaken limited clinical research with regard to various methods of contraception, but there have been no announcements of findings.

The Social Science Department of the University of Indonesia in 1967 conducted a survey of 2,000 respondents in the Djakarta area to determine attitudes toward family planning. The survey showed that a majority was favorably inclined but that few had any real knowledge of the subject. The survey was valuable mainly for proving the feasibility of more extensive and comprehensive studies.

The Indonesian Family Planning Association in 1967 sponsored a Ford Foundation-financed KAP survey (Knowledge, Attitude, and Practice) conducted by an American demographer with the assistance of local interviewers. The sample consisted of 2,246 married respondents in the Djakarta area, aged 15–49, half of them male, half female. The main findings were as follows: Levels of public information with regard to family planning are extremely low but there exists a strong positive attitude toward the acquisition of information. Only a small percentage of people as yet actually practice contraception or have any accurate knowledge of the various methods. Of those who know about family planning but do not practice it, the reasons given were as follows, in order of frequency: they feel no need; they want another child; they lack information on methods; they think the methods are unsafe; they have religious objections; they think the cost is too high; they have difficulty in getting assistance; their spouses object. Of those persons who do practice contraception, 42 per cent use "traditional" methods (rhythm, sponge, withdrawal); 23 per cent use "indigenous" methods (massage, herbs, etc.); 19 per cent use "conventional" methods (diaphragm, condom, foam); 16 per cent use "modern" methods (pill, loop, injection). A majority of the sample mentioned 17–20 as the ideal marriage age for women, 24–25 for men. With regard to the ideal number of children, far fewer respondents favored one, two, or three than those who voted for four, five, six, or seven. There was no significant indication of preference for male over female children. Asked whether they were interested in learning more about contraception, 72 per cent of the males and 56 per cent of the females said yes; 28 per cent of the males and 44 per cent of the females said no.

International agencies have met the major part of the cost of family planning in Indonesia to date and it is to be anticipated that the same agencies which financed previous projects will finance the new one. The United States A.I.D. Mission, which provided $270,000 in 1968, $1,050,000 in 1969, and $480,000 in 1970, was budgeting on the basis of $2–3 million for the early 1970s. The Ford Foundation was an early and major sponsor of the IFPA, to which it made various grants totaling $180,000 in 1968, $245,000 in 1969, and $50,000 in 1970. The International Planned Parenthood Federation has financed, inter alia, the National Training Center in Djakarta and certain conference expenses both in Indonesia and overseas. United Nations Agencies have contributed to various projects—$30,000 from UNDP in 1969, $5,000 from UNESCO in 1969. The World Bank contributed $34,000 in 1969. Various foreign governments have made significant gifts in cash or supplies and equipment: the Netherlands $200,000 in 1968; Japan $30,000 in 1969 and $250,000 in 1970; Sweden $28,500 in 1969 and $50,000 in 1970. The Pathfinder Fund has made relatively small grants at earlier but critical times for such special projects as visits of Indonesians to training centers overseas.

Conclusions

The Indonesian nation, with its immense human and natural resources, represents today one of the greatest gambles of the contemporary world for the national and international investor—or speculator—interested in early identification of a genuine growth area. Its economy is capable of improvements, provided the political and social turmoil of the national revolutionary period have now really subsided and the new leaders can channel into constructive programs the energies which their predecessors all too commonly wasted on agitation. As a result of the brilliant successes and the grim failures of the Sukarno era, the level of social, cultural, and political development is now far above what the economy can sustain. While the population has doubled since 1945 and its intellectual horizons have vastly expanded, the nation has become economically less and less viable. The financial gap between government revenue and expenditure is now on the order of $650 million per year—a still growing deficit which is made up by a consortium of aid-giving nations headed by the United States and Japan. The economic gap between Indonesia and certain of its neighbors, let alone the Western world, has steadily widened, and even the most heroic measures cannot within a decade produce results commensurate with the needs.

The present Five-Year Plan, of which the family planning program so far remains an unintegrated element, aims at achievable rather than ideal objectives. It is in danger of being oversold as a panacea both at home and abroad and hence of proving gravely disappointing. The Plan is no answer to the basic problem of the intolerable pressure of people upon resources. It will perhaps only provide the answer to the question of whether the Indonesians are now joining the international community of presumably scientific problem solvers. Too few thousands of qualified administrators and other professionals must now swiftly inspire too many tens of millions of peasants and laborers much more systematically than ever before to work, to save, to plan—ofttimes joylessly to forego present satisfaction for the sake of hypothetical future rewards. The recent record of the ruling elite, unhappily, has been one of profligacy, not of prudence. That of the masses has been one less of stability than of inflammability. And there persists from the Sukarno era an element of political and economic fetishism—the concept that national development cannot be scientifically calculated but only magically, mystically inspired.

Family planners have been subjected to heavy pressure to propose bigger and better programs before the earlier ones have taken hold, and to do so according to the approved contemporary international model of preparing and presenting for higher approval thick documents weighted with tables, charts, and appendices. The Indonesian method would be to operate on the basis of instinct, impulse, inspiration, and invention, and to do so with a fine show of verve and vigor. The expenditure of labor upon the document tends to distract and to exhaust, and to create the conviction that what follows will be yet another document, that the project itself will somehow eventually either be abandoned or else become self-fulfilling.

The disposition to view planning as a rite of passage into modern statehood rather than as a guide for immediate action is reinforced by the enormous difficulty of actually getting anything done in Indonesia. This is especially true if it depends upon the initiative or at least the noninterference of the vast, cumbersome, incompetent, corrupt bureaucracy. It is difficult to exaggerate the problems inherent in coping with the very machinery of government which must be utilized, for although the individual official can be both capable and cooperative, he himself is trapped within the system. The new family planning program will face the dual hazard—and opportunity—that its success will be contingent upon the creation of what will be in many respects a parallel and even a competing official organization. In this brand new government agency, personnel can perhaps be carefully screened, rigorously trained, efficiently utilized, adequately compensated, and hence will perhaps be highly motivated. None of this is true of existing agencies, although the Ministry of Health, with its relatively high percentage of professionally qualified personnel, is far better off than most. It remains to be seen whether the INFPCB sets any such electrifying precedent. If it does, it may make as important a contribution to administrative as to economic and social progress.

The enormous problems of organizing and implementing the new family planning program will be greatly simplified by the fact that it is to be confined to the three islands of Java, Madura, and Bali. Here it is relatively easy to extend the program rapidly from urban into rural areas because the communications and the logistics are more readily arrangeable. But while the 70 per cent of the nation's population which lives on Java, Madura, and Bali may be being persuaded to reduce its birth rate, the other 30 per cent in the outer islands may still be reproducing at least as exuberantly as before. A 3 per cent rate of increase for 40 million people is by no means as frightening as a 3 per cent rate for 120 million, but it does constitute a population problem of no mean dimensions. It is at least four times as formidable as that of adjacent Malaysia, where an apparently effective project is already under way, and over 10 per cent greater than that of either Thailand or the Philippines, about which demographers have become much alarmed. In effect, then, even if the new program of Java, Madura, and Bali suddenly proves effective, a population of 40 million—larger than that of any other Southeast Asian nation—may still be almost unaffected. Any major project with regard to what is the second biggest population problem in the area is now being postponed at least until the year 1975.

On the cost-accounting basis the Indonesian project to date has probably been one of the least efficient and most expensive ever undertaken. In 1969, for instance, an outlay of $3 million in foreign aid plus another $300,000 in direct Indonesian government subsidy and much more than that in indirect support resulted in a highly dubious score of 50,000 acceptors. This means an average cost per acceptor of well over $60, and although strict cost accounting cannot and should not yet apply, the project is clearly not cheap. Four hundred clinics, normally open once or twice per week for two or three hours per day, seem to have cost an average of $7,500 per clinic for services to 1.2–2.4 clients per session. The Five-Year Plan to recruit six million acceptors at a cost of $31 million must involve major improvements in efficiency. It is based upon the assumption that strenuous effort will be directed not only toward opening the clinics but also, as has not happened in the past, upon keeping them filled. The INFPCB therefore proposes—as has repeatedly been proposed before—to develop an effective propaganda program which will include not only the massive utilization of the mass media but also the employment of thousands of individual field workers for home visits and recruitment. To date, however, there has been no really convincing proposal as to how it may be possible genuinely to persuade the ordinary Indonesian to participate on a continuing basis.

Indonesian experience is not yet extensive enough to reveal how potential acceptors respond to the standard approaches. It seems safe to conjecture, however, that the average Indonesian is much less likely to be motivated by any reasoned argument about private or even community or national advantage than he is by social pressures. Few are likely to deny that limitation of offspring means increase of opportunity, or to express strong convictions that limitation is undesirable. Few, on the other hand, are likely to engage or to persevere in any such self-disciplining unless they quite clearly attract community approbation. It is conceivable that the reputedly devious Javanese may devise some arcane means of exacting compliance by bestowing or withholding the seal of social approval. On the basis of recent national experience, it would seem that if family planning is to be made popular, it must somehow be made exciting and spectacular. This might imply emphasis upon "volunteers" rather than "acceptors," and the staging of pageants featuring public citations for heroes and heroines and penalties for malefactors. All of this, however, would lead toward 1984 down the Orwellian roadway which the Suharto regime does not now at least care to travel.

The choice of tactics need not be between some opaque neo-Javanese super-subtlety or totalitarian crudity, although there is real danger of one or the other, or both, being tried. But tactics must be found, and in the choice the Indonesians will be addressing themselves to a truly critical national task. In this instance, the degree of success or failure and the distribution of credit or censure will be susceptible to fairly swift and objective determination. Regardless of all the aid and advice and even pressure which will undoubtedly be forthcoming from abroad, this is a task which only Indonesians can accomplish for themselves.

References

Nitisastro, Widjojo, *Population Trends in Indonesia* (Cornell U.P., Ithaca, N.Y.), 1970.

Pelzer, Karl J. "Physical and Human Resource Patterns," *Indonesia.* Ed., Ruth McVey. New Haven, 1963.

Sensus Penduduk, 1961—Seluruh Indonesia. (*Angka² Sementara Hasil Pengolahan 1% Sample—Diperluas.*) [Population Census of 1961—All Indonesia. (Preliminary Figures of 1% Sample—Extended.)] Djakarta, 1963.

The Author

WILLARD A. HANNA has maintained an interest in the Far East since he first went to China in 1932 as a teacher. After four years there he returned to the United States and completed his work for doctorate in English literature at the University of Michigan. During World War II, Dr. Hanna served with the U.S. Navy, reaching the rank of Lieutenant Commander. Under Navy auspices he took Japanese language training and earned an M.A. in international administration at Columbia University, and later was Chief of the Military Government Office of Education and Cultural Affairs on Okinawa. In 1946 he entered the U.S. Foreign Service and served as Chief Public Affairs Officer in Djakarta and Tokyo before joining the AUFS in 1954. Dr. Hanna has published a book on Southeast Asian Statesmen, *Eight Nation Makers,* and three collections of his AUFS Reports, *Bung Karno's Indonesia, The Formation of Malaysia,* and *Sequel to Colonialism.*

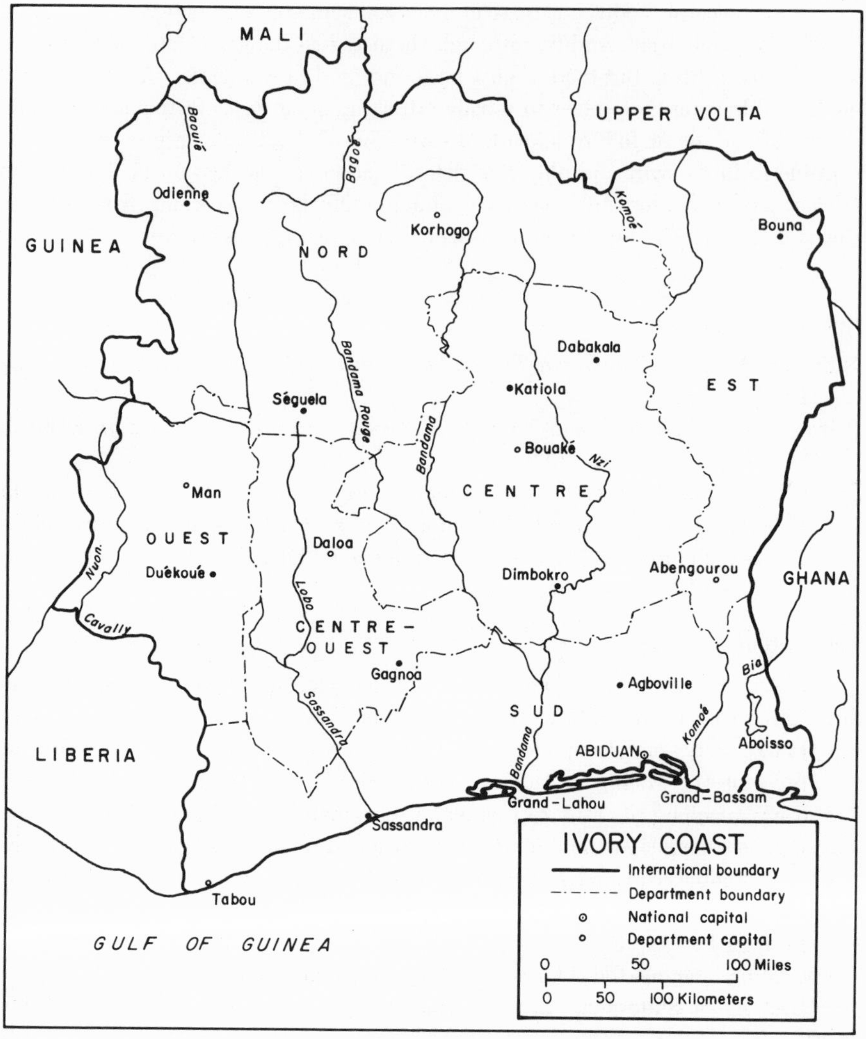

MALI
UPPER VOLTA
GUINEA
LIBERIA
GHANA
GULF OF GUINEA
NORD
EST
CENTRE
OUEST
CENTRE-OUEST
SUD
Odienne
Korhogo
Bouna
Dabakala
Katiola
Séguela
Bouaké
Man
Daloa
Duékoué
Dimbokro
Abengourou
Gagnoa
Agboville
ABIDJAN
Aboisso
Grand-Lahou
Grand-Bassam
Sassandra
Tabou
Baoulé
Bagoé
Komoé
Bandama Rouge
Bandama
Nzi
Nuon
Cavally
Lobo
Sassandra
Bia
IVORY COAST
International boundary
Department boundary
National capital
Department capital
0 50 100 Miles
0 50 100 Kilometers

Ivory Coast

Victor D. Du Bois

"Anomaly" and "miracle" are two words often used to describe the Ivory Coast. Though far from precise, both expressions convey something of the sense of awe which people come away with after visiting this country, even if only for a brief time. For this is one of the rare countries in Africa to have escaped the afflictions which in recent years have plagued so many other nations on the continent: tribal warfare, secession, military coups, financial bankruptcy, or economic stagnation. The Ivory Coast always has been the deviation from the rule—a kind of Garden of Eden where things somehow seem to be working out for the better for almost everyone concerned.

The situation is all the more remarkable in that there are many obstacles which might be expected to prevent such a state of affairs. In a land area of 123,-000 square miles, two thirds consist of savannah or semidesert, land ill suited for anything but the most primitive type of farming or stock-breeding. There are some 60 different tribes in the country, making it one of the most ethnically fragmented states in all of West Africa, second only to Nigeria. Its climate is regarded as one of the most oppressive in Africa with the mean temperature averaging 80 degrees the year around and a four to five month long rainy season. For nearly its entire history as a former colony it had to take a back seat to Senegal, long France's most favored Territory in Black Africa. Unlike Guinea, its neighbor to the west, it had no significant mineral resources and, like so many other nations in West Africa, it was a virtual prisoner of the one-crop economy (coffee) imposed on it by the colonial government. It was totally dependent on France to provide its imports and to absorb its exports.

Today the situation is vastly different. The Ivory Coast is the most prosperous of all of the former French territories south of the Sahara. Per capita income in 1970 stood at $300, foreign reserves at $150 million, and the agricultural base had been expanded to include rubber, cotton, timber, bananas, cocoa, pineapples, and palm oil products as well as coffee. Its industrial base has now surpassed Senegal's and a solid infrastructure of all-weather roads, dams, and electrification projects is being laid country-wide. Schools and hospitals are multiplying with the result that the population not only is being educated but is also being protected against diseases which formerly decimated its ranks.

What is perhaps most remarkable is that this is being accomplished under a one party political system which is one of the most liberal in Africa. In striking contrast to Guinea—richer in natural resources but plagued by economic stagnation for the past decade—there is a refreshing absence of strident xenophobia attributing all the nation's ills to outsiders, to enemies, real or imagined. Instead, there is a high degree of introspection, both on the part of President Felix Houphouet-Boigny, and on the part of other government officials.

Yet, curiously enough, this most enlightened of African countries has not undertaken a serious program of family planning. The government not only does not support family planning, but, in principle, opposes it. The dissemination of information regarding birth control methods is proscribed by law. This attitude is more surprising in that the government is fully aware that the Ivory Coast is already facing critical problems which emanate from overpopulation: a shortage of jobs; overcrowding in the cities; a severe taxing of social facilities such as schools and hospitals; and a growing tension among native Ivoiriens and the large number of foreigners who have come to settle in their country.

The reliability of statistics relating to the population of the Ivory Coast, and to other countries in ex-French West Africa, is at best problematical. Until 1958, many demographic data were subsumed under rubrics referring to the entire eight-member Federation of French West Africa (*5*). Even when demographic studies were made of individual territories, the sampling was often insufficient to warrant the kinds of extrapolations that subsequently were made. Moreover, extrapolations sometimes were based on censuses conducted in different parts of the country at different time intervals ranging up to five years.

The census of 1957–58 was the last general census conducted in the Ivory Coast. Since that time there have only been regional censuses. In the 1957–58 census and subsequent restricted censuses, several shortcomings seriously compromise the reliability of some of the data. Chief among these is the limited scope of the 1957–58 census itself. Certain important urban centers, including Abidjan and Bouaké, the two largest cities, as well as Korhogo, Agboville, Man, and Dimbokro, were excluded from the census entirely—either because they had been the subject of separate demographic investigations, or because they were scheduled to be in the future (*6*). The demographers who directed the 1957–58

POPULATION PROFILE. BASIC STATISTICS (*1*)

Total	3.1 million (1958); 3.4 million (1960); 4.1 million (1969)
Crude birth rate	51–55/1000 (1968)
Death rate	27–29/1000 (1968)

Rate of natural increase	2.2–2.8 (1968)
Immigration, emigration	Little data are available. The historic trend has generally been for people to immigrate to rather than emigrate from the country. One source estimates that as much as 40 per cent of the male working force at present comes from neighboring African countries (*2*). It is estimated that approximately 25 per cent of the total population of the country consists of foreigners, over 95 per cent of whom are from neighboring African states (Upper Volta, Mali, and Guinea predominating).
Population structure	Age-Sex Specific Structure: 43 per cent under 15 years; 47 per cent between 15–49 years; 10 per cent over 50 years (1958). No breakdown of data according to sex available.
Fertility factors and patterns	Little information is available concerning differences in fertility patterns based on social class or rural-urban distribution. The Ivory Coast is about 22.8 per cent Muslim. Polygamy has been traditionally practiced among this part of the populace as it has been among the 45 per cent who are pagan. Since 1964, however, polygamy has been officially prohibited by the government. The percentage of registered births born to women less than 20 years old in 1957–58 was 17. The median age of women registering births during this period was 26.
Mortality levels and trends	The number of deaths per 1,000 population in 1961 was estimated by one source to be 33.3. By 1968 this figure had declined to 27–29. This was still higher, however, than the average listed in the *UN Demographic Yearbook* for the ensemble of West Africa which had a higher death rate in the years 1960–1968 than the African Continent as a whole (*3*). Statistics relating to infant mortality and causes of death are not available. Life expectancy (1958) was 38–40 years.
Morbidity, causes of death	Data not available.
Estimates of future trends	Most estimates of the rate of natural increase fall somewhere between 2.2 and 2.8 per annum. At this rate it will take approximately 28 years for the population to double itself. The Economic and Social Council of the Ivory Coast estimated that the nation's population would grow to 4,400,000 by 1970 and to 5,700,000 by 1980 (*4*). Abidjan, which had a population of 550,000 in 1970, is expected to grow to 800,000 inhabitants by 1975 and to 1,100,000 by 1980.

census were keenly aware of this government-imposed limitation and were constantly handicapped by it.

Another defect derives from the insufficient attention devoted to the factor of population mobility. It was subsequently found that field investigators had not made sufficient differentiation between those persons who were permanent residents of an area and those who were merely visitors or temporary residents. Thus many individuals probably were counted twice or, what is equally bad, not counted at all. This problem was evident even in several regional censuses undertaken between 1962–1964. Subsequent analysts have claimed that, as a result of such imprecision, underestimation of the population may range from 10 to 20 per cent (*7*).

A further drawback is the scarcity of information relating to morbidity. There has been no attempt to systematically collect such information from hospital records, doctors' reports, insurance claims, etc. As a result, in the Ivory Coast as in other developing areas of the world, the state of the nation's health has tended to be evaluated almost entirely in relation to statisics of mortality, an index which can often prove to be deceptive.

Yet another factor which compromises to some extent the reliability of the 1957–58 statistics is inadequate sampling. The figure given for the general life expectancy for both sexes (35 years of age), for example, was based on a survey made of only 69 villages.

Of the sources cited in this Report, official documents of the Ivory Coast, those of the United Nations, and those of such organizations as the Office of Population of the Bureau for Technical Assistance A.I.D., none are more useful to the researcher than those emanating directly from the Ivoirien government. The statistical data are the most complete, and the numerous commentaries help to elucidate their meaning.

Population Distribution and Movement

In 1965, 23 per cent of the population of the Ivory Coast was classified as urban, while the remaining 77 per cent lived in rural areas (*8*). Table 1 gives a breakdown of the population, rural and urban, from 1965 to 1970 as well as a projection into the years 1975 and 1980.

In 1965, out of a total population of 4,300,000, only 980,000 people lived in urban centers; of these some 330,000 lived in Abidjan alone (*9*). By 1970, the total population was estimated to have increased to five million, of whom 1,450,000 lived in urban areas and 500,000 in Abidjan. Projecting on the basis of the current rate of increase (2.2–2.8), by 1975 the total population will be 5,800,000, of whom some 2,030,000 will inhabit urban areas, with Abidjan absorbing 820,000. By 1980, the last date for which such projections are available, it is expected that the nation's total population will reach 6,700,000, of whom 2,640,000 will live in urban areas with Abidjan reaching a population mark of 1,100,000.

When the first census was completed in 1958, it was estimated that of the three million persons then living in rural areas, approximately 3 per cent resided in areas other than those in which they were born (*10*). When subsequent regional

Table 1. Projected Population Growth of the Ivory Coast, 1965–1980, in thousands

	1965	*1970*	*1975*	*1980*
Urban population	980	1,450	2,030	2,640
Rural population				
Savannah region	1,460	1,520	1,410	1,460
Forest region	1,860	2,030	2,360	2,600
Total	3,320	3,550	3,770	4,060
Total population	4,300	5,000	5,800	6,700
Urban population	980	1,450	2,030	2,640
Abidjan	330	500	820	1,100
Other urban centers	650	950	1,210	1,540
Rural centers	200	230	250	270
Rural population	3,320	3,550	3,770	4,060
Resident	3,020	3,200	3,350	3,620
Transient	300	350	420	440
Europeans	30	35	40	45

Source: République de Côte d'Ivoire. Ministère du Plan. *Première Esquisse du Plan Quinquennal de Développement 1971–75. Document de travail à l'usage des Commissions de Plantification* (Abidjan: 1968), p. 24

studies were undertaken in 1962–1963, this figure was found to have declined to 73,000. A comparison of these two figures suggested to demographers that not only had internal migration from one rural area to another declined during this period, but almost one-third of the migrants who had been counted in 1958 had returned to their place of origin before 1963 (*11*).

Within the country the dominant migratory trend has been away from the savannah regions of the north and central parts of the country down toward the forest and coastal regions of the south. Approximately 90 per cent of the internal rural migration follows this general pattern (*12*). This demographic movement has been stimulated primarily by two factors: the attraction represented by Abidjan with its whole complex of new industries and the multiple job opportunities which have been created there as a result of the city's extraordinary economic expansion; and the growing number of plantations in the south which offer the prospect of prosperity to those fortunate enough to obtain land to cultivate, and those able to find employment as manual laborers on such plantations.

A further stimulus to migration toward the south, but this time to the southwest rather than toward Abidjan, is the building of the new port of San Pedro near the Liberian border. A completely new city carved out of the wilderness, San Pedro, according to some optimistic reports, within ten years after its scheduled completion in 1973 is expected to become the nation's second largest city.

Rural-urban migration. A notable demographic trend in the Ivory Coast in recent years has been the exodus of people from rural areas to urban centers. Although a number of Ivoirien cities have undergone substantial growth over the last 15 years, none has increased in size and stature as rapidly as Abidjan. In 1955 the city had a population of 125,000; by 1960 it had grown to 250,000; by 1964 to 350,000; by 1967 to 450,000; and by 1970 to half a million. The city's annual rate of growth averaged 11.5 per cent during the period 1948–1963. Since then it has increased to 14.5 per cent per annum (*13*).

Professor Michel Bloch-Lemoine, a French sociologist who has made the most comprehensive study to date of Abidjan (*14*), points out that while about 17 per cent of the city's population at any one time consists of migrants, in fact, only 8 per cent actually remain in Abidjan; the other 9 per cent leave the city within five years to return to their place of origin (*15*).

One of the most striking demographic characteristics about Abidjan is the youthfulness of its population. Citing figures for 1967, Bloch-Lemoine estimated that 36 per cent of the population was under ten years of age; 44 per cent was under 15; and 57 per cent was under 20. Only 3 per cent was older than 50 years of age (*16*).

It is also notable that although Abidjan is the political and administrative capital of the country, as well as its commercial center, only one half of its population in 1965 consisted of Ivoiriens; the other half was made up of a melange of Africans from neighboring countries, Europeans, and Levantines. Of the 50 per cent of the population in Abidjan that was Ivoirien, only one half was actually born in the city, including those children born in the Ivory Coast of non-Ivoirien parents (*17*). The Baulé, the largest ethnic group in the country, still maintained a precarious majority over all other ethnic groups living in the capital (30,000). Immediately after them, however, the largest single ethnic group in the city was the Mossi (25,000), natives of the Upper Volta (*18*).

Emigration. Traditionally, people have migrated to the Ivory Coast rather than from it. Numerous peoples—mainly from neighboring African states, but also from Europe and the Middle East—have come to the Ivory Coast because it has offered them the opportunity of making a better living than they could at home. Immigration has been continuous, varying in intensity depending on the political and economic climate prevailing at the time (*19*). Today (1970) it is estimated that about one quarter of the total population is of foreign origin. The overwhelming number of these foreigners (95 per cent), of course, are African (*20*).

Although reliable statistics relating to the national origin of the foreigners residing in the Ivory Coast are very difficult to come by, it is estimated that, of the million or so living in the Ivory Coast in 1969, approximately 500,000 were Voltaics; 200,000 were Maliens; 150,000 were Guineans; 40,000 were Senegalese; 35,000 were Europeans, mainly French; 15,000 were Ghanaian; 10,000 were Nigerian; 10,000 were Dahomeans or Togolese; and 4,000 were Nigérien; the remainder were from other African countries.

It is estimated that fully 70 per cent of the foreign Africans, prompted by

economic considerations, have settled in the southern third of the country (*21*).
This has been especially true of the Voltaics, most of them Mossi, who have flocked there by the tens of thousands. It is in the southern forest and coastal regions that the land is most fertile and therefore where the greatest number of jobs has been available. During the period 1954–1958 when the government undertook to increase its agricultural production of coffee and cocoa—its two principal cash crops at the time—Ivoirien planters were encouraged to expand their fields. Many did so, using Voltaics as the principal source of labor, often on a tenant-farmer basis. So great was the influx of these Voltaics and so great was their contribution to the local economy that between 1950 and 1965 agricultural production on southern plantations more than quadrupled (*22*).

Thousands of other Voltaics were attracted to the urban centers along the coast, and especially to Abidjan, where a rapidly expanding economy held out the prospect of finding jobs in the new factories, stores, port facilities, and other business enterprises being created there; thousands more went to work as domestics in the houses of well-to-do Europeans and Africans.

The entire demographic picture in the south began to change as the Mossi emigrants started to appear as transient and in some cases as permanent residents of the towns and rural areas. The large, industrial plantations, particularly those producing palm oil, came to be overwhelmingly dependent on foreign migrant labor (*23*).

One of the most striking demographic features of the migrants—both native Ivoiriens who come from the poorer, northern regions of the country and foreign Africans—is their youth. Extrapolating on the basis of a sampling of 75 villages, it has been estimated that 60 per cent of those persons who had left their native villages to work elsewhere were between the ages of ten and 30 (*24*). In many of the villages studied, fully one third of the economically active male population was away for at least six months of the year in search of work in the south.

Certain economic repercussions are immediately apparent. On the one hand, both the northern part of the Ivory Coast—the most unfavored part of the country—and the nations from which the foreign migrants come are being deprived of a substantial portion of the youngest and most dynamic part of their population. There are fewer active people left to cultivate the land and contribute to its development. On the other hand, part of the country is being flooded by large numbers of people in search of work. The abundant supply of cheap labor has contributed substantially to an increase in agricultural production averaging 7 per cent over the last fifteen years (*25*). This has not been due to the introduction of any technical innovation in farming techniques but to a more extensive cultivation of the land. In a number of cases, most notably in the production of coffee, yield per acre is still regarded as mediocre (*26*).

Harmful effects one might expect to ensue from the draining of the northern part of the Ivory Coast and of the neighboring African states of a substantial portion of their most able young men have to a considerable extent been offset by the funds which these migrant workers remit to their relatives who remained at home. Lecour Grandmaison estimates that the average migrant sends home to his family about 20,000 CFA francs ($80) per year (*27*). In most cases, he points out, this is as much if not more money than the individual could earn from working the land in the parched savannah regions of the north. In both the poorer regions of the Ivory Coast and in a number of neighboring African states (especially the Upper Volta and Mali), this steady flow of funds from migrant workers has been a major factor contributing to economic stability.

Population and the Economy

The Ivory Coast's major natural resources are the exceptionally fertile soil in the southern part of the country and vast timber resources. Its traditional export crops have been coffee and cocoa but in recent years palm oil products, coconuts, bananas, pineapples, cotton, and rubber have been introduced or greatly expanded in an effort to diversify the country's agricultural base. In addition, some minerals, notably manganese, diamonds, gold, bauxite, and iron ore, have also been discovered but have not yet been extensively exploited.

Since 1958 the economy has been expanding at over twice the rate of the population (7–9 per cent per year for the economy vs. 2.5 per cent per year for the population). The future seems to augur well, at least for the time being. As a French colony, moreover, the Ivory Coast was and has remained since independence a member of the franc zone. France continues to be its chief trading partner, providing most of its imports and absorbing most of its exports.

The government of the Ivory Coast defines the economically active population as "persons of working age" (*28*). The definition sets no limits at either end of the age continuum but it is meant to exclude both young children and elderly people who do not contribute actively or substantially to the productive capacity of the nation. In 1958, the government estimated that, of a total population of 3,100,000, there were 1,700,000 persons of working age (*29*). Of this number, 1,500,000 were classified as rural workers, and of these approximately 80,000 received wages of some kind. There were also some 65,000 persons working in what was termed the modern sector, of which some 2,000 were employers while the rest were employees (*30*). By 1960 the total population in the Ivory Coast had climbed to 3,225,000, of whom approximately 1,455,000 were classified as inactive (*31*).

After 1960, the government discarded this dichotomy in favor of a more detailed breakdown into general categories of employment. Table 2 is a projection of the growth of salaried workers in the Ivory Coast from 1965 to 1980 (*32*).

Employment in Abidjan. Between 1955 and 1963 the number of jobs available in the Abidjan area increased at the rate of 8 per cent, and during the period 1958 to 1964 the average African wage also increased by 8 per cent (*33*). This expansion of the job market, however, was inadequate to meet the needs of all the newcomers who had migrated to the city. To meet these needs, Abidjan will have to create approximately 125,000 new jobs during the decade 1965–1975 (*34*). That there is an increasingly serious shortage of jobs in Abidjan is attested to by the huge crowds of unemployed which gather every day in front of the Office de la Main d'Oeuvre, the state employment office. According to official

Table 2. Public and Private Sector Employment by Industry in the Ivory Coast, 1965–1980

	Number of workers 1965	*Number of workers 1970*	*Number of workers 1975*	*Number of workers 1980*
Agriculture, forestry & fishing	118,000	173,000	246,000	281,000
Industry	26,900	43,400	70,000	93,900
Construction	15,400	26,200	36,200	41,800
Transport	19,000	25,100	34,600	43,300
Commerce & service industries	22,600	33,200	44,800	58,300
Government	30,500	42,400	57,700	76,700
Totals	232,400	343,300	489,300	595,000

Source: République de Côte d'Ivoire. Ministère du Plan. *Première Esquisse du Plan Quinquennal de Développement 1971–75. Document de travail à l'usage des Commissions de Planification* (Abidjan: 1968), p. 26

figures submitted by this agency to the government, it received 28,404 requests for jobs from Africans during the year 1965. The number of jobs it offered the African population, however, totaled only slightly over 9,000, and of this number only 6,688 actually resulted in confirmed placements.

Figures for both African and non-African (i.e., European) employment requests and placements are given in Table 3. Of the total number of requests

Table 3. Employment Requests and Placements through the Office de la Main D'Ouevre, Abidjan, 1965

Type of request	*Number of requests for employment*		*Number of offers of employment*		*Number of actual placements confirmed*	
Abidjan's central office . . .	21,582	1,175	8,426	817	5,946	468
Neighborhood offices	3,793	—	764	—	742	—
Mail	3,029	1,826	—	—	—	—
Total number of requests . . .	28,404	3,001	9,190	817	6,688	468
Totals	31,405		10,007		7,156	

Source: Situation Économique et Sociale de la Côte d'Ivoire, Conseil Économique et Social (Abidjan: Imprimerie nationale), p. 242

made for jobs by the African population, less than one-quarter were satisfied.

These figures, moreover, present only a partial view of the real unemployment figure. Many Africans in Abidjan, despairing of ever finding employment through the Office de la Main d'Oeuvre, simply do not register with it but choose instead to go job hunting on their own.

Population and Development

In the Ivory Coast, as in a number of other West African countries, large migration streams which once were almost entirely rural in destination now are being increasingly absorbed by the country's urban centers, especially by Abidjan, which by 1969 was growing at the rate of 50,000 persons per year. It is in this city that the material aspects of population pressure are most acute.

Abidjan is already faced with a serious housing shortage. In 1965, President Houphouet-Boigny publicly announced that the goal of the government was ". . . that within ten years, there will no longer be a single slum in the Ivory Coast" (35). If this utopian goal is to be reached within this time limit—a most unlikely event—then in the remaining years there will have to be a sharp upturn in both urban and rural construction. The government will have to build some 6,000 dwellings a year just to keep up with the influx into the capital, and it will have to build an additional 2,000 housing units to replace those already existing that fall into ruin or are otherwise rendered uninhabitable.

Two ecological problems, moreover, seriously threaten the Ivory Coast at the present time: the erosion of land in the northern savannah regions resulting from slash and burn agriculture; and the gradual denuding of the forest region of the south resulting from excessive cutting of timber for export. The government has been slow, thus far, to implement a vigorous reforestation program.

Of more immediate concern, however, is a third problem. It emanates from the proposed resettlement of some 70,000 persons in new lands made arable by the construction of the giant Kossou Dam, which will harness the Bandama River and create a huge backup lake. Eighty per cent of the people involved in this resettlement scheme are Baulé, the Ivory Coast's largest ethnic group. And although the areas into which they will be moved also are populated mainly by Baulé, there is considerable concern in government circles over how well they will be received by the established population. Land pressures in the populous forest regions are already great and a number of conflicts between the newcomers and the old settlers have occurred.

Social-attitudinal aspects. Social status in the Ivory Coast is determined largely by one's economic position and the amount of political influence one is thought to wield with other important people in the social system. Other determinants of social class—education, living standard, especially the possession of external signs of wealth such as a fine house, car, clothes, etc.—are subordinate. During the colonial era, race and the ability to speak French correctly also affected one's ascription to a particular social class. As was common in other parts of the colonized world, Europeans, irrespective of how humble their own financial situation, merely by virtue of being white automatically were regarded as members of the ruling class.

More specifically, the social hierarchy in French African colonial society was divided roughly into five groups, all of which merged rather gracefully into one another instead of being rigidly differentiated. At the top were the elite French (mainly top colonial officials, the directors of important business enterprises, senior military officers, and well-to-do planters) and the elite Africans, the latter consisting principally of high-ranking government officials (deputies to the French Parliament and local territorial assemblies, senior civil servants). Next were the rest of the European settlers (lower-ranking civil servants, business employees, teachers, military personnel, owners of small shops, etc.—the whole gamut of people usually referred to by the derisive term "petits blancs"). Then came the lower-ranking African civil servants, teachers, small businessmen and employees; after them came African laborers and low-ranking African military personnel. And at the very bottom of the social ladder came everyone else—the masses of ordinary Africans who usually were both illiterate and jobless.

With the coming of independence this social structure remained basically the same. Most of the changes that have taken place have occurred at the upper two levels. The government elite is now almost entirely Ivoirien rather than French, although there were still in 1969 some 3,000 Frenchmen attached to the Ivory Coast government in some advisory capacity. Foreign diplomats and the directors of important but non-French business concerns new to the country have easily melded into the old elite structure. Further down the social ladder, a growing number of European entrepreneurs and ordinary employees have flocked to the Ivory Coast since 1960—because of the higher wages they can earn there —and have swelled the ranks of the *petits blancs.*

The spread of education, the growth in the government bureaucracy, and the thousands of new job opportunities resulting from the economic boom over the last two decades—all have provided a great deal of impetus for the upward mobility of many Africans who previously had no chance for advancement. While in the rural areas social stratification is still structured along more traditional lines involving kinship, caste, age group, these criteria tend to play a much less important role among the growing urban classes.

Insofar as prospective programs of family planning are concerned, therefore, it is clearly among the growing urban middle class that the chance for success is likely to be greater. These people—caught between the spiraling cost of living and their inability to enhance significantly their own standard of living because of excessive burdens thrust upon them by the large numbers of relatives they must support—are showing a greater interest in the practice of birth control.

Population and Society

The cultural availability of the average inhabitant of the Ivory Coast to influences favoring family planning is at present minimal. Not only is the dissemination of information regarding such programs officially forbidden by law, but there are few forces at work conducive to their growth. There are at present no family planning programs in operation in the Ivory Coast, and none is projected for the foreseeable future.

The educated—concentrated for the most part in the urban centers—have not as yet been systematically exposed to the kind of propaganda necessary to get a family planning program off the ground. Their access to information is extremely limited and their membership in the Roman Catholic Church has tended to discourage many of them from thinking of participating in such programs even if they were available.

In the hinterland the situation is worse. All of the retrogressive factors which mark traditional society and which impede modernization are present: rigid social structure; susceptibility to magic and superstition; confinement of women to an inferior status suited mainly for child-bearing; and resistance to innovation from any source. When to these rather formidable obstacles is added the fact that about 80 per cent of the populace is illiterate, the difficulties involved in communicating family planning information are readily apparent.

Moreover, there is on the part of many Africans, Ivoiriens, and others, a pronounced feeling of helplessness in the face of calamities. Concomitant with this feeling is a conviction that one ought not to try to interfere with events or try to influence them—especially where the birth of children is concerned—because such is God's will. This feeling is reinforced by the pagan religions as well as Islam and Christianity.

Public health situation. At the time of its independence in 1960, the Ivory Coast already had a solid and well-functioning medical infrastructure. Major hospitals and research institutes were working in close harmony with comparable institutions in other parts of French West Africa and in France; diseases such as yellow fever and smallpox, which formerly ravaged the population, had been brought under control, and efforts were being made to extend at least a modicum of medical facilities to all parts of the country.

Since independence, the public health situation has continued to improve. As of 1963 there was a total of 170 medical doctors (97 African, 73 European) in the country, 117 of whom worked in public health and the remainder of whom were engaged in private practice. There were also 65 pharmacists (10 in the public health service), 108 midwives, and 1,711 medical assistants, all of them in the public health service. Only nine dentists, four in public health service and five in private practice, served the entire population.

The ratio of medical doctors to number of inhabitants was 1/20,600, but even this figure is misleading since the available doctors were so maldistributed, with many practicing in the nation's urban centers, especially Abidjan, and comparatively few being available in the rural areas.

Educational profile. Since 1960, the Ivory Coast has made impressive progress in all domains related to education. In that year the enrollment rate at the primary school level for the entire country was 28.45 per cent and the number of children enrolled in primary schools stood at 200,046. By 1965 the enrollment rate for the primary level had climbed to 43.61 per cent, with a total of 347,133 pupils actually in school, an increase of 73.52 per cent. Table 4 traces this increase during the period 1960–1965.

The rise in the number of children attending secondary schools has also been

Table 4. Primary School Enrollment in the Ivory Coast, 1960–1965

School year	*Total estimated population*	*Total number of school-age children*	*Total number of children in school*	*Rate of enrollment*
1959–1960	3,350,000	703,000	200,046	28.45
1960–1961	3,435,000	721,000	238,772	33.11
1961–1962	3,520,000	739,000	263,452	35.65
1962–1963	3,605,000	775,000	310,820	40.10
1963–1964	3,690,000	787,000	330,551	42.00
1964–1965	3,780,000	796,000	347,133	43.61

Source: Report on Education in the Ivory Coast from 1960–1965 delivered by Mr. Lambert Amon Tanoh, Minister of National Education, Fourth Congress of the PDCI held in Abidjan on September 23, 24, and 25, 1965

spectacular. In 1960 there were only 8,326 students enrolled in secondary schools throughout the country. By 1965 this number had grown to 22,682, an increase of 172.42 per cent (*36*).

During the period 1965–1975, it is estimated that school-age children will increase to four times the present number. To provide for this increase during the ten-year period, the government will have to establish facilities for 2,000 new classrooms; and to achieve the 100 per cent enrollment it has set as its goal, it will be necessary to establish 3,700 new classrooms.

In 1965, there were also 3,909 students attending some 14 technical schools around the country. In addition to the schools mentioned above there are various schools run by certain government ministries to give specialized training to their own personnel. Among the most prominent are the École Nationale d'Administration, which, like its French counterpart, is an elite civil service school; the École des Mines in Daloa; the École des Cadres in Bingerville (agriculture); and the École des Beaux Arts et de la Musique in Abidjan.

The University of Abidjan opened in 1964 and now has an enrollment of about 2,000 students. Although the physical plant is still under construction the university already has faculties of law, arts and sciences, and letters. A new medical school is slated for completion in 1972.

The government has augmented its expenditures on education from 12.5 per cent of the national budget in 1960 to 21.8 per cent in 1965. It is doubtful, however, that even with this sizable increase it will be able to resolve the urgent problem of educating the nation's youth in view of the inordinately high cost which such education involves (*37*).

Population and Polity

The Ivory Coast government thus far has not encouraged the dissemination of birth control literature, going even so far as to prohibit it under law. This is not to say that the subject is completely ignored. Many of the nation's more enlightened leaders, including President Houphouet-Boigny, a former medical doctor, clearly recognize the merits of a family control program. For the time being, however, the problem is not felt by Ivoirien leaders to be sufficiently serious to justify an official change in policy. Nevertheless, for those who wish to practice birth control the government offers no really active opposition. Birth control pills and contraceptives of other types can be purchased openly in any pharmacy, usually without prescription, and doctors and pharmacists freely advise people on the matter whenever such counsel is sought.

Abortion does not pose the problem in the Ivory Coast that it frequently does in other, more industrialized nations. The few women who seek an abortion are usually European. African women, even unmarried ones, rarely do, in part because such operations generally are quite costly, but more important, because there is little stigma attached to having children out of wedlock. Given the prevalence of premarital sexual intercourse among so many of the Ivoirien youth and the common law marriage pattern, such "illegitimate" births are a common thing and do not inspire the fear of social ostracism that so often besets women in the West.

In 1964 the Ivoirien government passed a new Civil Code whose impact on social structure and family size is bound to be great. Among other things, it raised the civil status of women to the equal of men and completely revised the marriage code. With regard to the latter, it forbade child betrothal and polygamy (38), and also did away with the practice of charging an excessive bride price. Although they were not intended as such, all of these measures are likely to result in a reduction of the birth rate.

Aside from a few people in the Ministry of Health and a small number elsewhere in the government, there are few in the Ivory Coast who openly champion the cause of family planning. The idea has never gained wide currency among the leadership of the country and there is no figure of primary political importance who has openly and unequivocably urged its adoption as official government policy.

Various factors may account for this lack of interest. Many members of the Ivoirien elite are Roman Catholic and the lay population, like the clergy, European as well as African, have felt impelled to submit to papal dictate. Pressure against the adoption of such a program also has been forthcoming from leaders of the Ivory Coast's sizable Muslim community (about a quarter of the total population), still resentful over the government's abolition of polygamy under the new Civil Code.

There is another, more subtle political reason why birth control has not been advocated. In the minds of many Ivoirien leaders there is a genuine fear that it will lead to a weakening of the country vis-à-vis its neighbors, especially Guinea and Ghana. While many of these leaders would no doubt favor the vigorous implementation of such a program among the foreign Africans who reside in the Ivory Coast and compete with Ivoiriens for jobs, they are loath to see such a program established among themselves. For the foreign Africans, on the other hand, the Ivory Coast is the ideal place to have large families precisely because conditions are so much better than back at home.

Finally, Ivoirien leaders display an almost unhealthy optimism that the continued prosperity of the country can accomplish any miracle, including that of solving increasingly serious population problems. According to this reasoning, the more the country develops its social and economic infrastructure, the quicker it will be able to convert the parched, arid lands of the northern savannah into pleasant, salubrious places easily able to accommodate the nation's peoples.

Attitudes toward population programs. The Ivory Coast shares with other nations of West Africa certain socio-psychological characteristics affecting in a crucial way the nation's attitude toward population control programs. One of the most important is the common desire for large families.

Among the nation's multiple ethnic groups, both indigenous and foreign African, certain factors have traditionally favored the having of numerous progeny. A man's prestige was intimately associated in the minds of his relatives and neighbors with the number of children he had. Until very recently, moreover, most of the population was engaged in subsistence agriculture rather than in the cash economy, and children were regarded as an economic asset. They were looked upon as not so much an extra mouth to feed as an extra hand in the field. Given the stringent social requirements to which they were held concerning the support of their parents and relatives in their later life, they were also regarded as a form of social security for old age.

Quite aside from this purely economic conception of children as instruments of labor value, however, various societal institutions and sanctions encouraged a vigorous fertility among the population. Marriage of women at a very early age (until quite recently the age of consent was 13), the widespread practice of polygamy, and the tradition of a man inheriting his brother's wife (or wives) at the time of his death, all abetted the growth in population.

It is important to note in this connection that neither the religions indigenous to West Africa nor those more recently imported into the Ivory Coast (Islam and Christianity—the latter, for the most part, Roman Catholicism) tended to discourage the having of large numbers of children. The absence of such traditional methods of controlling births as abortion, infanticide, coitus interruptus, or deliberate celibacy, coupled with the general absence of birth control methods and devices, due in large measure to the discouragement of their use by the government and their condemnation by religious leaders, all have figured as significant factors affecting the fertility rate.

Offsetting, though by no means counterbalancing, the factors contributing to an increase in the fertility rate has been the number of persons expiring as a result of the high degree of syphilis, gonorrhea, nutritional deficiency, psychoneuroses and other nonvenereal diseases.

There has never been a survey conducted in the Ivory Coast which has sought to determine whether the people were or were not in favor of seeing their government or even a private agency initiate a family planning program. And it is highly unlikely that such an initiative will be undertaken at any time in the foreseeable future.

Demographic Research and Training

Since 1958 the quality of demographic research in the Ivory Coast has been steadily improving. Several government and private agencies with a great deal of expertise have been entrusted with the task of compiling data. Among the most important of the government agencies are the Direction de la Statistique of the Ministry of Economic and Financial Affairs, and the Commissions de Planification of the Ministry of Planning. Of the private firms, one of the best known is the Société d'Économie et de Mathématiques Appliquées (S.E.M.A.), now engaged in doing a demographic study of Abidjan. At the École de la Statistique, students are obliged to take courses in demography in order to qualify for a diploma as an *agent technique* or *chef de travaux statistique*.

There are at present no international agencies in the Ivory Coast working on family planning programs, although the Ford Foundation did provide travel grants to a number of Ivoiriens so that they could take part in the summer family planning workshop held at the University of Chicago in 1969.

Conclusions

The government of the Ivory Coast is perhaps the most progressive in all of French-speaking Black Africa. Its leaders have earned the respect of the international community for the intelligence and foresight they have brought to bear on virtually every aspect of national planning. The prosperity the nation enjoys today, and the high degree of competence of many of its civil servants, both attest to the determination of Ivoirien leaders to build their country on a firm foundation. This is one of the few countries in West Africa where careful and objective feasibility studies, divorced from political delusions of grandeur, are undertaken before any major project is begun. Economic policy, of course, is not totally independent of political considerations. This is not, and cannot be, the case in the Ivory Coast or in any other country. What distinguishes the Ivory Coast from other West African countries (notably Senegal, Guinea, and Ghana under Nkrumah) is that economic policy has not been based to as great a degree purely on political expediency.

The one conspicuous exception to this otherwise laudable record is the government's failure to initiate a family planning program. In the absence of any official statement either from the President or from other high-ranking officials, one can only conjecture what their reasons are.

Certainly, Ivoirien leaders' disquiet over the unusually large number of foreigners in their country is a significant factor. There is a genuine fear on the part of many Ivoiriens that, unless this growing stream of foreign migrants can somehow be stemmed, they may one day find themselves a minority in their own country. Serious tensions have been developing for some years between Ivoiriens and non-Ivoiriens over competition for jobs, housing, schools, and other social benefits.

During the colonial era, popular dissatisfaction could be directed against the French. The cry then was for independence and "Africanization," for government power to be transferred from the whites to the blacks. This has been done. The cry that now is being heard with more frequency is for "Ivoirienization." In view of the fact that in the Ivory Coast, as elsewhere in the underdeveloped world, there simply are not enough jobs, there is an increasingly persistent demand being made by the more articulate elements in society that what jobs are available should first go to native Ivoirien citizens.

The complexity of the problem of citizenship is exacerbated by an ambiguous legal status: the government has not yet resolved the question of whether or not the foreign Africans should be accorded the same rights as Ivoirien citizens. Efforts in 1965 by President Houphouet-Boigny to equalize their status by awarding dual nationality at least to all of those who were citizens of the Entente states (39) met with such widespread hostility from the Ivoirien populace that the plan was hastily withdrawn and has not been revived.

The government has dealt with the problem by avoiding the issue. There have been no further debates either in the National Assembly or in other government councils concerning the rights and responsibilities of this huge foreign population. The government collects taxes from them and allows them limited rights with respect to schools, hospitals, and other social facilities, but it has quietly began to limit severely their access to the better-paying jobs in the country.

So long as prosperity in the Ivory Coast continues, and Ivoiriens and foreigners alike derive some tangible benefits from the government's present economic policies, a crisis may be averted. If for any reason the economy in the Ivory Coast should suddenly take a downturn and large numbers of people are unemployed, then the issue will rapidly come to a head. And in view of the acute sensitivity of the people on the subject, it would be a political risk of the highest order for the President or any other official to urge at this time the adoption of a birth control project that would seem to limit in any way the growth potential of the Ivoirien people.

The new Civil Code with its basic reform of traditional marriage practices is an indication that the government is aware of the population problem but is seeking to deal with it in a legalistic fashion rather than through a concerted family planning movement. Such an approach is in many ways more radical than the implementation of a birth control program could be, for unlike the latter, which is essentially limited in scope and voluntary in nature, the former is mandatory and applies to everyone in the nation.

Other provisions of the new Civil Code call for the recording of all births and deaths, the registration of all aliens, the performance of all marriage and divorce proceedings before civil rather than before traditional authorities, and a periodic census of the nation—all giving evidence that the government is attempting to bring greater rigor into the field of population control.

To introduce a family planning program into the Ivory Coast, it will first be necessary to enlist the support of influential people both within the government and outside of it. It will also be necessary to overcome the resistance of the Catholic hierarchy and of the leaders of the Muslim and pagan religious communities, all of whom, for the moment at least, are unalterably opposed to the introduction of such a program. That the government itself is beginning to give ground is indicated by the fact that it allowed several of its citizens to participate in the summer family planning workshop that was held at the University of Chicago in

1969. This may have been only a modest concession, but at least it was a promising first step in the right direction.

Notes

1. The statistics cited in this paper from the 1957–58 census, the last complete census taken in the Ivory Coast, were taken from the following source: République de Côte d'Ivoire. Ministère des Affaires Economiques et Financières. Direction de la Statistique. *Enquête Démographique 1957–1958, Résultats définitifs. Supplément Trimestriel au Bulletin Mensuel de la Statistique,* 8e Année, No. 1, 1er Trimestre 1966 (Abidjan: 1966), p. 6.

   The more recent statistics (those from 1960 on) cited in this immediate summary were taken from various sources, the most important of which were: U. S. Government. *Population Program Assistance. Aid to Developing Countries by the United States, Other Nations, and International and Private Agencies.* Agency for International Development, Bureau for Technical Assistance. Office of Population (Washington, D. C., October 1969) [hereafter referred to as PPA] (A.I.D., 1969); and United Nations. Department of Economic and Social Affairs. *Demographic Yearbook: 1968.* Statistical Office of the United Nations (New York: 1969).
2. Amin, Samir. *Le Développement du Capitalisme en Côte d'Ivoire.* Les Éditions de minuit (Paris: 1967), p. 284.
3. During this same period, by comparison, the number of deaths per 1,000 population in West Africa was 26; in Africa as a whole, 21; in Europe, 10; and in North America, 9. *U.N. Demographic Yearbook: 1968,* p. 104.
4. République de Côte d'Ivoire. Conseil Économique et Social. *Rapport sur l'évolution économique et sociale de la Côte d'Ivoire 1960–1964* (Abidjan: Imprimerie Nationale, Décembre 1965), p. 185. Hereafter referred to as *Conseil Économique et Social, Rapport 1960–1964.*
5. The other territories were Senegal, Guinea, Niger, the Upper Volta, the French Soudan (the present Republic of Mali), Dahomey, and Mauritania.
6. In 1955 a separate census was taken of Abidjan; in 1956–1957, of the towns of Abengourou, Agboville, Dimbokro and Man; and in 1958, of the city of Bouaké.
7. République de Côte d'Ivoire. Ministère du Plan. *Côte d'Ivoire 1965: Population* (Abidjan: 1967).
8. The Ivory Coast government defines an area as urban if it has a population of 5,000 or more.
9. These and other statistics immediately following are drawn from the following source: République de Côte d'Ivoire. Ministère du Plan. *Première Exquisse du Plan Quinquennal de Développement 1971–1975, Document de Travail à l'Usage des Commissions de Planification* (Abidjan, 1968), p. 24. For purpose of brevity hereafter referred to as "Première Esquisse du Plan Quinquennal."
10. This figure and other statistics immediately following are cited from B. Lecour Grandmaison, "Migrations et Croissance Economique en Côte d'Ivoire,"

paper presented at the Congrès International des Etudes Africaines, Montreal, 15–18 Octobre 1969 (mimeographed form), p. 3.

11. One reason which may account in part for this was that the government, which is the chief purchaser of coffee—the nation's major cash crop—lowered its purchase price of this crop at that time in an effort to discourage further planting of coffee in order to reduce its surpluses.
12. Lecour Grandmaison, *op. cit.,* p. 7.
13. Michel Bloch-Lemoine, *Abidjan, Mythes et Réalités.* Conférence prononcée le 17 Octobre 1967 à la Fraternité Saint-Dominique [mimeographed] (Abidjan: 1967), pp. 4–5.
14. The monograph cited above is but one of the many studies which Professor Bloch-Lemoine has made of the Ivory Coast capital. A number of others have never been published.
15. Bloch-Lemoine, *op. cit.,* p. 5.
16. *Ibid.*
17. *Ibid.,* p. 6.
18. *Ibid.*
19. Prior to 1958 this movement of people from one state to another was facilitated by the fact that most of the various territories in Francophonic Africa, south of the Sahara, were constituent territories either of the Federation of French West Africa or the Federation of French Equatorial Africa. Inasmuch as all the people were either French citizens or French subjects, they were free to travel and settle anywhere within the French Empire. This resulted in the emigration of large numbers of people from the poorer, less economically developed states such as Dahomey, Togo, Mali, and Niger to the richer, more economically advanced states such as Senegal, Guinea, and especially the Ivory Coast.
20. The crucial role played by the European minority in the economic and cultural life of the Ivory Coast has been discussed in Victor Du Bois, *The French as a Minority in the Ivory Coast,* an unpublished manuscript prepared for the A.U.F.S. Conference on Minorities, 1969.
21. Lecour Grandmaison, *op. cit.,* p. 8.
22. *Ibid.,* p. 15.
23. It is estimated that on the Sodepalm plantations, one of the largest palm oil producing industrial plantations in the country, at least 85 per cent of all the workers are foreign Africans—the vast majority of them Mossi from the Upper Volta. Lecour Grandmaison, p. 15.
24. Demographic survey undertaken in 1968 by ORSTOM in the Sub-Prefectures of Broho and Jiaho at the request of the Ministries of Agriculture and Planning. Cited by Lecour Grandmaison, *op. cit.,* p. 11.
25. Lecour Grandmaison, *op. cit.,* p. 1.
26. For example, in the Ivory Coast a hectare of land (2.4 acres) produces only about 450 to 500 kilograms of coffee whereas in Latin America a hectare often produces 2 tons.
27. Lecour Grandmaison, *op. cit.,* p. 17.
28. Conseil Economique et Social, Rapport 1960–1964, p. 184.

29. *Ibid.*
30. *Ibid.* The remaining members of the so-called active portion of the population consisted of such people as students, military personnel, and self-employed persons.
31. *Ibid.*
32. It is interesting to note that different analysts, working for different government agencies but examining the same data, sometimes came up with strikingly different figures. Thus B. Lecour Grandmaison of the ORSTOM Centre des Sciences Humaines de Côte d'Ivoire estimates the total number of persons engaged in commerce and government administration in 1969 as 44,000 and 32,000 respectively. Table 2, on the other hand, estimates that in 1970 the figures would be almost the reverse, i.e., 33,200 persons in commerce and 42,400 persons in government. The possibility of a typographical error is not to be excluded. See Lecour Grandmaison, *op. cit.*, p. 3.
33. Bloch-Lemoine, *op. cit.*, p. 6.
34. *Ibid.*, p. 3.
35. Statement made on September 25, 1965, at the Fourth Congress of the Parti Démocratique de la Côte d'Ivoire (PDCI).
36. This and other statistics immediately following are cited from *Rapport sur l'enseignement en Côte d'Ivoire de 1960 à 1965,* delivered by M. Lambert Amon Tanoh, Minister of National Education, at the Fourth Party Congress of the Parti Démocratique de la Côte d'Ivoire (PDIC), held in Abidjan, September 23–25, 1965 [mimeographed] (Abidjan: Agence Ivoirienne de Presse, 1965).
37. In his report to the Fourth Party Congress of the PDIC, mentioned previously, M. Lambert Amon Tanoh, the Minister of Education, cited the following figures as the cost to the state for educating its children: for a primary school certificate (CEPE), $1,080; for a junior high school certificate (BEPC), $5,112; and for a high school diploma (BAC), $14,000. The Minister attributed these costs, which rank among the highest in the world, to the fact that many students repeat a grade several times before being promoted to the next higher level, and that the state assumes virtually the entire cost of caring for the child (lodging, board, books, etc.) during his entire school period.
38. Polygamous marriages entered into prior to the passing of the new Civil Code are not affected by this measure.
39. The members of the Council of the Entente, a loose form of political union, are the Ivory Coast, Upper Volta, Dahomey, Niger, and Togo.

References

Ivory Coast Government, Ministère des Affaires Économiques et Financières. Direction de la Statistique *Enquête Démographique 1957–1958, Resultats definitifs.* Supplément Trimestriel au Bulletin Mensuel de la Statistique. 8e Année, No. 1, 1er Trimestre 1966 (Abidjan: 1966).

Republique de Côte d'Ivoire. Ministère du Plan. *Republique de Côte d'Ivoire 1965: Population* (Abidjan: 1967).

Ivory Coast Government. Ministère du Plan. *Première Esquisse du Plan Quinquennal de Développement 1971–1975. Document de travail à l'usage des Commissions de Planification* (Abidjan: mai 1968), pp. 23–24.

Lecour Grandmaison, B., "Migrations et Croissance Économique en Côte d'Ivoire" [monograph], presented at the Congrès International des Études Africaines, Montreal, le 15–18 Octobre 1969 [mimeograph].

The Author

VICTOR D. DU BOIS has a particular interest in West Africa, especially the nations that once comprised French West Africa. Under a Ford Foundation Fellowship in 1959 he did the field work for a doctoral dissertation on Guinea. His research brought him into close contact with government officials, business and labor leaders, scholars, and other persons connected with or active in the Guinean political scene. As an undergraduate at Northwestern University he majored in anthropology. Shifting to the field of political science, he studied first at Northwestern and then at Princeton University which awarded him the Ph.D. in 1962. Dr. Du Bois has been associated with Consultants for Overseas Relations, Inc., has lectured on Africa, and has contributed chapters to books on African education and political affairs. He joined the AUFS in 1962 to observe and report on developments in the newly independent French-speaking countries of Sub-Saharan Africa.

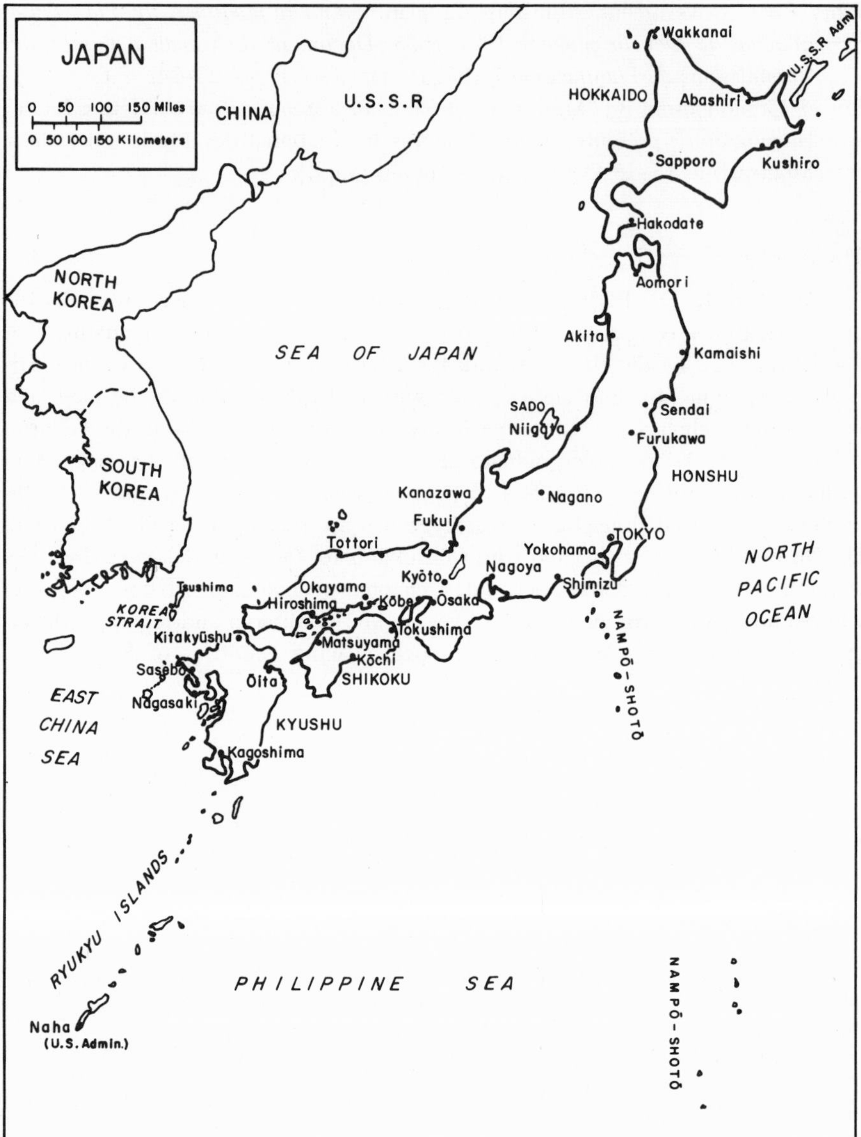

JAPAN
0 50 100 150 Miles
0 50 100 150 Kilometers
CHINA
U.S.S.R
(U.S.S.R Adm)
Wakkanai
HOKKAIDO
Abashiri
Sapporo
Kushiro
Hakodate
Aomori
NORTH KOREA
SEA OF JAPAN
Akita
Kamaishi
SADO
Niigata
Sendai
Furukawa
SOUTH KOREA
HONSHU
Kanazawa
Nagano
Fukui
Tottori
TOKYO
Yokohama
NORTH PACIFIC OCEAN
Kyōto
Nagoya
Shimizu
Tsushima
Okayama
Hiroshima
Kōbe
Ōsaka
KOREA STRAIT
Kitakyūshu
Tokushima
Matsuyama
Kōchi
NAMPŌ-SHOTŌ
Sasebo
SHIKOKU
Ōita
EAST CHINA SEA
Nagasaki
KYUSHU
Kagoshima
RYUKYU ISLANDS
PHILIPPINE SEA
NAMPŌ-SHOTŌ
Naha
(U.S. Admin.)

Japan

F. Roy Lockheimer

From the early part of the seventh century, when Japan began to import and adapt Chinese methods of government organization and administration to its own needs on a large scale, the Japanese have been inveterate record keepers. Continuing this tradition, in the early part of the eighteenth century, the Tokugawa military government (shogunate) began to conduct population surveys on a nation-wide scale every six years. These Tokugawa records indicate that from the outset of the surveys until the fall of the Tokugawa in the 1860s Japan's population was stagnant at approximately 30 million.

When Western methods of government and administration were introduced in Japan in the last third of the nineteenth century, especially French and German (Prussian) concepts, Japanese traditional attention to record keeping and statistical surveys was modernized and reinforced. Today, all Japanese nationals and their children, whether resident at birth in Japan or not, are supposed to be recorded in an official family register (*koseki*), which is kept up to date at an appropriate bureaucratic office. Regular national population censuses have been conducted in Japan every five years since 1920. The results of the census surveys are officially published by the Bureau of Statistics of the Prime Minister's Office (see Appendix A). Although there is an unfortunate delay of about five years before the official results of the quinquennial nation-wide population surveys, with complete demographic statistics, are made publicly available, there is every indication that these surveys, as well as other official publications of demographic statistics, are remarkably accurate and reliable. At much more frequent periodic intervals, the Institute of Population Problems, which is funded by the Ministry of Health and Welfare, publishes its research findings, including regular estimates of the national population.

At the turn of the century, about two thirds of the population of Japan lived in rural areas, with only one third in urban areas. By 1965, however, the situation more than reversed itself, with almost 70 per cent of the population living in areas that are officially classified as urban districts. In 1969, for example, 50.6 per cent of the total population was concentrated in the Tokaido megalopolitan area (extending from Tokyo to Osaka), which contains only 18.9 per cent of Japan's total land area. Tokyo, which recorded the greatest amount of growth, increased at the amazing rate of 82 per cent for the nineteen-year period from 1950 to 1969.

The population growth of industrial prefectures (provinces) is especially noteworthy. In the 49 years from 1920 to 1969, the rate of population increase for the seven major industrial prefectures and metropolitan areas of Tokyo, Kanagawa, Aichi, Kyoto, Osaka, Hyogo, and Fukuoka was 159 per cent. With one exeception, the rate for the rest of Japan in the same period, which was mostly agricultural, was only 50 per cent. The only exception was Hokkaido, which increased its population 122 per cent in the period concerned, largely owing to official support for its agricultural development.

During this century and perhaps until very recently, Japanese increasingly have left the countryside for the cities in search of higher wages and better conditions. As a result, Japan now has 565 districts that fall into the official "city" classification. The number of Japanese cities with 100,000 or more inhabitants reached 144 in March 1969. Estimates were that the results of the 1970 national population census would reveal that about 80 per cent of the Japanese population is involved in industrial occupations. Agricultural prefectures have also shown a decline in fertility, and, as a consequence of these developments, many of them have recently revealed a net decrease in their population. (See Appendix B)

Mortality rates in 1968 ranged from a low of 4.7 deaths per 1,000 persons in Tokyo to highs of 9.7 in Shimane and 9.9 in Kochi, both predominately agricultural prefectures. During 1968, for the whole of Japan, 1,870,000 babies were born alive while 686,000 deaths occurred, which resulted in a net natural increase of 1,184,000 persons, or the equivalent of 11.7 per 1,000 persons.

Internal migration. Japanese internal migration has long been considered as being within the traditional pattern for industrialized countries, wherein movement is from rural to urban areas. In Japan's case, this movement from the countryside has been directed towards two large cities, Tokyo and Osaka. However, according to Mr. Toshio Kuroda, chief of the Migration Research Division of the Institute of Population Problems, recent trends indicate that a movement towards the redistribution of population may have begun in Japan around 1965 (*1*).

A gradual movement may be beginning away from the two large urban centers of Tokyo and Osaka, and towards local prefectual urban centers. Mr. Kuroda, who feels that new data will have to be observed carefully before definite conclusions can be reached, believes that the data for Japanese internal migration since 1965 show the following three trends: (1) an increase in the rate of return migration to local areas from metropolitan areas; (2) a decrease in the rate of out-migration to metropolitan areas; and (3) a remarkable growth of local medium-

and small-sized cities through their absorption of people from surrounding areas. Dr. Kuroda tentatively has concluded that a period of decentralization may have begun for Japan's population.

Emigration. Emigration no longer plays as significant a role in official Japanese population control programs as it once did. The first instance of state-sponsored emigration from Japan occurred in 1885, when a group of 945 settlers was sent to Hawaii. In the ten years following until 1894 a total of some 30,000 Japanese were settled in Hawaii. The Japanese movement to Hawaii, which saw as many as 30,000 people settling there in one year (1906), came almost to a halt in 1908, however, with the conclusion of the restrictive "Gentlemen's Agreement" between the United States and Japan on emigration to Hawaii.

Emigration from Japan did continue, of course, to other areas in the continental United States, as well as to South America (especially Brazil) and, to a lesser extent, to Southeast Asia. After 1931, Japanese emigration to China (Manchuria) reached a rate of approximately 20,000 a year. But at the end of World War II more than three million Japanese were repatriated from Taiwan, Korea, China, Southeast Asia, and Micronesia. Of that number, estimates are that at least 1,230,000 people were prewar settlers and their families.

After Japan's defeat in 1945, resumption of government-aided emigration did not occur until 1952, when 54 persons were officially sponsored to settle in the Amazon valley. Government-sponsored and self-financed emigration reached an average of more than 15,000 annually after 1956. For comparative purposes, the number of government-aided emigrants in 1958 (7,609 cases), however, was only about half the number of such cases for Latin America alone during the 1925–35 period. In 1967 the number of Japanese residents who departed Japan for long-term or permanent residence abroad actually was exceeded (by some 2,400 cases) by the number of similarly-minded arrivals in Japan. For the present, since the Japanese government feels that the country is experiencing a labor shortage, officially-sponsored emigration is not being encouraged; and since political tensions do not permit an active program to welcome foreigners into Japan to alleviate the "labor shortage," immigration to Japan remains a difficult and time-consuming process.

Population and the Economy

Japan's total area of about 142,700 square miles makes it a medium-sized country, larger than Britain, smaller than France, slightly smaller than California. With an estimated population density of 278 persons per square kilometer of area in 1970, Japan appears considerably more densely populated than the United States, with its estimated 21 persons per square kilometer in 1967, but less densely populated than the Netherlands, with its estimated 375 persons per square kilometer in 1967. These figures are deceptive in Japan's case, however, because only about 16 per cent of its total area is arable and well-suited to human habitation. In terms of density of population per square kilometer of arable land, therefore, Japan is the most densely populated nation in the world.

Japan's comparative scarcity of arable land is somewhat alleviated by its resort to the resources of the sea for a source of food. Although Japan is self-sufficient in rice production, it does not produce sufficient sources of protein to meet the requirements of a modern diet. As a result, about 15 per cent of Japanese imports in 1968 were in the food and beverage category.

Minerals and raw materials for industrial purposes are all in short supply from domestic sources. Domestic oil and iron resources, for example, supply only 2 and 5 per cent respectively of Japan's industrial needs. It should not be surprising, therefore, that in 1968 more than half of Japan's total imports were in the categories of crude materials and mineral fuels.

With such a limited land area, poor natural resources, and a large population, the Japanese believe that foreign trade is their life line. The United States is by far the largest single national unit with which Japan trades. About one third of Japan's total world trade in 1968 was with the United States, as it has been throughout the 1960s. Trade with Asian countries makes up another third of Japan's world-wide trade, while the remainder is divided among Europe (c. 14 per cent), the Middle East (c. 7 per cent), Africa (c. 6 per cent), and Latin America (c. 6.5 per cent).

The supply of Japanese labor is at present considered to be inadequate within some industrial and political circles. Several Japanese demographic experts, Dr. Minoru Tachi, director of the Institute of Population Problems, among them, have acknowledged that a labor shortage does technically exist. Given the density of Japan's population, however, and its economic size and supply of raw materials, the answer is not political pressures for a dramatic increase in the birth rate, as Prime Minister Satō has urged, but a more economic use of the present sources of labor supply (*2*).

Projections of the Institute of Population Problems indicate that the rate of entry of middle school graduates into the labor force has been declining from a peak figure of 760,000 in 1963. By 1985 the Institute estimates that only 340,000 middle school graduates will be entering the labor force. A similar reduction, but not quite so severe, is anticipated in the rate of high school graduates entering into the labor market. A trend towards recovery is not expected to begin until the late 1970s (*3*). Dr. Tachi and others feel that a manpower shortage is likely to become endemic in Japan, as it appears to be *currently* in Western Europe, and that a possibly satisfactory answer to the problem in Japan's case is a "mobilization" of hitherto "untapped female labor power reserves" (*4*).

Population and Development

The rapid rebuilding and amazing expansion of the Japanese economy in the postwar period, as well as the continuation of a high rate of growth down to the present, have produced a number of serious dislocations in Japanese society, along with obvious benefits for the material well-being of the population. Japan's gross national product has skyrocketed to the point where the country is now approaching $200 billion a year economy, making it already the third greatest productive power in the world. This high rate of growth since the early mid-1950s has led to an important improvement in the standard of living, in the national income, and in the availability of a dazzling variety of durable consumer goods. It has also meant that Japan's national social overhead needs, roads, hospitals, schools, sewers, housing—public facilities of all sorts—have been given only a secondary emphasis. On the other hand, the industrial sector of the economy was given powerful support by the government for the rebuilding and modernization of production facilities.

Japan today, as a result, finds that its large industrial facilities, although generally bright and shiny, are increasingly being surrounded by the blight of industrial pollution, of the atmosphere, the countryside, the rivers, and the coastal sea. Housing is woefully inadequate; environmental engineering has only begun to be developed; and the rapidity of the spread of the urban sprawl remains relatively unmanaged. It is possible that the recent decline in the Japanese birth rate is directly related to the inadequacy of social overhead conditions.

The demographic impact of the high rate of growth of the Japanese economy over the past twenty years has meant that the transitional labor shortage, which appears to have resulted, has encouraged the movement of workers from small-scale enterprises, where traditionally disguised unemployment occurred, to large-scale industrial production lines. Twenty years of fast-paced growth has also meant a general increase in income as well as a recent improvement in its distribution. Starting in the mid-1950s, a new urban middle class was formed, composed of professional people, managers, clerical workers, salesmen, and service personnel. During the same period, the number of people engaged in agriculture and fishing declined dramatically. A gradual and continuing proportional decrease has also occurred in the number of Japanese engaged in manual work. In 1955, for example, 67.5 per cent of all employed persons in Japan were engaged in manual occupations, but by 1965 the number so engaged had dropped to 60.3 per cent (5). Along with these changes in income and occupation, class self-identification has also changed, with increasing numbers of people identifying themselves as members of the middle class.

The current Japanese labor pinch, which became apparent in the early mid-1960s, has also begun to cause the beginnings of a breakdown in traditional labor practices: lifetime employment and promotions by seniority gradually, for example, are being modified, but only very slowly. Just as the traditional Japanese family pattern of large extended families was modified into a smaller nuclear mold as urban areas regrew and spread throughout Japan all during this century, estimates are that modern labor practices—including job-to-job labor mobility, incentive pay, and promotions based on ability—will be accepted and utilized at an accelerating rate during the 1970s.

Population and Society

With more than 99.8 per cent of the 6–15 year old population at present enrolled in elementary and lower secondary schools, illiteracy in Japan is nearly nonexistent, and has been for some time. Even during the Tokugawa period (1600–1867), it is estimated that more than 40 per cent of the adult male population was literate; by 1910 the population of Japan was more than 95 per cent literate. In book publication and in total newspaper circulation, Japan ranks only behind the United States and the Soviet Union. Japan is one of the leading nations in the world in its use of mass media, a fact that partially stems from its high literacy rate as well as from its unified use of a single language as a medium of national communication. Although individuals, especially those in academic positions, are not so mobile as their counterparts are, say, in the United States, both the availability of information and the receptivity of the Japanese to new ideas are now and historically have been extremely high.

Public health situation. National programs for family health and maternal welfare are—on paper at least—well developed in Japan. A national system for public health insurance came into operation in Japan as early as 1926. There are now four major nation-wide programs for public health, three of which operate through various levels of government, while the other is managed jointly by a group of labor unions. Medical costs tend to be low and good medical care readily available as a result, but facilities are overcrowded—still one more indication of the government's reduced emphasis on social overhead investment. In 1968, nevertheless, the number of hospital beds available was almost double the figure for 1958. There are about 900 persons per doctor in Japan, a figure which is approximately that of Sweden or France.

With advances in public health administration and with the development of preventive medicine in Japan, mortality from infectious diseases has been practically eliminated. Tuberculosis, which had been a major factor before World War II, has been replaced by those diseases associated with advanced age in the list of the major causes of death in Japan today.

Dr. Minoru Tachi, director of the government-sponsored Institute of Population Problems, in urging greater employment of the female labor force, has suggested that national programs be developed to provide a supply of home-care and day nursery centers, complete with trained personnel whose main responsibility would be to look after the children of working mothers. Such facilities are at present totally inadequate in Japan.

Educational profile. Education traditionally has been highly regarded in Japan, so much so that one of the most honorable titles in Japanese society is *sensei*—teacher. On the compulsory educational level, Japanese student enrollments include nearly all children, no matter how remote their homes may be located. Almost 80 per cent of all Japanese children in 1968 sought some kind of schooling beyond their compulsory education. In the same year (1968), some 845 junior colleges, four-year colleges, and universities were operating in an attempt to attend to Japan's formal educational needs. About 1.5 million students were enrolled in Japanese colleges and universities in 1968.

The quantity of education in Japan, therefore, is enormous; the quality is not always so high. In its best institutions, however, the quality of Japanese education is on the same level as that for the world's most outstanding institutions. The national government's secondary emphasis on social overhead needs, and the demands of Japan's education-minded population, have produced too many academic institutions that are overcrowded, inadequately staffed, and without sufficient operating, not to mention endowment, funds. There has been a traditional overconcentration of institutions of higher education in the Tokyo metropolitan area. Local universities—other than the prestigious system of national universities—only recently have begun to receive the attention, development, and support they require. The turmoil in Japanese higher education over the past several years has been caused largely by the inability of Japanese institutions of higher learning to respond adequately to new demands; these demands are placed on them by numerous frustrated would-be students anxious to secure a place on the first rung of the ladder to professional success in Japan—higher education. The government's initial response was to repress student radical extremist activity and to curb some traditional campus freedoms. Later, official promises were made for extensive studies on the reorganization of higher education. Although some of these studies have now been concluded and the preliminary results published, the feeling is still strong among many observers that wholehearted government support for the *independent* growth, adjustment, redistribution, and further development of facilities for higher education in Japan on all levels can come none too soon.

Population and Polity

Family planning programs, government-sponsored and otherwise, as well as a variety of contraceptive devices and methods, with a few important exceptions, are all legal in Japan. Most contraceptive devices, especially condoms, which are sold openly on supermarket shelves, are easily available. Condoms alone or in foam-jelly-tablet combinations are, incidentally, the most frequent contraceptives employed in Japan, often alternating in combination with the rhythm method. This combination of methods appears to be highly successful in Japan. Statistics for 1966, which according to ancient oriental superstition was an unfortunate year for the birth of female children, reveal a dramatic drop in the birth rate, a fact that clearly indicates that modern-day Japanese are capable of exercising a significant amount of control over their fertility.

The two legally restricted types of contraceptive devices in Japan are the oral pill and intrauterine coil or ring devices (IUD). Both are without the approval of the Ministry of Health and Welfare, which prohibits their public distribution without entirely denying the public access to them. Upon a patient's request, physicians may prescribe one of the restricted methods. Japanese gynecologists have long opposed intrauterine coils and rings on the grounds that they may cause a rupture of the uterine wall. The oral pill is opposed on the grounds that it is still too new and insufficiently tested for possible pernicious side effects. Under a different trade name, however, the pill is readily available in Japan in large urban pharmacies as a method of controlling the onset of menstruation. Strangely enough, the fact that the two products are essentially the same is generally unrealized—probably because of the lack of advertising.

Abortion became legal in Japan with the passing of the Eugenic Protection Law in 1948. Historically, abortion as well as infanticide had been practiced—

rather widely in poor rural areas during Japan's heavily agricultural days—but these methods were never officially approved in those times. Infanticide, which historically was usually opposed by the *samurai* (military-bureaucrat) leadership class, is of course illegal and unknown in the prosperous Japan of 1970—as it has been during this century.

The Eugenic Protection Law was approved in 1948, when economic conditions were far from prosperous during the height of the postwar baby boom, ostensibly ". . . to prevent the increase of the inferior descendants from the eugenic point of view and to protect the life and health of the mother as well" (*6*). The law's real purpose was a manifold effort to reduce the birth rate through the national establishment of family planning centers for the dissemination of contraceptive information, as well as to allow physicians, *at their own discretion,* to perform "eugenic operations" or "artificial interruptions of pregnancy," *providing* certain conditions are met (*7*). A "eugenic operation" is defined as a surgical operation to ". . . incapacitate a person from reproduction without removing the reproductive glands" (*8*). An "artificial interruption of pregnancy" is defined to mean ". . . the artificial discharge of a fetus and its appendages from the mother at the period that a fetus is unable to keep its life outside of the mother's body" (*9*).

"Eugenic operations," according to the revised 1948 law, may be performed at a physician's discretion on any consenting individual under the conditions listed below, providing that the consent of the spouse concerned is also obtained. Exceptions may be made for minors and mental patients. The required conditions are summarized as follows: (1) hereditary mental disease in the person concerned, or in the spouse, or in a relative within the fourth degree of consanguinity; (2) leprosy in the person concerned or in the spouse; (3) danger to the mother from pregnancy or from delivery; and (4) a general unhealthy condition in a mother who has already borne several children (*10*).

The revised 1948 law also specifies that an "artificial interruption of pregnancy" may occur at a physician's discretion under the conditions listed below if the physician concerned has been approved and designated by the Medical Association in his local prefecture. The consent of the mother and her spouse are also necessary. The required conditions for legal abortion are summarized as follows: (1) mental illness in the mother, or in her spouse, or in their close relatives within the fourth degree of consanguinity; (2) leprosy; (3) serious danger to the health of the mother from the continuation of pregnancy or from delivery from a *medical or economic* viewpoint; and (4) rape of the mother concerned (*11*).

The 1948 law also established a Eugenics Protection Law Consultation Office under the aegis of the Ministry of Health and Welfare. Under its direction, some 850 regional and local health centers disseminate information and provide counseling in family planning throughout Japan. As a result, information on contraception is widely and easily available to the Japanese public, whose general level of education, as pointed out above, is high enough to have allowed them to comprehend and utilize this information with demonstrated effectiveness.

Current political situation. Until very recently there has been almost universal approval in Japan of national family planning and population control programs. Political parties have yet to take up the question as a major campaign issue. During the past two years, however, several groups have begun to question some aspects of the programs, among them the Kōmeitō (or Clean Government Party), the political arm of the militant Buddhist support group Sōka Gakkai. Conservative Prime Minister Eisaku Satō, reflecting concern over labor shortage among his business supporters, has called for an increase in the birth rate (*12*). Some sectors of the Japanese public, perhaps reflecting the ethics of new and increasing prosperity, have begun to question the morality of a large-scale program for easy and cheap abortions for economic reasons. Major newspapers have now joined the debate. With official minimum estimates at more than one million legal and illegal abortions performed annually in Japan, and with minimum estimates of more than 20 million abortions performed since 1948, general concern about the status of public morality is increasingly evident. Some have urged that a national investigation be conducted to determine whether abortions are too easily achieved in Japan. Generally speaking, when the great nationally-circulated newspapers each year publish the annual abortion statistics, a degree of moral shock is clearly discernible among many groups within the populace.

Consequently, the government requested (December 1969) the Japan Association for Maternal Welfare, a national organization of obstetricians and gynecologists, to conduct an investigation of the actual conditions under which induced abortions are performed. The results of that survey, along with a public opinion poll, will form a basis for a review of the Eugenic Protection Law by the Ministry of Health and Welfare. It could well be that increasing prosperity has provided a basis for the development of the luxury of a new morality of anti-abortion sensitivity in Japan—abetted of course by big-business concern over decreasing national sources of cheap labor.

Both population work and demographic research in Japan are on high levels, generally well respected throughout the world. Appendix C lists the various family planning programs and research agencies with a brief description of their major activities.

The Institute of Population Problems, under the direction of Dr. Minoru Tachi, conducts the most advanced demographic research in Japan. Dr. Tachi's and the Institute's prestige and influence seem intertwined and are both very high. Relatively high levels of efficiency are maintained throughout the population research field in Japan, although there are occasional delays in the publishing of final research findings. Private and public demographic research findings, however, are both considered seriously by the government in the making of national population policy.

Japan currently faces the problem of attracting sufficient numbers of students to enter the demographic field. Better career incentives, more academic courses, and better research facilities are needed if the present high level of Japanese demographic research is to be sustained so that it can meet the increased demands of the future.

Attitudes toward population programs. With a new concern in the government and in big business over the labor shortage, and with a new moral concern over the status of legal abortions within the general populace, population control programs will undoubtedly undergo a general review of Japan over the next several years. Except for the case of the Sōka Gakkai mentioned above and Japan's very small Roman Catholic Christian minority, religious groups in Japan—overwhelmingly Shinto-Buddhist—traditionally have not entered into public discussions concerning population problems. There is at present no indication that they are about to change their policies.

The response of the Japanese public to the first national debate on population problems since 1948, when large-scale population control programs were adopted, is a popular subject of speculation. Will it elect to pursue the Prime Minister's call for an increase in the birth rate? Or will adjustments be made in its population control program without stimulating a significant increase in the birth rate? Will big business tap new sources of labor supply and utilize more modern methods of labor management, or will it continue to press the pro-business conservative government to create pronatalist programs? Will the regulations concerning legal induced abortions be made more stringent? Will alternatives to induced abortion, such as sterilizations, which up to the present have not been popular in Japan, become more acceptable? The Japanese public today is somewhat confused; strong, well-informed government leadership will be required for the maintenance of a balanced program of population control.

Conclusions

Regardless of the public commotion over the labor shortage and its consequences for the existing national population program, there are several other important aspects to the question that should receive more attention over this new decade. The entire issue of labor efficiency and low labor productivity—in a phrase, labor waste—has not yet received proper attention. More rational use of the available sources of labor supply, including female sources, must be achieved in Japan before hasty talk about increasing the birth rate can be given just consideration. In every aspect of production, sales, and deliveries, Japan's use of its present sources of labor supply can and must be made more efficient during the 1970s.

Beyond the area of labor efficiency, the improvement of labor quality is another major task. Programs to provide for more educational opportunity are required, including better vocational programs—in school and out. Improved government programs for child-care centers and better-trained nursery personnel are also needed so that mothers can be freed to enter the labor force.

The 1970s, therefore, will be a crucial period for population control programs in Japan. Several important problem groupings now present serious challenges: (*1*) national adjustment to the current labor shortage; (*2*) provision for more social overhead capital funds for improved public facilities of all sorts; (*3*) careful observation of what might be a new trend in internal migration movements—away from the huge urban centers of Tokyo and Osaka and towards local prefectural urban centers; and (*4*) improvement of labor force efficiency and quality. These challenges are already clear to Japanese demographers and population specialists. The responses of government, big business, and big labor have yet to be heard. The public, in the middle, remains somewhat confused, making it seem all the more certain that the 1970s will be a population crossroads for Japan.

Notes

1. *Source:* Institute of Population Problems, Ministry of Health and Welfare, *Selected Statistics Indicating the Demographic Situation of Japan* (Tokyo: Institute of Population Problems, April 1970). See this publication for more detailed statistics.
2. For a fuller discussion of Dr. Tachi's views, see F. Roy Lockheimer, *Japan's New Population Politics* (FRL–4–'70), Fieldstaff Reports, East Asia Series, Vol. XVII, No. 5, 1970.
3. Minoru Tachi and Yoichi Okazaki, "Japan's Postwar Population and Labor Force," *The Developing Economies,* Vol. VII, No. 2, June 1969, pp. 177–179.
4. *Ibid.*, p. 186.
5. Hiroshi Komai, *Changing Pattern of Japanese Attitudes toward Work: A Consequence of Recent High Economic Growth* (Tokyo: Institute of Population Problems, Ministry of Health and Welfare, January 10, 1969), p. 10.
6. *Eugenic Protection Law in Japan,* latest rev. ed. (Tokyo: Institute of Population Problems, Ministry of Health and Welfare, March 1, 1969), p. 3.
7. *Ibid.*, pp. 3–4.
8. *Ibid.*, p. 3.
9. *Ibid.*
10. *Ibid.*, pp. 3–5.
11. *Ibid.*, pp. 10–11.
12. See F. Roy Lockheimer, *Japan's New Population Politics, op. cit.*

References

A. In English

1. Bureau of Statistics, Office of the Prime Minister, *Statistical Handbook of Japan, 1970* (Tokyo: Japan Statistical Association, May 31, 1970).
2. *Eugenic Protection Law in Japan,* latest rev. ed. (Tokyo: Institute of Population Problems, Ministry of Health and Welfare, March 1, 1969).
3. Institute of Population Problems, Ministry of Health and Welfare, *Selected Statistics Indicating the Demographic Situation of Japan* (Tokyo: Institute of Population Problems, April 1970).
4. Toshio Kuroda, *A New Dimension of Internal Migration in Japan* (Tokyo: Institute of Population Problems, Ministry of Health and Welfare, August 15, 1969).

5. Minoru Tachi, *Implication of Population Trends for Planning Social Welfare Services* (Tokyo: Institute of Population Problems, Ministry of Health and Welfare, February 1, 1964).
6. Minoru Tachi and Toshio Kuroda, *Interim Report on Teaching and Research in Demography in Japan* (Tokyo: Institute of Population Problems, Ministry of Health and Welfare, November 15, 1969).

B. In Japanese
1. Minoru Tachi, *Jinko Mondai no Chishiki [A Handbook of Knowledge on Population Problems]* (Tokyo: Nihon Keizai Shimbun-sha, 1969).
2. —, *Nihon no Jinko Mondai [Population Problems in Japan],* (Tokyo: Institute of Population Problems, Ministry of Health and Welfare, March 1, 1969). Title page and foreword in English.

The Author

F. ROY LOCKHEIMER has been a student of Japanese affairs since he was an undergraduate at Tufts University, where he received an A.B. in history in 1959. By 1961 he had earned both an M.A. and an M.A.L.D. in Japanese studies from the Fletcher School of Law and Diplomacy. After intensive language preparation at Harvard and Yale, doctoral research took him to Japan in 1962 for a study of conservative politics at the Graduate School of Keiō University. For several years, as a guest in the household of a conservative party politician, as an Exchange Research Fellow and Lecturer at Keiō, and as a columnist for the *Japan Times,* Mr. Lockheimer immersed himself in Japanese life and studies. Subsequently, he became Assistant Professor of History at Wisconsin State University (Eau Claire), where his assignment was to create a program in Asian studies. He joined the AUFS in 1966 to report from Tokyo on developments in Japan.

Table 1. Crude Birth Rate (per 1000)

Year	*Birth rate*
1900–04	32.1
1940–43	30.7
1947	34.3
1950	28.1
1955	19.4
1960	17.2
1965	18.6
1969(est.)	18.4

Source: Institute of Population Problems, Ministry of Health and Welfare, *Selected Statistics Indicating the Demographic Situation of Japan* (Tokyo: Institute of Population Problems, April 1970). See this publication for more detailed statistics.

Table 2. Crude Death Rate (per 1000)

Year	*Death rate*
1900–04	20.4
1940–43	16.3
1947	14.6
1950	10.9
1955	7.8
1960	7.6
1965	7.1
1969(est.)	6.8

Table 3. Life Expectancy at Birth

Year	*Male*	*Female*
1935–36	46.9	49.6
1947	50.1	54.0
1950–52	59.6	63.0
1955	63.6	67.8
1960	65.3	70.2
1965	67.7	72.9
1968	69.1	74.3

Table 4. Rate of Natural Increase (per 1000)

Year	*Natural increase*
1900–04	11.7
1940–43	14.4
1947	19.7
1950	17.2
1955	11.6
1960	9.6
1965	11.4
1969(est.)	11.7

Table 5. Gross Female Reproduction Rate

Year	*Rate*
1925	2.51
1940	2.01
1947	2.20
1950	1.76
1955	1.15
1960	0.97
1965	1.04
1967	1.08

Table 6. Net Female Reproduction Rate

Year	*Rate*
1925	1.56
1940	1.44
1947	1.67
1950	1.53
1955	1.05
1960	0.92
1965	1.00
1967	1.05

Table 7. Population by Age Group, as a Percentage Distribution of Total Population

Year	*0–14*	*15–64*	*65+*
1920	36.5	58.2	5.3
1940	36.0	59.2	4.7
1950	35.4	59.7	4.9
1955	33.4	61.3	5.3
1960	30.0	64.2	5.7
1965	25.6	68.1	6.3

Table 8. Estimates of Future Population by Age Group, as a Percentage Distribution of Total Population

Year	*0–14*	*15–64*	*65+*
1970	23.8	69.2	7.0
1975	24.0	68.1	7.9
1980	24.1	67.1	8.9
1990	22.1	67.5	10.5
2000	20.9	65.7	13.4
2020	20.8	62.1	17.1
2025	20.7	62.9	16.4

Table 9. Estimates of Future Labor Force Population by Sex, 15 Years Old and Over (in thousands)

Year	*Total*	*Male*	*Female*
1955	40,027	24,435	15,591
1965	48,294	29,519	18,775
	"Medium" Estimation		
1970	53,148	33,057	20,091
1975	54,998	35,130	19,868
1980	56,116	36,702	19,414
1985	57,081	38,027	19,054

Table 10. Induced Abortions (Cases reported according to Eugenic Protection Law only)

Year	*Number*
1950	489,000
1955	1,170,000
1960	1,063,000
1965	843,000
1968	757,000

Table 11. Stillbirth Rate (per 1,000 births)

Year	*Rate*
1900–04	93.3
1940–43	42.8
1947	44.2
1950	84.9
1960	100.4
1965	81.4
1969(est.)	68.8

Table 12. Infant Death Rate (per 1,000 live births)

Year	*Rate*
1900–04	153.3
1940–43	86.8
1947	76.7
1950	60.1
1955	39.8
1960	30.7
1965	18.5
1969(est.)	14.2

Table 13. Population Growth of Japan

Date	*Population*
1900	43,847,000
1920	55,391,000
1930	63,872,000
1940	72,540,000
1950	83,200,000
1960	93,419,000
1969	102,648,000

APPENDIX B. Economically Active Population and Distribution by Sectors, with Unemployment and Underemployment Estimates

Table 1. Labor Force Status, as a Percentage Distribution of Total Population

Year	*% of Total population*	*Employed*	*Unemployed*	*Not in labor force*
1950	65.4	64.1	1.3	34.6
1955	67.3	66.0	1.3	32.7
1960	67.4	66.9	0.5	32.6
1965	66.0	65.1	0.9	33.9

Table 2. Employed Persons by Industrial Sectors, as a Percentage Distribution of Total Number of Employed Persons

Year	*Primary*	*Secondary*	*Tertiary*
1950	48.3	21.9	29.7
1955	41.0	23.5	35.5
1960	32.6	29.2	38.2
1965	24.6	32.2	43.0

Source: Institute of Population Problems, Ministry of Health and Welfare, *Selected Statistics Indicating the Demographic Situation of Japan* (Tokyo: Institute of Population Problems, April 1970). See this publication for more detailed statistics.

Table 3. Employed Persons by Class of Workers, as a Percentage Distribution of Total Number of Employed Persons

Year	*Self-employed*	*Unpaid family workers*	*Employees*
1950	26.1	34.4	39.5
1955	23.9	30.3	45.8
1960	22.1	24.0	54.0
1965	19.6	19.5	60.7

Table 4. Internal Migration. Net Migration in Selected Regions of Japan

Region	*1920–25*	*1930–35*	*1947–50*	*1950–55*	*1960–65*
1. Hokkaido	−110	− 24	+116	+ 44	− 177
2. Tohoku (agricultural)	−145	−238	−167	− 474	− 677
3. Kanto (Tokyo area)	+512	+482	+656	+1,136	+1,739
4. Keihanshin (Osaka area)	+456	+778	+395	+ 618	+ 950
5. Sanin (agricultural)	− 32	− 55	− 54	− 62	− 128
6. Shikoku (agricultural)	− 91	−177	−111	− 237	− 278

Source: Adopted from Toshio Kuroda, *Continuity and Transformation of Migration Behavior in Japan* (Tokyo: Institute of Population Problems, Ministry of Health and Welfare, February 5, 1970), p. 5.

APPENDIX C. POPULATION AND WORK RESEARCH

A. Family Planning Programs
  1. Government
    a. Ministry of Health and Welfare
      (1) Eugenics Protection Law Consultation Office
        (a) Dissemination of information.
        (b) 850 Japanese regional and local Health Centers, each of which provides counseling on family planning.
  2. Private
    a. Family Planning Federation of Japan (FPFJ)
    The major agency for the coordination of privately sponsored family planning activities in Japan.
      (1) Institute for Research on Population Problems
        (a) Critical examination of government policies.

(b) Responsibility for the family-planning activities of the "new life movement," which was originated by 80 large Japanese enterprises for the improvement of the workingman's living conditions.

(2) Various small private groups active within Japan in family planning. Nominal coordination.

(3) The FPFJ is also nominally the Japan Chapter of the International Planned Parenthood Federation (IPPF).

B. Demographic Research and Training

1. Government

a. Ministry of Education

(1) National Institute of Genetics Research.

b. Ministry of Health and Welfare

(1) Bureau of Families and Children

(a) Maternal and Child Health Section

(2) Bureau of Public Health

(a) Health Center Section

(3) Institute of Population Problems. A semi-autonomous research body within the Ministry of Health and Welfare with the prime responsibility for the government's demographic research effort.

(4) Institute of Public Health

(a) Department of Public Health Demography
Medical and technical research.

c. Population Problems Inquiry Council
Policy advisory group of 42 members from public and private sectors.

2. Private

a. Population Problems Research Council of the *Mainichi* newspaper
Publishes articles, studies, and surveys in an effort to increase public interest in population problems.

b. Population Association of Japan
An academic organization which holds annual meetings and publishes its proceedings and its members' research findings.

c. Foundation-Institute for Research in Population Problems
Established in 1933 for population studies. Makes recommendations on basic policy for population control, labor-force problems, and regional development.

d. Demographic Study Group
A special study group established in 1959 and composed of qualified demographers. Conducts a broad variety of activities in the population field.

e. Study Group on Population Science
Established in 1958 and composed of qualified demographers. Holds monthly seminars and publishes monographs on specific population problems.

C. Indigenous Institutions with Significant Activities

As shown in this outline, all of the institutions with significant population activities in Japan are native Japanese organizations, a fact that well testifies to the high quality of Japanese population work and research.

The Ministry of Health and Welfare's Institute of Population Problems, under the direction of Dr. Minoru Tachi, conducts the most sophisticated demographic research in Japan.

D. Cooperation with Foreign National and International Agencies

1. Government
   a. Ministry of Foreign Affairs
      (1) Overseas Technical Cooperation Agency
      Training and overseas programs as part of a technical assistance program to the underdeveloped world.
   b. Ministry of Health and Welfare
      (1) Institute of Population Problems
      Informal exchange and liaison with similar organizations and researchers in other countries.
2. Private
   a. Japan Organization for International Cooperation in Family Planning
   Support for private family planning programs in the developing countries of Asia.
   b. International Planned Parenthood Federation (IPPF)
      (1) West Pacific Regional Office
      Located in Tokyo with responsibility for Japan, South Korea, and Hong Kong.
      (2) The Japan Chapter of the IPPF is nominally the Family Planning Federation of Japan (FPFJ).

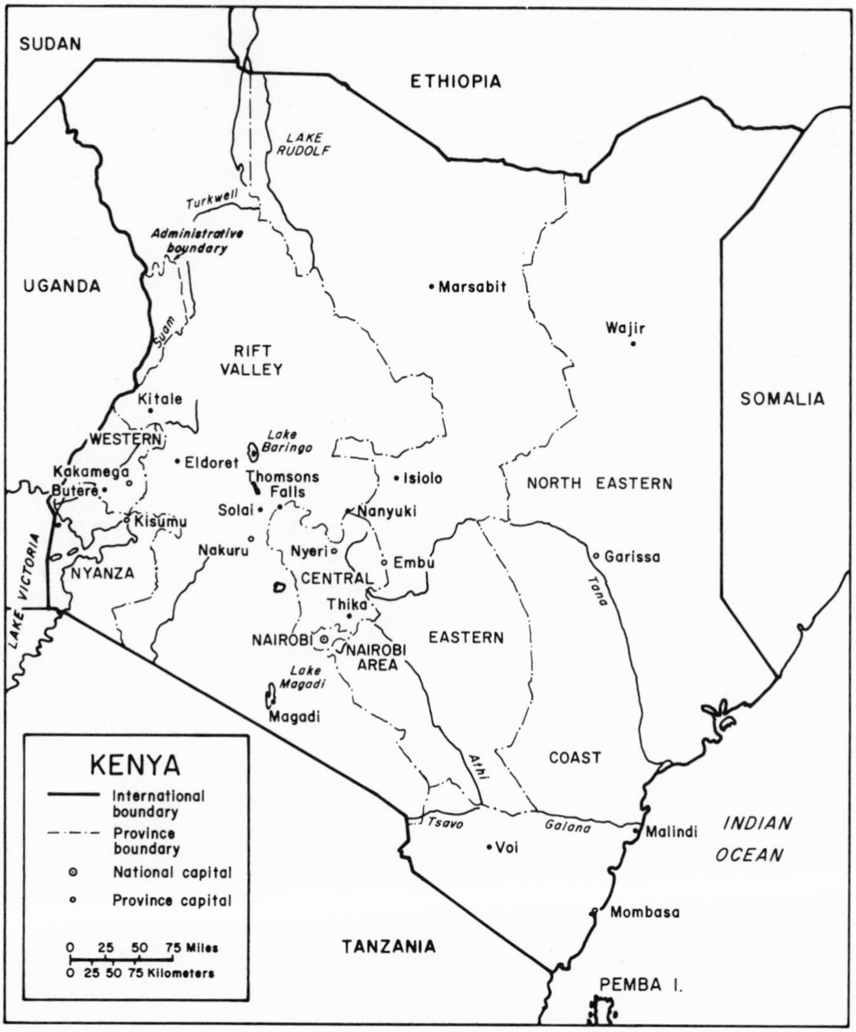
SUDAN
ETHIOPIA
LAKE RUDOLF
Turkwell
Administrative boundary
UGANDA
Suam
Marsabit
Wajir
RIFT VALLEY
SOMALIA
Kitale
WESTERN
Lake Baringo
Eldoret
Kakamega
Butere
Thomsons Falls
Isiolo
NORTH EASTERN
Solai
Nanyuki
Kisumu
LAKE VICTORIA
Nakuru
Nyeri
Embu
Garissa
NYANZA
CENTRAL
Tana
Thika
NAIROBI
NAIROBI AREA
EASTERN
Lake Magadi
Magadi
KENYA
International boundary
Province boundary
National capital
Province capital
0 25 50 75 Miles
0 25 50 75 Kilometers
Athi
COAST
Tsavo
Galana
Malindi
INDIAN OCEAN
Voi
Mombasa
TANZANIA
PEMBA I.

Kenya

Norman N. Miller

Introduction

The Republic of Kenya, located astride the equator on the Indian Ocean, enjoys the distinction of being the first tropical African nation to initiate a serious government program in population analysis and family planning. Ghana, Botswana, and the Reunion Islands off the African coast recently followed suit and have positive programs underway. By contrast, most other African states remain apathetic toward their own population problems, and a few are vigorously pronatal. Perhaps the most extreme example is Kenya's island neighbor, Zanzibar, which reportedly has introduced the death penalty for illegal abortions, and banned the sale of all contraceptives.

Kenya's achievements in family planning are doubly impressive when some of the obstacles are known. The nation is over 90 per cent rural, a majority of its people living either as farmers or herdsmen. Three fifths of the land mass is desert or semidesert, and the total productive land is estimated at only 17 per cent of the nation. Even in the fertile highlands, with the impressive agricultural wealth in coffee, tea, cereals, and pyrethrum, the land shortage is such that the densities soar to over 2,000 per square mile, exceptionally high for Africa. The diversity of the soils, the vagrancies of climates that range from tropical coastline to alpine snows, the maldistribution and underemployment of the people further compound the nation's problems. The result is that a majority of the people are trapped by their physical environment and encased in belief systems that traditionally tend to reject family limitation, family spacing, and the basic idea of reducing the birth rate.

The data relative to the demographic condition of Kenya fall into two main categories, the basic statistics and an evaluation of the reliability of the information. The 1962 census is the only complete information available although volume one of the August 1969 census, published in November 1970, does contain totals by age, sex, area and density, tribe or nationality, and by districts and provinces (Table 2).

Table 1. Basic Statistics

Total population:	10,942,705 (1969); 11,250,000 (mid-year 1970), est.
Crude birth rate:	51/1000 (1969), est.
Crude death rate:	18/1000 (1969) est.
Rate of natural increase:	3.3 (1962–1969)
Gross reproduction rate:	3.4 (1962)
Net reproduction rate:	2.1 (1962)

Table 2. Tribal Population

	1962	*1969*
1. Kikuyu	1,642,065	2,201,632
2. Luo	1,148,335	1,521,595
3. Luhya	1,086,409	1,453,302
4. Kamba	933,219	1,197,712
5. Kisii	538,343	701,679
6. Meru	439,921	554,256
7. Mijikenda	414,887	550,520
8. Kipsigis	341,771	471,459
9. Turkana	181,387	203,177
10. Nandi	170,085	261,969
11. Masai	154,079	154,906
12. Ogaden	121,645	90,118
13. Tugen	109,691	130,249
14. Elgeyo	100,871	110,908
15. All others	983,234	1,070,288
Totals	8,365,942	10,673,770

Immigration-Emigration: No data for 1962, although estimated to be substantially zero. Mid-1970 expulsion of an estimated 50,000 workers plus families from Uganda creates high current migration. *Statistical Abstract,* 1968, notes resident arrivals: 113,030, resident departures: 121,709.

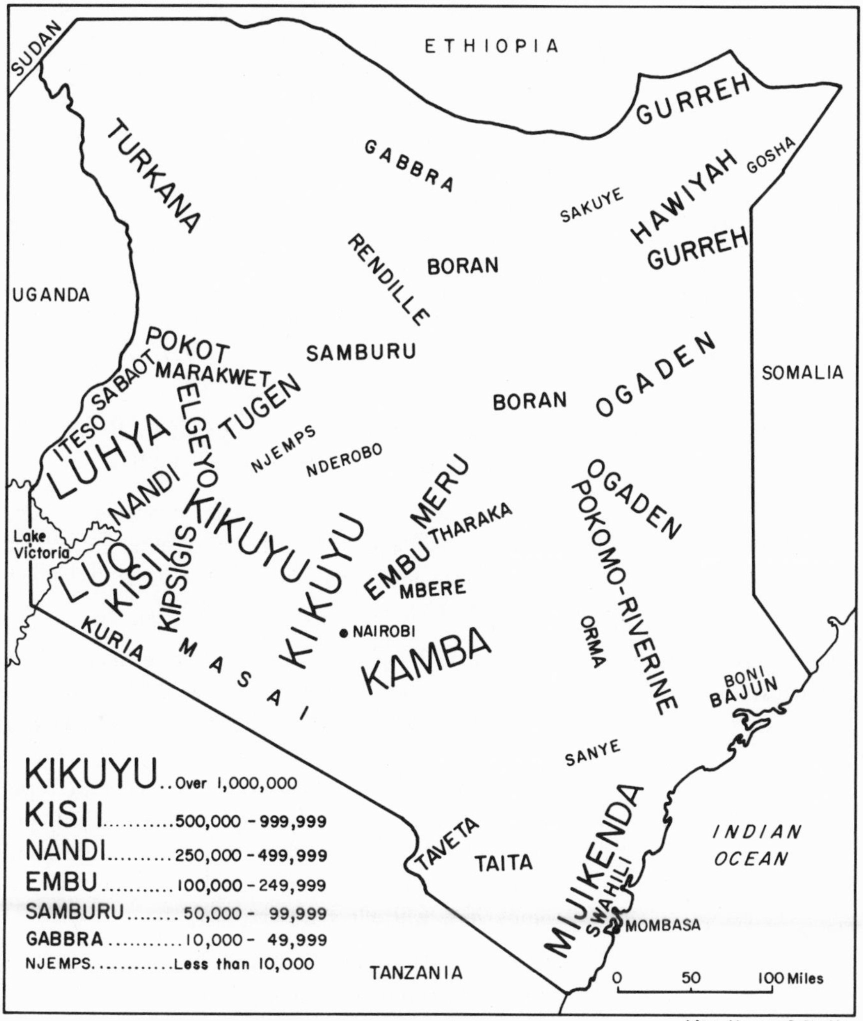

After Morgan & Shaffer

Tribal distribution of Kenya

Age-Sex Specific Structure:	46 per cent under 15 years, 4 per cent over 60 years, dependency ratio 106. Average age of marriage for males: 24.1 years, females: 18.9.
Total Fertility Rate:	6.8 (1962); 7.1 (1969) est.
Fertility Patterns:	Very little is known of fertility patterns regarding social class or rural-urban distribution. The coastal Muslim areas are reported lower. Polygamy is a minor factor compared to Tanzania where 21 per cent of the men are polygamous; no figures are available for Kenya, although the 3 per cent Moslem

rate compared to Tanzania's 30 per cent indicates far less. Age patterns indicate lower fertility in early childbearing years. Women who survive to 37–9 have an average of 7.1 children, those over 45, 8.5 children, indicating a strong tendency to continue to have children as long as possible.

Mortality Levels, Trends: There is high child mortality between ages two and five due particularly to malaria. The trend is slowly downward due almost entirely to public health measures. Life expectancy (1962) at birth was 39.0 years (1969 estimate is 45.0 years). See Table 5, appendix.

Infant Mortality Rate: 126/1000 (1969) est. as compared to 18/1000 for registered European, non-African children.

Morbidity/Cause of Death: Rank order, 1968: pneumonia, digestive system, enteritis, meningitis, TB, heart disease, nutritional deficiencies, measles, malaria, unknown or ill-defined. *Registrar General's Report, 1968.*

Estimates of Future Trends: At present 3.3 per cent growth rate, estimate of 22 million in 1990. Estimates for year 2000 as high as 34 million, low of 16 million if family planning programs initiated and effective. Present Nairobi (capital) growth doubles every ten years (7.1 per cent growth), other urban areas at 6.5 to 7.0 per cent. Outside events, such as triparte agreement (1970) to ask 10 per cent employment increase of employers, will effect trends.

Other trends: mortality down, fertility up, higher population growth in short term for 10–20 years, thereafter dependent on success of family planning. Possible rate of 3.8 to 4.0 for year 2000.

Other Factors: Number of households: 1.50 to 1.75 million
Average size of household: African, 6.25 persons (1962)
Ideal family size: women's ideal, 6.03 (Heisel); women's ideal, 6.70 (Dow)

Achieved Family size: 6.8 children
Difference rural-urban: rural slightly higher

Number of females, 15–44: 2.4 million total, 2.1 married.

Urban population: 8.0 per cent

Potentially Productive Acres Per Person: 4.2 (1965), 2.6 (1980), 1.5 (1995), 1.3 (2000).

Religion (excluding traditional faiths): Roman Catholic 21.8 per cent, Protestant 36.0 per cent, Hindu-Sikh 38.3 per cent, Muslim 3.8 per cent.

Ethnic groups (mid-1969)	
1. Kenya African	10,673,770
2. Non-Kenya African	59,432
3. Non-African	
a. Asian (*1*)	139,037
b. European	40,593
c. Arab (*1*)	27,886
d. Other	1,987

African Ethno-linguistic groups:
1. Central Bantu
2. Western Bantu
3. Coastal Bantu
4. Nilotic
5. Nilo-Hamitic (Kalenjin speaking)
6. Other Nilo-Hamitic
7. Western Hamitic (Rendille and Galla speaking)
8. Eastern Hamitic (Somali speaking)

Evaluation of data. Several factors affect the reliability of census data in Kenya. Although four enumerations were taken in 1911, 1921, 1926, and 1931, they are today of little value because Africans and Somalis in Kenya were not counted. The first census to include both Africans and non-Africans was in 1948 (estimated 5.4 million). The next census, 1962, however, makes comparisons between 1948–62 misleading because of changes in boundaries and in the degree of coverage. Figures for 1962 have been considered accurate, although preliminary figures for 1969 suggested there was undercounting in 1962.

The August 1969 census was probably the most accurate of the six enumerations. De facto head counting was done for the first time, post-enumeration checks done in some areas, and vigorous efforts made to train enumerators (mainly students and teachers). Several problems occurred, however, which will affect the accuracy for certain districts. Directions regarding random sampling were not followed in some areas, in others the sample obtained was too small. Response errors, particularly concerning age and marital status, also occurred. The discrepancies will only affect the local figures. The national figures are considered accurate. As with 1948–62, boundary changes affect the comparability of the 1962–69 figures. Enumeration in the remote northern seminomadic areas, probably covering 50 per cent of the land area of Kenya, was exceptionally difficult, and figures are essentially guesses. Other problems, common to many developing nations, include fear of enumerators, some failure to cooperate, and confusion over relation of the census to tax assessment. The fact that district offices were responsible for the census caused some administrative confusion when the forthcoming December elections were announced, shortly before the numeration. Senior officials tended to focus their attention on voting activities, and to disregard the enumerators. Over-all, however, the census was the most exhaustive and should be considered generally reliable.

Population Distribution and Movement

Urban-rural distribution. The general distribution of Kenya's population is reported at 8 per cent urban and 92 per cent rural (1962). The urban population is heavily concentrated in Nairobi, Mombasa, and two or three smaller trade centers. The rural population is located mainly in the southern one-third of the nation on some 17 per cent of the total land. The population density (1969 census) is 29 persons per square mile over-all. A total of 930 trade centers is considered by the Ministry of Lands and Settlements to have some degree of centrality and to merit consideration as local distribution points for education, health, markets, and social services. Some 70 centers have more than 2000 inhabitants. Migration from the rural areas to the urban centers is one of the country's continuing problems. The flow is caused mainly by the shortage of agricultural land plus the economic attractions of the city. Census projections for the rural areas are not particularly hopeful. The agrarian economy will have to support more people on less land than the present 4.3 acres per person and ostensibly do so with wages somewhat comparable to urban areas. Even with rapid economic gains and a ten-fold increase in urban employment, the rural areas will have to provide for three times the present population (*2*).

Unemployment and underemployment. Nairobi, the capital, and Mombasa, the major Kenya seaport, are the economically most active areas, employing the majority of the wage earners. Economically, socially, and politically, the unemployed and underemployed are the most serious problems in present day Kenya. Government estimates divide wage employment into three sectors, the total of which equals about 10 per cent of the population (*3*).

Table 3

	1967	*1969*
Modern sector	600,600	627,200
Smallholdings, settlement schemes	365,600	363,400
Rural, non-agricultural activities	60,600	81,700
Totals	1,026,800	1,072,300

Source: Economic Survey, 1970, p. 128

Between 1967–69 employment rose 46,000, while the total labor force rose 220,000 for the same period. The latter are mainly school-leavers. Of the 627,200 employed in the "modern" sector (firms, large farms, rural enterprises, and public employment), about 38 per cent were employed by the public sector. The breakdown by industry follows in Table 4.

Table 4. Public and Private Sector Employment by Industry, 1969 (Provisional)

	Total Employment ('000)	*Percentage distribution*		
		Public sector	*Private sector*	*Total*
Agriculture and forestry	195.0	8.4	91.6	100.0
Mining and quarrying	2.6	—	100.0	100.0
Manufacturing and repairs	72.7	21.4	78.6	100.0
Building and construction	28.9	43.6	56.4	100.0
Electricity and water	5.2	50.0	50.0	100.0
Commerce	44.2	5.4	94.6	100.0
Transport, storage and communications	51.8	69.1	30.9	100.0
Other services	226.8	67.2	32.8	100.0
Totals	627.2	37.9	62.1	100.0

Source: Economic Survey, 1970, p. 131

Totals by population:	*1964*	*1969* (Provisional)
All private industry	415,886	389,600
All public services	173,721	237,600
Total wage earners	589,607	627,200

Source: Economic Survey, 1970, p. 131

Although no firm figures are available Russell estimates there are 250,000 hard-core unemployed (*4*). In July 1970 there were approximately 200,000 signed up as unemployed. In addition some 60,000 overseas Kenyans, mainly in Uganda, faced prospects of losing their jobs. This essentially occurred in October 1970, with Uganda forcing most noncitizens out. At the present growth rates some 230,000 males will be added to the labor force in the year 2000. The long-term employment estimates, even considering an extraordinary rate of economic growth, indicate enough employment opportunities will not be generated to provide for the oncoming labor force. Projections also suggest very serious land pressures in the Central Province and Victoria Basin areas (*5*).

The problem of urban unemployment, as a direct result of the rural to urban migrations, has several consequences. High costs are incurred for housing, water, and power facilities, and other amenities such as schools are severely taxed. As in other new states, crime, social upheaval, and political instability also follow rapid urbanization. Solutions planned by the government include major rural development programs, and the geographical decentralization of industry. Both programs would help alleviate the rural-urban migration and unemployment problems, although the exact costs, the explicit benefits that outweigh costs, have not been assessed.

One of the problems surrounding unemployment concerns who exactly is unemployed. During registration periods to assist the unemployed, several of the messengers and clerks in the Ministry of Economic Planning itself registered as unemployed in order to secure better jobs. The same problem arises when officials attempt to learn how many people are landless.

Internal migration. Reports for the census year 1962 indicate some 604,000 interprovincial migrants moving to the Nairobi area, the Rift Valley, or the Coast Province. The major trends in internal migration are from the Central Province and the Victoria Basin to the farms of the Rift Valley and the plantation areas of west Kenya and the coast. These are mainly young men in rural-to-rural migrations. The major movements from rural-to-urban centers are those from the Central Province, and the western Victoria Basin areas, to Nairobi and Mombasa port. A large part of the female outflow is probably due to marriage migrations. The patterns are mainly explainable as responses to different economic opportunities. Data on fertility and migration are not available, except that there is apparently little difference in fertility between rural and urban areas. Overall, there is major movement within the high density Central and Western areas, to the Rift Valley, Nairobi, and Mombasa (*6*).

Emigration. Kenya provides relatively few migrant workers to other parts of Africa, particularly in comparison to her neighboring states. The present trend is for Kenyans to return from work in other countries rather than to increasingly emigrate. This does not include non-Africans (Asians and Europeans) who are emigrating at a high rate, especially European teen-age school-leavers and Asians holding British passports. In 1968 there was an excess of permanent immigrants over emigrants by some 5,400, considering all racial groups. This reversed the trend that had persisted between 1961–67 of permanent departures outnumbering permanent arrivals by up to 4,000 in a single year (*7*).

A reverse in trend also occurred in the European outflow in 1968. Between 1960 and 1967 Europeans tended to have up to 3,500 departures a year, with 1968 showing 2,500 more arrivals than departures. Most European departures were settler families; the inflow, particularly in 1968, was predominantly American commonwealth people concerned with technical or other aid. Since 1968 there has been an increased exodus of Asians, as work and trading permits become more difficult to obtain. The main emigrant tribes in the past (1948–57) have been Kamba, Taita, Kikuyu, and Baluhya.

Population and the Economy

National economy. Kenya is overwhelmingly an agricultural nation, with farming and stock-raising the main occupations of all but 8 per cent of its population. The natural resources lie mostly in the exceptionally fertile soils in the central and western parts of the nation. Some oil is found, and further exploration is under way in several sectors. Mineral exports include cement, soda ash, and small amounts of gold, diatomite, graphite, meerschaum, gypsum, silver, and asbestos.

The scenic diversity of the country, from tropical coastline and semidesert areas to highland and alpine areas, along with the national parks and wildlife promotes a tourist industry that is the leading foreign income earner. The agricultural economy is well diversified, and industrialization is under way. The high growth in per capita output in the last five years and the relatively high savings have been supplemented by inflows of technical assistance and capital from many nations of the world.

The major agricultural items for export are coffee, tea, sisal, pyrethrum, hides, meat, and dairy products. Wattle extract and maize, forest products, and both fresh and salt water fish are also exported in modest amounts. The major trade links in Africa are with Uganda and Tanzania, partners in common trade agreements, and to a far lesser degree with Ethiopia. Overseas trade is largely with the United Kingdom, Western Europe, and the United States, although agricultural products exported to India, Pakistan, and Japan are important. Trade with Russia, Eastern Europe, and China is not significant.

Public finances have been well managed, and because the foreign exchange reserves are sound and political stability has continued, general investment confidence exists for Kenya. The balance of payments is favorable, due in part to the inflow of capital from international aid projects. The balance of trade, however, is less favorable, with Kenya importing some $140 million per year more than she exported between 1966–1969 (*8*). The 1968 Kenya importation of goods was $336 million with expectations to reach $560 million by 1974, mainly in raw materials for manufacturing, equipment, and machinery. Exports for 1968 were $228 million, estimated to reach $336 million by 1974.

The East African Community, a partnership of Kenya, Uganda, and Tanzania, was established in 1967, with headquarters in Arusha, Tanzania. Its main objectives are to facilitate relations in terms of customs, tariffs, research, and income tax collection. East African Corporations for railway, mail and telecommunications, airways, and harbors are also in operation under the agreements. The common market created within the community attempts to remove trade restrictions between partner states, and discussions have been held with other neighboring states, particularly Ethiopia and Zambia, for inclusion in the market.

Kenya's labor problems lie in the shortage of trained technical skills and as noted, a shortage of wage-labor positions for the potential labor supply. Although the country has had a relatively long period of economic growth and the over-all standard of living is on the rise, the lack of a large industrial base forces most newcomers to the labor force to find employment in agriculture or other rural employment. Temporary solutions have included the government's request that employers take on an additional 10 per cent of their staff (1970) and a computerized job-placement program.

Although the general economy looks healthy there are several danger areas. The population growth and unemployment create potential unrest for many sectors. There seems to be a growing gap between the rich African elite in the urban areas and poor rural population. The increased pace of Africanization, particularly since early 1969, may cause serious loss of managerial and technical skills.

The nation's economic growth rate, in October 1970, is about 6.6 per cent. It is misleading because the country as a whole faces a serious problem in income distribution. Sizable wealth is held by a very few. A growing number of high school educated, unemployed individuals who are divorced from the land make up a potentially unstable proletariat. The economy does enjoy overseas confidence, and has a high inflow of capital. But at the same time, problems of wealth distribution persist. Whether the national leaders, who are mainly an entrenched African elite, will be able to cope with the growing economic malcontent, is a major question facing Kenya.

Population and Development

Demographic aspects of development. Several barriers exist for a greater portion of the population to be involved in wage earning capacities. The technological changes occurring in the nation are limited to a few urban areas. Power, transport, communications, and other infrastructural facilities do not exist for most of the nation. Industrial development, which is occurring at an impressive rate, considering East Africa as a whole, is still limited to three or four urban centers. Agricultural innovations have occurred, particularly in the central highlands, but range development, meat development, irrigation schemes, and other schemes for the improvement of the more arid regions have yet to meet with marked success, or to support any significant wage labor.

Ecological problems continue to hinder general development and to affect the population picture. For many settled areas the necessity to protect wildlife for the tourist industry decreases usable land and places man in competition with animal. The balance between wildlife and the expanding population has not been worked out, as witnessed by the continued poaching of game, encroachment of squatters, and debates in Parliament to reallocate protected areas for human use.

Each of the Kenya Five Year Development Plans (1966–70 and 1970–74) has called attention to the impact of a high population growth on the general economy. The policy, generally stated, is that the population growth should be curtailed by family planning services. Economic officials know that the undue pressure of numbers presently exerted on Kenya resources retards the speed of development. Given present technology, population pressures accentuate the rate at which natural resources are used while simultaneously increasing the cost of their use (9).

Several other factors are important in the relationship between Kenya's population growth and its economic development. Because of limited supplies of land and other resources, long term diminishing economic returns for the people will result, unless more capital, more trained labor, and technological innovations come into the equation. Cultivated land is currently limited to 4.3 acres per person, capital is still in short supply, and the improvement in labor skills is slow. The "back to the land" intense labor policy leads to diminishing returns, particularly when farmers have slack periods and lay off marginal laborers, thus aggravating the national unemployment situation.

Estimates in 1968 of the Kenya economic growth rate at 5.3 per cent, with population increasing at 3 per cent, gives a differential of 2.3 per cent per year. Under these conditions the income per capita would take 31 years to double.

If population were to grow at 2 per cent, income would double in 21 years, at 1 per cent in 16 years. Both economic growth and population growth are now considered higher, but the income per capita changes would be about the same.

In terms of age the dependency ratio in Kenya is high; 100 adult workers support themselves plus 106 children and old people. Their work is diverted for dependents, rather than efforts that lead to capital formation. If we accept the idea that capital formation is a key to development, then the dependency figures are basic to Kenya progress. The fact that nearly 46 per cent of Kenya's population is under 15 years suggests continued high dependency for many years.

In short, population growth impinges on development by increased pressure on the land, by speeding up the consumption of nonreplaceable natural resources, by slowing the rate at which capital is accumulated, and by reducing the rate of growth of resources and equipment that can be used by the labor force (*10*).

Life expectancy (Appendix, Table 4) and projected growth rates further cloud the future. The Population Council estimates for Kenya's population, projected from 1965, show over-all growth under present fertility conditions, and reduced conditions.

Table 5. Projected Total Population of Kenya, 1965–2000 (in Thousands)

Year	*Fertility unchanged*	*Fertility reduced by 50% in 15 years*
1965	9,100	9,100
1970	10,600	10,400
1975	12,400	11,700
1980	14,700	12,900
1985	17,500	14,100
1990	20,800	15,500
1995	25,000	17,100
2000	30,300	19,000

Source: Family Planning in Kenya, p. 4

The present trend in population is leading to a consuming populace of high dependency, large unemployment, and few skills. The situation will hinder the rapid development of the economy, as well as the standard of living (*11*).

Social-attitudinal factors. Social-attitudinal changes that affect the population as a whole are distinguishable by economic class. The social stratification of the colonial period was in three parts: the European managers and administrators, the Asian artisans and tradesmen, and the African unskilled labor force and farmers. Since independence in 1963 an elite class of educated Africans has moved to the top as government leaders, and in some cases managers or co-managers in private firms. The European influence is waning. Many settler families left the country after independence, and although expatriate Europeans and Americans came on development projects or commerce, the total white population is down over one third. The Asian population continues to dominate many of the craft and commercial sectors, although pressures by leaders to promote

African skilled craftsmen and entrepreneurs has somewhat reduced these numbers. The unskilled labor force is still made up almost exclusively of Africans.

Social class barriers of the colonial days in other respects remain intact. The European population, although only 40,000 in 1970, still enjoys disproportionate influence. Little social interaction occurs with non-Europeans outside business obligations, particularly for the remaining settler elements. Other European expatriate groups coalesce largely on the basis of nationality. Asians continue the old pattern of nearly total social exclusion of Africans, avoidance of Europeans, and rigid subgroup clannishness. African social mobility tends to follow occupational position and economic status. Educated Africans in government and university circles have a relatively new mobility with social networks and friendships still very much in formation. Basic social patterns tend to run along tribal lines, with old schoolboy ties and approximate age groupings also important. Status in the bureaucracy also dictates general social contact. Social classes in the rural areas follow more traditional lines, with family position and kinship ties of major importance. The acceptance of family planning seems to be strongest among European and educated African classes. Asian fertility is considered high, as is the case for the rural African population as a whole.

Restraints to economic development in the rural areas center around the inclination to regard any innovation with suspicion. Gradualism, chauvinistic male demands, and the belief that large families are economic necessities promote high birth rates and hinder economic development. Women who participate in family planning programs often do so at considerable personal sacrifice. Conflicts with husband and husband's family, ridicule, economic punishments, and loss of status are some of the costs. Strong pressures also exist for women to consult local medical practitioners or herbalists in lieu of clinics when health and child care problems arise.

Population and Society

General cultural conditions. The cultural availability of the educated Kenya populace to family planning innovations has been remarkably high. The initial success of the program instituted by the Ministry of Health occurred in high density areas, with women who had some education, and some exposure to government information programs. The acceptance rates, per month, in the program, however, have leveled off. This is probably because most of the more innovative women have taken advantage of the service, with the remaining bulk of the female population representing the more conservative, less educated elements.

Important factors that affect the cultural receptivity of family planning innovations for the conservative rural woman lie in the diverse economic life styles in Kenya. The majority of the population are engaged in subsistence farming which is typified by a low level of technology, labor intensive conditions, and limited, often overworked acreage. Most farm families have little capital, little or no savings, and no self-sustaining growth potential. Wealth-level mechanisms affect those families who do attain something economically. They are often obliged to spend their resources for communal purposes, including ritual feasts, religious ceremonies, and other activities which consume personal wealth. Others are expected to give inordinate time and resource to communal offices and status positions.

Social-psychological characteristics affecting family planning that would apply to much of rural Kenya include a high degree of fatalism, or the individual's feeling that he lacks the ability to control the future. In terms of achievement motivation measured as a desire for personal accomplishment, the individual would be generally apathetic. Agricultural innovativeness, assessed as the rapidity of adopting new ideas, would be low. Political knowledge is mainly limited to local institutions and vague ideas of a few national leaders. Economic knowledge centers on local prices paid and market value of crops grown, or the goods and services sought. Both educational and occupational aspirations, for one's self and one's children, should depend on contact with the outside world. Aspirations tend to rise in terms of the individual's cosmopolitan experience. There would also be little sense of empathy in that older villagers have scarce capacity to identify with new aspects of their environment or see themselves in another individual's situation.

Over-all, the rural villager has a short time horizon, the future is unsure, and there is a tendency to view the coming events in narrow time periods, often conceived of as cycles or repetitions of events that are known and vaguely linked to the planting and harvesting cycle. There is little knowledge of the outside world and little interest in gambling on future events. The individual in the poorer areas lives in constant insecurity, plagued throughout his life by the threat of natural disaster. The upshot of these conditions is that the probability of family planning ideas gaining widespread acceptance is low, particularly without major educational efforts.

The estimates on literacy vary in the nation. Some 35–40 per cent of the population are probably literate, with up to 70 per cent literate in the urban areas. Two high density sectors in Kenya, the Victoria Basin and the central highlands, have higher literacy than most other rural areas, and it is here that most family planning programs have been launched. The initial success has been encouraging.

In terms of socio-intellectual mobility, a large portion of the young adult male population would at some period migrate for work or to seek work, and gain a degree of understanding outside their home areas. By and large the magnetism and security of the home village, and the lack of opportunity for the uneducated or semi-educated, keep travel to a minimum.

Public health situation. The current public health situation for urban Kenya is considered excellent by continental African standards, although the lack of trained staff for the rural clinics makes the nation-wide health picture mixed. The physical facilities for medical treatment are considered adequate, with one hospital bed for every 715 persons (1967). The financial allocations from the government, for major medical purposes, is about 7 per cent of the total national budget, with some 0.25 per cent for family planning, maternal and child health services specifically.

Family planning services are offered as an integral part of the government health program, with about 200 clinics offering free IUD and oral contraceptives. The major problem lies in the gross shortage of trained personnel for both family planning and general medical practices. The ratio of doctors to the population in 1970 was about one for 10,000. However, the poor distribution of the staff—about 80 per cent of the 1,080 doctors are in private urban practices—give the rural areas an approximate ratio of one doctor for 250,000 people. The same shortage exists for nurses and other medical staff. In the nation as a whole there were some 400 KRNs/Ms (Kenya Registered Nurses or Midwives) and some 1,200 KENs/Ms (Kenya Enrolled Nurses or Midwives). About 400 medical assistants, with about four years of training, are also employed in local clinics and hospitals.

The demands on the professional time of these personnel are such that in 1969 the average patient was seen for a period of some 53 seconds. This theoretically includes time for the patient to come into the room, to undress, to be diagnosed, to be treated, to be given medication, to dress, and to leave the room (*12*). The general conclusion is that higher level medical personnel cannot under any circumstances handle family planning cases in addition to their other duties. The solution proposed is for the junior staff to be trained to handle family planning responsibilities currently carried by doctors, including loop insertion and pill distribution. The present acceptance of family planning devices is estimated at 30,000 women per year. The retention rates are not known, but probably not over 60 per cent.

Educational profile. The Kenya government places major emphasis on education, and although there has been recent criticism of the overproduction of liberal arts graduates, in lieu of engineering and technical graduates, the nation has an impressive educational record. Three goals have been pursued by the government: (1) the production of people with sufficient skills, knowledge, and expertise to support the modern economy; (2) the provision of universal elementary education; and (3) the implanting of cultural values "for a productive society and developed personal lives."

In the decade 1960–69 the number of schools increased by 28 per cent to a total of 6,879 institutions. Pupil enrollment increased 75 per cent to 1.3 million, and the number of teachers doubled. The expenditure by the government on education rose from $16.7 million in 1963–64 to $30.8 million in 1968–69.

Specific figures for educational enrollment in 1969, and the increases between 1964–69 and 1968–69 indicate the emphasis government places on education (Table 6).

Table 6

		Percent	*Increase*
	1969	*1964–69*	*1968–69*
Primary school (1–8)	1,282,297	26%	6%
Secondary school (9–14)	115,246	22%	14%

Source: Economic Survey, 1970, pp. 171, 173

During 1969 some 6,111 primary schools operated with an average enrollment per class of 32. Secondary education has grown far faster since independence in 1963, particularly in the rural areas. In 1969 a total of 694 secondary schools was under way. School locations follow population densities. Central (171 schools) and Nyanza (127 schools) are the most numerous provinces; the Coast (42 schools) and North Eastern (one school) provinces have the fewest schools.

Trade schools have relatively small enrollments, some 3,000 students in 1969. The government is switching its emphasis to education in this sector, however, and substantial growth can be expected. Teacher training colleges in 1969 had some 6,126 training to be teachers. Over 44,000 teachers were in service in 1969.

There were some 1,725 Kenya students enrolled on the three campuses of the University of East Africa in 1969–70, 1,226 in Nairobi. The three branches dissolved and became separate universities in 1970, the Nairobi branch becoming the University of Nairobi. Kenya students abroad total 901, with the United Kingdom, United States, Soviet Union, and India hosting nearly two thirds. The number of medical students at home and abroad total approximately 250.

The 1970–74 Development Plan calls for university enrollment to double, with increased numbers of graduates in mathematics, engineering, and science. New faculties of law, agriculture, and journalism are scheduled to open by 1974. Students will increasingly receive government loans rather than grants, with repayment expected after graduation. Some pressure on students to accommodate their interests to national needs and to skills for which they will find ready employment can also be expected. As the development plan notes, "unemployed university graduates are a luxury the country cannot afford."

The population growth projections probably affect the primary school age children most directly. Currently some 60 per cent of primary age children are enrolled. The government plans an annual increase of 4 per cent. Under present population growth rates the total number of children receiving no education in 1990 will be twice the present number. If fertility were reduced by 50 per cent in the next 15 years, the government's goal of universal primary education would be possible by 1990.

Population and Polity

Legal situation. As a result of a report submitted to the government in 1966 by the Population Council, Kenya was the first tropical African state to officially establish a family planning program. After careful consideration the government decided to ". . . pursue vigorously policies designed to reduce the rate of population growth through voluntary means." In 1967, under the supervision of the Ministry of Health, the program began providing information, counsel, and various contraceptives. Free clinics in government hospitals and health centers provided the services. The program continues to be presented in coordination with maternal and child health, and works in cooperation with the Family Planning Association of Kenya, and other private groups.

Although the Kenya government took decisive steps in 1967, it does not have a totally committed policy. In the early debates government leaders exercised caution and avoided taking strong stands on family planning. Tom Mboya, then Minister for Economic Planning, illustrates the feelings:

> I must also warn against those who in their enthusiasm for family planning go around preaching the scare of population explosion. This may be the problem in some countries but it is certainly not the prompting factor in Kenya . . . . It has never been the Government's intention to introduce birth control or family planning by compulsory or legislative measures (*13*).

Earlier Mboya had pointed out that population growth could exceed economic growth, and the resulting per capita income would fall far short of the government's hopes. He further argued that the family planning programs must also assist families with infertility problems, thus avoiding "involuntary inferiority" frequently ascribed to barren women.

Perhaps the strongest policy statement has been articulated in the 1966–70 Development Plan. "The population problem has such an impact on the future development of the country that the Government has decided to place strong emphasis on measures to promote family planning education. . . ." The plan notes that fewer children who are more widely spaced would reduce the annual cost of schooling to the family and allow more children to reach higher levels of education. Pressures on the family's housing, water, and food supplies would be diminished, and a higher standard of living would be possible.

Kenya's family planning services were first started by the Pathfinder organization in 1952. This early program and those launched by the churches and the Family Planning Association of Kenya were largely limited to the urban areas, and to the heavy population sectors of Central Province. International agencies, particularly SIDA and USAID, have more recently provided the contraceptives free of charge.

No abortion laws exist in Kenya at the present time; abortion is neither legal nor illegal. The operation can be obtained in the urban areas, although some doctors refuse the service and others only do so with the concurrence of two other doctors that it is necessary for the mother's welfare. Indications are that professional abortions are rare. On the other hand, attempted abortions by amateur practitioneers are commonplace. The frequency with which such cases need hospital attention prompted a question in Parliament asking about the numbers admitted to government hospitals and why the government did not "legalize abortion in order to facilitate family planning." The Attorney General replied that there were 4,210 cases in 1968, and an average of 4,079 per year between 1963–67. He further stated that the increase was not significant, and there was therefore no need to amend the law (*14*). Some indications are that pressures are building up to have the question debated in Parliament, although most observers feel it is too sensitive a topic, politically, and that any such debate would be sidetracked to the need for sex education or more family planning programs. Legal changes supporting abortion are improbable in the near future.

Current political situation. Basic political support for increased family planning came initially from the 1967 decision by government to institute a program. At that stage there was general agreement among most government leaders that the nation had a severe population problem that required immediate action. Political counterpressures, however, were quick to build up. The main arguments tended to center around six points: (1) a belief that Kenya needed greater manpower to take its rightful place of power among African states; (2) the belief, particularly during the political crisis of 1969 (*15*), that some tribes needed maximum growth to protect themselves against other tribes; (3) the idea that any form of family planning might lead to compulsory limitation and impinge on the individual's right of free choice; (4) the notion that the vastness of Kenya's unsettled areas could support greater population; (5) the expressed moralistic fear that contraceptives will promote promiscuity in women, a view that mainly prevails in rural areas; and (6) the belief that the military position of Kenya vis-à-vis its neighbors might be undermined by family planning. This fear incorporates the idea that with a successful Kenya program, Uganda would eventually have a larger population, and with Tanzania already larger, Kenya would be dwarfed by its East African neighbors.

The major political pressures in favor of the Kenya population program have been from two general sectors. First, local institutions such as the Ministry of Health, the Family Planning Association of Kenya, churches and other locally organized agencies, and second, the foreign agencies that provide the major staff and financial backing for the program.

Although the general theory is that the national program should move ahead with vigor, in reality the government continues to vacillate. The fact that the great majority of family planning activities are initiated by foreign donors and agencies, that the training and staffing of Africans in family planning has not been given top priority, and the fact that the financial contribution from the national budget remains small, all indicate a general inaction. Although the groundwork has been laid and impressive initial steps have been taken, most professional observers state that the top echelons of government are still ambivalent about family planning. The lobbies and pressure groups that do exist are mainly the international agencies and donors, but their efforts are largely uncoordinated and they have little significant influence on government policy or planning.

Attitudes toward population programs. Attitudes of government leaders toward population programs tend to be those of cautious approval. Most officials outside the Ministry of Health feel that it is that Ministry's responsibility. Agricultural officials are somewhat aware of the implications for their work, but there is reluctance to use extension workers to disseminate family planning ideas on the basis that they are already overworked. Officials feel such additional attempts would dilute the extension message, confuse the farmers, and further alienate older village leaders. The Ministry of Economic Planning and Development, in drafting the 1970–74 plan, called for a substantial increase in government spending on family planning, although even here a detailed commitment is lacking.

In the Ministry of Information and Broadcasting, family planning is grouped with educational material on maternal and child health. Until 1970 broadcasting in support of family planning was avoided because the material was considered to be of "private matters." Even in the Ministry of Health, the main rationale is that the family planning program has been mounted for the sake of maternal and child health. Discussions of the demographic or economic aspects of population growth are avoided.

The general view of government officials is that family planning is a health activity that must be couched in such terms as to avoid publicity and resistance. Most middle- and lower-range officials are uninformed or misinformed about the program. The major short-run problem, the lack of administrative and paramedical personnel, is generally unrecognized.

Attitudes of religious leaders toward family planning may be assessed as Christian, Muslim, Hindu, and traditional or pagan. The Family Planning Association of Kenya (FPAK), a private association which operates in cooperation with the national program, has encouraged many of the Christian churches and missions to sponsor educational programs and clinics. The National Christian Council of Kenya has coordinated conferences and conducted research, particularly on the population implications for education and school-leavers. The general attitude of Christian churchmen and missionaries would be similar to those in the United States, the more fundamental religious groups tending to be far less sympathetic to family planning measures. Muslim leaders have cooperated with the Family Planning Association in the preparation of brochures and information aimed at that community. The activities are mainly on the coast, and one of the leading lay figures in the Mombasa Muslim community is a member of the FPAK committee. Hindu religious leaders are less involved in family planning, in spite of a relatively high growth rate for that community. Traditional religious leaders usually counsel their followers toward arch-conservative, pronatal attitudes.

The attitudes held by the general populace are in many ways better researched and documented than those of elite or religious groups. For Kenya in general, Molnos has pinpointed many of the attitudes surrounding family planning. Pronatal beliefs stem from the view that children provide a labor force and material wealth for the family, that an easy life is gained when children work for the elders, and that old age insurance is provided by many children. Traditional concepts of life carry strong notions of lineage continuity and descent. The status of a man with many children continues to be equated with wealth, power, pleasant surroundings and peace with his ancestors. Similar attitudes toward the virtue of large families derive from the fear that many children will die before adulthood, a belief founded in the high infant mortality rates of the past. There is a further desire to have a proportionate number of male and female children to support the division of labor among the sexes. Expectations of bride-wealth revenue transactions are also important. Other attitudes that tend to resist family planning are found in the humiliation to which a barren woman is subject, in her fear of being accused of witchcraft, her fear of supernatural punishments, or her fear of other social stigmas.

Special investigation of urban attitudes toward family size by Dow found that some 200 women with an average of three children wanted three more and there was little difference in the desired family size by sex. One half of both the men interviewed (152) and women had some knowledge of family planning methods, and there was widespread interest in learning more (75 per cent of the men, 90 per cent of the women). Another question indicated that only 2 per cent of the women, however, had actually practiced family planning (*16*). The last finding calls the articulated attitudes into some question, and underscores that talk is easy, but practice much harder.

In his study of rural areas, Heisel noted a strong tendency to see children in an economic rather than a psychological or social context. All other considerations, such as the size of the family, risks to mother's health, or fear of infant mortality, were relatively insignificant (*17*). Probing attitudes surrounding the number of children desired, Heisel reports that the women he interviewed desired a mean of 6.03 in the rural areas. Heisel also found that there was considerable ignorance about methods of limiting family size and that the methods known were for the most part "either objectionable or ineffective." In view of the awareness of the economic strains created by large families, Heisel thinks it may be that "in the absence of knowledge of safe and reliable contraceptives, ideas of family size tend to remain near the level of achieved fertility." Given some success in family planning education, this finding is possibly a hopeful sign about the future success of family planning measures. Dow reported 6.20 for women, and 6.6 for men. Both findings are close to the actual number of children estimated per family (7.0). On the other hand there seems to be little interest in very large families. Only 15 per cent of Heisel's sample of women reported nine or more children as ideal. There is little difference between rural and urban attitudes on number of children desired.

An interesting specific finding by Martin shows the differences in attitudes on the question "A woman has a duty to her husband and his relatives to have as many children as possible."

Table 7

	Husbands		*Wives*	
Response	*Little urban experience*	*Much urban experience*	*Little urban experience*	*Much urban experience*
Agree	61%	53%	31%	20%
Don't know	4%	3%	6%	5%
Disagree	35%	44%	64%	75%
Total respondents	132	241	255	108

Source: Martin, p. 5

Positive attitudes toward family planning are usually traced to the aspirations of the parents to educate all children, to provide better material needs such as housing, food, and clothes. The need for more disposable cash and more pleasure and leisure time are also important. Many of these articulate beliefs come with education and with more confidence in the modern health services. In church-oriented families, the moral issue of the parents' responsibility to have only those children they can easily support tends to be a recurring attitude (*18*).

Population Work and Research

Family planning programs. Family planning initiatives were first taken in Kenya in 1952 by the Pathfinder Fund. Formal services through private efforts began in 1957 with the formation of the Family Planning Association in Kenya, (FPAK). The government program, launched in 1967, is headquartered in the Ministry of Health. Its basic aim is to provide family planning education, information, equipment, supplies, and medical service through free clinics which are mainly located in existing hospitals and dispensaries. The demographic targets of the program are not stated by the government beyond a desire to reduce the excessive rate of growth, while cutting down mortality. The main education thrust is to make every child a conscious choice. The Ministry of Health is adamant in stressing that the program is wholly voluntary and has no wish to encroach on religious beliefs and customs. Spacing of births is emphasized as well as methods of contraception and family limitation.

Organizationally, the Director of Medical Services in the Ministry of Health is responsible for the planning of a comprehensive program. He is chairman of a working committee on family planning which serves as an advisory and coordinating group. Under this committee is the family planning section, made up of two expatriate professionals and a Kenya nurse education specialist. They are assisted by the Epidemiological section in statistical analysis and a health education section which prepares materials. Foreign donor agencies provide a number of experts and equipment.

As of mid-1970 some 200 medical facilities were offering family planning on a regular basis (*19*). The key problem lay in the fact that most of the clinics are rural health centers or dispensaries which are genuinely overburdened. The number of trained personnel is inadequate, and most staff are too preoccupied with normal medical duties and health work to give family planning a high priority. An important decision was taken in 1969 to allow nurses and other paramedical personnel to begin training on inserting IUD's and dispensing other family planning services.

By 1969, some 2,600 women a month were accepting contraception after consultation, a figure that represents some fifteen-fold increase over 1967–68. In 1969 some 31,000 women were seen as first visitors, and 67,000 were seen on "revisits." During 1970 an average of 12,000 per month were visiting the clinics, with about 2,800 per month as first visitors (see Appendix, Table 2). Figures on retention rates for IUD acceptors and continuation rates for pill users were not available; estimates range from 40 to 80 per cent rejection in the first year. A majority of the clinics are operated by the government (80) or the IPPF mobile units (61). Some 40 are conducted by the Nairobi City Council, 19 by mission stations, and eight by the FPAK on a private basis. The frequency of the clinics is either weekly (99), at ten-day intervals (26), monthly (50), or on request (21). A recent study of a random sample of first visits to Family Planning clinics showed the following services being dispensed (December 1970): pill 51 per cent, IUD 29 per cent, injectables 4 per cent, other methods 2 per cent, none 13 per cent, unknown 1 per cent.

Clinical services include consultation with patients, general examination and diagnosis, history-taking, screening, dispensing contraceptives, follow-up instructions, referral of problem cases, record keeping, and general clinic management. The contraceptive methods employed are the free distribution of pills provided by SIDA (Ovulen and Eugynon in accordance with the Dunlop Committee reports), and the Lippes Loop. Throughout Kenya 55 per cent of the acceptors use the pill, and 45 per cent the loop, although major geographical variations occur. The Muslim-influenced coastal area, for example, has an 85 per cent use of pill and only 10 per cent use of IUD's. Therapeutic abortion is not practiced in the program, and other forms of control such as sterilization and injectables are rare. No incentives are provided to encourage participation. At the present time there is no organized opposition to the government's program. The provisional 1969 census reports, showing a higher growth rate than had been expected, have probably served to keep the family planning activities from becoming controversial and overtly political. Support, in fact, is forthcoming from the military which has several clinics on its bases.

Future plans are to increase the Kenya staff of medical and paramedical personnel in family planning schemes, and thus to alleviate the overburdened medical staff. Training, begun in mid-1970, was directed at a doctor group who will in turn act as supervisors for other personnel. Seminars are projected and a field staff of FPAK educators will join the 50 now working in rural areas. Such educators will make home visits as well as presentations at public meetings. In terms of projected financial support, the disproportionately high contribution by international agencies is expected to be reduced with increased funds, personnel, and equipment from the Kenya government.

Demographic research. One of the basic problems in Kenya's population program is the lack of enough trained demographic specialists. The University of Nairobi provides a second year sociology course in demography which includes techniques of population analysis. Although it is a thorough course, there is no direct link between those who complete the course and positions that entail the needed analysis for the Kenya government.

Other demographic activities related to family planning include the work of the Statistics Division of the Ministry of Economic Planning and Development. This office produces the *Kenya Statistical Digest,* a quarterly economic report, and other documents partially related to population. The Bureau of the Census conducts the primary analysis of the national census and provides mid-year estimates of population. Demographic work on the census data, however, is divided between several Ministries, and much of the work is carried out by expatriate officers on short-term assignments.

A registration act for births and deaths, amended in 1967, makes registration in certain areas of Kenya compulsory. It is voluntary in others. The high density Central Province has had compulsory registration since 1964, and other districts are gradually being brought into the program. There is also increased publicity on legal statutes which cover legitimacy, marriage, adoption, and divorce. This may lead to better registrations and aid future demographic research.

Indigenous institutions. The most important local institution working on family planning is the Family Planning Association of Kenya, which operates from grants by the International Planned Parenthood Federation. FPAK operates 17 clinics in areas where government programs do not yet operate, and in urban areas on a private basis. A major information program is also offered, and branches of the association are maintained in several areas. Six area officers promote close coordination between the branches, and some 56 field educators carry family planning information to rural families.

The Association was formed in the 1950s by several doctors in Nairobi and Mombasa to help avoid unwanted pregnancies. In 1961 the Association affiliated with IPPF. In 1969 an agreement over responsibilities was reached with the Ministry of Health whereby the Association would be working mainly in the education and information fields, with the Ministry providing technical and medical services.

Other local organizations working in family planning include:

(*1*) Family Service Council of Kenya, a voluntary organization, which focuses on such problems as juvenile delinquency, broken homes, divorce, and marriage counseling. A school program in "family life education" is also operated in which family planning topics are taught.

(*2*) University of Nairobi has developed a teaching program in demography within the department of sociology and a population specialist, supported by the Population Council, is on the staff. Several conferences have been held in conjunction with the University, and surveys on knowledge, attitudes, and practices in family planning have been conducted. Medical and nursing schools also train students in family planning.

(*3*) Churches, usually through mission medical facilities, offer clinical services and educational programs. Some also train their own medical personnel and receive direct support from their parent mission organizations.

(*4*) Private organizations, which include service-oriented clubs, groups for community welfare, economists, agricultural extension groups, and school groups provide lectures on family planning. Discussions are also underway to provide family planning teaching in the schools, including the primary level.

International agencies. The major support for the Kenya population program comes from several foreign agencies working in conjunction with the

Ministry of Health. During the fiscal year 1969–70 contributions from these organizations equaled $934,680.00. The Ministry of Health contributed $28,000 as a line item plus two or three times this amount in facilities and health personnel salaries. The specific contributions from the international agencies include the following (1969–70):

(*1*) British Overseas Development provided equipment for the epidemiological section, office equipment, and ten vehicles. Estimated contribution, $78,400.

(*2*) Ford Foundation provided a grant for a training and education project, supports a research survey on family planning attitudes, and keeps a population program officer for East and Central Africa. Estimated contribution, $19,600.

(*3*) International Planned Parenthood Federation makes a major financial contribution to support the FPAK, provides seven mobile teams giving family planning services and training, and finances and operates a Family Welfare Center. Contributions estimated at $368,480.

(*4*) Netherlands provided a technical staff of seven, including two gynecologists, and medical equipment. Estimated contribution, $126,000.

Royal Dutch Institute of Tropical Hygiene organizes and evaluates statistical data and helps train field staffs in mobile units.

(*5*) Norway provided equipment for 50 family planning clinics, valued at approximately $12,600.

(*6*) Population Council provided one medical advisor and one nurse-health educator for the Ministry of Health, plus support for university teaching staff in demography and sociology. Estimated contribution, $72,800.

(*7*) SIDA provides one advisor on administration for the Ministry of Health and supplies contraceptives for free distribution. Estimated contribution, $70,000.

(*8*) USAID provides two experts working on the population census, an expert in health education, and one audio-visual professional working with educational materials. Basic equipment for the health education unit and three vehicles are also provided. The estimated contribution is $159,600.

The total contribution by international agencies, estimated by Fendall between 1965 and early 1970, was $1,319,000. This included other contributions by The Oxford Committee for Family Relief to train midwives, the Pathfinder Fund contributions for nurse education and contraceptive pills, and the American Friends Service Committee for population consultants and advisors.

Evaluation. The major advances made in family planning lie in the clinical services, in the strides in education, and in the backing international donors continue to provide. Problems lie in the lack of trained personnel, the failure of the program to establish reliable research service, and the ambivalence of top politicians. The program's efficiency is commendable, as the growing number of participants in family planning services illustrate. Precise evaluation, however, is difficult because it is not known how many initial acceptors reject the loop or discontinue the pill. The over-all commitment Kenya women have to family planning is unknown.

One of the major problems in establishing a viable family planning program has been the discoordination in the financial sector of family planning. Donor agencies have been slow to deliver contracted items, such as equipment for data processing, vehicles, and chemical supplies. Pills, far more costly than the IUD, have been preferred. The actual financial input of the Kenya government has been small, and because of lack of coordination, even these funds in the past have not been completely used. The trend has been reversed.

Conclusions

Kenya has been called the Japan of Africa, an aggressive, driving nation determined to reap the fruits of industrialization and to have for its people the benefits of the modern world. In terms of population, this nation early on took a long and sober look at its burgeoning growth rate, and began doing something about it. In just three years a major national program has reached over 100,000 women. Family planning leaders can be justly proud of this first tropical African program. It is highly rational, highly pragmatic, and, like Japan, inextricably linked to the economic development of the state.

Probing below the surface, however, one finds that the inevitable cross-pressures and difficulties in establishing such a national effort begin to emerge. In reality family planning is largely run by non-African expatriates. About 80 per cent of all contraceptives are handed out by European doctors and nurses. The organization and infrastructure of the program are indeed intact, but strong commitments from major African leaders are still lacking. The financial imbalance at which international donors support the program, a rate of 30 times that of the Kenya contribution, indicates its priority. There is a feeling that the Kenya leaders are drawing on some ancient proverb that portrays the foreigners coming with their new wares, as wise old men watch and wait and ponder the implications.

The political pressures on the family planning program spring from the basic problems of Kenya national integration. Competition between the leading tribal groups for power has characterized Kenya since independence, and particularly after the assassination of Tom Mboya in mid-July, 1969. The divisions run deep between Mboya's Luo people, the second largest tribe (1962 census), and the larger, economically dominant Kikuyu of the central highlands. The general trend, therefore, has been for politicians to cautiously ignore or soft-pedal population questions. Those who may have wished to bring family planning up as a controversy have been temporarily put off by the fact that no African politician has embraced the cause sufficiently to make him a worth-while target.

The more meaningful criticism that the population program is still largely a paper program supported by foreign monies and basically run by "two-year visitors" has not been leveled as yet. The charge would probably reach too far into the question of foreign advisers and foreign aid. Such criticisms have been unfashionable except for the mild comments as ". . . we have more aid than we can chew . . " or ". . . the aid bottleneck is the lack of trained personnel . . . ."

Specific organizational problems lie in the day-to-day operations of the program. A decrease in the monies appropriated by the government for family planning has been due largely to the fact that the funds available were not spent. Funds were given up at the end of the last three budget years, and the next budget subsequently reduced. The 1970 budget reversed the downward trend, up from $28,000 to $42,000.

More basically, there have been no specific targets set for the Kenya family planning program other than a general decrease in the population. There has been no research and evaluation about ideal population figures in terms of distribution. Research problems also lie in the lack of solid demographic information for some districts, and the lack of data or research on the actual clinical operations. Little is known of techniques and their effectiveness or ways to improve upon them. Data problems also exist concerning the effects of contraceptive pills, particularly in terms of attitudes and what is articulated by users to non-users.

One possibility of major expansion of the family planning program lies in the use of injectable contraceptives. The widely-held belief that an injection is far superior to any other medicine makes the needle the most respected form of treatment for the mass rural population. The development of such injectables in Kenya has only been used in private clinics and for women with five or more children. This caution is due mainly to the uncertainty that fertility can be re-established. Other techniques such as sterilization are rarely used, often due to the unavailability of surgeons and the shortage of beds. Most surgery is done on an emergency basis and there is little time for preventive practices. Male contraceptive pills and other methods have been discussed but not tried. A further problem exists in medical staff orientation, which tends to be curative rather than preventive. There is also a lack of interest by medical staff in serving as instructors. The shortage of counselors and advisers for educational purposes impairs the program. Personnel problems are further complicated by rapid transfer, leave-taking for long periods, and pregnancies by medical staff. Other problems in the past have stemmed from conflicts between voluntary programs and the national program, particularly regarding services to those who do not have or wish to have access to government clinics.

In a positive sense the national family planning program has shown steady progress. The number of clinics offering services has increased, and among the educated population there is a growing realization that the existing medical facilities and improved health conditions reduce infant mortality and thus reduce the need for large families. A further advantage for the Kenya program is the relative smallness of the Catholic population of the nation which keeps the complicated lay beliefs on birth control shared by Catholics in French-speaking African states from entering the picture. Perhaps most important, both religious and lay leaders of Kenya have commitments to improving the status of the people, and there is general realization that this cannot be accomplished without a significant decrease in fertility.

Pressures in support of the program can also be expected to come from bureaucrats and some members of Parliament, particularly those concerned with economic analysis. Here there is a growing realization that the population increases seriously challenge Kenya's development. Over-all, population equals the power game. For the moment there is relative peace on this front, but it would be unrealistic to expect the tranquillity to continue. As pressures go up for leaders to take strong stands on population control, so too will the political counterpressures emerge in terms of localism, tribalism, and other vested interests.

Acknowledgments

I am particularly indebted to Mr. David Radel, Ford Foundation, Nairobi, Dr. S. Kanani, Dr. James Russell, and Mr. Jorgen Ahlinder of the Kenya Ministry of Health, Mr. William Wamalwa, chairman, Dr. Giceha Kigondu, executive director, and Miss Freda M. Mudoga of the Family Planning Association of Kenya, for providing materials and commentary on their respective family planning interests. Dr. Donald Heisel, Population Council in New York, gave me a number of source materials as well as the benefit of his Kenya experience. The writer remains solely responsible for the findings herein.

Notes

1. The term "Asian" in census terms denotes an individual from the subcontinent of India, but does not include Ceylonese, who with Chinese, Japanese, or other persons from the Far East are classified as "others." People of Arab affiliation are those with ancestry in Saudi Arabia, Yemen, Muscat, Aden, or Oman.
2. Source: Kenya Ministry of Economic Planning and Development, *Economic Survey, 1970* (Nairobi: Government Printer, 1970), p. 128.
3. Wage employment includes self-employed farmers who work on other farms as casual laborers. Wage employment in small-holding sector is only those hired by others.
4. See Russell, James J., "Kenya: Country Profile," Population Council and Kenya Ministry of Health, October 1970, mimeo, draft, pp. 8–9.
5. See Etherington, D. M., "Projected Changes in Urban and Rural Population in Kenya and Implications for Development Policy," in J. R. Sheffield, ed., *Education, Employment and Rural Development* (Nairobi: East African Publishing House, 1967), pp. 54–74.
6. See Map in Appendix. Also see Ominde, S. H., *Land and Population Movements in Kenya* (London: Heineman, 1968), pp. 83–196.
7. Kenya Ministry of Economic Planning and Development, *Statistical Abstract-1969* (Nairobi: Government Printer, 1970), p. 22.
8. Kenya Ministry of Economic Planning and Development, "Statistical Digest," Vol. VIII, No. 2, June 1970, p. 12.
9. Angwenyi, Charles P., "The Effects of Population Growth on Economic Development in Kenya," Seminar on Population Growth and Economic Development, University College, Nairobi, Dec. 14–22, 1969 (mimeo), pp. 1–5.
10. Angwenyi, p. 12, and Spengler, J. J., "Population Obstacles to Economic Development," in J. J. Spengler and O. D. Duncan, eds., *Population, Theory and Policy* (Glencoe, Ill.: Free Press, 1956), p. 311.

11. Angwenyi, p. 20.
12. J. J. Russell, speech, Kenya–American Conference on Family Planning, Nairobi, Sept. 25–26, 1970.
13. Mboya, Tom, "The Place for Social Welfare in the National Development Plan," Conference on Social Welfare (Nairobi, September 1967), speech.
14. Question in Parliament, No. 573, July 23, 1970. Regarding abortion, see also section 156, 159, 160 of the Penal Code, Laws of Kenya.
15. See Norman N. Miller, *Assassination and Political Unity: Kenya* (NNM–5–'69), Fieldstaff Reports, East Africa Series, Vol. VIII, No. 5, 1969.
16. Dow, Thomas E., Jr., "Attitudes Toward Family Size and Family Planning in Nairobi," *Demography,* Vol. 4, No. 2, 1967, Part I.
17. Heisel, Donald, "Fertility Limitation Among Women in Rural Kenya," IDS papers, University College, Nairobi, 1969. See particularly pp. 638, 639.
18. Molnos, A., *Attitudes Towards Family Planning in East Africa* (Munchen: Weltforum Verlag, 1968).
19. Indicates clinics reporting in government program; other private clinics exist.

References

Kenya Ministry of Finance and Economic Planning, *Kenya Population Census,* 1969, Vol. 1, Nov. 1970.

Molnos, A., *Attitudes Towards Family Planning in East Africa* (Munchen: Weltforum Verlag, 1968).

Ominde, S. H., *Land and Population Movements in Kenya* (London: Heineman, 1968).

Russell, James, J., "Kenya: Country Profile," Population Council and Kenya Ministry of Health, October 1970, mimeo, draft.

Soja, Edward W., *The Geography of Modernization in Kenya* (Syracuse, N. Y.: Syracuse University Press, 1968).

The Author

NORMAN N. MILLER has been concerned with East Africa's anthropology and politics for more than a decade. In 1950–60 he travelled extensively in East and Central Africa and subsequently, with research support from the Ford Foundation and the Carnegie Corporation, lived in Tanzania or Kenya on four separate occasions. Dr. Miller has also done research under grants from Michigan State University and has taught at the University of East Africa in Dar es Salaam. Receiving the M.A. and Ph.D. degrees from Indiana University, in 1966 he joined the faculty of Michigan State where he is the editor of *Rural Africana,* a research bulletin in the social sciences. On leave from Michigan State, Dr. Miller is a Faculty Associate of the American Universities Field Staff and resides in Kenya. The author of numerous articles and chapters on local politics in Africa, his interests include documentary film-making, and he has recently completed a 16mm. instructional film entitled *East Africa: Myth and Drum.*

Table 1. Number of Clinics under Ministry of Health

Year	*Month*	*National program*	*Nairobi city council*	*Totals*
1969	Jan.	85	14	99
	April	73	27	100
	July	102	28	130
	Oct.	116	33	149
1970	Jan.	133	35	168
	April	142	39	181
	July	150	39	189
	Oct. (unofficial report)	—	—	198

Source: Kenya Ministry of Health, Epidemiology and Medical Statistics, Report Aug. 18, 1970

Table 2. Attendance 1967–70, Clinic Visits and Re-visits

Year	*1st Visit*	*Re-visit*	*Total*
1967	1,519	7,879	9,397
1968	11,711	17,891	29,602
1969	30,303	71,967	102,270
1970 (Jan.–June)	16,743	54,149	70,892

Source: Kenya Ministry of Health, Epidemiology and Medical Statistics, Report, August 18, 1970

Table 3. Acceptors by Education (1968 Visits), Years of Schooling

	Number	%
None	2261	25.0
1–3	1149	12.7
4–7	3256	36.0
8–10	1474	16.3
11–13	117	1.3
14	27	0.3
Unstated	760	8.4
Totals	9044	100.0

Source: Kenya Ministry of Health, Epidemiology and Medical Statistics, Report Oct. 21, 1969

Table 4. Life Expectancy for Kenya Africans (1962)

Age	*Expectancy*	*Age*	*Expectancy*
0	39.0	45	19.9
1	43.6	50	16.9
5	44.6	55	14.0
10	43.4	60	11.4
15	39.4	65	9.1
20	35.9	70	7.2
25	32.9	75	5.7
30	29.7	80	4.6
35	26.4	85	3.5
40	23.2		

Source: Calculated from Estimates in Kenya Census, 1962, Vol. III, p. 92. Compiled by James Cramer

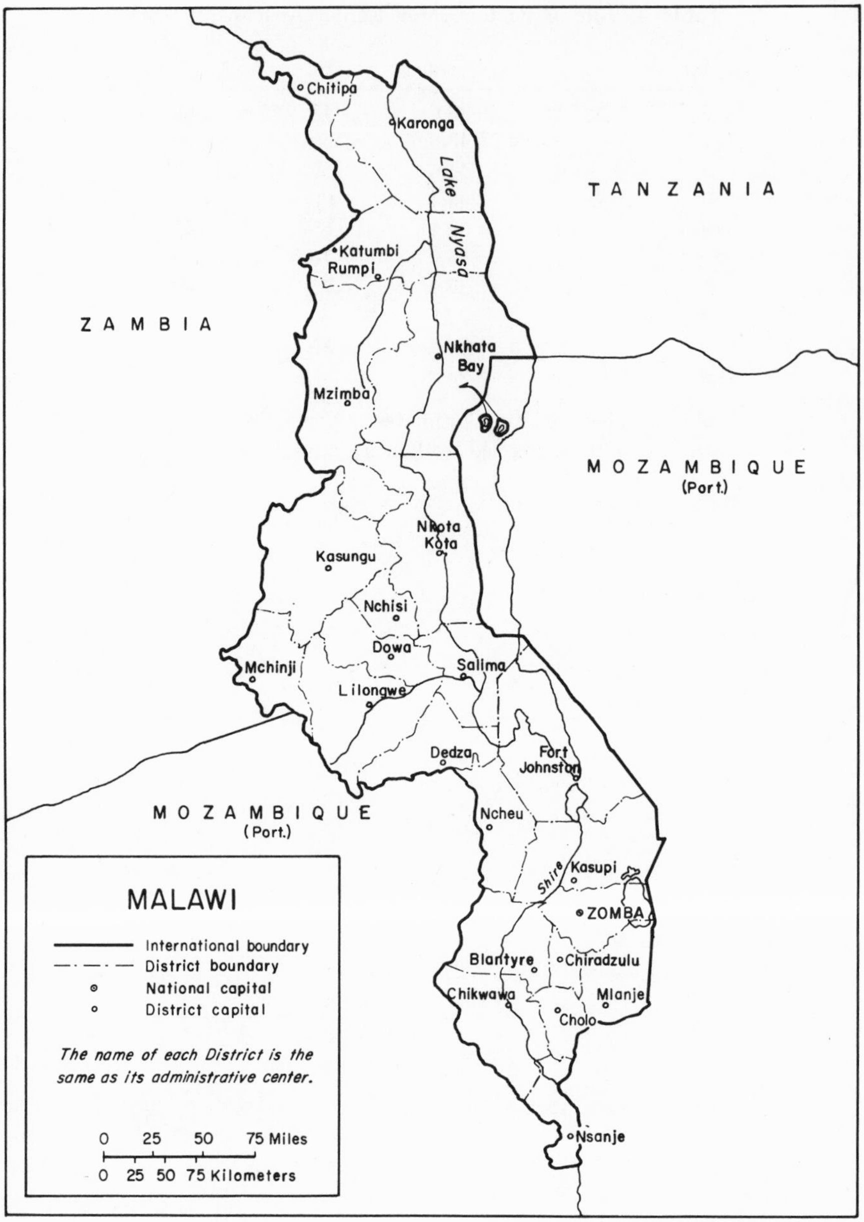

TANZANIA
ZAMBIA
MOZAMBIQUE
(Port.)
MOZAMBIQUE
(Port.)
Chitipa
Karonga
Lake
Nyasa
Katumbi
Rumpi
Nkhata
Bay
Mzimba
Nkota
Kota
Kasungu
Nchisi
Dowa
Salima
Mchinji
Lilongwe
Dedza
Fort
Johnston
Ncheu
Shire
Kasupi
ZOMBA
Blantyre
Chiradzulu
Chikwawa
Mlanje
Cholo
Nsanje
MALAWI
International boundary
District boundary
National capital
District capital
The name of each District is the same as its administrative center.
0 25 50 75 Miles
0 25 50 75 Kilometers

Malawi

James R. Hooker

Malawi is a small country (36,000 square miles) with an unusually high population density: in 1966 it had an average of 111 persons per square mile, half that of Western Europe and four times greater than the figure for all Africa. On the continent, only Rwanda, Burundi, and Nigeria (accepting that nation's last census, which requires considerable faith) appear to have greater pressures on land.

On the assumption that the rate of growth indicated in the censuses of 1945 and 1966 still obtains—3.3 per cent per annum—Malawi today has about 4.6 million people. The demographic profile is interesting. The median age is 17.5 years; there are only 90 males per 100 females; 19 per cent of the populace is below five years; the child/woman ratio is an astounding 82 (number of children below five divided by number of women aged 15–44 times 100). By 1990, there should be nine million Malawians. There are so few figures available, that almost nothing can be said of mortality and life expectancy. At any time there are perhaps nearly 200,000 Malawians working outside the territory. Within the country there is considerable migration, especially seasonal. Latest estimates set the urban growth rate at about 2.9 per cent per annum. About 43 per cent of the women, who form nearly 54 per cent of the population, are in the prime fertility years.

Are the materials from which these assertions are drawn reliable? The 1966 census was the first conducted by trained enumerators working in clearly delimited districts. It was *de facto,* counting only those present in the country, though separate lists of absentees were maintained. The technique used had been selected previously in Zambia. Every one of the more than a million dwelling units in the country was visited between August 9 and September 15, and people were asked to give particulars of all who had slept in each house the previous night. The quality of the workers (VSO, PCV, teachers, and students), the use of an American computer, and a sophisticated postenumeration survey technique suggest that the margin of error was reasonably small, the government's estimate being an undercount of 2.6 per cent. There is nothing like the Nigerian necessity for censal figures to prove political points in Malawi, so I am inclined to believe that the basic data available are reasonably accurate.

Population Distribution and Movement

Malawi is undergoing a shift from the land to the city. Over 90 per cent of the people still live in villages, and much of the so-called urban 5 per cent actually dwells in traditional villages which have been surrounded by vastly expanded city administrative limits. Current estimates by the National Statistical Office hold that towns are growing at roughly 3 per cent per annum, predominantly as a result of natural increase. Although the country is overwhelmingly rural, there is evidence of increased urbanization. The main picture is of an internal migration, at least seasonally, away from the Northern Province into the other two, as well as out of the country. There is, however, little data available on emigrants.

Approximately half the population lives in the Southern Province, which also contains the largest cities. Greater Blantyre has just over 100,000 inhabitants, so the word urbanization may conjure up misleading images. Probably only 3 per cent of the urban population has "nowheres else to go." There is little value in talking about reverse migration because almost no one completely leaves the land. Nearly every male in an urban area owns some land, whether or not he is using it. Internal migration is important, but can be exaggerated: 88 per cent of those counted were living in the district of their birth. And yet, Malawians have a deserved reputation for traveling (the President, Dr. H. K. Banda, was away 43 years). One supposes that as with air travel in the United States, a small determined group is doing all of it. In 1966, about 266,000 Malawians were out of the country, and about the same number of foreigners, mostly from Mozambique, were resident here (*1*). Nevertheless, certain districts do lose population (27.4 per cent from Nsanje), and others, notably the glamour spots, do gain (14.9 per cent to Blantyre).

Sex ratios are skewed badly by male migration. In the 15–49 age group there can be as few as 73 males per 100 females. Indeed, not until age 60 is parity reached. The over-all ratio, as mentioned above, is 90/100. By comparison, in Zambia and Kenya it is 98, while in Rhodesia, a migration terminus for, among others, Malawian laborers, there are 106 males for every 100 females. The remittances which these emigrants send to Malawi are important economically, probably amounting to more than $10 million per annum. Moreover, the absence of males does not seem to disrupt family life in the predominantly matrilineal and matrilocal societies of southern Malawi. It appears that the end of the normal 18–24 month work tour in South Africa or Rhodesia comes at about the time mothers begin to wean their babies, and hence are once again available for sexual congress. The temporary absence of the husband thus has a negligible effect on the birth rate.

Every person at least ten years old was asked by the enumerators if he had earned cash in the past year, and if so, how. Of males, 63.1 per cent had some access to money; among females the figure was 52.3 per cent. Two-thirds got their money from the sale of farm produce. The population which identified itself as wage- or salary-earning was 246,000. However, the government in 1970 reported 140,000 wage and salary workers, including only those employed in enterprises with 20 or more workers. At the very best only a fraction of available manpower is at work for wages, and of this fraction not quite 50 per cent had worked for twelve consecutive months. Service occupations and tea/tobacco agriculture lead the list, with 41,000 and 38,000 respectively. Manufacturing and construction each employ about 17,000, while other sectors range from 8,000 engaged in transport to 1,000 in quarrying.

Though there has been a recently renewed interest in a considerable bauxite reserve on Mlanje mountain, Malawi's only mineral deposit found to date, its exploitation depends upon developments over which the country has no control. For ore mining to be profitable, new aluminum plants must be built in South Africa, the Portuguese must construct the Cabora Bassa Dam on the Zambesi, and good rail or water links must connect Mlanje with the Indian Ocean ports.

As President Banda has remarked tirelessly, Malawi's gold is its soil. The country seems destined to remain an agricultural country, but one which is turning from the monoculture plantation economy of most such states. Smallholder tea and tobacco schemes, though in their infancy, have been remarkably successful. The country is a strong exporter of foodstuffs such as maize (produce accounted for 75 per cent of exports and 50 per cent of national product in 1969), most of which is peasant-planted. A small secondary industry catering to the needs of the domestic market has also emerged.

Historically, Malawi has been linked to the London tea exchange, but in most other instances closely tied to Rhodesia and South Africa. Since Rhodesia's unilateral declaration of independence in 1965 (UDI), certain changes have occurred, notably the establishment of trade with other countries, such as Japan (2). Generally speaking, since independence in 1964 the balance of trade has run against Malawi because of heavy imports of fixed investment indispensable for development. Moreover, the nation is one of 13 land-locked African states and must deal with the reality of Portuguese existence. The port of Beira until recently was necessary for goods transfer. Now this dependence may be shifted to the new Portuguese deep water port at Nacala, recently connected to Blantyre by rail.

Population and Development

Malawi is among the very few states in the Third World which have faced the agricultural facts of life. While urging the entry of manufacturing interests, and encouraging the growth of local industry, the bulk of the government's effort has been expended in the area of natural resources. There is an intensive afforestation program; the game parks are being enlarged and equipped with camps and access roads; indiscriminate setting of bush fires (associated with slash and burn agriculture) and hillside logging are treated increasingly as serious offenses; soil surveys and aerial mapping programs are being conducted; and courses in farming are beginning to appear as compulsory subjects in schools. "Our gold is our soil" is not an empty Presidential phrase.

In the realm of agricultural development, perhaps the two most successful donor countries, at least in the private opinion of some government officials, have been Israel and China (Taiwan). The Chinese have concentrated their 49-man team in six specific rice projects, but they have also been producing enormous onions and other vegetables in demonstration plots. The Israeli mission is one of the larger they maintain in Africa. Whereas the Chinese aim only at increasing agricultural productivity, the Israeli effort is funneled through the Malawi Young Pioneers, who are trying to create citizens pledged to return to their villages as social activists. In both instances, the emphasis is on the village world, the small farm, without much in the way of machinery or reliable transport. The Chinese avoid ideology, except to preach the gospel of private enterprise in farming. The Israelis openly declare they are helping to weld a nation out of disparate elements. They wage war upon tribalism, stress the *lingua franca* chi-Cewa, and clearly hold that in certain circumstances "civics" might be as important as ditching and diking.

Forests and wildlife resources are also being developed. The timber industry here has a sound basis, and there appears to be no section of the country where soil erosion is a threat.

Urban sprawl exists, to be sure, but as yet this is nothing more than ribbon development. Nowhere can one see the slums so characteristic of many other African cities. Malawi is one of the dozen poorest countries in the world by United Nations criteria, but such statistics do not adequately describe the actual life of Malawians. There is no land hunger, no landlord class, no powerful church, no reactionary government, no caste system, no regional grievances which are unmanageable, and only a tiny alien minority (7,000 Europeans and 11,000 Asians in 1966). Little cash jingles in the pockets of Malawian peasants, but there are few starving beggars either. Development is the constant preachment of the President and the party, and many people have come to think that enthusiastic support of the government's development policies not only earns cash but also proves political loyalty. Whether this enthusiasm can be maintained is a guess, but current indications are positive.

The government is not foolish enough to believe that people will find farming glamorous; rather, it hopes to persuade the talented that there is money in the land, and the mediocre that there is no point in going to Blantyre. Admittedly, left and right policy hands often fail to clasp: in the English-instruction course on the Malawi Broadcasting Corporation's program for schools, listeners practice such sentences as "When I grow up and live in Blantyre I shall have a car." But almost every public utterance of any official of consequence contains the obligatory exhortation to look at the land and prosper. In the most thorough analysis of agriculture in Malawi, Horst Dequin (3) suggests 7.5 acres as the upward limit for hoe agriculture holdings. This seems high to anyone who has handled one. Cutting his figure back to four or five acres, it still is possible to find men whose financial arrangements are expressed in hundreds of pounds rather than shillings. Without touting them as heroic figures, it should be possible to establish a class of rich peasants who would earn sufficient foreign exchange and produce enough comestibles for local consumption to switch Malawi's balance of payments from red to black. In this connection Dequin's speculation that the projected new capital in the north (Lilongwe) might remove much of the population from contact with the fleshpots of the European south makes sense.

Population and Society

Malawians have a reputation throughout southern Africa for their hard work, thrift, and high regard for education, characteristics at least partly the heritage of those Scots missionaries who followed Livingstone up the Shiré River. Judging by government expenditures, however, Malawi may be alone on the continent in the relatively low priority it now attaches to education, except in the agricultural field. Of the 9 million pounds devoted to development last year, only 700,000 pounds went to education, while communications and resources together got 6 million pounds.

Only a minority of Malawians are literate in any language. About 17 per cent of the school-age population was in school in 1966. The 51 secondary schools cannot cope with the qualified demand for places, let alone do anything for those who failed, or failed to get exposed to, lower education. Slightly less than 6 per cent of the total Malawi population understand English. There are about 1,000 students in the five divisions of the University. In all, it is doubtful if more than a third of any age set is exposed to formal education. What can be said is that Malawi has no "Muslim north," as in Nigeria and the Sudan, so that standards are fairly uniform throughout the country, although the better teachers are likely to be in the city schools. Last year's graduates in Liberal Arts were the first to find jobs scarce. At least in government, it appears that the market for degree holders already has been satisfied.

Population and Polity

The government, the ruling party, and the Life President all are opposed to birth control, to population planning, and to the dissemination of any information about sex, which is considered to be a topic unsuited to the sensibilities of decent people. There is no pressure group here which seeks to challenge this position, no crusading journalist, daring educator, or distinguished medical man to deride or deplore official attitudes. This is not a permissive society. Europeans may favor contraception, and their private views are respected, but the government has shown a marked aversion to any publicity on the subject. Birth control is perceived by some Malawians, at least by those in a position to influence policy, as a European idea, perhaps appropriate to Europeans and Western medicine, but not to Malawians. One can obtain an abortion in Malawi. The operation is performed for therapeutic reasons only and this fiction seems to satisfy everybody. The willingness to determine the therapeutic necessity varies widely. There is one school of thought, however, that argues for abortion rather than contraception, on the ground that it offends no traditional belief, and can be jusified to a modern government.

The President views the projected doubling of population with favor. To those who declare that Malawi already is overpopulated, he retorts that it is untrue, and especially so when one considers new ways of using land and other resources. He is fond of reminding people that when he got the chance, one of the first ministries he took over from the British was Natural Resources. From the start he was determined that Africans would enter commercial agriculture, and they have. It is too early to say much about tea, for the first acres are only beginning to yield, but smallholders now produce more tobacco than do the European estate owners. All together, peasant agriculturists are producing nearly a million pounds sterling more of export crops than are their white counterparts, who previously monopolized the field. From an American perspective, it might not seem worth mentioning that Africans can grow cash crops. From the viewpoint afforded in the field, however, things look different. It *is* important to boast of African performance, to cite those men who now earn more than Members of Parliament, for Europeans, when they ruled, loudly proclaimed, and now privately insist, that Africans cannot grow cash crops. Dr. Banda can be proud of this achievement.

There are, of course, people in and out of government who view unrestricted population growth with alarm. They express this privately. (One of the rumors one cannot avoid being told concerns the master plan for birth control which is filed discreetly in the Ministry of Health awaiting the Life President's demise.) For the moment, however, no agency, private or public, is concerned openly with the topic. Consequently, there are no projects which touch upon family planning, no national bodies associated with related research, no cooperation with foreign organizations.

Those who wish to criticize the President usually do so on other, more narrowly political grounds, and the entire issue of the relationship of population to resources gets obscured. Development is the primary theme in Malawi, and according to President Banda's interpretation of the nation's needs, population expansion seems implicit. Agricultural production *is* increasing, cultivated acreage *is* expanding. The balance of payments runs against Malawi, but there are good reasons—none of which are associated with overpopulation—to account for this. In short, neither President Banda nor his advisors seem to view 111 persons per square mile as ominous.

Conclusions

One of the major problems facing Malawi in the demographic field is an excess of fertile females—nearly a quarter of the population. Welfare workers have suggested several reasons for the apparently overwhelming pronatal attitude among women: there is nothing else for girls to do; it at least gives them a sense of purpose, a justification for living. Others have argued that, *per contra,* women are avid for contiaceptive education, that given the chance they express a very lively fear of being trapped into successive pregnancies, and that this distaste is exacerbated by rising school fees and a chronic shortage of places.

Nevertheless, the girl who does not marry young and give birth often remains an object of concern to her family and embarrassment to her friends, provided, that is, that she maintains contact with her family and village. Since mobility in Malawi is more commonly found among men, who also tend to monopolize literacy and jobs, the chances are very good that women will remain close to their birthplaces. Some of the Christian churches traditionally have opposed birth control measures, but this seems to matter little, for clerical dislike or condemnation merely reinforces existing attitudes among the rural masses.

This is not to say that girls brought into the modern world feel the same way, but their numbers are small and their opportunities quite limited (Radio Malawi, Air Malawi, certain expatriate firms, some government ministries). Moreover, they tend to meet married men, a relationship which loses its appeal after a short interval in most cases. For the great bulk of Malawi women, life will continue to be lived in the village, presumably as mothers. Only a small percentage yet enter the cash economy, and then only in a nickel and dime way as small-scale market women (there are no great female entrepreneurs, as in Ghana or Nigeria). There is prostitution, but as everywhere, the girls do not tend to profit much. On Broadway, it might be possible to imagine the successful courtesan—grown old and prosperous in the life—who retires to contemplate her career. In Blantyre's satellite townships the idea is risible.

If the predicted rate of population growth continues, as it has for at least a generation now (and may have done for many years without detection), and the sex ratio also remains steady, then Malawi will produce more and more girl babies who will during most of their fertile years have more and more girl babies. With such a population, even the number of unpremeditated, unwanted children might be quite large. As urbanization proceeds, one anticipates a loosening of traditional family restraints, and an increase in the number of "illegitimate" (paternity unknown or denied) youngsters. The female population, then, will get larger, and in absolute figures more and more impressionable and pregnable.

The second problem which Malawi will confront during the rest of this century, and most likely well before it ends, is the question of youth, more especially male youth. In brief, the young and vigorous lack things to do, and may turn to those who claim to offer something. Even now, and Malawi is not altogether unique here, there is a huge population of teen-age males, a majority not in school and not at work. Many dozens of thousands compete for the approximately 5,400 secondary school places. Naturally, competition is severest in the urban areas, which have most of the teachers and facilities. The wives of civil servants frequently fill the teaching posts, and by consequence cluster around the bureaucratic strongholds. Like every other place in Africa, Malawi is experiencing what is perceived to be a rise in crime, especially against property. Along with several other African states, Malawi also is canvassing the idea of a mandatory death penalty for robbery (armed) or with violence.

One organization exists to cater to youth, the Young Pioneers, a uniformed quasimilitary outfit with 21 training camps scattered throughout the land, usually in remote places. At these camps 18–24-year-old males predominate, but at the principal center several dozen girls are also schooled in citizenship and improved village agriculture, with the understanding that their nine to ten months of paid training (room, board, clothing, and a pound a month) will equip them for life.

Like many youth groups they are intolerant, quick to interpret the President's remarks as directives, severely criticize students, and spend too much of their time acting as police adjuncts. They have been informers in schools, have taken it upon themselves to chastise women whose dress was thought too daring (the President has an obsessive fear of the collapse of Western standards, as evidenced by the drug scene and nudity in theatre; he may introduce legislation banning miniskirts), and generally busied themselves with a censorial role.

The national training advisor of the Pioneers, an Israeli general officer named M. Tavor, rejected my suggestion that they were paramilitary, nor did he allow that their training smacked of the more militant *kibbutzim*. Indeed, he specifically mentioned the Malawi government's suspicion of anything socialist. Nevertheless, the Young Pioneers certainly give the appearance of being something more than civilian in outlook. (Their headquarters guardpost has a large mirror with the admonition "Stand like a Young Pioneer!" stencilled on it.)

The Taiwanese in charge of their agricultural mission implied that he thought the Pioneers perfunctory in their approach to the farming life. He contrasted them unfavorably with an economically motivated peasantry working its own land. The Young Pioneer training program falls under the rubric of "nation building," i.e., large doses of recent history, explanations of the structure and workings of government, the role of the Congress party, and the need for self-help. None of this can be faulted, but one may wonder at the advisability of marshalling youthful cadres in this way. There has as yet been no effective follow-up, so that no one knows what has happened to graduates who have returned to the countryside. Theoretically, there is a tie-in with Education and with Community Development. Some Pioneers have been seconded to the Chinese: for instance, those who man the President's private farm in Kasungu, near his birthplace. But it remains to be seen whether they will, in fact, work effectively once out in the rural areas. The Young Pioneers were formed when the party was struggling to wrest control of the country from the British. It may not be easy to downgrade their political role in the aftermath of independence.

Land is the ultimate factor, as President Banda proclaims constantly. When in 1970 he toured parts of the north and far south which he had rarely visited, what he saw apparently cheered him. In the districts affected, particularly Cholo and Mlanje in the south, a number of small farmers have made successful cash crops. The idea of competing with Europeans has caught on, and the President is largely responsible, though he has a dedicated European staff to back him. Why, Dr. Banda asked in October 1970, should men go to Rhodesia to earn \$50 to \$100 a year, when they could get three times that from an acre of tobacco in Malawi? Maize, he is fond of saying, will feed you, but tobacco will feed you and send your wife to the shops and your children to school as well. (I suppose there are certain ironies in a physician who is a nonsmoker urging the production of carcinogens, but life in Southeast Africa is harsh.)

On paper, Malawi's plight seems worse than a ground inspection would suggest. President Banda is correct when he asserts that there are many additional acres which could be brought into use. The Southern Region, which carries half the population, has 7.8 million acres, of which half is, theoretically, arable; only 20 per cent is being farmed. Communications and water are needed, of course, to bring the rest under the hoe, and this is what the government is attempting to do. Moreover, a closer look reveals that of the 1.4 million acres now cultivated, only a quarter million is in anything but subsistence maize; thus the President's pleasure over the modest but measureable progress made in cash cropping. Dependence upon the great exchanges of London and New York for the sale of crops seems inevitable. Short of a hermetic system, such as mainland China's, however, what can anyone do about relations between the West and the rest? President Banda is attempting to work with the givens, and Malawi seems to be making progress.

Malawi's landscape now looks something like what one imagines England did before the consolidation of estates and inclosure of lands: Piers Plowman's "field full of folk." The arguments for population control in the Third World are suspect at best when they come from our mouths, and particularly when they are directed at a country which by serious effort is changing its situation. Malawians, after all, are not wasting half the world's resources. Indeed, from their view they are increasing the globe's supply of consumables. They cannot be persuaded that life is getting worse. Discussion of the "quality of life" which so pervades American journals seems singularly grotesque here. Americans have persuaded themselves that man has over-run the universe; in this part of Africa that assumption is rather silly. In sum, there is little evidence which Malawians have seen to suggest that what animates Westerners is not just old-style racism tricked out in new garb. They are not impressed.

I have referred to the President constantly, and it is time to consider him more directly. One does not have to be in Malawi long to realize that a parlor game played with regularity is called "what happens after Banda?" Depending upon one's companion, the answer is liable to be bleak, confident, or Pollyanna-like. There is little room in present-day Malawi for overanxious claimants to the throne, nor has there been a school for princes established by the potentate. His recent decision to accept the offer of the Life Presidency should put an end to any illusions about his intentions on that score.

What physical opposition there was has been stifled by force of arms, and what generally is regarded as the support of the populace. Deportation has become institutionalized as a means for dealing with obnoxious Europeans and Asians. The University is pretty well at heel (all research projects must have approval from the President's office, which means there are some frustrated sociologists here). Press and radio are under control. Foreign missions are unlikely to press hard in delicate places, particularly as this is one of the few countries where the United States does not have to defend its Asian policy.

One would not expect, therefore, that Dr. Banda hears much in the way of direct criticism of his views about population. He does not believe in birth control; indeed, he is strongly opposed to it. The position taken by the American Medical Association when Dr. Banda was a student (not that black men belonged to that professional body at that time) is about where Malawi stands today.

Malawi, President Banda believes, needs a larger, not a stable, populace. It has become fashionable to wonder whether he really does have Greater Malawi aspirations, but it seems unlikely. Nothing that he has said could be used against him. He usually says that he is referring to indubitable historical fact, that there once was a Maravi state spilling across northern Mozambique, eastern Zambia, and southern Tanzania, but his evidence is vague Portuguese utterances about places they had not seen before filling in their seventeenth century maps. In any case, he does not openly contest the national boundaries arbitrarily established in Africa by Europeans. Nevertheless, the topic of population is, in the State Department phrase, "sensitive" in Malawi, for whatever reason.

So long as he rules, I doubt that President Banda will revise his opinion. So long as he sits in the Presidential Lodge, or in raincoat, sunglasses and fedora, glides through the streets in his Mercedes, Malawi will not experience radical shifts in policy, and ordinary life will go on as usual. Girls will become pregnant, boys will be unemployed unless they have an agricultural bent, and the population will go on increasing at the same or a greater rate. Should the President be right that the produce of the land will be sufficient to meet the population's foreseeable needs, he will be remembered as the expert. But if his estimate of resources proves optimistic, and his disregard for the population's profile turns out to have been a mistake, the Ngwazi may receive a bad press from historians.

Notes

1. Malawi does not compile official statistics on emigrants. The figure 266,000 is drawn from records of remittances transmitted by post, from answers to questions asked by census enumerators (how many relatives do you have outside the country? where are they? do they intend to stay?), and from records kept by countries to which Malawians emigrate.
2. For an account of affairs through 1969, see Edwin S. Munger, *Trading with the Devil* (ESM-2-'69), Fieldstaff Reports, Central and Southern Africa Series, Vol. XIII, No. 2, 1969.
3. Horst Dequin, *Agricultural Development in Malawi* (Institut für Wirtschafsforschung, Munchen, 1969).

References

Malawi Population Census, 1966 (Department of Census and Statistics, Zomba).

Tables from *Compendium of Statistics for Malawi, 1970* (Zomba). *Vision of Malawi* (Blantyre, September 1970).

Financial Times Survey, Malawi (London, July 2, 1970).

Horst Dequin, *Agricultural Development in Malawi* (Institut für Wirtschaftsforschung, Munchen, 1969).

JAMES R. HOOKER is currently on leave from Michigan State University where he is a professor of African history. Receiving his Ph.D. from MSU in 1957, he has been teaching and writing on East Africa for more than a decade. His interests have included such diverse topics as the development of trade unions, separatist churches, and Pan-Africanism. Dr. Hooker has served as a consultant to the House of Representatives Subcommittee on Africa and as Associate Editor of the Bulletin of the African Studies Association. Widely travelled in Latin America and the Caribbean, he has maintained a particular interest in that area's connections with Africa. The author of *Black Revolutionary,* Dr. Hooker has edited several books and contributed numerous articles to journals in the humanities and social sciences. As a Faculty Associate of the Field Staff, he reports from Malawi, Zambia, and Rhodesia.

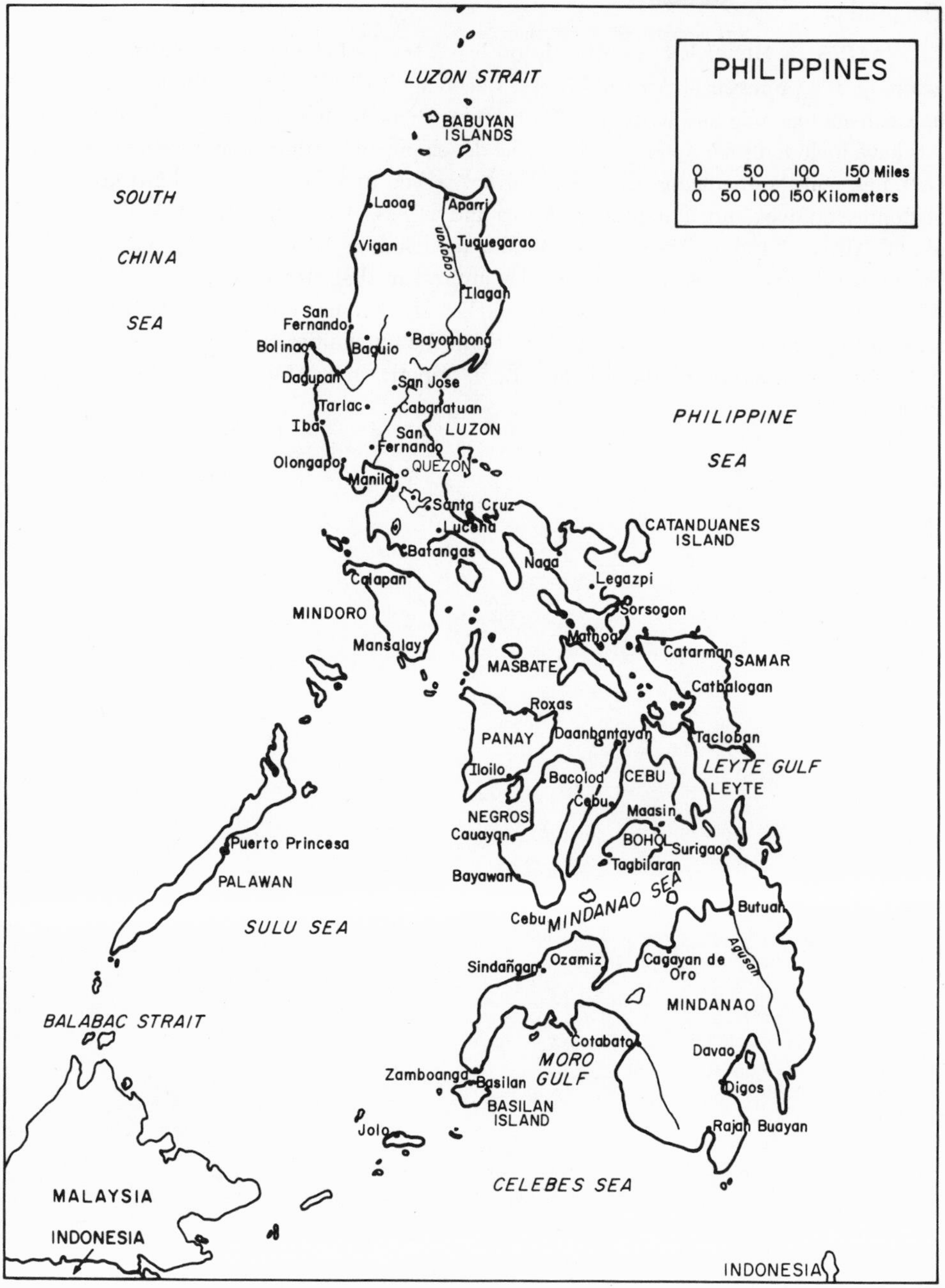

PHILIPPINES
0 50 100 150 Miles
0 50 100 150 Kilometers
LUZON STRAIT
BABUYAN ISLANDS
SOUTH CHINA SEA
Laoag
Aparri
Vigan
Cagayan
Tuguegarao
Ilagan
San Fernando
Bolinao
Baguio
Bayombong
Dagupan
San Jose
Tarlac
Cabanatuan
Iba
San Fernando
LUZON
PHILIPPINE SEA
Olongapo
QUEZON
Manila
Santa Cruz
Lucena
CATANDUANES ISLAND
Batangas
Naga
Calapan
Legazpi
MINDORO
Sorsogon
Mansalay
Mathog
Catarman
SAMAR
MASBATE
Catbalogan
Roxas
PANAY
Daanbantayan
Tacloban
LEYTE GULF
Iloilo
Bacolod
CEBU
LEYTE
Cebu
NEGROS
Maasin
Cauayan
BOHOL
Surigao
Puerto Princesa
Tagbilaran
PALAWAN
Bayawan
MINDANAO SEA
Butuan
SULU SEA
Cebu
Agusan
Sindañgan
Ozamiz
Cagayan de Oro
MINDANAO
BALABAC STRAIT
Cotabato
Davao
MORO GULF
Zamboanga
Basilan
Digos
BASILAN ISLAND
Jolo
Rajah Buayan
CELEBES SEA
MALAYSIA
INDONESIA
INDONESIA

The Philippines

Albert Ravenholt

Were the pressure of a burgeoning population upon available resources the major hazard of the global demographic dilemma, then the problems confronting the Philippine Republic would compel concern. For changing human values, often expressed as expectations, have a way of engulfing material circumstance like a tropical typhoon snapping up a frayed coconut palm frond. It is these expectations that are generating a special kind of crisis for Filipinos. As the only predominantly Christian—and largely Roman Catholic—nation in Asia, theirs has become a society indelibly conditioned from the West over four centuries of first Spanish and then American colonial rule and later continued ties. Thus, a population explosion under way in this archipelago of 7,100 islands prompts consequences compounded by this heritage. For both Christian and democratic values foster aspirations galloping far ahead of employment and income opportunities.

As nowhere else in Southeastern Asia, the imprint of these values proliferates in the Philippines with uninhibited mass communications, joined with education as a major industry. Shared familial traditions among the ethnically mainly Malay peoples in the region suggest that in time this Filipino conundrum may be experienced by their neighbors. The threat of rendering illusory recent advances, particularly in rice production, symptomizes how fast these economies must expand just to maintain presently unsatisfactory consumption and other living levels. Despite such overwhelming physical and psychological odds, the Philippines does offer promise. There is evidence of what a small cadre of concerned leaders and citizens can do to make pressures of population growth more manageable, utilizing especially outside assistance from international organizations, foreign foundations, and the United States Agency for International Development. Equally vital are achievements of the press and radio, chiefly within the past three years. First, they made respectable public discussion of population problems and use of contraceptives, earlier inhibitions notwithstanding, then prompted both public officials and religious leaders to sanction action, and now are beginning to make family planning a topic of conversation even among otherwise traditional rural or *barrio* folk.

Population Profile

With approximately 37 million inhabitants as of mid-1970, the Philippines ranks fifteenth among nations of the world in population and is among the 15 countries with the highest rate of natural increase. The less than exact statistics available indicate to knowledgeable demographers an annual crude birth rate of 45–50/1000. They calculate that the crude death rate annually is about 10–12/1000 of the total population. Life expectancy at birth now averages 55 years, with an insignificant difference between men and women; five years ago life expectancy was about 53 years. The rate of natural increase is "thought" to be 3.45 per cent. Preliminary figures from the 1970 census suggest that since the 1960 census there has been an average annual increment in the number of Filipinos of 3.1 per cent. Immigration contributes insignificantly to the population of the islands, primarily due to restrictive official policies. The only exceptions are the small numbers—untabulated for obvious reasons—of Chinese and Indonesians who are smuggled in by fast, small vessels usually via the "back door" from Sabah and the Celebes to the south. Emigration is again a difficult figure to determine with accuracy. The United States Embassy now is granting over 20,000 immigrant visas annually; the numbers admitted to Canada, Australia, and Spain—other "Meccas" for Filipinos wanting out—are much smaller. Additionally, some thousands of Filipinos yearly go to these and other countries on student visas, temporary visitor visas, or in other classifications and manage to remain. Likewise, there are some 8,000 Filipino civilians working in Vietnam and fewer numbers in Laos and Thailand. Roughly 60,000 Filipinos are now in Sabah, where many have acquired residence and some citizenship. By these and other means, it is estimated that less than 70,000 Filipinos emigrate in any one year.

The gross reproduction rate calculated on the number of female births per woman in the reproductive age of 15 to 49 is 3.5 and the net reproduction rate is believed to be 2.8. A look at the population structure shows 45 per cent of all Filipinos under 15 years. Another 52 per cent of the population is between the ages of 16 and 64 years, and only 3 per cent is 65 years and older. According to the 1960 census—figures for the 1970 census were not at the time of writing available—the sex ratio for all ages was 50.1 male and the remainder female. The fertility pattern is suggested by the fact that when she reaches the age of menopause the average Filipina has delivered 6.8 children. Infant mortality among live births under one year is still four to five times that of most developed countries; registered infant mortality shows 60/1000, although sample data and other indications suggest that this figure actually is about 100 or more per thousand live births. Tragically, the mortality among children age one to four is among the highest recorded anywhere, or about 14 times that of more developed countries in Western Europe. Chief among the causes of reported death is tuberculosis, while other diseases related to malnutrition also take a terrible toll among the youngest. Malaria still is endemic in frontier regions like Northern Luzon, the provinces of the Sierra Madre Range of Eastern Luzon, Palawan, Samar, Leyte, and parts of Mindanao. Schistosomiasis afflicts several million Filipinos, especially in Southern Luzon, Leyte, Samar, and Eastern Mindanao. Compared to its Southeast Asian neighbors, except Singapore and Malaysia, the Philippines has far more doctors and nurses per capita, more clinic and hospital facilities, and greater availability of modern drugs. Unfortunately, these tend to concentrate in the cities, leaving much of the rural population without access to adequate curative treatment and reliant upon *herbolarios,* healers utilizing local herbs and drugs.

Estimates of future population trends in the Philippines are hostage to a host of imponderables. Extrapolating with the compound interest formula from the 3.1 per cent annual growth rate indicated by the increase between the 1960 and 1970 census figures yields a population of about 92 million in the year 2,000. However, should the crude birth rate remain at its present level of better than 45/1000 and the death rate drop by the year 2,000 to 7/1000—this latter trend appears distinctly probable—then there will be roughly 111 million Filipinos by the close of this century. Should family planning become an integral feature of the Filipino life scheme, then it is possible that the crude birth rate would decline, as suggested by experience in the West and such modernized Asian societies as Singapore, to 24/1000. Such a trend combined with the drop in the death rate to 7/1000 would produce a Philippine population by the end of this century of 72 million. The difference of 37 million between high and low projections equals the present entire population of the Republic and indicates just how crucially decisive the operative programs and attitudes that condition family size will become over the next three decades.

All of the above figures and calculations are necessarily educated estimates. Registration of vital statistics for the country as a whole is grossly inadequate. An indication is the fact that recorded statistics now yield a crude birth rate of 25/1000 and a crude death rate of 7/1000. Everyone concerned recognizes that registered figures are incomplete, especially in the rural *barrios.* The most reliable figures result from sample surveys of selected communities and population groups. One of the first of these—by a United Nations team 17 years ago—compelled the Philippine government to abandon its official assumption at the time that the net rate of increase was 1.5 per cent annually. Since then, the Census Bureau, the Population Institute of the University of the Philippines, and other organizations have applied greatly improved methods of demographic investigation.

Population Distribution and Movement

Efforts to classify the Philippine population as either rural or urban compel arbitrary distinctions that do not entirely hold in practice. During 1970, some 7,283,000 Filipinos were living in the 58 chartered cities whose administration is independent of the 66 provinces. These chartered cities, holding 19.7 per cent of the population, often extend to vast stretches of rural landscape. Zamboanga City, for example, includes within its boundaries coconut plantations, fish ponds, and areas of near virgin jungle. In the event that residents of *poblaciones,* forming the seats of government for nearly 1,500 municipalities roughly equivalent to American counties, are included among urbanites, then they would total about 30 per cent of the population. Vital statistics are too fragmentary to allow an over-all national comparison of fertility and mortality differences beween these urban and rural sectors of the population. Still, the health services available most adequately in the cities suggest that particularly infant mortality is significantly lower among urbanites. Their public water supplies are better, school feeding programs function more effectively, they can get to a doctor or a pharmacy, and certain endemic diseases like malaria, schistosomiasis, and gastrointestinal ailments are less of a problem.

As is traditionally true of most rural societies, Filipinos become economically active at an early age; even a young boy can tend a *carabao* (water buffalo) and girls very early become their mothers' helpers. At seasons when there is a peak labor demand to plant or harvest rice or cut sugar cane, most able-bodied members of the family may be mobilized in the fields. The latest published figures that classify the economically active sectors of the population are for 1967. They record that of the population ten years and older, 54.7 per cent was in the labor force. Among males aged ten and over it was 69.3 per cent and for females 40.1 per cent. Of those then in the labor force, 92.3 per cent were listed as fully employed. This included 94.7 per cent of the males and 88 per cent of the females. These figures are necessarily a bit misleading. In the provinces, an attorney may consider himself employed although he advises one or two clients a month and has returned from Manila after passing the national bar exams to live off the rentals of inherited family lands. Likewise, it is almost impossible to calculate underemployment, especially in rural areas. Much depends upon the character of agriculture. In predominantly coconut growing regions of Southern Luzon, the Eastern and Central Visayan Islands, and the fringes of Mindanao, harvesting of nuts and making of copra is a year-round enterprise. Where the monsoons more distinctly affect the weather and create a five to seven month dry season, as on Western and Central Luzon, only limited areas have irrigation for growing a rice crop at this time.

It is these weather patterns that condition internal migration of Filipinos—plus the flow of young people who come to the cities to study and return home to the provinces during vacation, principally from April to July. In the Central Luzon Provinces of Bulacan, Pampanga, and Nueva Ecija, many farmers go to the cities looking for work during the dry season from January through May, when construction activity is at its peak. In July, they are back in the fields plowing and planting a wet season rice crop that is weeded and otherwise cared for until it is harvested about December. A similar pattern holds for Rizal and Laguna Provinces east of Greater Manila and to a limited extent to the south in Cavite and Batangas. From Pangasinan on the shores of Lingayen Gulf, men go off to work in the mines in the mountains of Northern Luzon, yet try to return even briefly to help with planting and harvesting of the rice they then carry back to provide for themselves. From western Panay Island, *sacados* (temporary laborers) migrate during the sugar cane harvesting season to the Iloilo area or neighboring Negros

Island and again try to return home for the wet season rice growing and corn planting on which their family subsistence depends.

As indicated earlier, the number of Filipinos who emigrate appears to be less than 70,000 annually to all foreign destinations. This is only about 6 per cent of the annual increment in population. The 108,260 Filipinos registered as present in the United States by the Bureau of Immigration and Naturalization in the fiscal year ending June 30, 1969, have an important influence here at home. This is particularly true of the 75,546 Filipinos who as of that date had established permanent residence in the United States. Although their remittances home to family and other relatives are not completely tabulated, this has been a traditional source of extra cash in many communities, like the Ilocos region of Northwestern Luzon, whose inhabitants are noted for their venturesome search for opportunity abroad, as in Hawaii and California. Some 15,000 Filipinos serving in the United States Navy provide important cash for their families, especially in provinces like Zambales and Cavite where American naval bases are located. When these servicemen retire to their home *barrios*, their steady stipends in dollars often make them the envy and target of less affluent relatives, many of whom become adroit at anticipating when the monthly check is due. As more Filipino specialists have gone to work in Vietnam and even distant Afghanistan, and doctors, nurses, and technicians in larger numbers move either temporarily or permanently to Canada, Australia, and other countries seeking skilled persons, their remittances home also become important. Separation from their relatives often creates acute pangs of homesickness among these Filipinos and many begin to wonder whether the extra earnings justify being away from all the kinetic warmth of an extended family. In the past, those who emigrated were predominantly male and any single Filipina who arrived in one of their neighborhoods, as in Alaska and Puget Sound where many worked in the fishing industry, was courted relentlessly. Now this sex balance is being redressed as many more nurses, medical technicians, pharmacists, and teachers go abroad.

Population and the Economy

Measured against its present population, Philippine natural resources are relatively abundant. However, utilization of these resources to provide for the present inhabitants and their expected increase leaves much to be desired. Both ineffective and wasteful use of resources suggest that in the future the common Filipino assumption that "come what may, I can always get by and somehow my family will make out," may prove a myth. The problem is compounded by the fact that in the older settled regions, like Central Luzon, Ilocos, Cavite, Batangas, and the Central Visayan Islands of Cebu, Bohol, and many smaller islands there already is an acute problem of securing an adequate living with present patterns of principally subsistence farming and fishing. Frontier regions like Northeastern Luzon and Mindanao offer promise, provided roads and ports are developed and land title problems can be solved. Absence of effective peace and order in many regions also is a deterrent to maximum agricultural and other production.

Philippine trade patterns are one indicator of emphasis in the economy. The largest dollar earners among exports are the products of the coconut tree, which in recent years have been yielding an average of about US$260 million annually—the archipelago has been providing about 60 per cent of all the coconut products in world commerce. These include copra, or the dried meat of the coconut, oil expelled from copra and shipped in tankers, copra pellets exported to Europe, America, and Japan as cattle feed, and desiccated coconut. This industry, which is the chief source of livelihood for about one fourth of all Filipinos, is particularly vulnerable to both drought and typhoons. Once a strong typhoon has passed through a coconut region, even when the trees survive (they require seven years to reach production), almost a year's crop is lost since this is the time elapsing from flowering to harvest.

The next two important exports are sugar and timber products. The Philippines, as the largest foreign supplier of the American market, now ships about 1,250,000 tons of mostly centrifugal sugar annually and provides roughly 11 per cent of United States consumption. At least a dozen new sugar centrals now are under construction—chiefly on Japanese credits—and the prospect is one of abundant supplies for the growing domestic market plus possibly a surplus for which there may be difficulty in finding a foreign market.

After World War II, when the timber industry first emerged as an important exporter, it was chiefly as a supplier of logs to the Japanese, Korean, Taiwanese, and other foreign mills manufacturing Philippine mahogany plywood. During the past six years, domestic manufacture into veneer, plywood, finished lumber, and many other products has become more sophisticated and important. Unfortunately, prospects for sustained yield timber management are threatened by both the irresponsible logging techniques of some companies, who fail to protect residual trees or replant, and the constant pressure of "slash and burn" agriculture. As roads are pushed into the forests, these settlers follow and burn the trees to raise a crop for three or four years—usually upland rice, corn, bananas, and sweet potatoes—and then abandon the area to useless *cogón,* or tough, high grass, as they move on to the next site in virgin areas. Although such "slash and burn" farming has been traditional in Southeast Asia, its expansion over the past two decades threatens the ecology there as elsewhere.

Mining is the most rapidly expanding sector of the Philippine economy. Before World War II, the archipelago was important as a gold producer; other important metals were refractory chromite—of which the Philippines was a major exporter—manganese, chrome, modest shipments of iron ore, and limited copper and silver. During the past 15 years, copper mining has become ever more important. Mined and milled here and shipped chiefly to Japan as concentrates, present production equals about 175,000 tons of contained copper metal annually and is being expanded rapidly as present mines enlarge capacity and new ones are opened. Once an importer, the Philippines now is a major cement producer and has surplus production for export. Magnetite iron sands are being exploited on a growing scale and there is a new interest in massive lateritic nickel deposits. Depending upon world market prices for metals, mining promises to become the major export industry of this next decade and, in the process, to open many hitherto remote communities to commercial contact.

Other less important exports include canned pineapples, bananas, abaca or Manila hemp, cigar tobacco and cigars. Handicrafts are becoming important as dollar earners. These include the carved "monkey pod" or acacia woodenware first popularized by Hawaiian manufacturers and now made in the Philippines. Embroidery, woven bags, furniture, carpets, and numerous other items similarly bring a profit from Filipino skills and artistry.

As would be expected, the largest import is petroleum products—next after Japan, the Philippines has the greatest number of motor vehicles in the Far East. Equipment is a major import, as is cotton for the textile industry and raw materials for many other import-substitution manufacturers. Until recently, motor cars—often the most expensive models—and other consumption items prized by the wealthy absorbed considerable foreign exchange. Imports that count for the ordinary Filipino include milk products, usually reconstituted and tinned here, canned fish, rubber for manufacture of tires and numerous other items, paper, transistor radios; for the cities television sets and pharmaceuticals; for the farmers fertilizer and pesticides and engines for fishing and other vessels. Although the Philippines produces superior rum, scarce foreign exchange is squandered on whiskey, gin, brandy, and other such imports.

Within the past five years, the Philippines has progressed from importing about 600,000 tons of rice annually to self-sufficiency. Prospects are that, barring unseasonable drought or a succession of typhoons during the approaching harvest season—as occurred in the autumn of 1970—the archipelago can produce a surplus for export. However, the Philippines has yet to develop the milling, storage, grading, and other facilities that will be essential to become a competitive exporter in what is increasingly a buyers' market for rice. Only about one eighth of some 3.4 million hectares (one hectare equals 2.47 acres) planted to rice has dependable year-round irrigation. Water rights legislation, financing of gravity irrigation construction, geological surveys of underground water geology, operation and maintenance of irrigation systems, and effective engineering for all present problems must be mastered before the potential offered by the new rice technology emerging from the International Rice Research Institute at Los Baños can be more substantially realized.

Corn is the second most basic staple in the Filipino diet—it is prized particularly in the Central Visayan Islands and for cultivation in newly settled frontier regions. Among roughly one fifth of the population preference is for corn, a white flint that is cracked and cooked to be eaten as corn grits. Corn also is in increasing demand for the manufacture of starch and for poultry, hog, and cattle feed. Areas devoted to corn have expanded from 580,000 hectares in 1910 to 2,256,000 hectares in 1970. Average yields per crop, however, have remained almost constant at about 12 *caváns* per hectare (one *cacán* of shelled corn weighs 57 kilograms of 2.2 pounds each), depending somewhat upon the weather. Where rainfall is well distributed, farmers may grow two or even three crops of corn annually. Both the College of Agriculture of the University of the Philippines and the Bureau of Plant Industry have released improved varieties of corn that can yield 70 to 120 *caváns* per hectare. Most are "synthetics" allowing the farmer to produce his own seed. Their extensive use will require mastery of skills and application of fertilizer and other inputs that are at present beyond most ordinary farmers.

Like nearly all of Southeastern and Southern Asia, most of the Philippines remains deficient in protein foods—the soya bean never has become important in agriculture and the diet as in China where it fills much of this gap. The *mungo,* a small green or yellow bean, is grown and used in cooking, although only to a fraction of its potential. Several other legumes suited to the tropics and cultivated as vegetables are underutilized. Meat is available primarily to Filipinos in the middle and upper income groups—the raising of pigs is both a backyard enterprise and increasingly a commercial venture, but the cattle and *carabao* population has yet to recover fully from World War II decimation of herds. Fish are the most valued of animal proteins and relatively available at reasonable prices where caught. The problem for most consumers living away from the coasts is underdevelopment of transport and preservation. Consequently, the average Filipino lives on a predominantly starch diet. Aside from rice and corn, these include sweet potatoes, cooking bananas, *cassava* (manioc), taro, which is known as *gabi,* and other root crops. Especially in the cities, bread, noodles, and other wheat products are gaining popularity, although high prices charged by the flour millers inhibit this shift in eating habits.

According to the most recent data published detailing occupations as of October 1967, 58 per cent of all employed Filipinos identified themselves as farmers. The next largest group were the craftsmen, some 12.4 per cent, including carpenters, bricklayers, mechanics, painters, and others where skills are demanded as in the cottage industries. Third and fourth in importance numerically were service occupations and salesmen, numbering 7.8 and 6.4 per cent, respectively. Professionals constituted 4.1 per cent, managerial 3.6 per cent, and clerical 3.3 per cent. Transport workers included 2.6 per cent of the work force and only 1.5 per cent chose to be listed as manual workers, which all suggests that at least some sellers of sweepstake tickets and car watch boys, like others with casual employment, chose to report more prestigious occupational categories.

Population and Development

Subsistence farming and/or fishing remains the economic way of life for most rural Filipinos. And among them innovation comes slowly and occasionally in odd ways. The small, air-cooled gasoline engine, usually a Briggs & Stratton, a Clinton, or a Wisconsin of about 12 horsepower, has become the most consequential mechanical introduction for those who live by the sea. Powering the *banca,* a craft hollowed from a log and fitted with outriggers, these engines allow a mobility for fishing, trading, visiting of relatives, and occasional smuggling almost unknown 15 years ago. Ever since the close of World War II, when explosives became readily available and law enforcement lax, dynamite fishing has become the surest way to bring home a catch. In some communities, despite legal prohibition, catching fish in lagoons is augmented by poisoning, occasionally with cyanide, toxic insecticides, or the juice of plants that stun the fish. Among commercial fishermen, chiefly concerned with supplying Greater Manila's roughly

4.5 million inhabitants, trawling has been modernized and more recently purse seining has become an important technique for larger fishing boats. When these more modern, large-scale operators move in and begin netting fish in the traditional grounds of local subsistence fishermen, conflict often ensues and the latter may be compelled to move their families to better sites.

The subsistence farmer has yet to be touched significantly by the "green revolution" that offers such promise of expanded yields through use of better seeds and modern technology. Even under the special circumstance where he has learned of their potential, the fact that he does not participate in a commercial economy for his primary livelihood denies him the cash required for inputs of fertilizer, insecticides, and much else. Also, he is hesitant to risk his narrow margin for survival upon methods yet to be proved in his presence when the stake involves the family food supply. Consequently, upland rice, native corn, *camotes* (sweet potatoes), *cassava*, bananas, and a few pigs and chickens—including usually the prized fighting cock—are his primary productive concern. Only in areas like Central Luzon, Laguna, Rizal, Cavite, Camarines Sur, Eastern Panay Island, the sugar producing lands of Negros, and the more intensively cultivated sections of the Cagayan Valley of Northeastern Luzon and Mindanao is there substantial use of new technology in agriculture. There particularly sugar, rice, and corn as commercial crops move out of the community and bring back cash. Except on a few larger plantations—where rat control with metal bands on the tree trunks is used and fertilizer may be applied together with inter-cropping—coconuts are managed and harvested as always. A specialized exception are the primarily pineapple and banana plantations of Del Monte and Dole in Mindanao, where scientific techniques are fully utilized.

It is around the burgeoning cities, and particularly Greater Manila, that a new kind of modernizing agriculture is most evident. The establishment of commercial feed mills has encouraged farmers to specialize in raising laying hens for eggs and large-scale broiler production. Likewise, vegetable growing for sale has become important. In the dry season, eggplants, squash, and beans may be planted in rice fields in Bulacan Province. In neighboring Pampanga Province the dry-season growing of watermelons, cantaloupe, and cucumbers generates new cash income for farmers, as do onions further east in Nueva Ecija. Around the summer capital of Baguio and farther north in Mountain Province farmers now specialize in tomatoes, cabbage, carrots, beets, cauliflower, and numerous other temperate zone vegetables for which city consumers have created a market. The city and its ways reach out into the countryside in many an interesting manner; postwar development of the jeepney, converted from United States Army military surplus jeeps to carry passengers, bananas, pineapples, chickens, rice, and whatever is to be hauled, now is augmented by the Honda tricycle that is replacing the horse-drawn *calesa*. The small power tiller and the irrigation pump powered by a diesel engine are beginning to appear in the countryside. Often they are paid for by a son who has gone to work in the city, as may be the concrete block addition to the bamboo and *nipa* palm thatched family home in which he grew up.

Although manufacturing of all kinds provided an income for only 11.3 per cent of all Filipinos classified as employed in all occupations as of 1967, it already is becoming important both economically and in the attitudes that result. Textile plants, automobile assembly firms, paint factories, ceramic tile producers, plumbing fixture manufacturers, food canning, flour mills, cement plants, makers of concrete pipe, steel fabricators, office furniture manufacturers, and numerous other industries all shape an increasingly complex economy. They also foster a new awareness of potentials in applied technology, both among capital and managerial groups and among workers. The search for opportunity that draws ever more Filipinos temporarily or permanently from the land into the city creates burgeoning problems not only among the unemployed. Squatter shacks that arose among the wreckage in the cities of World War II now usually have been replaced with sturdier homes. However, newcomers to the cities also create new slums as they seek housing within their means. Renting a few hundred square meters (one square meter equals about ten square feet) or simply squatting on public land, as along the tracks of the Manila Railroad, they collect galvanized metal roofing, scraps of lumber, and hammer flat five-gallon kerosene cans to erect close-packed shacks. Water for these proliferating communities usually is available from public faucets. Sewage pipes rarely are laid in and garbage collection is at a minimum. Resulting health problems can prove even more stubborn to correct than they were in the rural *barrios* whence these migrants came.

Social and attitudinal changes are less readily identified. Certainly World War II and the widespread guerrilla movements resisting the Japanese military occupation generated a major social upheaval. Young men who had been farmers and mechanics emerged as guerrilla chieftains who led their bands of armed followers in the mountains and after Allied liberation rose to the fore as a new elite. *Hacienderos* who traced their social dominance usually to land and status acquired under the Spanish regime that was supplanted by American rule in 1898 now had to make way and share their political leadership. Particularly in the cities and on the newly settled frontiers the tumultuous postwar quarter century has witnessed the emergence of another and equally significant group; the self-made Filipino entrepreneur. He may be welding together barges from wartime scrap or imported new steel or grinding rock to provide ingredients for a new paint factory. Regardless of the means employed, he emerges among the new leaders of the community. And the very success of both legitimate entrepreneurs and others who have gone up through manipulating political advantage lends credence to the faith in social mobility first instilled by American schoolteachers at the start of this century.

As Philippine society has become both physically and socially more mobile with young people seeking careers in the cities, the dominance of family elders over the young is weakened. As an impatient young Filipino on the make said: "I could not do anything, really, until I got away from my home town. There my parents and even my grandparents held the money and told me what I could do. Now, at least I can try on my own. Whether or not I make it is up to me." As men and women with this attitude emerge in business and the professions, the often traditional rural "gambling-luck" social syndrome of assuming that one's fortunes are ordained from outside ebbs before new values. Gradually, as these attitudes seep into the countryside and appetites for consumer goods are aroused by the numerous transistor radios, ever fewer Filipinos are content with circumstances of the past and impatiently join in demands for rewarding change.

Population and Society

Although some 156 ethno-linguistic groups inhabit the Philippine archipelago and eight major native languages predominate, Filipinos share a remarkable degree of national unity. Since theirs became an independent Republic on July 4, 1946, no substantial moves toward fragmentation have challenged this common political identity. Unlike many of the newly independent nations of Asia and Africa, the Philippines has successfully moderated within an elective and democratic governmental framework the contending demands of regional, linguistic, and economic pressure groups. History and religion both contributed to this achievement. The Spanish, who just over four centuries ago initiated colonization and Christianization of the islands, first gave Filipinos a sense of unity that set them apart culturally from the great and ancient Asian civilizations—a stubborn exception were the Mohammedan Moros of Mindanao and the Sulu archipelago, whose warlike prowess enabled them to resist—and pagan minorities of the mountainous hinterlands. When Americans at the turn of the century replaced the Spanish, opened the archipelago to Protestant missionaries, and established a public school system with English as the language of education, government, and commerce, they further fortified this sense of a unique Filipino common culture, more attuned to the West than to the East.

As literacy in English grew with the public schools, establishment of teacher training institutes and the University of the Philippines, and expansion of private collegiate education, chiefly by Catholic and Protestant effort, new values entered the society. Encouragement of political institutions representing popular electorates after 1902, when the United States Congress made municipal councils elective, and 1907, when Filipinos chose their first National Assembly, fortified faith in democratic teachings. When ordinary Filipinos saw that graduates of these schools actually could enter government on merit and sometimes quickly become prominent, they developed an extraordinary confidence in education as an avenue to advancement. It became the goal of nearly every Filipino family to send at least one child through college. He in turn was expected to help younger siblings and advance family interests within the administrative-political power structure. Such a popular faith in education largely accounts for the ability of roughly two-thirds of all Filipinos to read and write—although sometimes only simple sentences—in English or one of the major dialects. In rural areas the average youngster receives only four years of schooling. A chronic shortage of textbooks plus overcrowded classrooms means that many acquire but a smattering of learning. For those who do not master English—the language of instruction from the third year onwards—opportunities are circumscribed. Nevertheless, faith in education as the means to furthering individual and family fortunes persists and is evident particularly in the rapidly expanding middle class.

Public health was among the first concerns of the early American administrators. They acted energetically to control smallpox, cholera, typhoid, plague, and other infectious diseases that in some years had occasioned a net drop in the population of the islands, which at the start of this century numbered slightly over 7 million. Safe water supplies and modern sewage disposal systems were among the innovations Americans introduced, at least in the major cities. While preventive medicine was the first and chief concern of these pioneer doctors, they also established modern government hospitals. As the College of Medicine of the University of the Philippines developed to become the leading center for training physicians in Southeast Asia, schools of nursing were established both with government assistance and by private universities. Likewise, training in pharmacy facilitated establishment of *boticas* (drugstores) in all cities throughout the archipelago where modern drugs could be purchased. Continued expansion of such institutions since independence and popularity of medicine and nursing as a career gives the Philippines a far larger pool of trained health personnel per capita than any of its neighbors, except Singapore and Hong Kong. They also allow the Republic to provide roughly one fourth of all foreign doctors working in the United States, plus several thousand nurses.

Family and maternal health and welfare programs, although relatively developed and important in national life, are also very uneven. In the cities and provinces most touched by modernization, a Filipino family with means has the choice of often first-rate facilities. These are also the areas where the national government's Department of Health and provincial and city hospitals and clinics tend to have the best equipped facilities and ablest staff. By contrast, many a public health doctor and nurse in a more remote province may be desperately handicapped for lack of sometimes even simple surgical instruments and drugs. Appropriations for the Department of Health chronically lag behind actual needs. Perhaps inevitably, hospitals and clinics closer to the center of supply tend to fare better. During postwar years the training and outfitting of midwives has been affected by the same disparity between generally higher quality performance, as in and around Greater Manila and other cities, and meager facilities, drugs, and even skills in the hinterland. Disparity between recorded and actual vital statistics on birth and death is but one indication of the uneven health facilities to which most Filipinos have access. Similarly, when disaster strikes, as in the form of a typhoon or flood, it is the cities and islands with modern communications that are heard from first and where relief efforts tend to be concentrated. While national government and private organizations do mobilize to assist stricken areas, many remote *barrios* must survive and rebuild almost entirely with their own resources. During the past three months when a succession of typhoons and tidal waves ravaged the eastern coast of Luzon, logistical problems delayed for weeks the arrival of relief goods and medicine in these remote communities, many of which lack road connections with the outside that are passable except in the dry season.

Although the Philippines usually is thought of as a predominantly Roman Catholic country, this is only partially correct and claims of the Church hierarchy to representing some 80 per cent of the population merit scrutiny. Culturally, Filipino society bears the stamp of Roman Catholicism as the Spanish first carried it from Mexico to these islands in the sixteenth century. Massive Catholic churches dominate most plazas that are the center of life in the *poblaciones*. The tradition of selecting *compadres*, who become ritual kinship extensions of the family as invited sponsors at baptisms and weddings, is integral to most of the society. Every *barrio* has its patron saint, honored at the annual fiesta. Yet, in actual religious practice, although dominant among the elite and organizationally potent, Roman Catholicism is less consequential. Since there are only some 5,000 Catholic priests in the archipelago and nearly one half of these are engaged in education, the Church is unable to provide the majority of Filipinos with substantial religious instruction, despite the mobilization of lay volunteers.

Anticlericalism was a key element in the late nineteenth century revolt against Spain, often furthered by members of the Masonic lodges inspired from Europe. Out of this independence movement emerged the Philippine Independent Church, often called Aglipayan after its founder and first bishop, Gregorio Aglipay. Numbering perhaps three million members, this church has received apostolic succession and now has intercommunion with the American Episcopal Church. In the Philippines, however, it tends to be a church of the less privileged and is especially strong among Ilocanos and some Visayans of the central islands. Methodists, Presbyterians, Lutherans, Seventh Day Adventists, and Baptists—all have won a significant following, particularly within the emerging Filipino middle class. Their leadership in education, medicine, rural literacy, and social service makes them more influential than their combined membership of nearly 1.5 million would suggest. Jehovah's Witnesses is only one among the newer denominations rapidly gaining adherents among ordinary Filipinos. Largest and most enterprising among the numerous indigenous churches without foreign ties is the Iglesia Ni Kristo. Claiming more than two million members who are socially cohesive, this church has superior organization and has become politically potent. Construction of numerous modern "chapels" of distinctive architecture and equipped occasionally with theater-type seats and air conditioning fortifies the sense of status of those belonging. Excluding an estimated 8 to 10 per cent of the population who are Muslim or pagan, the available figures indicate that non-Catholics have more full-time ministers in parish work than do the churches looking to Rome. Neat division of Filipino membership in different Christian churches, however, tends to obscure an eclectic trait—especially among rural Filipinos, worshipping most frequently in one church does not always preclude having a child baptized at another church of a different denomination where such services are cheaper or more available.

Regardless of affiliation, most Filipinos have an intense feeling of religious involvement reminiscent of nineteenth century Midwestern America. On market day in the provinces evangelists may preach to the assembled folk through an electric loudspeaker mounted on a jeep. The Bible is the most basic popular literary source in small towns and the hinterland—although comics are fast gaining headway. All consequential mass movements at least over the past century have had a religious dimension. Even the Communist-led Huk guerrillas in their unsuccessful rebellion against the Philippine government two decades ago drew justification for their program from the scriptures. Poetic jousts disputing religious interpretations between champions of Roman Catholicism and Protestant denominations can draw enthusiastic listeners in rural areas. Although not necessarily formalized, religious sanction of personal action is sought by most ordinary Filipinos and does substantially condition their actions.

Population and Polity

Public and official changes in Philippine attitudes and policy towards population and family planning over the past three years have been both dramatic and consequential. Formerly, birth control and contraceptives were subjects that all except a very small and concerned minority of professionals and scholars discussed only furtively. Government officials and politicians with rare exceptions studiously avoided expressing any opinion publicly. Now all of this is changing and family planning is becoming a popularly discussed issue, although opinions differ greatly on what should be done and the appropriate means. While these are disputed, family planning clinics offering a range of services from the rhythm method to IUDs and pills are multiplying. Undoubtedly, a large number of Filipinas wish to delay childbearing, space pregnancies, and limit births. Unanswered questions, however, include how promptly and effectively services can be made available to them, especially in rural areas, and at what stage do efforts at controlling births conflict with entrenched attitudes and values.

Official action both reflecting changing public views and fostering them started in 1968—the previous year U.S.A.I.D., after quiet preparatory work, was allowed to make modest grants chiefly for research followed within about eight months by assistance to action organizations. Formal government effort began in December 1968, when the Executive Secretary to the President, Rafael Salas, met with two dozen concerned leaders and proposed creation of a Commission on Population to study the problem and recommend policies and programs. On February 19, 1969, President Ferdinand Marcos signed an Executive Order establishing the Commission on Population—some 14 months earlier he had signed the United Nations Declaration of Population. With the Secretary of Education, O. D. Corpus, serving as Chairman, the Commission includes 22 members representing government and private groups. A nine-member Executive Committee under the chairmanship of the Secretary of Social Welfare, Gregoria Feliciano, includes the Secretary of Health, Dr. Amadeo Cruz, plus the Secretary of Education and the Commissioner of National Integration representing non-Christian minorities. Among its members are the presidents of the Catholic Bishops' Conference, the Philippine Medical Association, and the Family Planning Organization of the Philippines and the director of the National Council of Churches. Mercedes Concepción, who heads the University of the Philippines Population Institute, also manages the Secretariat of the Commission and is a member of this Executive Committee.

On December 6, 1969, less than a month after he was re-elected to an unprecedented second term, President Marcos approved the statement on population policy and program that the Commission had prepared. Essentially, it committed the government to adopt quantitative population goals, promote family planning education, modify legal and administrative restrictions on family planning, reduce rates of morbidity and mortality, guide internal migration, and cooperate with international public and private organizations concerned with population. Meanwhile, the Secretary of Justice quietly lifted the ban on the import of contraceptives. Although it is practiced surreptitiously, abortion remains illegal unless deemed medically necessary to save the life of the mother. Executive Order No. 233 of the President dated May 15, 1970, commits the government to proceed with the program outlined by the Commission on Population. Significantly, the Philippine Congress has yet to add its endorsement or appropriate specific funds. Given the realities of political life in the Republic, only when Congress does so act will there be assurance of long-term official support for what is otherwise a forward-looking population policy.

The role of political and other pressure groups in shaping action on family planning is not easily delineated—so many forces are at work and population programs occasionally become entangled with other competing enterprises and personalities. When President Marcos in his State of the Nation Address on January 26, 1970, called for a national program to cope with the population explosion, he removed the inhibitions that have held in check other elected political leaders. After the First Lady, Mrs. Emelda Marcos, later in 1970 indicated her interest in action on family planning, it became socially respectable and gained a potent supporter. An indication of how rapidly the official climate is changing is a recent ruling by the Secretary of Health that government clinics may offer all forms of family planning, but rhythm is the only "recommended" method of contraception. By contrast, two years earlier the National Economic Council had insisted that U.S.A.I.D. discontinue assistance to two private associations involved in family planning because they offered all forms of contraceptives.

In mid-1969 the Conference of Roman Catholic Bishops of the Philippines issued a revealing statement on family planning. Endorsing the government's exploration of the necessity and alternatives of a population policy, they also called for a program that would be "Filipino-planned." Their statement warned: "External aid presents a peculiar difficulty. It arises from the right of those who grant aid to determine the purposes of such aid." While the argument was phrased in terms of nationalism, it also served the purposes of conservatives within the Church. More progressive Roman Catholic bishops, priests, and laymen now are gaining support and a hearing in numerous publications. The Bishops' Conference has endorsed "responsible parenthood" but offered only the rhythm method in the context of community development. Possibly, what they have not done is more important than positive action—through the efforts of the more concerned Church leaders Roman Catholic opposition to government action on contraception has remained *sotto voce* and thus allowed others to move ahead.

Protestant churches, colleges, and universities continue to champion a broad program of population control short of allowing abortion, with one exception; the Iglesia Ni Kristo. This concern with family planning is in harmony with major attention to the medical missionary enterprise that has been so much a part of Protestant efforts in Asia. It also reflects the conviction Protestants share with concerned Catholics that fundamental Philippine economic and social ills can only be managed provided population growth is checked. While the Iglesia Ni Kristo has not openly explained its noncooperation, past policies suggest its leaders are primarily concerned with building membership, and limiting family size would conflict with this objective. It is unlikely that either Muslims or pagan tribesmen in the Republic will soon show much interest in family planning. Infant mortality is exceptionally high among these groups, reflecting the primitive quality of health services available to most and their remoteness from cities and modern influences. Also, as minorities they feel threatened by the Christian majority—as indeed they are in some areas—and they have few educated leaders they trust to guide their people toward a more enlightened view.

Population Work and Research

Just a decade ago the Pathfinder Fund opened an office in Manila and quietly began helping couples with family planning. Today, there are at least 20 different Filipino organizations and government agencies active in family planning and others are drafting proposals for assistance. This is indicative of the Philippine pattern; it is a mix of public and private effort which meshes congenially with the character of the society where volunteer groups of many kinds are important. This inevitably entails some overlapping and confusion: it does promise better results than would an attempt at rigid coordination and centralized direction that could become hostage to the least common denominator of bureaucratic efficiency. As it is, there is scope for spontaneity and individuals who want to "do something" have good prospects of finding a role.

A listing of all these organizations and their programs will not be attempted; some in their formative stage are organizing staff and procedures and others are regrouping. A sketch of several, however, will characterize developments. Within the government the over-all responsible agency is the Project Office for Maternal and Child Health. Established two years ago in the Department of Health, it is directed by Dr. Flora Bayan and screens proposals presented for assistance from A.I.D. Indicative of a trend toward cooperation among private groups was the creation, in February 1969, of the Family Planning Organization of the Philippines. It joined the four-year-old Planned Parenthood Movement of the Philippines, Inc., which was essentially Protestant supported, and the Family Planning Association of the Philippines in which liberal Catholics were active. Led by Dr. Ruben Apelo of the University of the Philippines College of Medicine and its Executive Director, Dr. Raymundo Rivera, Jr., this organization has 44 special family planning clinics and cooperates with another 185 general clinics, mostly in Greater Manila and on Luzon. Another important effort is that of the Institute of Maternal and Child Health, directed by Dr. Fe del Mundo. Aside from training personnel, as of mid-1970 the Institute had 94 clinics reporting on acceptors. Others who have taken initiative in establishing clinics offering family planning include the Manila City Health Department, Laguna Province, the Philippine General Hospital and the University of the Philippines College of Medicine, Silliman University Medical Center in Dumaguete City, the Asian Social Institute, Pathfinder Fund, the Philippine Rural Reconstruction Movement, the National Land Reform Council, and health departments of several outlying cities.

Although information is beginning to accumulate from these clinics and arrangements have been made to computerize the returns, it is much too early to evaluate results. Nor is it possible at this stage to measure accurately how rapidly Filipinas will avail themselves of different methods of family planning from rhythm to IUDs and pills—initial indications were that new acceptors might number between 115,000 and 130,000 for all of 1970. In some communities there is evidence of avid interest and follow up by women returning to the clinics. Elsewhere, after overcoming their initial hesitation and visiting a clinic, Filipinas for yet to be determined reasons lost interest. Research is under way at the University of the Philippines Population Institute and the Institute of Philippine Culture at the Jesuit-managed Ateneo de Manila which should begin to provide some answers. However, given the chaotic character of record keeping common to many Philippine organizations compounded by the physical handicaps to be overcome, it appears essential that carefully chosen social laboratories be selected and studied over a period of time to develop reliable data for judgment of these programs.

By far the most important source of funding for this proliferating Philippine family planning program has been the U.S.A.I.D. This fiscal year roughly one half of A.I.D.'s budget of US$10 million for the Republic is devoted to population and assistance is going to 14 institutions. This compares with an A.I.D. expenditure for the previous fiscal year of about US$2,394,300—a portion of this was channeled through the Pathfinder Fund and the International Planned Parenthood Foundation and helped pay for import of pills and other supportive services. Present plans under study contemplate A.I.D. assistance to make family planning services available in from 1,800 to 2,000 clinics throughout the islands by 1974. Included will be at least one clinic in each of some 1,500 municipalities and thus the program would come within reach of most rural areas.

Foreign assistance to population efforts in the Philippines has come from a number of other sources. An early contributor was the Population Council which funded work at Silliman University. Over the past six years the Ford Foundation contributed $674,200 toward development of the Population Institute at the University of the Philippines and two years ago a grant of $113,000 was made to the University of Santo Tomás for development of an Institute for the Study of Human Reproduction. A $175,000 grant by the Ford Foundation to the Press Foundation of Asia headquartered in Manila and a smaller sum from the Pathfinder Fund to the Philippine Press Institute have also been important. With these funds the Press Foundation and the Institute brought Asian journalists together for intensive seminars that alerted them to demographic developments and methods of family planning. The Press Foundation established a Depth News service emphasizing reporting on development economics and population, contributing to a measurable improvement in Asian coverage. Other more modest contributions from abroad have come from the International Planned Parenthood Foundation and the Rockefeller Foundation. The Pathfinder Fund and World Neighbors provided direct assistance to clinics, and Church World Service sent supplies and educational materials to 18 mission-supported hospitals. The United States Peace Corps is helping through a program that also aims to show Filipino farmers how to raise more protein-rich mungo beans and teach mothers to improve child feeding. The United Nations Fund for Population Activities has helped with census processing and analysis. Although these programs are uneven in effectiveness, they have all contributed to the beginnings of progress.

Conclusions

Although the Philippines has begun to make promising headway on its population problem, which may now be the most explosive in Eastern Asia, major hurdles are in the offing. It is relatively easy to mobilize government agencies and private groups to initiate family planning in the cities and accessible nearby rural areas. Given sustained follow-through once the momentum of a program is achieved, it should be possible to make a real "dent" in the rate of population growth in these areas. Farther out in the countryside, however, it will prove much more difficult. Distance from the city is not only physical; it is also attitudinal, despite the rapid urbanization of values fostered by the transistor radio. *Barrios* not reached by all-weather roads are often missed by all kinds of services, including public health doctors and nurses, their devotion to the job notwithstanding. Even when there is a family planning clinic staffed and with free contraceptives available in every *población,* as now envisaged under the A.I.D.-supported program, it is difficult to imagine the wife of a subsistence farmer walking through the mud to attend it regularly during the rainy season. She has so much to do at home and it is difficult enough to make it to the weekly *barrio* market, which is much closer and where friends will be gathered.

Built-in social resistance must be anticipated, at least until there is a further evident drop in mortality among infants and preschool age children. For among rural Filipinos, children remain the only dependable old age insurance. It is often the grandparents who emphasize this and their views will not readily be reshaped by new values. Prevalence of share-tenancy, especially in most rice growing regions, fortifies this pressure for more children and especially sons. As self-defeating as it is in the national economy, the fact is that all the tenant has to sell is his labor and that of his family. It is only when he becomes at least a lease holder, or better yet, an owner, that the farmer's attitude changes—and then but gradually. As he begins to think of himself as a property holder, a new set of criteria conditions his actions. Does he want to have two or three sons among whom the farm must be divided? Will he be able to afford to send any of his sons to college and thus provide an alternative future for those to whom no land can be given? Even Filipinos who migrate to the cities are conditioned by whether their family owns rice land in the province—frequently they take pride and comfort in having their rice sent from home after harvest, even though it would be easier and possibly cheaper to buy it in the city market.

Ultimately, prospects for family planning in the islands devolve upon the Filipina, the pressures to which she is subjected and the values to which she is heir. Women have a status in Philippine society higher than anywhere in Asia—

next in relative importance of their role probably are Burmese women. The Filipina's stature is a product of many influences, not the least of which is Christianity. Although she can and does on occasion claim equality with men, as in the professions and politics, her role usually is less conspicuous. In family matters, however, hers is commonly the decisive voice. It is to his wife that a man normally brings his earnings on payday—and she gives him an allowance for personal spending. Once a family owns urban property, the wife tends to manage it. To augment family income she frequently starts a business and many a husband has later discovered he was better off to leave his job and join the enterprise she founded. Given the upward mobility to which particularly middle class Filipinas are committed, they can be expected to at least space their children further apart, once available family planning gives them greater choices in life style.

Even in pursuing these goals, however, the Filipina is subject to pronatalist counterpressures. This is particularly evident among the wealthier families who have longest had access to contraceptives, irrespective of the legal inhibitions. The Filipina within this class takes evident pride in bearing children. As a distinguished Filipina psychiatrist remarked: "She knows the role of mother and is more at ease as such than as a wife." Often after she has had six children, such a Filipina will say "that is enough," and still they keep coming. Since servants are abundantly available and inexpensive, the care of infants usually is left to them. When women in her peer group find she is out of sorts, a common remark is: "Maybe you should have another baby." Other subtle influences may be at work. Filipino male ego not infrequently is involved with *pagalalake* (manliness), which can be proven by taking a *querida,* as a mistress is known. The wife's defense is first of all in her children—should her husband become absorbed in another woman, these at least are her very own. And the *querida* in turn may be similarly motivated. Although the wealthy are a small minority, they tend to project a pattern of behavior toward which the less fortunate incline when opportunity allows.

Before a family planning program can substantially curtail Philippine population growth, the values which it represents must become an integral part of the culture. The rural Filipina, who now feels most comfortable with a baby on her hip or at least a child beside her whose hair she can stroke, must discover possible alternative satisfactions. Once she does, she will be a potent force for curbing her family's size. Especially for this reason it would seem wise to make Philippine family planning less a program that is offered from outside by government agencies and others and more a socially indigenous effort in which particularly Filipinas find a participatory, rewarding role.

References

The Manila Galleon, by William Lytle Schurz, E. P. Dutton & Co., Inc., New York, 1939. Available as D35, A Dutton Paperback.

A Half-Century of Philippine Agriculture, by scientists writing each on his special theme under the leadership of Dr. Gonzalo Merino, Director of Plant Industry. Published for the Bureau of Agriculture Golden Jubilee Committee by Graphic House, Manila, 1952.

Philippine Population in the Seventies, edited by Mercedes B. Concepción, Community Publishers, Inc., Manila, 1969.

Report on the Combined Conference on Evaluation of Malaysia Family Planning Program and Population Programs of East Asia, held March 1970 in Kuala Lumpur, "Country Statement on the Philippines," by Mercedes B. Concepción, Director of the Population Institute, University of the Philippines, presently unpublished.

The Author

ALBERT RAVENHOLT has worked on Asia and the Western Pacific since before World War II, serving as a correspondent in China, India, Burma, Indochina, and the Philippines. In 1947, as a fellow of the Institute of Current World Affairs, he went to Harvard University for advanced study of Far Eastern history and Chinese language. In 1948 he returned to China to cover the civil war. Mr. Ravenholt joined the Field Staff at its founding in 1951 and covers large areas of Asia from his base in Manila. He has written for *Foreign Affairs, The Reporter,* the *Chicago Daily News Foreign Service,* and other magazines, in addition to his regular Fieldstaff Reports. Published works include reports for the *Encyclopaedia Britannica Book of the Year* and the *World Book Yearbook,* a book entitled *The Philippines; a Young Republic on the Move,* and chapters in other volumes. Although a generalist on East Asian and Southeast Asian affairs, Mr. Ravenholt maintains a specialized knowledge of Asian and tropical agriculture.

YUGOSLAVIA
International boundary
Republic boundary
Autonomous area boundary
National capital
Republic or autonomous area capital
0 25 50 75 100 Miles
0 25 50 75 100 Kilometers
AUSTRIA
HUNGARY
ROMANIA
BULGARIA
GREECE
ALBANIA
ITALY
IT
SLOVENIA
CROATIA
BOSNIA AND HERCEGOVINA
SERBIA
VOJVODINA
MONTENEGRO
KOSOVO
MACEDONIA
ADRIATIC SEA
Maribor
Čakovec
Celje
Varazdin
Ljubljana
Zagreb
Karlovac
Rijeka
Pula
Zadar
Split
Dubrovnik
Okučani
Vinkovci
Subotica
Bačka Topola
Novi Sad
Vršac
BELGRADE
Banja Luka
Tuzla
Valjevo
Vreoci
Sarajevo
Foča
Titovo Užice
Paraćin
Niš
Trebinje
Titograd
Priština
Tetovo
Skopje
Gostivar
Titov Veles
Gradsko
Prilep
Strumica
Debar
Drava
Sava
Una
Danube
Tisa
Drina
Tara
Velika Morava
Nišava
Vardar

Yugoslavia

Dennison I. Rusinow

With a population of under 21 million in an area roughly that of Minnesota, Yugoslavia is a small country. In the remarkable ethnic diversity of that population and in extreme regional differences in levels of economic and social development, social structures, history, religion, and customs, it is nevertheless bewilderingly complex. Population growth rates range from extremely low—or even negative—to the highest in Europe; literacy rates and the quality and availability of health and social services display almost as wide a spread; regional extremes in per capita national income run from over $1,200 in Slovenia to around $200 in the Kosovo Autonomous Province; the country's five official nationalities and dozen ethnic minorities display the varying and often contradictory imprints of three major religions (Orthodox, Catholic, and Muslim) and three distinct foreign cultural heritages (Central European, Ottoman, and Veneto-Mediterranean). In such a society almost no generalization can be both valid and meaningful. Any discussion of demographic trends and problems and of family planning programs and attitudes must therefore take this complexity into account.

Population Profile

Since 1921, when the first census was taken in the newly created Yugoslav state, the total population has increased from 12.5 to an estimated 20.3 million in 1969. This growth was primarily a result of natural increase, although migration played some role, especially during World War II. Even in the interwar period, however, both the crude birth rate and the rate of natural increase tended, with some fluctuations, to fall slowly. The rate of natural increase declined from 15.8/1000 in 1921 to 11/1000 in 1939, while the crude birth rate moved downward from 36.7 to 25.9/1000. In some regions—notably Slovenia, Eastern Serbia, and parts of Croatia—the decline in fertility actually dates from at least the 1890s, as early as in most of Western Europe except France.

Yugoslavia lost 1.7 million of its citizens—11 per cent of the total population—in the holocaust of war and civil war from 1941 to 1945. After the war, in the period 1950–54, there was a compensatory rise in the crude birth rate, back to nearly 29/1000. Since 1955, however, the pattern of consistently falling birth rates has reasserted itself and has been extended to some previously unaffected regions. By 1969 the country-wide crude birth rate was 18.8/1000. With an also characteristically declining death rate, lately tending to level off at between eight and nine per thousand, the 1969 rate of natural increase was down to 9.6/1000, or just under one per cent per annum.

More interesting and significant are the rates revealed by a regional breakdown of these country-wide figures, into the Republican and Provincial components that roughly coincide with ethnic divisions, or at least ethnic concentrations (Table 1) (*1*). Here the 1969 crude birth rate ranges from 13.1/1000 in the multinational Vojvodina and 16.9/1000 in Slovenia up to 37.9/1000 in Kosovo, with its Albanian majority. The correlation between birth rate rankings and regional levels of economic development, education, health services, etc., is unsurprisingly direct and striking, with minor deviations a function of relevant differences in cultural or religious traditon.

The death rate, like the birth rate, has been declining for six decades in the more developed regions, where it has recently tended to level off at slightly above Western European standards. The largest improvements in mortality figures in the postwar period have occurred, not unexpectedly, in districts where the rate was previously the highest: Kosovo, Macedonia, and Bosnia-Herzegovina. Because of the resulting age structures, crude death rates are now lowest in these underdeveloped regions. (Montenegro provides an interesting exception. A very poor region—next to the bottom on most indices—life for its legendarily heroic warrior-peasants, scratching a meager livelihood from the barren rocks of the Black Mountain, has always been rugged and often violent. Yet Montenegro has long enjoyed the lowest death rate in the country: under 10/1000 ever since the War and 5.8 in 1969. A Montenegrin male's life expectancy, which was 66.7 years in 1967, is the longest in Yugoslavia. No pollution? best yoghurt or strongest plum brandy? life style? or natural selection, with centuries of precarious life and continual warfare eliminating weaker strains and leaving unusually sturdy stock?)

Although the death rate pattern consequently does not display quite the tidy set of correlations with levels of development found in the birth rate pattern, regional variations in death rates are now quite low and so have a much smaller effect on population growth than variations in birth rates. Thus the ranking of the regions in rates of natural increase corresponds to their ranking in birth rates and (with minor exceptions as noted) to development levels: from 3.1/1000 in the Vojvodina and 5.7/1000 in Slovenia up to 17.2/1000 in Macedonia and 29.4/1000 in Kosovo.

The Yugoslav gross reproduction rate has meanwhile declined from 1.89 in

1950 to 1.26 in 1967; the net reproduction rate from 1.54 in 1950 to 1.11 in 1967. The regional pattern for these rates again deviates slightly from the birth rate pattern, as a function of different sex ratios among the newborn in different areas. In three regions, together including five ninths of the total population, the net reproduction rate has been less than unity in all years since 1957: in 1967 it was .93 in Croatia and .88 in Serbia proper and in the Vojvodina. Kosovo again marks the other extreme, with a 1967 gross reproduction rate of 2.78 and net reproduction rate of 2.12.

Although there are more women than men in the total population, partly a consequence of two world wars, in all classes up to 39 years of age there are at present more males than females, the result of a constant ratio of 106–107 male to 100 female live births since 1921.

Yugoslavia has a net emigration balance. According to official statistics, the difference between the number of permanent emigrants and the number of immigrants averaged 7–8,000 per year between 1962 and 1969. More accurate unofficial estimates put the total closer to 12–15,000 per year. The majority of permanent emigrants are from Croatia and Macedonia.

Finally, it should be noted that the mean life expectancy in Yugoslavia—at 64.7 years for males, 69 years for females in 1966—is still shorter than in most European and other developed countries primarily because the mortality rate among Yugoslav infants and small children has remained relatively high. Infant mortality was still 64/1000 among live births for males and 60/1000 for females in 1967, down from 122 to 109, respectively, in 1950–54. Regional extremes in 1967 were 31/1000 male and 23/1000 female live births in Slovenia, 102/1000 males and 114/1000 females in Kosovo.

The head of the Center for Demographic Research in Belgrade summarizes the over-all picture as follows:

> The transitional demographic period, which is characterized by falling birth and death rates and by changes in the age distribution of the population, is virtually at an end in areas with a low birth rate, fully established in areas with a medium birth rate, and just beginning in areas with a high birth rate (Kosovo and some other smaller regions) (*2*).

The Center's projection of future population growth presupposes a continuation of present rate trends, with leveling off in low birth rate regions partly balanced by the onset of the "transitional demographic period" in Kosovo and other high birth rate pockets. Given also the age structure of the present population, the absolute number of births per year is expected to rise slowly through the 1970s (with a peak of just over 500,000 per year, 1976–81—cf. 499,280 in 1952, the previous peak), and then to sink slowly in the early 1980s. According to the Center's projections for the next fifteen years, the total population should be about 20.8 million in 1971 (the decennial census was due in March 1971), 21.9 million in 1976, 23 million in 1981 and 23.5 million in 1986 (*3*).

In these projections, as in all Yugoslav demographic statistics, the present writer knows of no reason to suppose that the accuracy of the data and the competence of the statistical analysis deviate significantly from European standards.

Population Distribution and Movement

Rapid industrialization since the Second World War has brought a significant change in urban-rural population distribution in favor of the urban sector. In Yugoslavia, however, the shift has been far less dramatic than in most developing countries with much lower economic growth rates. There has been a strong tendency, particularly marked in the most industrialized Republics, for nonfarm labor to maintain a rural domicile; this is true both for full-time industrial workers and for the numerous "half-peasants" who oscillate between farm and nonfarm employment. Thus Slovenia, the economically most developed Republic, ranks just above underdeveloped Kosovo, Montenegro, and Bosnia-Herzegovina in per cent of urban population.

As a result, Yugoslavia remains one of the least urbanized countries in Europe. In the 1961 census (more recent data will not be available until the 1971 census has been taken and analyzed), only 5.2 million persons or 28 per cent of the total population lived in the 348 communities defined by Yugoslav criteria as urban (*4*). Of these communities, only 14 had 50,000 or more inhabitants, with another 44 registering populations of 20–50,000. The seven towns with over 100,000 inhabitants accounted for 32 per cent of the total urban (and 9 per cent of the total Yugoslav) population.

The growth of the urban population—by 29 per cent between the 1953 and 1961 censuses, excluding the 107 communities reclassified as urban in the interval—is largely a function of rural-urban migration rather than natural increase. No data are available on migration balance vs. natural increase as factors in urban population growth. It seems reasonable, however, to assume that (with the probable exception of Macedonia and Bosnia-Herzegovina) rapid urbanization has not had a major specific effect on fertility.

Most of the rural-urban migrants in Slovenia, Croatia, and Serbia have come from districts where the trend toward smaller families was already under way, or was soon to develop in tandem with similar trends in urban environments. Mortality rates, of course, do tend to be lower in urban settings, with better health services and standards of hygiene.

Other significant aspects of internal migration can be roughly summarized as follows:

Yugoslavs as a whole are surprisingly un-mobile for a people undergoing such rapid economic and social change. A recent survey has reconfirmed 1961 census data showing that about two thirds live in the place in which they were born (*5*). Of the rest, 11.4 per cent have moved within the commune of birth (mostly women who moved at the time of marriage), 7.5 per cent within the Republic, and only 18.5 per cent to another Republic or abroad.

Ethnicity is the chief barrier to internal migration. Thus the economically developed Slovenes, the most mobile of all in terms of intra-Republican migration, and the Macedonians—both nations with distinct languages and new-found national pride—rank just above the least mobile ethnic and religious minorities

(Albanians, Bosnian Muslims, Hungarians) in the percentage of their people who cross an ethnic frontier.

In inter-Republican and inter-Provincial population movements Bosnia-Herzegovina, Montenegro, and Kosovo are areas of net emigration. If longer-distance, intra-Republican rural-urban migration is included, other traditional emigration areas in Croatia (Lika, the Dalmatian hinterland) join the list. All are following a tradition of great antiquity: the secular tendency of the desperately poor but fecund Dinaric highlands to export surplus population to the "fat" lowlands, frequently by means of invasion or conquest. Some have interpreted the Communist Partisan takeover of 1944–45, staffed predominantly by "highlanders," as essentially the latest in such a series of demographically derived socio-political revolutions.

Finally, since 1964 there has been an annually growing volume of temporary migration of manpower to Western Europe, particularly the German Federal Republic. Latest estimates put the present total at over 500,000. The demographic effect of such family separations is, however, reduced by a widespread tendency to return home every year or two, often specifically for breeding purposes. (Again a long-standing tradition is involved. In Dalmatia and other areas of traditional pre-1914 emigration to America, well-spaced families were effortlessly achieved by triennial or quinquennial visits by the *pater familias* working in the United States. In some predominantly Muslim districts a more remarkable solution was once in favor: if a married temporary emigrant could not return home often enough to maintain customary fertility levels himself, he would entrust this particular family chore to a stay-at-home brother or best friend.) Moreover, the economic aspects of temporary migration frequently make it economically possible or easier to start a family or enlarge one: recorded remittances from migrant workers abroad are presently running at more than $200 million annually.

Population and the Economy

In 1939, 75 per cent of all Yugoslavs were dependent for their livelihood upon agriculture, most of it subsistence farming on peasant smallholdings. Today the equivalent figure is about 45 per cent. It is a country in transition from an agrarian to an industrial-agrarian society. In the early postwar period industrialization was carried out in accordance with Soviet doctrines: extensively and at high speed, with little concern for costs or profitability, but with a commitment to full employment that disguised unemployment as underemployment. In the psychological atmosphere engendered by such a system and its values, the only new socio-economic factors that might inhibit a large family size were the rapid rise in the number of working women (from 200,000 in 1939 to 1,033,438, or 30 per cent of the total employed, in 1968, plus 42 per cent of the economically active rural population) and the perennially acute housing shortage in the new industrial centers.

In Yugoslavia the transition from a command to a market economy, which took place legally in the early 1950s and effectively in the 1960s, altered the parameters within which economic and demographic development would interact.

Intensive and profit-oriented investment gradually and unevenly replaced extensive, jobs-for-everyone-everywhere development. With the major reform inaugurated in 1965, "passive" regions and economic sectors entered a period of crisis and were told that labor mobility to profitable regions and sectors was their principal long-run hope. Unemployment was accepted and grew rapidly, with a critical situation avoided only by the safety valve of unrestricted temporary emigration abroad. The total number employed stagnated and in 1967 actually fell by 21,000, and this at a time of maximum demographic pressure on employment, as products of the postwar baby boom came on the job market. (From 1953 to 1961 the average annual increase in the population of working age was 94,000; in the mid-1960s it was double that figure.)

On the other hand, the economic reforms of the '60s meant improving living standards and prospects for those who were employed, since they included a shift in the investment-consumption ratio in favor of consumption and an increased emphasis on the production of consumer durables, housing, and other amenities. At the same time, a final surrender to the private peasants, in the form of increased incentives to produce for the market and improved opportunities to do so, led to both a more optimistic atmosphere in the countryside (where 85 per cent of the arable land is owned and worked privately) and better supplies on the market; indicative of these changes are the ending, at least, of Yugoslavia's perennial postwar dependence on wheat imports and a visually staggering amount of new family dwellings in the richer rural districts.

Awareness of demographic trends, incidentally, may have contributed to the Yugoslav reformers' unexpected stubbornness in holding to the economic reforms despite a protracted period of consequent stagnation in growth and rising unemployment, but in anticipation of a decline in demographic pressure on employment after 1971 (*6*). If this is true—and it is purely speculative at this point—it also suggests that Party and government support for expanded family planning programs in recent years (see below) may be based in part on awareness of the economic benefits of lower birth rates with the post-1965 model and at the present stage in economic development.

Population and Development: Social-Attitudinal Aspects

Sociological research conducted in rural Yugoslavia between the wars confirmed what the onset of significantly declining birth rates in many districts more than 60 years ago suggested: that some form of birth control, primarily coitus interruptus and primitive abortion, was already a widely-accepted practice. Under the present Communist regime, wider practice of birth control and further reductions in family size have been encouraged by several factors. Among them are legal sanction and legal availability (primarily abortion, see below), the rural-urban shift of population compounded by the acute urban housing problem endemic in socialist states, and the impact of both changing values and the regime's agricultural policies on peasant attitudes toward ideal family size.

Only the last of these factors is specifically Yugoslav. When the Communist regime abandoned attempts at forced collectivization of agriculture in the early

1950s, it placed a ten hectare (26 acre) limit on the size of a single peasant household's holding of arable land. In 1965, when hopes had proved vain that the more enterprising peasants would voluntarily choose to join the "socialist sector," after observing the advantages of scale and mechanization there, restrictions on peasant access to privately-owned means of mechanization were lifted and market production encouraged by higher prices for farm products.

Both of these political acts affected peasant attitudes toward family size. The superordinate value that Yugoslav peasants in almost all districts had traditionally placed on becoming a *gazda* (a rich peasant) through the acquisition of more land, implying a need for more hands to work it, had become unrealizable. Then the possibility of acquiring mechanized equipment further reduced the perceived value of more family manpower, while the aspiration for such equipment increased the relative value of cash income and the peasant's marginal propensity to save. Add to these factors decay of extended kinship ties and the shift in values and status symbols from land and family to consumer goods and education, typical of societies in Yugoslavia's present state of modernizing transition. The usual conclusion has been that more mouths to feed now, and more heirs dividing the farm later, are not good things.

One other legal change also affects attitudes to family size. Before WW II only male children could inherit agricultural land; in socialist Yugoslavia the law requires equal treatment of male and female heirs. The postwar law has been implemented only gradually and is still not observed in many areas. While it may be only a minor factor, a Belgrade sociologist who has done extensive demographic field work tells me that she finds a significant correlation between the rate of fertility decline and the extent to which the law is observed—i.e., she sees this as one reason why the birth rate has declined much more rapidly in rural Serbia, where the law is now widely implemented, than in Macedonia or Montenegro, where it is not.

Even without access to the results of attitude surveys (7), an observer who has traveled extensively in rural Yugoslavia can accumulate enough firsthand evidence to confirm these generalizations about changing values and their impact on family size. Among peasant acquaintances in the Vojvodina, Slovenia, Sumadija and eastern Serbia, inner-Croatia and Slavonia, families with more than two children are exceptions of increasing rarity. The reasons offered: not enough land and a desire to avoid further splintering of already small holdings; the value of education, its cost, and hence a desire to have no more children than one can afford to educate; the good things of life that one can hope to acquire if there are fewer mouths to feed (the consumer mentality, or the rising elasticity of substitution between children and goods on the market); or, more negatively, the lack of any real "prospects" (*perspektive*) in the village, so that children go away to the city when they grow up, so why have them? Or, in a related variant of the negative rationale: things are getting worse, the future—under socialism or in general—is grim, modern children are in any case ungrateful wretches who have abandoned the familial values of their fathers and so offer no security against the vicissitudes of old age, etc., thus self-interest or a sense of responsibility, or both, indicate few or even no children. And the method: abortion, almost exclusively (but often *presumably* after coitus interruptus has failed), frequently annually, increasingly done in hospitals or health centers, but in primitive areas—like eastern Serbia—homemade by traditional and dangerous means.

Population and Society

It is probably fair to say that a Communist system of administration and control has at least the technical capability to raise the level of "cultural availability" of the populace of an underdeveloped country more rapidly to near totality than any other existing system. The Party and its associated "socio-political" and cultural networks make it possible for all kinds of directives, "guidelines" and information to be passed to the most remote communities and brought, superficially at least, to the attention of all but the most determined citizens. Moreover, despite a theoretical belief in the primacy of economics, the Marxist concept of development displays in practice a better grasp of the wholeness and the totalistic nature of the process than most, if not all, competing models for modernization. What is communicated through the various "transmission belts," therefore, concerns wide aspects of social change—culture, education, family mores, value systems, et al.—as often as it does economic and political systems as such. On the other hand, exposed to a continuous barrage of often spasmodic but repetitive "campaigns" mounted by these interlocking networks in favor of this or that policy, value, or program, the citizens of such states, including Yugoslavia, develop a protective layer of deafness and apathy that makes them less "available" than the technical effectiveness of the ubiquitous networks would suggest—except, perhaps, in some "subliminal" sense.

Literacy rates are among the least reliable of Yugoslav statistics, primarily because they record as literate anyone who has been to school and overlook the very large number of school drop-outs who have subsequently forgotten how to read and write. For what they are worth, official statistics show, as of 1961, 2.8 million illiterates ten years of age or older; 19.7 per cent of the population so defined. The ranking is the usual one, with only 1.8 per cent illiterate in Slovenia (probably fairly accurate), 10.6 per cent in the Vojvodina, and 12.1 per cent in Croatia, the rate then increasing to 32.5 per cent in Bosnia-Herzegovina and 41.1 per cent in Kosovo. Younger age groups, as usual in societies with rapid recent development, have far higher literacy levels than their elders (even in Kosovo, where the certainly optimistic 1961 official illiteracy figures run: 13 per cent in the age group 10–19 years, 36 per cent in the 20–34 age group, 65 per cent in the 35–64 age group, and 80 per cent among the over-65s).

Social and educational mobility suffers little restriction on the basis of class origin, even in the inverted sense in which educational and career opportunities were long denied to offspring of the previous "privileged" classes in other Communist states. It is, however, restricted by the cultural environment (familial and communal) of early years, as elsewhere, and by ethnic barriers, which particularly limit the mobility of members of less numerous minorities. At the same time, the style of economic development—with a relatively low rate of accompanying urbanization and a consequent high level of retained psychological links and physical movement between urban and rural or modernizing and traditional sectors—has meant relatively easy mobility for ideas, values, and fashions between the two sectors. (The superficially unchanging face and life-styles of much of the Yugoslav countryside are in this sense misleading.) This aspect of the social structure is also, of course, another and important aspect of the "cultural availability" of the populace.

Despite intensive efforts and encouraging results in the past two decades, the Yugoslavs still have far to go in extending an adequate public health service to the entire country and in improving the quality of existing services. By 1964, the latest figures at hand, the country was served by 15,274 physicians (cf. 4,747 in 1938). The country-wide ratio was one physician, including those engaged in administration and research, to every 1,260 persons (cf. one to 3,240 in 1938). But the distribution, both in personnel and adequate health centers, remains woefully uneven: in the worst-served area, Kosovo, the 1964 physician-population ratio was still 1:3,185. The country still ranks first in Europe in the incidence of diseases, like tuberculosis, typically associated with underdevelopment. It should be added, however, that the Yugoslavs have long been ahead of their times and level of development in their broad conception of what a public service should be doing—in education, public hygiene, and preventive medicine—and in basic organization and effort to this end, a philosophy of public health that dates back to the 1920s (8).

Education presents a similar picture: rapid expansion and notable progress, but still inadequate to the needs of the country. Eight years of education are compulsory and most children now start school. The drop-out rate after as little as two to four years remains high, especially in rural areas. Widely-dispersed population in the rugged mountains of much of the interior presents special problems for elementary schooling, while a basic and necessary commitment to separate but equal schooling for every ethnic group raises per pupil costs. One extreme set of statistics is illustrative: the one million members of the Albanian minority in Kosovo, Macedonia, and Montenegro, who had no schools of their own before the war (and less than 12,000 students in Serbian primary schools), possessed by 1968–69 a total of 1,015 primary schools, 74 vocational schools, and 27 classical secondary schools (*gimnazije*). The Albanian primary schools had a total enrollment of 211,000 pupils (cf. 119,000 in 1963–64), out of over 250,000 children of primary school age. In Yugoslavia as a whole, at the end of the 1968–69 academic year, 263,161 pupils completed primary school (cf. ca. 406,000 14-year-olds in the country that year), while 171,316 students graduated from secondary schools, 18,131 from specialized post-secondary schools, and 13,358 from universities and colleges.

Population and Polity

The Titoist regime has always been passively profamily planning, and actively so since about 1963. Philosophically the League of Communists and state agencies oppose family planning as an aspect of a population policy; all such policies, whether pronatalist or antinatalist, are in fact officially condemned as "inhuman" because they are seen as implying state interference in the right of the individual to make free choices. Official attitudes are based instead on the regime's construction of Marxian concern with human freedom and responsibility: family planning is therefore supported as a vital aspect of the "emancipation" of the individual. Frequent reference is made to the "possibility that parents themselves determine the number of children they will have and the time intervals between births" as "one of the basic human rights and duties" (9).

Family planning programs are supported by the Party and the state, both with greater intensity in the past three years. In accordance with the Yugoslav concept of "social self-management" by autonomous institutions sensitive to "guidelines" and "resolutions" passed by Party forums and parliamentary bodies, tasks in this field are entrusted to such institutions in the social welfare and public health sectors (see Table 1).

Contraceptives and contraceptive information are consequently freely available in principle, the former through medical centers, some practitioners, and pharmacies and the latter through medical centers, through the work of the Councils for Family Planning, and recently through courses in sex education and human relations being introduced in schools in some areas. By 1969 the Federal Council for Family Planning counted about 500 health institutions concerned exclusively or partially with contraception, with 12 contraceptives available on the market (five oral, three mechanical, and four chemical). The distribution is uneven, and so are the results.

Abortion was first legalized in 1952, the motivation at the time being a desire to reduce the incidence of illegal abortions performed under unsatisfactory conditions, with attendant dangers to life and health. The law was amended in 1960 and a new general law on the interruption of pregnancy was passed in 1969. The effect of all these acts has been to make clinical abortion available to anyone desiring it, with a minimum of formality (*10*). The 1969 law attempts to tighten the conditions in only one important way: the applicant must be warned of the dangers and advised to desist, and she must be given information about contraceptive techniques and availability. In addition, the new law requires that appropriate "social and educational institutions" should "acquaint women and youth with the harmful consequences of the interruption of pregnancy and with the advantages of the use of means and methods of contraception."

The potentially most important recent legal change in the field is a provision, in the latest Federal law on health insurance, authorizing the Republics to extend the availability of *free* contraceptive means to all such means and all citizens. Heretofore only the pill has been free—as a prescribed medicine—and only to those covered by health insurance. (Such coverage is automatic in Yugoslavia for people employed in the "socialist sector" and their families, but is voluntary for those not so employed—meaning primarily private peasants.) Republican action on this provision is, however, inhibited by the unsolved problem of financing such an extension of services.

Two other recent, quasi-legal acts deserve mention. On April 25, 1969, the Federal Assembly (parliament) passed a Resolution on Family Planning, a lengthy document which (1) firmly supported both the principle of planning

Table 1. Selected Demographic Indicators

							Serbia			
		Yugoslavia	*Bosnia & Herz.*	*Croatia*	*Macedonia*	*Montenegro*	*Serbia proper*	*Kosovo*	*Vojvodina*	*Slovenia*
Population, 1961, in thousands		18,549	3,278	4,160	1,406	472	4,823	964	1,855	1,591
Live births	1950–54	28.8	38.2	23.2	38.4	32.7	26.1	43.5	23.3	22.8
	1965–69	19.7	25.0	15.7	26.5	22.1	15.2	38.3	14.4	17.8
	1969	18.8	27.3	14.6	25.4	20.3	15.6	37.9	13.1	16.9
Deaths	1950–54	11.8	12.0	11.7	14.5	10.0	11.4	18.0	12.4	10.9
	1965–69	8.7	7.0	9.7	8.2	6.3	8.5	9.4	9.5	10.1
	1969	9.2	6.9	10.7	8.2	5.8	9.5	8.5	10.0	11.2
Natural increase	1950–54	17.0	26.2	11.5	22.9	22.7	14.7	25.5	10.9	11.9
	1965–69	10.0	18.0	6.0	18.3	15.8	6.7	28.9	4.8	7.7
	1969	9.6	15.4	3.9	17.2	14.5	6.1	29.4	3.1	5.7
Gross reproduction rate	1950	1.89	2.53	1.49	2.83	2.08	1.70	3.60	1.54	1.49
	1967	1.26	1.51	1.00	1.66	1.35	.96	2.78	.96	1.17
Net reproduction rate	1950	1.54	1.93	1.27	2.13	1.67	1.44	2.28	1.31	1.36
	1967	1.11	1.30	.93	1.39	1.18	.88	2.12	.88	1.13

Sources: Demografska Statistika 1967 and Breznik, *art. cit.* in *Yugoslav Survey*, X, 2

new and extending existing programs, (2) demanded the extension of sex and contraceptive education in schools and other institutions, and (3) expressed concern about the continued high incidence of abortion, recommending measures to shift popular preference toward contraception. (These measures were mostly educational, but included a suggestion that "material incentives" be considered, perhaps including a charge for abortions with contraceptive means free.) A month earlier the League of Yugoslav Communists (the Party), at its Ninth Congress, had included among its resolutions a section in support of family planning.

The Councils for Family Planning and other concerned organizations are presently lobbying for two further legal changes. The first would additionally tighten those provisions of the 1969 abortion law designed to encourage a shift to contraception by requiring that the local commissions which must approve each abortion be formed or continue existence only if they include a "council for preventive means," i.e., contraception. The second proposed change would make sex and contraceptive education obligatory instead of optional in the country's schools.

Population and Polity: Attitudes to Programs

In 1967, the latest year for which statistics are available, a total of 276,249 abortions were performed in Yugoslav health institutions. With 389,640 live births in the country that year, officially recorded abortions alone therefore equalled 70 per cent of all live births. Regional figures are even more striking (Table 2): while in Macedonia recorded abortions in 1967 were only 21 per

Table 2. Abortions Carried Out in Yugoslav Health Institutions

	1963	*1964*	*1965*	*1966*	*1967*	*1968*
Yugoslavia . . .	215,063	227,665	245,391	265,391	276,249	
Bosnia-Herzegovina	27,272	28,644	31,103	34,396	34,917	
Croatia	35,531	38,979	43,418	45,300	44,178	
Macedonia . . .	5,211	6,121	6,909	9,300	8,582	
Montenegro . .	4,242	4,655	5,571	5,870	6,898	
Slovenia . . .	15,468	15,385	15,987	14,886	14,465	13,500 (est.)
Serbia	127,260	133,881	142,403	155,542	167,209	
(of which in the Vojvodina) . . .	40,575	44,423	46,181	47,579		

Source: Faits et Tendances, no. 6 (1970), pp. 46, 117, 138

cent of live births, and in Bosnia-Herzegovina 30 per cent, the incidence then rises through Slovenia at 48 per cent and Montenegro at 60 per cent to Croatia at 66 per cent and Serbia at 113 per cent of live births. In the Vojvodina Province in 1966 recorded abortions equalled a staggering 167 per cent of live births. Thus the incidence was highest, relatively as well as absolutely, in the two most populous Republics and the Vojvodina (*11*).

Moreover, while these figures do include 65,515 technically illegal but in-hospital abortions in 1967 (i.e., with a side payment to the doctor to avoid the inconvenience of the legal procedure and its commissions), the number of other illegal interruptions of pregnancy, performed outside health institutions, is anybody's guess. Representatives of the Federal Council for Family Planning presume that the total of such abortions may be still greater than the total of recorded legal and illegal interruptions.

These figures and estimates alone bear sufficient witness to the lack of significant popular social-psychological or effective pressure group barriers to acceptance of birth control in general and of legalized abortion in particular. They also bear witness, however, to relative lack of success in the regime's efforts to induce a switch from abortion to contraception as a means of family planning, at least so far and in most areas.

A comparison between abortion figures and the distribution of the population by religion suggests that religious sanctions, including particularly efforts by the Catholic hierarchy to propagate the official views of their church, do not play a major role in determining popular attitudes, although they have some effect. The incidence of abortion in Catholic Croatia is less than in Orthodox Serbia but greater than in all other Republics. The lowest abortion rates are recorded by Muslim and Orthodox areas (Macedonia, Kosovo, and Bosnia-Herzegovina, the last with a Catholic minority but predominantly Muslim and Orthodox), whose common denominator is underdevelopment and a still traditional, "closed" status (*zatvorenost*) for women. The Catholic Church in Yugoslavia, it should be added, has recently been increasingly free and activist in social as well as liturgical matters; but the hierarchy's only specific intervention in the family planning controversy known to this writer, aside from generally favorable episcopal and religious press commentaries on the Papal position on contraception, has been an alleged effort (reported in the Croatian press) to persuade Catholic doctors to refuse to perform abortions.

The attitude of the Orthodox Church seems, without detailed study, to be ambivalent and uncertain. When opposition to planned restriction of family size is preached from the pulpit, it would appear to be based more on national than on the theological grounds; if the Catholic Croats were to obey the admonitions of their church while the Orthodox Serbs practiced family planning, Serb priests occasionally warn, the Croats would eventually become more numerous than the Serbs, with disastrous consequences.

A recent small but potentially significant decline in the incidence of abortion in the Catholic Republics of Slovenia and Croatia seems indeed to be less attributable to the influence of *humanae vitae* and supporters of the Papal position than to the first signs of a shift to contraceptives—in turn an index of the Catholic Republics' higher level of economic and social development and their spiritual and physical proximity to Western Europe. Thus a spokesman for the Institute for Family Planning in Ljubljana, Slovenia, reports that the total number of visits to "centers for contraception" in that Republic had jumped from 40,000 in 1966 to 100,000 in 1968, while in the same period sales of hormone contraceptives in Slovenian pharmacies increased from 65,000 "packages" (number of months per package unspecified) to 200,000. From 1966 to 1968 the number of recorded abortions in Slovenia declined from 14,886 to about 13,500 (*12*).

The country-wide pattern for the use of contraceptives—in terms of visits to "contraception centers"—is suggested by Table 3.

Table 3. Visits to Centers for Contraception in 1967

	Number of visits		*No. of 1st visits by age*				
	Total	*of which, first visits*	*up to 19 yrs.*	*20–29 yrs.*	*30–39 yrs.*	*40–49 yrs.*	*50+ yrs.*
Yugoslavia . .	399,304	160,817	12,823	75,616	60,088	11,558	732
Bosnia-Herzeg. .	38,959	22,765	2,006	9,735	8,771	1,989	264
Croatia . . .	42,519	18,283	1,115	8,696	7,280	1,272	20
Macedonia . .	26,742	19,376	713	8,209	8,318	1,922	214
Montenegro . .	3,169	1,869	65	683	856	230	35
Slovenia . . .	47,591	13,853	1,051	7,742	4,394	658	8
Serbia proper . .	135,593	58,558	5,237	27,504	21,824	3,926	68
Vojvodina . . .	101,143	24,308	2,420	12,215	8,114	1,438	121
Kosovo . . .	3,588	1,805	216	932	532	123	2

Source: Faits et Tendances, no. 6, 1970, p. 46

Concerned officials attribute the persistence of abortion as the exclusive effective means of family planning in most areas both to tradition and to an unintended side effect of Yugoslavia's liberal laws on pregnancy interruption, which (they feel) have created a widespread popular impression that abortion is *the* authorized means. The same officials also locate the principal opposition to extended availability of contraceptive information and means in two not unexpected groups: among conservative educators and school boards and among gynecologists who insist that only they, and not general practitioners, should prescribe or fit contraceptive means or even give information and instruction.

The preference for abortion meanwhile persists even in relatively modern urban environments like Belgrade, and at educational and cultural levels where knowledge of alternative methods is widespread (albeit curiously incomplete, as in a belief that hormone contraceptive pills must be taken just before intercourse). One survey of 300 high school students, for example, revealed that 98 per cent were familiar with the process of conception and with between two and five different types of contraceptives, but that "they prefer to resort to surgical interventions in the case of unwanted conception and do not make use of their knowledge about contraception with a view to preventing unwanted conception" (*13*).

The reasons offered at this level are the ones one would expect: "it takes the fun out of it" and "my husband wouldn't approve, but doesn't know when I have an abortion" are perhaps the commonest. There is, for example, a Vojvodina peasant who had five abortions that her husband was unaware of, all in the three years between the births of their first (female) and second (male) children; or of girls who insist that their partners use neither condom nor coitus interruptus because they "would rather take a chance." They know exactly where to go for a quick pregnancy test or an abortion, but are vague about other possibilities because they are simply not interested.

Population Work and Research

Yugoslav family planning programs, like the laws on the interruption of pregnancy, appear to have been born of the concern felt in women's organizations, public health institutions, and some Party circles over the high incidence of illegal abortion, with its attendant consequences. While the laws were designed to move abortions into medical centers, reducing the risks involved, concerned nongovernmental institutions were primarily interested in promoting a shift to contraceptives, for ethical as well as health reasons. The role of women's organizations, and particularly of one of their coordinating bodies, the Conference for Social Activity of Women of Yugoslavia, in voicing alarm and in initiating pro-contraception, anti-abortion programs meant that efforts in this field were to develop within a wider context of concern over the status of women, the problems of working women, family nutrition and hygiene, human relations in general, and relations between the sexes in particular. The internal logic of this wider framework quickly converted a pro-contraception campaign, based on medical and narrowly ethical arguments, into a full-fledged family planning program supported by a broader rationale.

The institutional commitment and interests of such sponsors and organizers also has meant that the rationale of family planning in Yugoslavia has emphasized, almost exclusively, its importance in widening human freedom and independence, emancipating women, and enhancing individual responsibility. In interviews with workers in the field, efforts to discuss family planning in the context of a worldwide population "explosion" or "problem" were invariably met with disinterest or reference to the absence of that kind of "problem" in Yugoslavia and principled opposition to any "population policies" as state intervention in a private sphere. The only exception was when discussion turned to the Kosovo, where "something must be done there" masked contemplation of a population policy after all; but it was usually balanced by a reference to the Vojvodina or eastern Serbia, where "something also must be done" about depopulation.

In the Marxian terminology required on such occasions, a member of the Presidium of the Conference for Social Activity of Women told an international seminar on family planning in Belgrade in November 1969:

> Family planning, as an important social problem with social, economic and ideological aspects, has been the object of continuous activity by the Conference . . . for the past ten years. In all this time, the social aspect

> of this question has always been emphasized . . . in our efforts to ensure that the position of woman, the condition of the family, and (in this connection) questions relating to the most intimate sphere of human life receive the place they deserve in the building of a socialist society which has as its goals the emancipation of labor and the individual and the realization of human relationships . . . . One of our society's most urgent tasks is to extend assistance to the individual so that he can acquire knowledge in the field of humanization of relations between the sexes and awareness of the means of preventing undesired pregnancy, in order to eliminate spontaneity in this delicate sphere of human life and to achieve, through family planning, the goal that each new-born child should be a wanted child (*14*).

To these ends, a Coordinating Committee for Family Planning was formed within the Conference for Social Activity of Women of Yugoslavia in 1963, and was upgraded to the status of a Federal Council for Family Planning in June 1967. This body acts as a roof organization for Republican and Provincial Councils for Family Planning, each of which is made up of representatives delegated by relevant organizations, institutions, and government services. In the case of the Serbian Council, for example, these include: the Institute for Health Protection of Young People of the Socialist Republic of Serbia; The Serbian Medical Association; the Serbian Red Cross; the Republican Institute for Health Protection; the Conference for Social Activity of Women of Serbia; Serbian Youth Federation; Serbian Student Federation; Serbian Trade Union Federation; Republican Ministeries of Health and of Education and Culture; the Federation of Pharmaceutical Societies; and fifteen other institutions, astutely including the Serbian Journalists' Association.

According to their statutes, these Councils engage in promotional activities in two basic fields: in education (including "humanized relations between the sexes" as well as sex and contraceptive education as such) and in "the prevention of unwanted pregnancy," which is subdivided into two related activities: providing knowledge and providing means.

The Councils' activities are, in effect, those of a chartered lobbyist: pressing for the passage of needed legislation or helpful resolutions at the Federal or Republican level; urging the introduction of sex education and human relations courses on local town councils and school boards and providing materials for such courses; engaging the mass media in efforts to popularize family planning (while also pressuring publishers to discontinue publications of the plethora of low-quality imitations of *Playboy* and near-pornography that has sprung up in Yugoslavia during the past three years); pressuring hospitals or local "health communities" to establish contraception centers; cooperating with demographic research institutions in attitudinal studies; providing encouragement to those wishing to start families in depopulation areas like the Vojvodina by helping them find or finance housing, organize day nurseries for working mothers, etc.; and cooperating with foreign national and international agencies active in the field, e.g., the international seminar of November 1969 referred to above, which brought together 30 delegates from 20 countries—all European except Tunisia and India (*15*).

Demographic research, including KAP-type studies, is conducted by two subinstitutes of the prestigious Institute of the Social Sciences in Belgrade—a Center for Demographic Research (director, Dušan Breznik) and a Center for Public Opinion Research (director, Ferdus Džinić)—by corresponding institutes at Republican levels, and by individual sociologists at the various universities. Demographic statistics are collected and analyzed by the Federal and Republican Institutes for Statistics and published by the Federal Institute for Statistics.

Conclusions

The limited effectiveness of family planning programs to date—in contrast to widespread acceptance of abortion—is admitted by spokesmen of the Councils. The basic reasons have been suggested in earlier sections of this Report. Traditional reliance on abortion, reinforced by legally sanctioned, easy, and relatively safe availability (in 1967 no deaths resulted from legal abortions and only 67 from illegal ones), are primary factors in low birth rate areas. Traditional values and a male-dominated society in which women are restricted to the home and *should* be kept "barefoot in the summer and pregnant in the winter" are important in Kosovo and other, usually Muslim, high birth-rate areas (*zatvorenost* of women is felt by one Belgrade sociologist to be a primary source of high fertility in southern Yugoslavia).

The only serious population problems at the present moment are these two: dependence on abortion as the principal means of family planning, and still unsatisfactorily high rates of natural increase in some areas. In both cases there are sound reasons for cautious optimism. Recent figures on declining abortion and increasing use of contraceptives in the most developed Republics, Slovenia and Croatia, look like the beginning of a trend that may be expected to spread, with delays and unevenness, to Serbia and beyond. And while the rate of natural increase is still slowly rising in the Kosovo, birth rates there already show a downward trend; economic and social developments in the Province since 1966 give additional reason to hope that the "transitional demographic period" will soon begin in earnest among even the hold-out Albanians.

In Yugoslavia as a whole, and in four of the eight regions considered here (with 60 per cent of the total population), the rate of natural increase is now below one per cent per annum. Reasonable projections, as noted above, foresee the continuation of a one per cent growth rate through the coming decade, followed by a renewed fall to about 0.4 per cent in the 1980s; these projections do not take into account the possible earlier impact of family planning programs that are still new, still building up steam, still not effectively reaching most rural areas and some whole regions.

Reversals of trends are always possible. In Yugoslavia in the coming decade or two the most likely reason for any upward swing of demographic indices would seem to be nationalism—a reaction to a real or imagined demographic threat posed by a national enemy. If the threat were external, the reaction could take the form of a governmental switch to pronatalist policies; the Romanians underwent such a shift in 1966, and for just such reasons, with impressive results. If the threat were domestic, posed by ethnic rivals within Yugoslavia's uneasy multinational community, the reaction could take the form of a kind of spontaneous conception, a local patriotic baby boom consciously undertaken by the threatened nationality.

Without such a specifically induced change, the Yugoslavs seem unlikely to grow in numbers at a rate much exceeding one per cent per annum for the foreseeable future. Is that low enough?

Notes

1. Yugoslavia is a federation of six Republics, the largest of which (Serbia) contains the Vojvodina and Kosovo Autonomous Provinces. Because these Provinces are demographically of special interest, representing the extremes in most sets of data, this Report divides Yugoslavia into eight regions: Serbia proper (excluding the Provinces), the two Provinces, and the other five Republics. All statistics are based, unless otherwise noted, on *Demografska Statistika 1967* and the *Statistički Godišnjak 1970* (both Savezni Zavod za Statistiku, Belgrade, 1970) or Dušan Breznik, "Demographic Trends in Yukoslavia," in *Yugoslav Survey*, X, 2 (May 1970).
2. Dušan Breznik, *art. cit.*
3. "Prognoza stanovništva prema starosti i polu," Table 1-5 in *Demografska Statistika 1967, op. cit.*
4. For the Yugoslav definition of an urban community and a detailed analysis of the urban-rural distribution, see "Increase of Urban Population," in *Yugoslav Survey* no. 18 (Sept. 1964) and "Communities in Yugoslavia," *ibid.*, vol. viii, no. 2 (May 1957).
5. By Dr. Ruža Petrović, Belgrade University sociologist. See a summary of her conclusions in *Borba* (Belgrade), September 15, 1970. For a detailed analysis based on the 1961 census, see Dr. Dušan Breznik, "Internal Population Migrations in Yugoslavia" in *Yugoslav Survey*, vol. IX, no. 2 (May 1968).
6. For relevant data since 1953 and projections of Yugoslavia's total, working age, and economically active population to 1986, see Table VIII and accompanying text in Breznik, *art. cit.* in footnote 1.
7. Access to a number of such studies by Yugoslav researchers could not be arranged on short notice.
8. See Dennison I. Rusinow, *Yugoslav Public Health from Rockefeller to Tito* [DIR-3-'65], Fieldstaff Reports, Southeast Europe Series, Vol. XII, No. 3, 1965.
9. From the "Resolution on Family Planning" passed by the Federal Assembly on April 25, 1969.
10. The key liberal provision in the 1969 law is Article 4: "The interruption of pregnancy will be done on the demand of the women if during pregnancy

and after birth she could fall into serious personal, family, material or other troubles" (Opšti Zakon o Prekidu Trudnoće, in *Službeni List* (Official Gazette) No. 20/69).

11. Unfortunately the available abortion statistics do not include the usual breakdown of Serbia into its components (Serbia proper, Vojvodina, Kosovo). The Serbian figure is therefore for the Republic as a whole, while the Vojvodina figure is from a separate source (*loc. cit.*, p. 138). It is reasonable to assume, however, that the unavailable Kosovo figure is very low—probably close to the Macedonian ratio.
12. Dr. Lidija Andolšek, Ljubljana, paper presented to International Seminar of Family Planning, Belgrade, November 1969 (printed in *Faits et Tendances* no. 6, Belgrade, 1970, pp. 115–7).
13. Nevenka Petrić, "Le planning familial en Yugoslavie," paper presented to international seminar in Belgrade, *loc. cit.*, note 12, p. 34.
14. *Ibid.*, pp. 33f. "Spontaneity," it should be noted, has intensely negative connotations in the Marxist vocabulary.
15. For a fuller discussion of family planning programs in Yugoslavia, see the paper presented to this seminar by Nevenka Petrić and others, *Faits et Tendances, loc. cit.*, pp. 15–156.

References

Dušan Breznik, "Demographic Trends in Yugoslavia," in *Yugoslav Survey,* vol. x, no. 2 (May 1970).

Dušan Breznik, "Internal Population Migrations in Yugoslavia," in *Yugoslav Survey,* vol. ix, no. 2 (May 1968).

"Increase of Urban Population," in *Yugoslav Survey* (Sept. 1964).

"Communities in Yugoslavia," *Yugoslav Survey,* vol. viii, no. 2 (May 1957).

Lidija Andolšek, paper presented to the International Seminar of Family Planning, Belgrade, November 1969 (printed in *Faits et Tendances,* no. 6, Belgrade, 1970).

Nevenka Petrić, "Le planning familial en Yugoslavie," paper presented to the International Seminar of Family Planning, Belgrade, November 1969 (printed in *Faits et Tendances,* no. 6, Belgrade, 1970).

The Author

DENNISON I. RUSINOW, who writes from Yugoslavia on Eastern Europe, has maintained an interest in Adriatic Europe since 1952, when he specialized in the problems of the Habsburg Successor States as a Rhodes Scholar at Oxford University and traveled in this connection to Vienna, Trieste, and Belgrade. He returned to the area in 1956 as an officer of the United States Sixth Fleet. In 1958 he was awarded a fellowship by the Institute of Current World Affairs, and after a year's residence in Vienna he moved to St. Antony's College, Oxford, where he continued his study of recent Italian, Yugoslav, and Austrian history.

He holds a B.A. from Duke University, and an M.A. and D.Phil. from Oxford. While at Oxford, Mr. Rusinow held an appointment as Extraordinary Lecturer at New College, teaching modern history, international relations, and political institutions. He joined the AUFS in 1963.

The Question

Harrison Brown

Recently a study was made under the auspices of the National Academy of Sciences on the consequences and policy implications of rapid population growth.* The group of distinguished population experts who made the study strongly stresses the need for nations to adopt two kinds of population policies:

(1) Those which are *responsive* to population change and (2) those which *influence* population change. In the former category are those policies which will ameliorate or overcome the effects of rapid population growth. In the latter category are those policies which will bring about a reduction in fertility, mortality, and growth rates.

Population-responsive policies include those aimed at increasing the supplies of manpower in health and educational services at rates which are greater than the rate of growth of population, at increasing food and agricultural production, at developing new urban areas, and at providing jobs for the increased flow of people from the farm to the city.

Population-influencing policies include those policies which set goals in time perspective for reductions in fertility and mortality and which provide the means, such as programs in public health and family planning, which will enable the goals to be reached. In this connection the report recommends that governments extend to families the freedom and means to determine the number of children in each family by making available "a full range of acceptable, easily used, and effective means of preventing births," by disseminating widely "full

---

* *Rapid Population Growth: Consequences and Policy Implications,* published for the National Academy of Sciences by The Johns Hopkins Press, Baltimore (1971).

information on all the means of preventing births," and by employing the diverse and numerous benefits of small family size.

As short-term goals, the report urges that countries in which rapid population growth is now taking place attempt to reduce within the next 20 years their growth rates to 15 per thousand persons per year, their death rates to 10–15 per thousand per year, and their live birth rates to 25–30 per thousand per year. The report also urges the adoption of multi-objective policies which would increase parents' interest in small families. Among those suggested are laws prohibiting child labor and laws effecting compulsory education, social security, pensions, educational and career opportunities for women, and reduction of infant and child mortality.

When we compare the situations described in these reports with the recommendations which emerged from the Academy study it would appear that most of the countries treated by this conference are far removed from the adoption of what might be called truly rational population policies. Nevertheless there is room for optimism.

Although it would appear to be some time before the official policies of Brazil and Malawi are altered, there is internal opposition to those policies and it appears to be growing. Attitudes toward family planning in the Philippines have changed dramatically in the last three years. President Suharto has taken official note of the fact that Indonesian population growth is outstripping food supplies. Increasingly the poor countries are coming to appreciate the severe limitations placed upon their development by shortages of land and capital, by inadequate education, by increasing unemployment, by unprecedented rates of urbanization, and by the emerging problems of the environment. Increasingly they are coming to realize that population growth is a factor that must be reckoned with in development planning.

This is indeed encouraging. But will full recognition come soon enough? That is the overwhelming question of our time.

Index

Index